WITHHOLDING TREATMENT FROM DEFECTIVE NEWBORN CHILDREN

Canadian Cataloguing in Publication Data

Magnet, Joseph Eliot

   Withholding treatment from defective newborn children

   Publ. en collab. avec Brown Legal Publications

   Bibliography:

   Includes index.

   2-89073-551-6

   1. Neonatal intensive care — Moral and ethical aspects.   2. Infants (Newborn) — Legal status, laws, etc.   3. Infanticide — Moral and ethical aspects. 4. Medical ethics.   I. Kluge, Eike-Henner W.   II. Title.

R726.M33 1985   174'.24   C85-094219-5

ISBN-2-89073-551-6

Legal Deposit
3rd Trimester, 1985
National Library of Canada
Bibliothèque nationale du Québec

WITHHOLDING TREATMENT FROM DEFECTIVE NEWBORN CHILDREN

by

JOSEPH ELIOT MAGNET

B.A., LL.B., LL.M. PH.D.
of the Ontario Bar
Professor of Law,
University of Ottawa

and

EIKE-HENNER W. KLUGE

B.A., M.A., PH.D.
Professor of Philosophy,
University of Victoria

BROWN LEGAL PUBLICATIONS inc.

C.P. 180 COWANSVILLE (QUÉ.) J2K 3H6

In Memory of my Father
Isaac Harry Magnet, M.D.
(1911-1985)

ACKNOWLEDGEMENT

Many research assistants worked on this book and I would like to record my thanks to them. I am particularly grateful to four, who deserve a special mention: Philip Marcovici, Jane Murray, Craig Robertson and Leslie Kelleher.

JEM

TABLE OF CONTENTS

CHAPTER ONE

CANADIAN NEONATAL PRACTICE DESCRIBED

CHAPTER ONE

CANADIAN NEONATAL PRACTICE DESCRIBED

I. INTRODUCTION

Canada's death rates for low birth weight and deformed newborns used to be cataclysmic. A short while ago, many doctors thought this was natural. Low birth weight infants suffered from immature respiratory systems which made breathing difficult.[1] High mortality in deformed populations was perceived to be nature's way of eliminating its mistakes.[2] Only in very select cases did doctors intervene with then available medical techniques.

Twenty-five years ago two pioneering Canadian hospitals[3] revolutionized the treatment of seriously ill newborn children. The hospitals created specialized centres for newborn intensive care to combat the unparalleled incidence of mortality then experienced by congenitally defective and low birth weight infants. Neonatal centers[4] coordinated separate advances in drug therapy, transfusion techniques, pediatric surgery and radiotherapy. From the start, the first units demonstrated remarkable success. Newborn death rates fell dramatically; incidence

---

1. P. Swyer, *The Intensive Care of the Newly Born* (N.Y., 1975), p. 1; G.W. Chance, *The Severely Handicapped Newborn: A Physician's Perspective* (1980), 1 Health Law in Canada 34.

2. G.E. Knox, *Spina Bifida in Birmingham* (1967), 13 Dev. Med. Child Neuro. 14; K. Laurence, *The Survival of Untreated Spina Bifida Cystica* (1966), 11 Dev. Med. Child Neuro. Supp. 10.

3. The Hospital for Sick Children (Toronto); The Children's Hospital (Montreal).

4. In referring to the neonatal intensive care unit, we contemplate tertiary care units. Tertiary care units are the highest level of intensive care possible and are distinguished from primary care units, which are basically observation and convalescent facilities, and from secondary care units which are an intermediate stage between the two, appropriate to moderate risk patients.

of long term disability was slashed.[5] Because of this great achievement the concept of an intensive care nursery has gained wide acceptance in Canada. Twenty-nine units now serve as regional centers to which most serious pediatric cases are routinely referred.[6]

The original units experienced start-up problems with recruitment of staff and funds for equipment. The staffing problem continues as a major obstacle to development of the concept. There are few qualified neonatologists. Turnover in neonatal nursing staff is exceptionally high.

The idea of newborn intensive care is inspired by an interdisciplinary approach to pediatric medicine. Neonatal units train, and then utilize the services of a new specialty, neonatology. Children are admitted to the intensive care nursery in the name of the neonatologist, who thus assumes primary responsibility for care. The neonatologist coordinates the work of increasingly specialized pediatric disciplines, including pediatric cardiology, pediatric urology, child development and so forth. In concept, assessment and management of serious pediatric cases is accomplished in concert by a neonatal team under the neonatologist's managership.

---

5. In Ontario, as appears from the following statistics, the units were an important factor in successfully attacking newborn mortality. The death rate per thousand live births at age 0-6 days fell dramatically. Death rate — 1950-19; 1955-16; 1960-15; 1965-13.5; 1970-12; 1976-7.6; See *A Regionalized System for Reproductive Medical Care in Ontario*, Report of the Advisory Committee on Reproductive Medical Care to the Minister of Health for Ontario, September, 1979, p. 3. However, the Ontario and Canadian death rates do not compare favourably with that of many other countries. *Id.*, p. 4. In 1977, Ontario had 122,757 births. In that population there were 930 neonatal deaths, 1,078 still births and 500 severely handicapped infants: *Id.*, p. 16.

6. *British Columbia*: Vancouver General Hospital — Health Centre for Children; *Alberta*: The University Hospital, Edmonton; The Royal Alex Hospital, Edmonton; Foothills Hospital, Calgary; *Saskatchewan*: Regina General Hospital Regina; University Hospital, Saskatoon; *Manitoba*: Children's Health Science Centre, Winnipeg; St. Boniface Hospital, St. Boniface; *Ontario*: McMaster Hospital, Hamilton; St. Joseph's Hospital, London; Kingston General Hospital, Kingston; Children's Hospital of Eastern Ontario, Ottawa; Toronto Hospital for Sick Children, Toronto; Woman's College Hospital, Toronto; *Quebec*: Maisonneuve Hospital, Montreal; Montreal Children's Hospital, Montreal; Royal Victoria Hospital, Montreal; Jewish General Hospital, Montreal; St. Justin Hospital, Montreal; University Centre Hospital, Sherbrooke; University Hospital; Quebec; St. Francois Hospital, Quebec; *New Brunswick*: Dr. Everett Chalmers Hospital, Fredericton; St. John's Regional Hospital, St. John: Moncton General Hospital, Moncton; *Newfoundland*: Dr. Charles Janeway Child Health Centre, St. John's; *Nova Scotia*: Grace Maternity Hospital, Halifax; St. Rita Hospital, Sydney; Isaac Walton Kilham Children's Hospital, Halifax. The units vary in size from 8 to 35 beds. The average unit has 20 beds and experiences 400 admissions annually. All units, save Dr. Everett Chalmers Hospital, report utilization beyond design capacity.

The interdisciplinary approach to pediatric medicine has proven most valuable in cases of multiple anomalies. Meningomylocele, for example, exhibits deficiencies in neurological, orthopedic and urological functioning. A urologist is not competent to treat meningomylocele, but, as a member of the neonatal team, he can assess the extent to which the urological system is repairable, and illuminate for other doctors the expected quality of the child's life from a urological point of view. Neurological and orthopedic data are appraised separately by pediatric neurologists and orthopods.

Neonatal units experience a diverse case load. The majority of patients referred are low birth weight newborns suffering from respiratory distress.[7] These cases pose a special problem because diagnostic techniques are imprecise. Unlike adults, one third of severely asphyxiated newborns recover completely, even if spontaneous respiration is absent for up to thirty minutes. The remainder, however, do not. In many cases catastrophic disability results, frequently destroying all capacity for self awareness or socialization. Many children become ventilator dependent vegetables.[8] A smaller population is admitted for developmental or congenital defects distinct from immaturity.[9] These cases bristle with similar treatment dilemmas.

The wonderful successes neonatologists have had in treating defective newborns have been accompanied by spectacular failures. A significant number of cases are salvaged to lead lives of incomprehensive

---

7. For example, at McMaster University Medical Centre (25 beds) in 1978, the intensive care unit had 735 admissions. Of these, 394 (53.6%) were under 2,500 grams; 158 (21.5%) were under 1,500 grams. In Ontario the incidence of low birth weight infants (less than 2,500 grams) was 71 per thousand live births in 1968: Ontario Council of Health, *Perinatal Problems*, Toronto; Ontario Department of Health, 1971, p. 12.

8. H. Steiner and G. Nelligan, *Perinatal Cardiac Arrest: Quality of Survivors* (1975), 40 Arch. Dis. Childh. 696; H. Scott, *Outcome of very Severe Birth Asphyxia* (1976), 51 Arch. Dis. Childh. 712; G.W. Chance, *The Severely Handicapped Newborn: A Physician's Perspective* (1980), 1 Health Law in Canada 34.

9. Spina bifida and associated hydrocephalus are the most common defects seen in neonatal intensive care. "Spina bifida" is a protrusion through the defect of a cystic swelling involving the meninges (meningocele), spinal cord (mylocele) or both (meningomylocele). The incidence of spina bifida is two per thousand live births: R.B. Zachary, "Ethical and Social Treatment of Spina Bifida" in *Moral Problems in Medicine* (ed. Corovitz et al., 1976), p. 342, 346. Since Ontario had 122,757 births in 1977, there would have been roughly 244 cases of spina bifida by this calculation. "Hydrocephalus" is an accumulation of fluids in the cranial vault resulting in enlargement of the head, atrophy of the brain, deterioration of mental functions, and convulsions. At the Children's Hospital of Eastern Ontario, where the neonatal intensive care unit has 400 admissions per year, 15-20 cases of spina bifida and 50-60 cases of hydrocephalus are treated each year.

misery. If no intervention is made, nature would take its course; most severely defective newborns would die.

Neonatal intensive care increases the number of grossly deformed survivors. Because this is so, pediatricians increasingly incline to the view that some seriously ill children should not be treated. All Canadian neonatal units practice selective treatment. With cases considered unsalvageable or without potential for development, active care is withheld. The child is allowed, in some cases actively assisted, to die.

A large body of literature in medicine, medical ethics and medical law has considered the medical wisdom, ethics and legality of withholding treatment from seriously ill children. Typically, the literature views the phenomenon in gross, and thus asks: is selective treatment good medicine? Is it ethical? Is it legal? A consistent disappointment of recent research has been the inability to break the problem apart. No serious inquiry has been made into important smaller aspects of selective treatment, such as the decision making authority, the decision making process, the use of paramedical data and the proper interim care.

The reason for this failure is all too obvious. Routines inside neonatal units are opaque. There has been no adequate description of the practices neonatologists adopt relative to the smaller issues.

It is the purpose of the present chapter to fill this gap. The research is based on interviewing with neonatologists, pediatric specialists, pediatricians, pediatric residents, neonatal nursing staff, parents, officials of Children's Aid societies, social workers, and prosecutors conducted during 1979-80. Interviewing was pursued into all Canadian tertiary care units.

The most promising interviews were transcribed. The interview extracts in the following pages were taken from this material. The transcriptions certainly lend themselves to quantitative methods of analysis, but the materials have not been utilized in that way. It is not that a statistical picture of neonatal intensive care is not useful;[10] it is only that we think debate can be furthered by a different presentation. Thus, practice in the intensive care nursery is described by using techniques analogous to those of an investigative journalist. Our intention is to paint a detailed picture of what really goes on inside relevant to

---

10. Indeed, we are highly impressed with Diana Crane's study: *The Sanctity of Social Life: Physicians' Treatment of Critically Ill Patients*, New York: Russell Sage Foundation, 1975, and recommend it to those interested in a quantitative presentation.

the smaller questions. Our method has been to ask questions calling for a descriptive answer, and also, to put interviewees on the spot. We have been concerned to elicit reactions and responses that would give the feel of actual intensive care practice. This could not have been done with a questionnaire or with other than a personal form of survey. We make no apologies for our view that this is what is needed to correct the abstract generalities of much medical, legal and ethical writing relevant to defective newborns.

It has thus become possible to redirect research into passive euthanasia of defective newborns. The smaller issues now cry out for legal and ethical investigation. Chapter 2 considers the law relevant to these issues. Chapter 3 considers relevant ethical theory. Chapter 4 applies this theory, to create a useable model for ethically acceptable deliberate deaths. Chapter 5 suggests new ways to regulate medical practice in the intensive care nursery.

II. WITHHOLDING TREATMENT IN CANADA

1. The Neonatal Intensive Care System

Neonatal intensive care developed haphazardly in Canada. Medical staff convinced certain hospitals to establish experimental nurseries to combat high rates of newborn mortality[1] and long term disability. No thought was given to hospital location. The pioneers did not perceive that certain facilities might utilize an intensive care department better than others. Nor did they consider coordinating intensive care nurseries with programs to identify high risk pregnancies. Governments did not become seriously involved in research and planning until development was well underway.

Lack of initial coordination has resulted in long term problems increasingly intricate to solve. Neonatal units are unequally distributed across Canada, and are concentrated exclusively in urban areas. Availability rarely conforms to community need. Access is difficult, particularly from outlying regions.[2]

Neonatal units perform better when integrated with fetal-obstetric care centres having programs to identify high risk pregnancies. Integration at this point, however, would be difficult and expensive. Although sixty to seventy percent of high risk pregnancies can be identified before birth, many neonatal units receive only referrals.[3] None

---

1. In Ontario, as appears from the following statistics, the units were an important factor in successfully attacking newborn mortality. The death rate per thousand live births at age 0-6 days fell dramatically (Death rate: 1950-19; 1955-16; 1960-15; 1965-13.5; 1970-12; 1976-7.6): see *A Regionalized System for Reproductive Medical Care in Ontario*, Report of the Advisory Committee on Reproductive Medical Care to the Minister of Health for Ontario, September, 1979, p. 3. However, the Ontario and Canadian death rates do not compare favourably with those of many other countries. *Id.*, p. 4. In 1977, Ontario had 122,757 births. In that population there were 930 neonatal deaths, 1,078 still births and 500 severely handicapped infants: *Id.*, p. 16.

2. P.R. Swyer and J.W. Goodwin (eds.), *Regional Services in Reproductive Medicine*, Report of the Joint Committee of Society of Obstetricians and Gynaecologists of Canada and the Canadian Pediatric Society on the Regionalization of Reproductive Care in Canada (Toronto, 1973), pp. 21-2.

3. In 1976, of 2,600 newborn infants cared for in level 3 centres in Ontario, 1,898 were referred as newborns: *A Regionalized System for Reproductive Medical Care in Ontario*, Report of the Advisory Committee on Reproductive Medical Care to the Minister of Health for Ontario, September, 1979, p. 49. Ontario has some facilities, such as Woman's College Hospital, which combine fetal-obstetric care with neonatal intensive care. However, these facilities generally do not handle surgical cases. Surgical cases must be transferred to tertiary care units. In addition, Ontario continues to establish new units, such as The Children's Hospital of Eastern Ontario, in hospitals that do not offer obstetric care. It appears that Alberta, Quebec and Nova Scotia have been persuaded to combine fetal-obstetric care with neonatal intensive care:

of their patients are born in the hospital. In many cases, effective treatment requires immediate postnatal action. By the time serious post-partem complication is diagnosed in the delivery facility, and transport to neonatal intensive care is arranged, it often is too late. This is particularly true in Canada where distances are relatively great and the climate presents serious obstacles to transport.

Neonatal units operate as regional collecting centres for low birth weight and defective newborns.[4] All units have specialized transport teams, operating by road and air. The teams pick up referred infants on request.[5] Seriously ill newborns are, or should be, referred routinely from non-specialized birth facilities to an intensive care nursery. Non-specialized hospitals have neither the equipment, personnel, or integrated systems to diagnose many types of neonatal illness properly, or to initiate the procedures available.

2. Decision-Making at the Birth Facility

Most defective children in Canada are born in hospitals which lack an intensive care nursery. Even if full integration of neonatal units and obstetric centers was achieved, the problem would not disappear.[6] Thirty to forty percent of risk pregnancies escape detection by current

---

See, D.A. Geekie, *Report of the Seventy-Second Meeting of the Alberta Medical Association* (1977), 117 C.M.A.J. 922; *Perinatal Intensive Care after Integration of Obstetrical Services in Quebec: A Policy Statement of the Quebec Perinatal Committee.* Que.: Ministry of Social Services, 1973; K. Scott and M. Goddard, *Assessment of the Role of Antenatal Referral in Reduction of Neonatal Deaths* (1978), 11 Ann. Roy. Coll. Phys. Surg. Can. 79.

4. The perception that intensive care is best equipped to handle all "difficult" cases creates a problem. Regional hospitals become overly anxious to refer all problem cases. They are "dumped" into metropolitan tertiary care units. However, some neonatologists strongly hold the view that the units must be limited to tertiary care. They resist admission of other than tertiary care patients. Many units are strained beyond design capacity because they are referred more than what they perceive to be their fair share of primary and secondary care cases. When this happens, it is not uncommon for the neonatologist to refer the child to some other facility.

5. For example, at the Isaac Walton Killam Children's Hospital in Halifax, all of the infants are referrals. Approximately one-third arrive by hospital road ambulance service; the rest arrive by ambulance run by the referring hospital, commercial aircraft, and armed forces search and rescue aircraft. The Ontario system of neonatal transport is described in a special report by the Ontario Ministry of Health, Project Team on Neonatal Transportation, January 31, 1978.

6. Integrated units are referred to as "perinatal" facilities. "Perinatal" is defined as the period from 28 weeks of intrauterine gestation through the first six days of life: See Ontario Council of Health, *Perinatal Problems*, Toronto: Ontario Department of Health, 1971, p. 11.

medical techniques.[7] These mothers would continue to deliver in general service hospitals where newborn intensive care is seldom available. The only way to protect this population would be to direct all pregnancies to centralized, integrated fetal-obstetric centers, thereby removing deliveries from the work load of all other hospitals.

Before a seriously ill newborn may benefit from the intensive nursery someone must refer him. This requires that the attending obstetrician or pediatrician recognize that the infant is seriously ill; that the doctor be aware intensive care is appropriate; and that someone positively refer the child to an intensive care unit.

Hurdles are encountered at all three stages of the decision. Many doctors do not recognize such specialized and relatively rare abnormalities as congenital heart disease or neurological anomalies. Diagnosis often requires specialized equipment and expertise. So too, many doctors are poorly educated about the potentiality of neonatal intensive care. They may fail to recognize that very low birth weight infants (600 grams) are salvageable or that certain seemingly monstrous dentofacial abnormalities are correctable.[8] In some cases, the doctor or parents decide not to provide active care for defective children. They choose not to refer.

A decision not to refer to neonatal intensive care is contrary to standard operating procedure in all hospitals. Generally speaking, as soon as it appears that something is seriously wrong with the child, he is referred to intensive care. According to a nurse:

A. It's done almost automatically — if there's anything seriously wrong with the baby, it is sent immediately.

A decision not to refer a seriously defective newborn to intensive care is equivalent to a decision to withhold treatment.

In theory, a decision not to refer is made by the child's parents on the advice of the attending obstetrician or pediatrician. Reality, however, usually is different. Speed is all important. The risk of death or deformity increases significantly the longer treatment is delayed. Many post-partum mothers are exhausted or under anaesthesia. The fathers of seriously defective children often are upset emotionally. Frequently, the attending doctor perceives that he has little choice but

---

7. *Second Report of Perinatal Mortality Study in Ten University Teaching Hospitals in Ontario.* Toronto: Ont. Dept. of Health, 1967.

8. Swyer and Goodwin, *supra*, note 2, p. 38.

to dispense with long discussions with the parents, and decide whether to refer himself.[9]

Where the parents are present, competent and concerned to play an active role in decisions concerning their child, differences of view sometimes erupt between the parents and medical staff. The parents may regard a seriously deformed infant as too much of a burden. They perceive that it would be better if he were allowed to die. They resist giving their consent to transfer the newborn to intensive care, even where the doctor urges the contrary. As well, the doctor may conclude that the infant should not be salvaged.[10] One senior resident pointed out that many survivors of intensive care have constant medical problems requiring frequent emergency admissions to hospital. The parents are tied to these children. While doctors may be skeptical about referring in some cases, parents may be unable to accept passive euthanasia of their children.

Where the parents and doctors form different views about referral to intensive care, the matter is resolved in a variety of ways. At one end of the scale, doctors engage parents in a constant interchange, largely of an educational nature. The doctors explain the advantages of intensive care evaluation, the advances in pediatric medicine, and the medical alternatives which a proper intensive care assessment can develop. In most cases, after these discussions, parents originally resisting referral comply with the doctor's request.

---

9. F.J. Ingelfinger, *Bedside Ethics for the Hopeless Case* (1973), 289 N. Eng. J. Med. 914, 915: ("Current attempts to de-mysticize and debase the status of the physician are compromising his ability to provide leadership (not exercise dictatorship) when health and life are at stake...").

10. Views here are exceptionally diverse. A very small sampling follows: E.M. Cooperman. *Meningomyelocele: To Treat or Not To Treat* (1977), 116 Can. Med. Assn. J., 1338, 1340: ("The special needs of individual families must be considered. Serious family stress is frequent in homes with a handicapped child."); L. Whytehead et al., *Considerations Concerning the Transit from Life to Death.* Report of the Task Force on Human Life, Anglican Church of Canada, 1972: ("When there is no doubt we must consider the suffering of the parents and the burden which society assumes particularly the diversion of services and opportunities which could better be used for the care of humanity as a whole rather than in sustaining a life that is not human."); M. Katyen, *The Decision to Treat Myelomeningocele on the First Day of Life* (1971), S. Afr. Med. J. (27 Mar.), 345, 347: ("It would therefore appear that active treatment should be attempted in all cases unless the child has associated abnormalities which would preclude survival."); J.R. Claypool, *The Family Deals With Death* (1975), 27 Baylor L. Rev., 34, 37: ("What quality of life can the patient reasonably expect to enjoy from these procedures? What economic impact will this treatment make on those the patient loves best? How much suffering should an individual be asked to endure?").

If the parents continue to refuse consent, doctors have the option of taking legal action to compel referral. Most doctors are reluctant to institute legal proceedings. Few cases appear clear cut to them. Although the doctor may differ with the parents' conclusion, the difference rarely is so fundamental that the doctor is unable to accept the morality of what the parents propose. One doctor said:

A. Probably once a year we go to the Children's Aid Society...I never pushed this. It's not my decision. I don't force this on the parents.

Children's Aid Society officials confirm that legal proceedings to control parental decision-making about newborn care are rare.

Doctors influence the parents without resorting to legal compulsion. The chief of an obstetrics/gynecology department described the case of a microcephalic child who had serious intestinal difficulties. A relatively minor operation was recommended to remove an intestinal blockage causing starvation. The parents were opposed to treatment. They preferred that the child die a natural, if somewhat painful, death rather than live with serious neurological deficit. The doctor, however, wanted to correct the child's intestines. He gave the parents a choice between leaving the child in hospital and letting him operate, or taking it home to die. The parents ultimately consented to surgery.

On occasion parents are provided with limited and highly selective information weighted all one way. The parents are not informed of all medical alternatives. As a urologist said:

A. I think I have an obligation to parents to make some sort of decision for them and I am just turning away from making a decision [by long explanations to the parents] and putting it on them which is unfair.

This particular doctor went on to say that if he favoured withholding treatment he would not advise the parents that a kidney transplant from a live donor could be performed.

A. If one says that little Johnny is going to die without a kidney...you put unbearable pressure on the family to submit to a nephrectomy, which is a life-threatening procedure.

Q. So in the kidney transplant situation — you would not tell the parents basically that a procedure is available?

A. As it stands now, no.

In between full disclosure and selective provision of information there is a range of decision-making practices constituting a continuum, with "back and forth, back and forth" between doctors and parents at one end, and grudging provision of biased information at the other.

Interaction between doctors and parents is the main forum for making decisions whether to refer. However, other hospital personnel participate actively, particularly nurses and residents. It is not uncommon for differences of views to erupt, especially in the case of nurses. Nurses are responsible for day to day care of the children. The pediatrician and parents may see the child infrequently, or not at all.

Where a decision has been taken to withhold treatment, vigourous disagreement by hospital personnel sometimes leads to legal interference or the threat of legal interference. In one case, pressure from nursing staff forced a doctor to operate after active treatment had been withheld for six weeks.[11] In another case, threats of legal action by a psychiatrist-administrator of a child welfare organization resulted in the reversal of the medical decision.[12] In a third case a nurse who disagreed with the medical/parental decision informed the Children's Aid Society. The Society intervened on the child's behalf and legal action was commenced before the provincial court. At a Christmas Eve hearing, the baby was made a ward of the court, and surgery compelled.[13] Similar cases have occurred in the United States.[14]

Decisions respecting defective newborns differ considerably from decisions respecting low birth weight infants. With defective newborns, it is merely desirable that treatment begin on the first day of life.[15] Long-term results are proportionately better the earlier treatment is begun. By contrast, immediate treatment for low birth weight infants is a matter of life and death. The child's respiratory system is immature, and requires immediate mechanical respiration to prevent asphyxia. There is no time for detailed explanations to the parents or consultation with other doctors. A snap decision must be made in the case room. There is no time for referral to an intensive care nursery in some other hospital or city.

---

11. F.M. Gutman, *On Withholding Treatment* (1974), 111 Can. Med. Assn. J. 520.

12. *Id.*

13. *Court Saves Mongoloid Baby*, The Toronto Star, Jan. 21, 1977, p. 1.

14. *Maine Medical Center v. Houle*, Maine Sup. Ct. No. 74-145, Feb. 19, 1974 (Roberts, J.); *In re Phillip B.* (1979), 156 Cal. R. 48 (Cal. App.); *In re Hofhauer* (1978), 411 N.Y.S. (2d) 416 (App. Div.).

15. J. Lorber, "The Doctor's Duty to Patients and Parents in Profoundly Handicapping Conditions", in D. Roy (ed.), *Medical Wisdom and Ethics in the Treatment of Severely Defective Newborn and Young Children*, Montreal: Eden Press, 1978, p. 18.

A wide variety of doctors make decisions whether to ventilate low birth weight newborns. If the mother's obstetrician is attending the delivery, he will make the decision. If he is unavailable, whatever doctor is in the case room will decide. Residents, including junior residents, could decide. Parents rarely participate in decisions whether to ventilate. Most doctors believe the situation does not call for parental involvement. As one doctor said:

> A.   I think in the case room one just has to make that a sort of arbitrary decision in actual fact.

He explained:

> A.   ... I don't think we would ever ask [the parents]. I don't think you can. I wouldn't think that that is a fair question to ask anyone, 'do you want me to ventilate your baby?' I don't think there is any way you can ask that question...I think at that point in time you've got to make one decision either this kid is really so immature there is really no hope at all or else, O.K., there's a chance, and I think most of us would agree that if you make that decision then you go ahead and do whatever has to be done.

In some cases, ventilation decisions are strictly medical. In others, para-medical factors become important.[16] Family profile, a first pregnancy, parents desperate to succeed with the particular child, parental ability to care for the child, and other socio-economic indications may be considered.

Doctors in the birth facility face considerable difficulty obtaining para-medical socio-economic or personal data. They must decide quickly. There is no time to make detailed investigations.

The medical chart will be available. Rarely will it disclose any, or sufficient, para-medical data. Increasingly few doctors know the parents well. The doctor's quickly formed personal impressions are usually based on quicksand.

Life-threatening, low weight deliveries are unanticipated. Few obstetricians compile para-medical dossiers for use in the unexpected event it will be needed.

---

16. Diana Crane's, *The Sanctity of Social Life: Physicians' Treatment of Critically Ill Patients*, New York: Russell Sage Foundation, 1975, leaves no doubt that non-medical socio-economic and personal information regularly influences decisions whether to treat. She administered questionnaires to large number of doctors describing roughly identical cases with non-medical factors varied. The resulting variation in answers as to whether the child would be treated is convincing proof that these factors are highly germane.

Q. Do you ask the parents that before?

A. No. I don't ask, because I think it doesn't help me very much...most of [the infants] don't have defects !

Certain hospitals employ standardized medical criteria to aid decision-makers in choosing whether to ventilate low weight or defective newborns. The factors considered include birth weight, length of gestation and APGAR scores.[17] If the child fits the criteria for resuscitation, he will be ventilated; if he does not fit, he will not be ventilated and will die. A second group of hospital employs no set criteria. Medical decisions are made on a case by case basis. The decision whether ventilation is medically indicated will be made by the duty doctor. A third group of hospitals errs on the side of caution. Virtually all low birth weight infants are resuscitated immediately after delivery. An assessment of the child's chances for survival is made later, and a decision whether to continue ventilation will be taken then. In many hospitals, duty doctors, including residents, make the subsequent assessment.

When a baby dies, parents are rarely informed of the decision not to ventilate. Typically, in the words of one doctor, parents are told:

A. I'm sorry, your child was just too small to make it. I'm sorry, your child was premature; it just didn't have what it took to live.

A difficult problem arises with neonates on respirators who are clinically dead;[18] who have no chance for survival; or whose chances for survival are perceived as not warranting continued ventilation. The respirator must be turned off. The problem is compounded by abuse of resuscitation technology. One resident reported experiments beyond established guidelines, to try to keep low weight children alive. Seven hundred gram infants would be ventilated; sometimes six hundred; even five hundred grams or less. In virtually all cases, subsequent decisions must be made to turn the ventilator off.

Procedures for deciding to discontinue ventilation are *ad hoc* in general hospitals. Attending pediatricians, including residents, have

---

17. This is a numerical expression of the condition of a newborn taken 60 seconds after birth. It is a sum which combines assessment of heart rate, respiratory effort, muscle tone, reflex inability, and colour.

18. The medical profession regards patients as dead when subject to necrosis of the cerebral cortex and brain stem: See Canadian Medical Assn. (1968), 99 Can. Med. Assn. J. 1266; *Report of the Ad Hoc Committee of the Harvard Medical School to Examine the Definition of Brain Death* (1968), 205 J.A.M.A. 85. The patient is in an irreversible coma; he has lost consciousness and automatic nervous functions. However, respiratory activity can be continued indefinitely by mechanical ventilation.

discretion to discontinue respiration. There is little formal machinery for consultation with senior staff or the attending pediatrician.

Parental consultation is erratic, differing from hospital to hospital, doctor to doctor. Some doctors do not significantly involve parents when deciding to discontinue ventilation. One doctor justified this as a need to accept medical responsibility. He described the following case where discontinuing respiration was under consideration:

> A. In one experience a few years ago, a girl phoned up the father and said, 'this is the situation. It looks terribly, terribly bad and I think we should stop. Do you agree with this'? He got very angry with this and said, 'how on earth can you ask me to make that sort of decision? It's your decision. You make the decision. You decide what you want to do' ...

In other cases, the parents are presented with the medical indications, a summary of the prognosis, and a recommendation.

> A. I think most people would be very willing to discuss this with the parents and say, 'here's the situation. We know neurologically the prognosis is very, very bad. We think we should probably stop at this point' — and you get varying responses of course, to this. Most parents, if they know what you are talking about, most parents will agree if you say to them, 'well look'. Most of them have seen what has happened to the baby as well, and if they have a little time to see them on the ventilator, it is pretty discouraging at the best of times, 'I'm sorry but the prognosis is bad', most of them will agree...

Ventilation is often discontinued without parental involvement. Sometimes respiration is initiated and discontinued without parental knowledge of either fact. Typically, as a senior resident said, the parents are told that everything possible was done for the baby. He continued:

> A. The parents are told that the kid didn't make it. They are not told he was resuscitated and that the ventilator was turned off.

Decisions whether to refer low birth weight or defective newborns to neonatal intensive care units are a small but significant part of many hospitals' routine. A typical report comes from one hospital in an outlying centre, having 1,200 births annually. The hospital refers between 6 to 12 neonates per year to a metropolitan intensive care nursery. In the past year, three decisions were made not to refer.

The hospital indicated that many children referred are subsequently returned to die. This creates a chilling effect on decisions to refer. Doctors are concerned that the exercise not be pointless, expensive and frustrating for parents.

3. Decision-Making in Neonatal Intensive Care

(a) Neonatologist's Discretion

Rotating duty lists insure that a neonatologist is always present or on call in neonatal units. When children are admitted to the unit, existing medical responsibility alters. Children are admitted in the neonatologist's name and become the neonatologist's patients. Responsibility passes from the referring pediatrician to the neonatologist.

Initially, the neonatologist assesses the child's over-all condition in order to identify proper treatment protocol. His freedom of medical decision is greatest at this point. The neonatologist may undertake treatment himself, alone; he may consult members of the neonatal team for specialist opinion or management; or he may be sufficiently convinced of the child's morbid outlook as to conclude further evaluation is unnecessary. The neonatologist may withhold active care.

Difficulties arise where the neonatologist opts for a one man approach. Neonatologists cannot properly appraise numerous diseases falling within the competence of particular pediatric specialties. Surgical cases, for example, require specialist training to evaluate correctability. Neonatologists without expertise in cardiology, neurology and urology are unable to assess properly such cases as cerebral palsy or spina bifida. Even diagnosis presents difficulties.

The neonatologist's authority to withhold treatment in all cases is more theoretical than real. In practice, the neonatologist's views are tempered against the advice of members of the neonatal team, the referring pediatrician, pediatric residents and neonatal nurses before deciding on important medical protocols. It is rare that neonatologists act alone. Unlike the birth facility, decision-making in neonatal intensive care tends to be a team process.

Low birth weight infants (less than 1000 gms) suffering from respiratory distress pose a particular dilemma. Techniques for estimating their prognosis are unreliable. In one third of extreme asphyxiation cases newborns, unlike adults, recover completely, even if spontaneous respiration is absent for thirty minutes.[18a] Two thirds, however, suffer severe damage, destroying, in many cases, all capacity for socialization and self-awareness. Many become ventilator dependent vegetables.

18a. H. Steiner and G. Nelligan, *Perinatal Cardiac Arrest: Quality of Survivors* (1975), 50 Arch. Dis. Child. 696; H. Scott, *Outcome of Very Severe Birth Asphyxia* (1976), 51 Arch. Dis. Childh. 712; G.W. Chance, *The Severely Handicapped Newborn: A Physician's Perspective* (1980), 1 Health Law in Canada 34.

Many low weight infants are assisted by ventilation commenced at the referring hospital. Decisions must be made whether to continue life support. For those not already ventilated, quick decisions must be made whether to start.

Decisions to initiate or discontinue ventilation are neonatologists' decisions. Unlike the birth facility, neonatal units impose tight controls on all ventilation decisions. Only neonatologists can stop respiration. Residents are not allowed to decide. Nor can the referring pediatrician. As a senior resident explained:

> A. ...the neonatal unit in this hospital is run as a closed unit. If Dr. X from the community refers the child here, the child is admitted under the neonatologist rather than Dr. X. It is not Dr. X's decision [to stop ventilation].

As in the birth facility, ventilation decisions are made without significant parental involvement. A decision to commence ventilation is regarded as ordinary care, well within the neonatologist's discretion. A chief neonatologist explained that such decisions were "standard". He continued:

> A. If the baby is born here and it is very small, he will be brought to this part of the hospital where the treatment will be started. This means without any signature. We will put the baby in an incubator and start an I.V., intravenous fluid, and give oxygen if we need to, and even put the baby on a respirator if it is needed, even without the signature of the parents.
>
> Q. So, if the baby is sent to this hospital from another hospital before you can put him on respirator, you need a consent?
>
> A. Oh no ! No. No. Oh ! I don't know if we need it. But we don't ask for permission to start these kinds of treatments which we consider standard treatments.

A decision to cease ventilation is viewed in the same way, but doctors perceive that they are on less secure ground. Potential legal liability looms ominously in their minds. As a result, neonatologists maintain closer liaison with parents when deciding whether to terminate respiratory support. While written consent is not thought desirable, it is common for neonatologists to obtain oral consent to disconnect ventilators. However, in some cases, neonatologists perceive that opting for passive euthanasia is beyond parental capabilities. One neonatologist gave the following typical description of what he would do when this occurs.

> A. There have been some times I discuss that completely with the parents and they said, 'Okay, stop', and there is some times that

the parents have so much invested in the baby themselves, they couldn't come to that. I mean, not that you said, 'look, I want you to tell us to stop'. That's cruel. But sometimes, just their whole response to what you are telling them is such that you can see they can't make that decision... So sometimes we, under those circumstances, have stopped the respirator, and told the parents that 'we're awful sorry, he's gone'.

(b) *Interdisciplinary Decision-Making*

Following initial assessment of newly admitted patients, neonatologists, in most cases, consult with the neonatal team. The neonatologist decides which specialists to involve. Commonly, if there are multiple anomalies, the neonatologist asks different pediatric specialists to assess the child's body systems separately. This occurs quickly. Meanwhile, neonatal nurses and pediatric residents care for and observe the baby.

The baby remains the neonatologist's patient. He is not transferred to pediatric specialists, who are consulted only in an advisory capacity. Consulting specialists develop information on one particular system, which data figures as a separate factor in a multi-faceted decision. Meningomylocele, for example, produces deficiencies in neurological, urological and orthopedic functioning. Different specialists assess each system. Urologists are not competent to treat meningomylocele, but, as a member of the neonatal team, a urologist can illuminate for other doctors whether the urological system is repairable. He can assess the capacity of the repaired system to function, and describe the expected quality of the child's life from a urological point of view.

> A. ...I could say that his sexual activity was to be normal or abnormal, or satisfactory or unsatisfactory...[that] development is possible and the patient will be continent, socially acceptable.

Neurological and orthopedic data are separately evaluated by competent experts under the neonatologist's leadership. The neonatologist collates, assembles, and discusses this data with participating members. Paradigmatically, decision-making is interdisciplinary. Decision are made in concert under the neonatologist's managership.

Team dynamics vary with the severity of particular system anomalies. This becomes clear in cases of moderate multiple anomalies, where one system stands out because of its poor prognosis. The doctor reporting on that system is the pivot man. His assessment determines treatment protocol. A urologist explained by describing a case in which the patient has five system anomalies.

A. Three are entirely correctable, one is partially correctable and the third is a question mark…It ends up being that last system's final decision as to whether [treatment] is worthwhile.

The importance of a particular system deficit sometimes alters the interdisciplinary process of decision. The parents focus their attention on the specialist evaluating the badly damaged system. Not uncommonly, that doctor regards the patient as *his* patient. This may affect his willingness to accept the advice of pediatric colleagues, or to consult with them.

Interdisciplinary decision-making crumbles markedly in neurosurgical cases. Once involved, the neurologist becomes *the* significant actor. Consultation withers. *De facto* decision-making power is transferred away from the neonatologist because, as a neonatologist explained:

A. …I can't force the [neuro-] surgeon to operate on the child. Clearly it is a decision that he is going to have to make…

Neurosurgeons jealously guard their perceived prerogative to decide whether to operate. For this reason, they are cautious in tendering or accepting advice about "their" patient. The team approach shatters.

Some neonatologists acquiesce in this, but with considerable unease. Others protest strongly, but with apparent lack of success. One chief neonatologist angrily described the typical decision-making process with respect to spina bifida in his hospital.

A. They don't consult very much. Some people don't consult. These neurosurgeon doctors don't consult very much.

Q. So it's often what they feel is best?

A. Yes, and it changes from here to there. They don't say exactly the same thing, but…

Q. Do you feel that's a problem at all?

A. It is a problem ! It's so much of a problem you don't know exactly what could be done.

The problem is that a one-man approach usurps the interdisciplinary *raison d'être* for neonatal intensive care. An ultra-sophisticated facility metamorphoses into a neurosurgical satellite.

Deterioration of the interdisciplinary approach sometimes becomes complete. The neurosurgeon *de facto*, and formally, treats the child as "his" patient. Inevitable problems arise.

Neurosurgeons have sharply limited parental contact as compared with the neonatologist or neonatal staff. Neurosurgeons usually lack socio-economic and personal information developed by the neonatal team and its para-medical organs.[19] Communication channels established between neonatologist and parents shut down. Parents who were receiving daily or hourly information from the neonatologist and intensive care staff find themselves in a vacuum. Neonatologists assess carefully the parents' capabilities and wishes as part of the decision-making equation. With neurologists, the parents become a greatly reduced factor, or do not enter the decisional formula as a factor at all. As one neurosurgeon said with great emphasis:

A. I don't let the parents make the decision. I don't think it's fair letting the parents make the decision. I think we [the neurosurgeons] are the responsible ones to make the decision...anyway, they should not be able to make a decision. They can't make a decision. Therefore, we make the decision for them after discussion back and forth with them.

When neurosurgeons consult parents, they deliver less neutral information than do neonatologists. Typically, the information is highly selective and packaged as a foregone conclusion. A neonatologist complained:

A. The parents are being told exactly what the [neuro-] surgeons would like them to decide...most of the [neuro-] surgeons have already made their decision when they saw the child, and he will see the parents, I guess, not completely neutrally, if you want.

Q. ...Do you think that there should be a different way of going about doing these things, or?

A. Yes. I would like the parents to know both sides of the problem — what will happen if they don't operate, and if the child doesn't die. They have to see what will happen, and the margin there could be about a foot wide.

(c) Para-Medical Data in Medical Decision-Making

The major consideration influencing decisions whether to withhold medical treatment is the expected quality of the child's life. That is not the only criteria. All units utilize para-medical socio-economic and personal data as a further aid to medical decision-making.

One factor considered important by doctors is the marital status of the baby's parents.[20] Many doctors surveyed indicated that if the

---

19. See below, Section II(2)(c).

20. This has been reported before in the literature: See Diana Crane, *The Sanctity of Social Life: Physicians' Treatment of Critically Ill Patients*, New York: Russell Sage Foundation, 1975, p. 50; D.B. Shurtleff, P.W. Hayden, J.D. Loeser, and R.A.

baby were cared for by a young, single, unwed mother, they would be more likely to withhold treatment. According to a cardiologist:

> A. ...the perfect example is the 16-year-old unwed mother. You can spend hours arguing about whether this mother can keep her child at all, whether it's normal or not. That's the classic example. There you may not bring it up, but it's certainly in everyone's mind.

In one case, a decision "to let the child go" was made where, in addition to dislocated hips and severe club feet, the baby had a high level spina bifida lesion. At this particular hospital, the policy is to treat all spina bifida cases, unless the lesion is very low down on the spine. The baby's parent was a single, 18-year-old girl, and that "bad situation", as the orthopod referred to it, was influential in deciding to withhold care.

Doctors are equally concerned about the quality of the child's family. If the parents have low intelligence, poor psychological adaptation, or for other reasons cannot provide an adequate environment, treatment is proportionately less likely. A chief neonatologist explained why:

> A. There is no use in sending a baby back who requires complicated management and care to a mother who is unmarried, who has an I.Q. of 70 and quite unable to deal with it. She may have part-time work or something like that, or six other kids in the family. We know it's not going to work...

"You *have* to consider", said a cardiologist,

> A. ...if you are dealing with a [poor] psychological situation...if you fix this child surgically, is he going to make it in the post surgery... It's a very big part of pediatrics.

Certain doctors try to appraise the effect which addition of a deformed child would have on the particular family.[21] These doctors

Kronmal, *Myelodysplasia: Decision for Death or Disability* (1974), 291 N. Eng. J. Med. 1005 ("For an initial decision to offer maximum therapy the following points were considered...a family (i.e. natural parents) with economic and intellectual resources living within reach of appropriate medical facilities..."); J. Lorber, *Results of the Treatment of Myelomeningocele* (1971), 13 Dev. Med. Child Neurol. 279, 290.

21. This is a point which has been noticed before in the literature. See E.M. Cooperman, *Meningomyelocele: To Treat or Not to Treat* (1977), 116 Can. Med. Assn. J. 1339, 1340; J.R. Claypool, *The Family Deals With Death* (1975), 27 Baylor Law Rev. 35; B.M. Freeston, *An Enquiry Into the Effect of a Spina Bifida Child Upon Family Life* (1971), 13 Dev. Med. Child Neurol. 456, 460-1 ("The moment the baby is born the parents will be submitted to a series of distressing situations.... When doctors are deciding what kinds of operation and treatment they will recommend, they should also bear in mind the ways in which it is going to affect the child and his family, and consider these effects alongside their decisions about clinical treatment"); R.B. Zachary, *Ethical and Social Aspects of Treatment of Spina Bifida* [1968], The Lancet

know that parents of handicapped children experience high divorce rates; feel much guilt; and express mutual recriminations. Strain is produced on the family by uncertainty and long periods of hospitalization. Other children frequently react adversely.[22] A neonatologist pointed out that it is senseless to ruin five people's lives in order to save a life of questionable quality. "It is very difficult for the parents", said a urologist,

A. plus the effects it would have on other members of the family, other children. There is certainly more attention to this child...is it worth destroying the family in the process?

Social welfare considerations are important.[23] A minority of doctors surveyed have a heightened awareness of the economic burdens handicapped children impose on society. This perception creates a greater overall resistance to treatment. A urologist explained:

A. We have an idea of what the success rate is, and we feel it can be improved with doing it... It's just that I am concerned about cost. It's easy to make another baby in most cases.

The economic position of the baby's family figures prominently in medical decision-making. Most doctors think that if the parents are well situated financially, it is more likely that they will be able to cope with a handicapped child. Consequently, in questionable cases, the child of economically comfortable parents has greater chances of receiving treatment. A neurologist pointed out that economic capability is:

A. ...very important to cope with it. That will not make definite the decision, but, you see, if you have a severely damaged child with hydrocephalus, paraplegia, and all that, it is not the same thing

---

274; K.J.P. Sargeant, *Withholding Treatment From Defective Newborns: Substituted Judgement, Informed Consent, and the Quinlan Decision* (1978), 13 Gonzaga L. Rev. 781, 803 ("...man, as a social animal, has certain limited obligations to others which society can reasonably impose...such as an individual's obligations to a family. Thus...complete social disruption of the family might occasionally justify nontreatment.").

22. See B.M. Freeston, *An Enquiry Into the Effect of a Spina Bifida Child Upon Family Life* (1971), 13 Develop. Med. Child Neurol. 456, 460; E.H. Hare, K.M. Laurence, H. Payne, and K. Rawnsley, *Spina Bifida Cystia and Family Stress* (1966), 2 Brit. Med. J. 757.

23. For reports of this in the literature, see J. Lorber, *Ethical Problems in the Management of Myelomeningocele and Hydrocephalus* (1975), 10 J. Roy. Coll. Phys. 47, 58 ("doctors and the public today have to consider whether the vast resources of learning, skill, manpower, time and money needed to keep some extremely handicapped person alive, maybe against their will, are wisely spent"); D.B. Shurtleff, P.W. Hayden, J.D. Loeser, and R.A. Kronmal, *Myelodysplasia; Decision for Death or Disability* (1974), 291 New Eng. J. Med. 1005.

to treat that child for a rich family that would be able to cope better with the child, than for a single...that will not influence definitely the treatment, but I think it may influence somehow.

Another paramedical factor repeatedly mentioned by doctors is the ability of the parents to have additional children. If it appeared that the parents had significant difficulties in carrying a pregnancy to term successfully — that this child was the parents' best hope in child-bearing — medical intervention would be attempted more aggressively. Conversely, parents who were young, healthy and had good chances of bearing other children, would be a factor weighing against active treatment of a particular deformed newborn.[24]

Special mention should be made of mental retardation. Properly speaking, mental retardation is a medical factor. Nevertheless, retardation is such an important consideration in doctors' minds that it transcends the purely medical.[25] There is widespread discomfort and fear provoked in many doctors, paramedical staff, and parents by retardation. Even a mildly handicapping situation can become ripe for a decision not to treat if retardation is a factor.[26]

Out of a series of fourteen pediatrics residents interviewed, thirteen said that, in the case of their own child, they would refuse consent to treat if serious neurological deficits were involved. The following is a typical response:

Q. Supposing that you had a defective child, severely retarded or brain damaged. Would you treat it?

A. I don't think so.

---

24. See J.M. Freeman, *To Treat or Not to Treat: Ethical Dilemmas of Treating the Infant with a Myelomeningocele*, 20 Clinical Neurosurgery 134, 145 ("The fact that the family was young and capable of having more children, despite the known increased risks, also entered into the decision".)

25. Diana Crane, *The Sanctity of Social Life: Physicians' Treatment of Critically Ill Patients*, New York: Russel Sage Foundation, 1975, p. 41. Professor Crane surveyed large number of doctors from several relevant medical specialties as to what treatment they would provide to selected cases. She found that patients (both salvageable and unsalvageable) having mental damage were significantly less likely to be treated than patients having physical damage and concluded (p. 46): "The medical standards which are applied to mentally retarded children are different from those which are applied to normal children".

26. A case arose at the Johns Hopkins Hospital involving a mongoloid baby with intestinal obstruction. The parents refused consent for rather simple surgery to remove the obstruction. The baby starved to death over a fifteen-day period. There has been much bitter criticism levelled at the medical decision: See R.A. McCormick, *To Save or Let Die: The Dilemma of Modern Medicine* (1974), 229 J.A.M.A. 172; J.M. Gustafson, *Mongolism, Parental Desires, and the Right to Life* (1973), 15 Persp. Biol. Med. 592.

Q. You make a different decision as a doctor than you would as a mother?

A. Yes, but I am operating on quite different levels when I operate as a physician and when I operate as a mother. When I am operating as a mother, I am operating out of total emotionalism. I will be shattered; I will be upset; I'm going to say no, no, no ! Don't do anything or whatever.

Most of the doctors said they would decide one way as a doctor (treat affirmatively) and another way as a parent (refuse treatment). All were perplexed at the inconsistency, which they found difficult to explain. But all were definite about the answers given, notwithstanding the inconsistency.

Failure to integrate fetal-obstetric centers with neonatal units creates difficulties in gathering para-medical socio-economic and personal data. At the birth facility, obstetricians may know the mother because they cared for her during pregnancy. They may therefore have some indication of the family's socio-economic profile, the mother's child-bearing difficulties, whether this is a first pregnancy or whether the particular child is perceived as the family's only hope for bearing children. Obstetricians may be aware of personal factors, such as marital stability or psychological profile, considered relevant to the family's ability to provide the child with a suitable environment. By contrast, very little para-medical data is available on admission to the intensive care nursery. Quick decisions usually are made with no organized socio-economic or personal information. A chief neonatologist described the typical case:

A. Most of the time, it is coming through the chart, because it has been said to the obstetrician or to the pediatrician at the other place, that will transfer the information to us, because, most of the time, we don't have time to wait until the parent comes.

Q. Oh, so you wouldn't have contacted the parents at all?

A. Not before, most of the time.

Where there is more time for decision-making, para-medical staff become important in gathering para-medical data for the neonatologist. Nurses are a prime source of such information. A neonatal nurse, in describing her role, said that she was expected to develop information as to:

A. How the parents seem when they come; what kinds of questions they ask; do they touch the baby; do they look at the baby; do they feel comfortable with the baby; will they hold it; will they not hold it... It is not infrequent that neonatal nurses will be

sent to the birth facility to speak with the parents... We do make
a large number of visits to these referring hospitals.

Many units employ social workers as para-medical fact-gatherers.
Social workers interview the family and prepare reports containing
socio-economic and personal data. In some facilities these reports are
attached directly to the child's medical chart.[27] The doctor may discuss
the information with the social worker and solicit the latter's general
perception of the family. Certain doctors rely on this information to
guide them in subsequent communications with the parents.

In some units the involvement of social workers is automatic in
all cases of particular types. Staff at one unit explained that immediate
involvement of social workers was routine in all spina bifida cases:

A. It starts as soon as the child is born. The name is given to the
social workers there and then. It is an automatic process when
the child is born with a spinal deficiency. This always comes into
play and the child is followed in clinics every month or two.

Social workers gather a wide assortment of data. Typically, they
develop information as to whether, emotionally and financially, the
family can care for a defective child, whether the mother would have
to give up a job, whether a single parent would be without support,
whether other children in the family might suffer, and whether marital
difficulties might be caused between the parents. Employment of social
workers as para-medical fact-gatherers varies greatly in different
intensive care units. However, it is clear that use of social workers as
para-medical consultants is acceptable intensive care practice. It is a
phenomenon on the rise in most Canadian units.

(d) Parental Involvement

Neonatal units try to maintain close contact with the baby's parents.
Daily, by phone or in person, neonatologists enlighten parents as to
the child's progress. Links between parents, neonatal nurses and
pediatric residents occur more frequently.

Doctors are perplexed about what to tell parents. Medical indications governing treatment protocol are technical. Assessment requires
professional medical expertise. Professional responsibility obligates the
physician to make this judgment. Most neonatologists assume a further

---

27. Certain hospitals are very anxious to attach social workers' reports to the medical
record. It is thought that the document thus becomes a mental health record within
the purview of *The Mental Health Act*, R.S.O. 1980, c. 262 and therefore more
immune from discovery in the litigation process under Sec. 29 of that *Act*.

duty. They superintend the decisional process in order to ensure that parents do not deprive a salvageable baby of help, or force treatment on the hopeless case.

In practice, doctors retain decision-making authority whether to initiate or withhold treatment.[28] This position is maintained with some anxiety because it cuts sharply across two fundamental values: the legal doctrine of informed consent,[29] and the ethical precept of self-determination. To soften the violence done to principle, neonatologists are astute to involve parents significantly in the decision-making process.

Although parental participation varies markedly from case to case, it is possible to describe a typical, if composite, decisional procedure.

Neonatologists reach their own conclusion as to proper treatment protocol before involving parents. "You have to have your own point of view", a neonatologist emphasized, "in order to advise the parents reasonably". Doctors form tentative views. With these opinions in mind the child's developmental potential is explained to the parents. The broad medical picture is described in layman's terms. Doctors tell the parents what their life, as well as the child's life, will be like. Parental wishes are ascertained. "Then", said a cardiologist, the parents and doctors "try to come to some reasonable decision that we agree with". In most cases doctors and parents agree about a proper medical course of action.

---

28. The proposition derived from the research is consistent with views expressed by doctors in the literature. See: R.M. Forrester, *Ethical and Social Aspects of Treatment of Spina Bifida*, [1968] The Lancet 1033; F.J. Ingelfinger, *Bedside Ethics for the Hopeless Case* (1973), 289 New Eng. J. Med. 914: ("So when Duff and Campbell ask, 'who decides for the child? the answer is 'you' — You, the child's doctor... Society, ethics, institutional attitudes and committees can provide the broad guide-lines, but the onus of decision-making ultimately falls on the doctor in whose care the child has been put".); J. Lorber, *Ethical Problems in the Management of Myelo-meningocele and Hydrocephalus* (1975), 10 J. Roy. Coll. Physic. 47, 56: ("Who should make the decision to treat or not to treat?... One cannot leave it to the parents because they are hardly ever sufficiently informed and because they are under severe emotional strain at the time. Further, whatever happens, they may later feel guilty for the decision they took if events turn out unexpectedly... Of course, the parents' wishes must be taken into account..."); J.M. Freeman, *To Treat or Not to Treat: Ethical Dilemmas of Treating the Infant with a Myelomeningocele* 20 Clinical Neurosurgery 134, 141: ("The only person capable of fully understanding the consequences of each decision is the physician...parents should obviously be part of such a decision, but their decision can hardly be an informed one").

29. Curiously, no doctor surveyed could state what the informed consent doctrine required. Most were completely ignorant of formal legal obligations in this vein. Nevertheless, several doctors referred to informed consent as "nonsense".

Some cases are on the line; the medical indications are not decisive either way as between withholding or initiating treatment. It is easy for parents and doctors to disagree about whether to salvage the baby.

Doctors are reluctant to superimpose their authority in these cases. If parents consider fully the information doctors provide and are firm in resisting treatment, doctors usually acquiesce. The parental decision is difficult; implications for their future lives are profound. "If this is what they say", conceded a neonatologist,

> A. "I would go along with them. If, in spite of my explanation...that is the way they feel...I don't feel that I should force them...I accept the morality on their side. I don't agree with it, but, I would say 'alright...it's fine'...

Distinct from these borderline cases, two further situations arise where parents and doctors disagree. First, doctors conclude treatment should be withheld. The parents think differently. They prefer to initiate treatment. Second, parents conclude treatment should be withheld. The doctor disagrees. In his opinion, treatment is required.

(i) Doctors Desiring to Withhold Treatment

Where doctors conclude that treatment is improper they retain decisional authority. Even if parents specifically demand surgery, doctors may refuse. "The decision is ours", said a chief neonatologist, "but we take the parents' wishes into every consideration". A chief resident explained that the parents are

> A. ...involved with the discussion. They are informed as to the condition of the child. They are informed as to what the expected outcome is going to be. They may express an opinion...but that opinion may or may not be acted upon. The decision is not theirs, although they have input into the decision-making.
>
> Q. So if...the parents said, 'well, we have been trying to have kids; this is the one we have; this is the one we are going to have. Treat it. Do everything you can and don't let go' — still you might not provide active life support?
>
> A. Yes. That might happen. That's a correct assessment.

In one case, a single mother of a spina bifida child was adamant that she wanted her child treated. The neurosurgeon refused. He perceived the mother as "a very poor girl". He told her that the child would die. The mother insisted on taking the child home. Spinal fluid was dripping out of the wound. No antibiotics were administered. The neurosurgeon described what happened:

A. ...but she insisted that she wanted the child treated. So she went almost to the point to beg for the treatment of the child. So, you know, after long talks with her, I explained that, at least, we would give a trial of life [provide no treatment for a few days to see if the child survives]. She wanted to take the child home. She took the child home without antibiotics, and this was a leaky meningocele. The child was leaking spinal fluid and all that. So everything looked..everybody was saying that this child most likely would die...Well, she came back, to our surprise, about 2 months later with the myelomeningocele area completely healed. The baby never got infected...So we had no choice, we had to treat the child [at that point]...

The parents' views about treatment are important to the medical team. They figure significantly in the decision-making formula.[30] Doctors explain the medical indications to the parents before eliciting their reactions. If sharp disagreement about medical protocol erupts, less objective information is forthcoming. The flow of medical information is used as a lever to control the decisional process. "They are not explained the two sides of the problem", said a neonatologist.[30a] In this way, doctors attempt to influence parental conclusions about the case.

In sum, where doctors favour passive euthanasia and the parents disagree, decisional power is retained by the doctors. Notwithstanding parental requests to the contrary, doctors may refuse to treat seriously deformed newborns.

---

30. The position stated in the text conforms to the view advanced by most doctors in the literature: see D.W. Hyde, H. Williams, H.L. Ellis, *The Outlook for the Child with a Myelomeningocele for Whom Early Surgery was Considered Inadvisable* (1972), 14 Dev. Med. Child Neuro. 304, 307: ("It has now become the custom at Oxford for each case to be examined by a pediatrician and a pediatric surgeon. Special attention is paid to [enumerated medical factors]... The family's own doctor is consulted and a full discussion then takes place with one or both parents; not until their views are made known is a final decision reached".); D.B. Shurtleff, T.W. Hayden, J.D. Loeser, R.A. Kronmal, *Myelodysplasia: Decision for Death or Disability* (1974), 291 New Eng. J. Med. 1005: ("...we do not leave the decision to the parents until we have described the full implications of maximum treatment or supportive treatment and rendered an opinion based upon evaluation by the group of professionals...").

30a. In Waitzkin and Stoeckle, *The Communication of Information About Illness*, (1972), 8 Advanced Psychosomatic Medicine 180, 198 the authors point out that "inconsistent and disorganized communication of information constitutes one of the most severe problems experienced by hospitalized patients." The authors include several citations from empirical studies in support of this proposition. They also conclude that pediatricians "do not view information transmittal as very important": p. 201.

(ii) Parents Desiring to Withhold Treatment:
Parental Consent and Substituted Consent

The views of doctors and parents are sometimes reversed. Doctors conclude that treatment is indicated. The parents, unable to accept a deformed child, refuse to consent. Decisional power is differently distributed in such cases.

Most hospitals require two parental consents before beginning significant procedures in the intensive care nursery. First, written consent to "all necessary treatment" is obligatory at admission[31]. A second, specific consent is compulsory prior to surgery.

Medical practice is not inhabited by the lawyer's preoccupation with a fully informed and freely given consent. Where lawyers assume an aroused sense of respect for patient autonomy, doctors introduce two further considerations. Doctors temper the legal ideal of self-determination against a perceived discretion to refuse personally to treat, and a perceived duty to protect the patient's best interests.

Neonatologists elicit parents' wishes about whether to salvage their seriously defective child. In many cases doctors respect parental decisions for passive euthanasia. However, there are limits beyond which doctors will not go. If it is considered that the parents' decision unreasonably cuts across the child's best interests, neonatologists refuse to implement it in most cases. "The prime consideration", said a chief neonatologist, "is the welfare of the infant. The secondary consideration is the welfare of the family".

When medical indications decisively warrant active medical intervention, doctors readily override the parents' decision to refuse treatment. Two mechanisms are used to control the parents' refusal of consent.

First, the neonatal staff, led by the neonatologist, engage the parents in constant dialogue attempting, as a neonatologist said, "to influence the decision". The neonatal staff explain the encouraging medical prognosis to the parents. They provide information about available social welfare programs, education for handicapped children, and

---

31. The consent is given in standard form. Such forms tend to be overly broad and legally unenforceable. The Ottawa Civic Hospital, at this writing, uses the following form:
    "I, the undersigned, do hereby give full consent to the attending physician and Hospital staff to carry out any form of examination, tests, treatment, operations, anaesthesia, photographs on _____ and do therefore absolve them from any consequences thereof."

the potential for handicapped children to lead useful, happy lives. "It is a question", explained a senior pediatrics resident, "of saying 'yes, there is this kind of possibility; there is a good outcome', and so on". In most cases, after this dialogue, parents consent to treatment.

In a small number of cases doctors resort to legal coercion. Hospital officials inform the Children's Aid Society that the child is in need of protection. The Society has jurisdiction to take proceedings on the child's behalf in order to obtain a legally recognized, substituted consent to treatment. Following treatment, depending on the family circumstances, the baby may be returned to the parents, or remain a ward of the Children's Aid Society. In one case, parents adamantly refused consent for surgery to remove an intestinal blockage from their mongoloid child.[32] Judicial consent for the relatively simple surgery was obtained by the hospital administration. In a second case, judicial consent for neurosurgery was obtained to salvage a baby born with myelomeningocele. According to the neonatologist, the parents of this child "decided they didn't want the baby, and agreed, in fact, they would give up the baby". In a third highly publicized case the British Columbia Supreme Court awarded interim custody to the Superintendent of Child Service and authorized him to consent to a shunt revision for a profoundly damaged child over the strenuous objections of the parents, and conflicting medical testimony.[32a]

In all cases where doctors obtained substituted consent, they described the test for resorting to legal compulsion as the "best interests" of the child. By "best interests" the doctors understand a calculus of medical probabilities based on medical indications that the baby would survive in a condition beyond the vegetative. Some doctors added to the "best interests" test distinct quality of life considerations. "Quality of life" embraces the child's expected capacity for physical and mental development. Beyond medical indications, quality of life includes family environment, access to medical services and economic resources.

(iii) Breakdown in Interdisciplinary Decision-Making

The team approach utilized in the intensive care nursery enhances the flow of information to parents. Where interdisciplinary decision-

---

32. Such cases are a not uncommon dilemma in pediatrics practice. They are discussed in D.P. Girvan and C.A. Stephens, *Congenital Intrinsic Duodenal Obstruction* (1974), 9 J. Pediatric Surgery 883; J.M. Gustafson, *Mongolism, Parental Desires and the Right to Life* (1973), Persp. Biol. Med. (summer), 529.

32a. *In re Stephen Dawson*, [1983] 3 W.W.R. 618 (B.C.S.C.) reversing [1983] 3 W.W.R. 597 (B.C. Prov. Ct.).

making deteriorates, parents are less fully informed. Their considered views weigh less in the decision-making balance. Opportunities increase for principal specialists to impose their conclusions on the parents by tailoring the information provided.

A particularly revealing example occurred in the case of a child with severe kidney deficits. The child had additional abnormalities, including deficits in the neurological system, and brain damage. In this case, the nephrologist assumed virtually total responsibility for medical management. Pediatric colleagues were not consulted.

During an interview, the child's parents described the medical prognosis as hopeless. They thought a kidney transplant was not warranted because death was imminent. The nephrologist explained the case quite differently.

Q. What about a kidney transplant?

A. I don't think it would be worth it because the kidney disease is not confined to the kidney. It is mainly a brain disease and it is a generalized disease.

Q. If he were to have a kidney transplant, would he probably live?

A. Oh possibly, oh yes.

The nephrologist, in deciding against transplantation, proceeded through a complicated calculus of medical indications involving all body systems. The high probability of brain damage was the critical factor in his mind weighing against transplantation. None of this was explained to the parents, nor were they given an opportunity to say whether they wanted to salvage the child, even if brain damaged. Moreover, the nephrologist by-passed hospital committee structures in coming to his decision.

A. Kidney transplant, oh we do have a committee...when it comes to accept, or particularly when we think we might refuse [transplantation] the committee has to be unanimous in their decision to refuse a child.

Q. And the committee in this case decided they would not go ahead?

A. No. We did not even admit him to the committee because chances are he will not live long enough to get a transplant.

At this writing, one year later, the child is still alive and doing well. The parents are still unaware that transplantation is being withheld. In discussing the parents' role, the nephrologist said:

Q. Would the parents enter into the decision of transplant?

A. Yes. They would. But like always in medicine, the decision of the parents is strongly influenced by the opinion of the doctor.

Where interdisciplinary consultation occurs as it is supposed to occur in neonatal intensive care, distortion or restriction of information provided to the parents occurs much less frequently. Generally speaking, neonatologists regard parental liaison, including the obtaining of informed consent, as an important part of their responsibilities. Failure to obtain informed consent is significantly more probable where the process of interdisciplinary decision-making breaks down.

4. Care Provided Where Treatment Withheld

Where it is decided to withhold active treatment from a defective newborn, difficult questions arise as to the level of care the baby should receive. Should resuscitation efforts follow cardiac arrest? Should a fever be controlled with antibiotics? Should the baby's fluids be managed? Should he be fed?

The questions are troublesome because, *ex hypothesi*, the child's condition is incompatible with life, or with a life worth living. On that view, it seems pointless to lengthen the life by medical means. Nevertheless, withholding necessities such as food, warmth or basic medicines implies an ethic repellent to many.

Doctors respond to this dilemma with emotion and doubt. Nevertheless, there is a discernible consensus in Canadian neonatal units.

The consensus is that the baby should be fed, kept warm and made comfortable. His fluids should be managed. Beyond this, nothing should be done. No resuscitation should be attempted. No minor surgery should be performed. No antibiotics should be administered.[33] The baby's suffering should not be drawn out, because, as a resident said:

A. ...if you have made a decision not...to maintain a life support system, then it makes equally little sense to treat infection. What's the goal of treating infection?

Although most doctors accept the logic of this consensus, they find it difficult to implement. Practicing by these rules brings doctors face

---

33. Leading practitioners have expressed similar views in the existing literature. J. Lorber, for example, "The Doctors Duty to Patients and Parents in Profoundly Handicapping Conditions" in D. Roy (ed.) *Medical Wisdom and Ethics in the Treatment of Severely Defective Newborn and Young Children*, Montreal: Eden Press, 1978, p. 21 says:

"It is essential at this point to state clearly that one hopes that those who are not treated should not live long. It is imperative that non-treatment should really be non-treatment, not just no operation. Nothing should be done to prolong life; *no incubators; no tube feeding, no antibiotic drugs* and most certainly *no resuscitation*."

to face with their inability to assist or cure. To some, it appears indistinguishable from euthanasia. A senior resident, when asked whether antibiotics would be given, said excitedly:

A. You're asking me if I'm chicken or not. That's what you are asking. Am I chicken or am I not chicken. You know what I mean?

Q. No. I don't know what you mean.

A. A chicken is chicken liver, you know, weak liver, how brave I am about making this kind of decision.

Q. O.K. you make a decision not to treat and now he gets a little fevery, are you going to give him an antibiotic?

A. I probably would.

Q. You would?

A. Yes. It depends. If his lesion is such that he is not compatible with life and I am not treating him, it doesn't make any difference whether I give him antibiotics or not.

Q. But you'd give it to him anyway?

A. Sure. If he has an infection, there is no reason why I can't treat him because my original premise has to be of the lesion that I cannot treat is that the lesion is incompatible with life. The problem of a fever shouldn't be handled, but I think I would handle it.

Q. In other words, you don't think you should handle it because the idea is that he should die as quickly as possible?

A. Right.

Q. But yet you would treat it?

A. True.

....

Q. I don't understand though that when you decide not to treat a child and then the reason is the child's going to die, and this has to go to your remark about being chicken, why shouldn't you help him along a little bit? Why should you prolong the misery?

A. When you are wrong, you feel quite rotten.

A controversy exists with respect to use of painkillers such as morphine and demerol. The prevailing view among pediatricians is that, because the nervous system is immature, newborns do not experience pain in the same way as adults. For that reason, painkillers are not used in most neonatal units, even in aid of surgery. However, because there is uncertainty about the child's capacity to experience pain, certain units have adopted different practices with respect to the use of painkillers. To some extent, different practices are utilized by different doctors in the same unit.

5. Pediatric Euthanasia

For obvious reasons, it is very difficult for the researcher to describe accurately the incidence of pediatric euthanasia.[34] However, two types of euthanasia can be documented. First, increasing dosages of painkillers, particularly morphine, may be administered. Although the purpose is said to be relief of pain (if, indeed, neonates experience pain), the hastening of the baby's death is a clear and well understood effect. Second, the doctor or nurse may hold back part of the morphine dosage recorded as administered. When a sufficiently large amount is collected, a lethal dosage will be administered all at once, causing cardiac arrest and death.

Administration of increasing dosages of painkillers creates problems in the unit. Doctors are responsible for ordering the medication. Nurses are responsible for administering it. Because the doctor may have little contact with the baby in question, the consequences of his orders do not impact on his conscience with the same immediacy as occurs with the nurses. The doctor will not suffer from the same sense of anxiety or guilt. However, his orders may require nurses to administer painkillers to the baby on a regular schedule, even if the child shows no sign of pain, or is sleeping. It will be crystal clear to the nurse that she is giving medication to a baby for whom such medication is not medically indicated. Furthermore, the medication sometimes produces anomalous results. In one case, the situation became traumatic for the nursing staff because, despite large dosages of morphine administered, the child continued to live. A nurse described what happened:

A. We put him on high doses of medication. We kept increasing the medication and it became more traumatizing for the staff because essentially we knew we were poisoning the child. So there was a little anxiety there naturally. What happened was the child refused to die. He was there three months, and eventually we cut out the morphine completely, and stopped the drugs completely, and sent him upstairs to another unit where he was just given feeding by tube, and now he is eating pablum...He is a child who refused to die.

It is impossible from our survey to say how common is the second situation - actively causing the child's death by a lethal dosage of morphine. Not surprisingly, neonatologists surveyed were reticent

34. One *per cent* of respondents (residents and physicians) to a questionnaire said they would be likely to give an "intravenous injection of a lethal dose of potassium chloride or a sedative drug" to an anencephalic infant; three *per cent* said that they might do so": Diana Crane, *The Sanctity of Social Life: Physicians' Treatment of Critically Ill Children*, (New York: Russel Sage Foundation, 1975), p. 72.

about discussing this subject. Some cases were described at second hand. In a much publicized case an Edmonton resident ordered a lethal dose of morphine for a severely brain damaged newborn. "It's happening everywhere" the doctor said in a newspaper interview, "but nobody's talking about it".[34a] At the Hospital for Sick Children (Toronto) a Royal Commission of Inquiry probed the mysterious deaths of 36 infants between June, 1980 and March, 1981.[34b] The hospital's chief cardiologist suggested under cross examination that euthanasia might explain the deaths. "The motive would perhaps be that of mercy killing", he stated. Most of the babies were "very ill with severe heart defects",[34c] a fact which itself indicates the possibility of pediatric euthanasia. A Harvard University cardiologist is reported as saying that mercy killings are now done behind closed doors.[34d] The information gathered, however, is too fragmentary to allow any general conclusions as to frequency of euthanasia to be stated with confidence.

6. Effect on Neonatal Staff

Babies who are not treated are kept in neonatal intensive care or transferred to a convalescence unit. It is rare that parents take their child home.

Neonatal staff are seriously affected by these cases. The units have high mortality rates; in some cases close to one death per day. The staff works under constant stress produced by a case load of dangerously ill patients. Morale suffers. There is high staff turnover because, as a nurse said, "it's depressing".[35]

Instances of bonding between nursing staff and particular children certainly occur.[36] But this seems to be rare. Typically, the staff feels,

---

34a. *Euthanasia 'happening everywhere' doctor says*, Toronto Star, June 6, 1983.

34b. Ontario Report of the Royal Commission into certain deaths at the Hospital for Sick children and Related Matters 1984.

34c. *Euthanasia raised as motive for baby deaths at hospital*, The Globe and Mail (Toronto), Aug. 26, 1983, p. 1.

34d. *Let hopeless cases starve to death: MD*, Toronto Star, June 2, 1983.

35. A Shaw, *Doctor, Do We Have A Choice?*, The New York Times Magazine, Jan. 30, 1972, p. 54: ("It is easy at a conference, in a theoretical discussion, to decide that such infants should be allowed to die. It is altogether different to stand by in a nursery and watch as dehydration and infection wither a tiny being over hours and days. This is a terrible ordeal for me and the hospital staff — much more so than for the parents who never set foot in the nursery".); J.M. Gustafson, *Mongolism, Parental Desires and the Right to Life* (1973), 16 Persp. in Biol. and Med. 529: "The nursing staff who had to tend to the child showed some resentments at this. One nurse said she had great difficulty just in entering the room and watching the child degenerate — she could 'hardly bear to touch him' ".

36. See J.M. Gustafson, *Mongolism, Parental Desires and the Right to Life* (1973), 16 Persp. in Biol. and Med. 529.

in the words of a neurosurgeon, "It is not very nice to have these children around...They are going to die". This takes a significant toll from the staff in terms of morale, job satisfaction and turnover.

III. CONCLUSION

Certain practices uncovered in the present survey cry out for comment and analysis from both legal and ethical points of view. However, it is necessary to sound a note of caution. There is a danger in concentrating attention on individual cases of abuse; one becomes lost in a wilderness of single instances.

Analysis of the survey must be sufficiently general to capture all cases of a particular type, as contrasted with all particular cases surveyed. The method of analysis must rise from the empirical to the inductive. Broad .categories of questionable intensive care practice need to be synthesized from the individual cases. It is those categories of questionable medical practice which require legal and ethical analysis; not individual cases of abuse. The present survey contains a sufficient wealth of detail to allow the researcher to state such categories.

The incidents described in the present chapter are parts of a larger whole. They reveal general agreement among the medical profession on a number of issues raised by treatment of defective newborns. The actual incidents uncovered in the research are, in the majority of cases, authentic manifestations of a larger professional consensus reached on particular problems encountered in the intensive care nursery.

By their practice, Canadian doctors have developed standards of acceptable medical conduct for the difficult ethical dilemmas faced daily in neonatal intensive care. These practices may be said to constitute a professional tradition. They condition the behaviour of new staff in the units. Doctors learn by doing. They usually do what they observe others doing. A pediatrics resident in intensive care will observe and absorb, or be instructed in, these practices. He may modify them, but the practices are certain to shape the resident's professional orientation more than he shapes the practices.

The professional consensi to which we refer amount to more than a tradition: they constitute an ethics of medical practice - a guide to medical conduct. Rarely will this ethics be stated or formally codified. By nature, such ethics are professionally established in the routines of institutional medical life. They are practical ethics, not abstract or ideal ethics. They are practical in the sense that this is what doctors actually do and feel pressured to do, even if not certain that what they are doing is right.

The present research reveals that a professional consensus exists on the broad question whether passive euthanasia of defective newborns is tolerable in some cases. Where the anticipated physical and mental quality of the child's life is perceived as being exceptionally poor, passive euthanasia, by withholding medical care, is acceptable medical management. The evidence for this consensus is that all units surveyed report selective treatment and management of defective newborns. Beyond this, the present research demonstrates that a professional consensus exists on six particular issues relevant to passive euthanasia of defective newborns.

First, a professional accord exists as to the identity of the proper authority - between parents, courts, variously constituted committees, and doctors - to make decisions to initiate or withhold lifesaving medical treatment. The consensus established in neonatal intensive care is that doctors are the proper decision makers. This point was observed repeatedly throughout the survey. Doctors in the birth facility decide for the parents whether to refer to neonatal intensive care;[37] doctors exclude parents from decisions whether to ventilate low weight or defective neonates in the birth facility[38] and in neonatal intensive care;[39] standardized medical criteria are used by doctors in some units to decide whether ventilation should be commenced;[40] ventilation is discontinued by doctors without parental, court or committee involvement in the birth facility[41] and in neonatal intensive care;[42] doctors refuse to operate when the parents request that treatment be initiated;[43] doctors fail to inform parents of available lifesaving medical procedures in the birth facility[44] and in neonatal intensive care;[45] doctors by-pass established hospital committee structures in deciding whether to withhold lifesaving treatment;[46] doctors fail to provide the parents with adequate or objective information relevant to medical decision making;[47] doctors resort to legal means to compel compliance with their view that treat-

---

37. *Supra*, p. 10-11.
38. *Supra*, p. 14.
39. *Supra*, p. 18.
40. *Supra*, p. 15.
41. *Supra*, p. 16.
42. *Supra*, p. 18.
43. *Supra*, pp. 21, 28-29.
44. *Supra*, p. 12.
45. *Supra*, p. 32.
46. *Supra*, p. 32.
47. *Supra*, p. 12.

ment should be initiated;[48] doctors resort to moral and peer pressure to compel compliance with their view that treatment should be initiated;[49] doctors initiate treatment without parental, court, or committee consent.[50]

The particular incidents referred to in the survey are not presented as examples of what every doctor would do if similarly situated. However, the examples are all related in that, in various contexts, they reveal paradigm instances of medical practice where the doctor reserves for himself decisional power to initiate or withhold treatment in neonatal intensive care. The thread which links all of these examples together is an established professional consensus — a practical ethics expressed in the routines of institutional life — that doctors are the proper decision-makers with respect to passive euthanasia of defective newborns.

A second ethical dilemma in the intensive care nursery relates to the procedure by which decisions to withhold treatment are made. Assuming that doctors are the decision-makers, which doctors should decide, and, if more than one, what procedure should govern the decision-making process? A professional consensus exists on that issue. While the neonatologist retains formal responsibility for the decision, established procedure requires that this formal authority be tempered against the necessities of an interdisciplinary specialty. There is a professional understanding that the neonatologist must initiate appropriate consultation with pediatric colleagues and neonatal staff in order to coordinate a decision in concert by the neonatal team.

The evidence for the existence of this consensus is as follows: patients are admitted to neonatal intensive care in the neonatologist's name as his patient;[51] residents in neonatal intensive care, unlike residents in the birth facility, have no decision-making authority to discontinue treatment;[52] residents and nurses, who actually care for the child, are encouraged to express their opinions daily to the neonatologist on ward rounds; vigorous disagreement by neonatal staff, especially nurses, may lead to legal interference with any decision taken;[53] neonatologists almost always consult the referring pediatrician;[54] neonatologists

---

48. *Supra*, pp. 13, 31.
49. *Supra*, pp. 11, 13, 30-31.
50. *Supra*, p. 14.
51. *Supra*, pp. 4, 17, 18.
52. *Supra*, p. 18.
53. *Supra*, p. 13.
54. *Supra*, p. 17.

routinely consult pediatric colleagues in cases of multiple anomalies,[55] even where the appropriate course of medical action appears relatively clear to the neonatologist; cases of neonatologists acting alone are rare;[56] consultation with pediatric colleagues does not transfer responsibility for the patient away from the neonatologist,[57] pediatric colleagues who are consulted view themselves as advisors in a collegial decision-making process;[58] failure by pediatric specialists - especially neurosurgeons - to consult extensively with pediatric colleagues provokes sharp criticism from neonatologists;[59] inadequate consultation, when it occurs, is perceived as a problem needing correction.[60]

A third problem concerns the information which must be developed prior to making a decision for passive euthanasia of defective newborns. Doctors in neonatal intensive care are generally agreed that the child's anticipated quality of life must be determined by extensive medical assessments of the child's separate body systems. "Quality of life" refers to the child's potential for physical and mental development, and environmental factors which bear on the potential for development. Where the anticipated quality of life does not decisively indicate whether treatment should be initiated, further information must be developed. The parents' wishes are ascertained, and figure as a separate factor in the decision whether to treat.

Evidence in support of the existence of this consensus is as follows: doctors use the child's "best interests" as the primary test for deciding whether to treat;[61] "best interest" is understood as the medical probabilities based on medical indications;[62] the child's body systems will be separately assessed by different pediatric specialists in order to estimate anticipated quality of life;[63] it is standard policy for birth facilities not having the capacity to make extensive separate assessments to refer to neonatal intensive care;[64] the parents' wishes become a secondary test in doubtful cases;[65] the parents' wishes are a significant

---

55. *Supra*, p. 19.
56. *Supra*, p. 17.
57. *Supra*, p. 19.
58. *Supra*, p. 19.
59. *Supra*, p. 20.
60. *Supra*, p. 20.
61. *Supra*, pp. 30, 31.
62. *Supra*, p. 31.
63. *Supra*, pp. 19, 20.
64. *Supra*, p. 10.
65. *Supra*, p. 28.

factor in the doctor's decision;[66] the doctors are astute to involve the parents in discussions to determine their wishes;[67] neonatologists criticize pediatric colleagues who fail to determine the parents' wishes adequately.[68]

A special difficulty of information development related to the use of para-medical socio-economic and personal data for the purposes of deciding whether to treat defective newborns. It is generally agreed that para-medical information properly figures in the decision-making formula. Most of the units take initiative in developing para-medical facts.

However, the consensus established is narrow. It exists only as respects the propriety of using paramedical data. The units have evolved no uniform practices for gathering para-medical facts. There is no substantial agreement on how to control the quality of para-medical data developed. Nor are there common practices respecting the weight properly accorded to certain contentious information, such as economic data. In sum, the units are anxious to acquire para-medical facts, but differ in their methods of fact-gathering, quality control and the use of any data obtained.

Evidence for the existence of this consensus is as follows: the child of a young unwed mother has diminished chances of receiving treatment;[69] the only child of an older mother, or a mother who has had many unsuccessful pregnancies, has greater chances of receiving treatment.[70] The child of a family who appears well able to cope with the deformity is significantly more likely to receive treatment. "Being able to cope" refers to the economic position of the family,[71] the emotional maturity of the family[72] and the intelligence of the family.[73] The child of a family which is likely to be torn apart[74] or to have other children injured[75] by the addition of a deformed infant is less likely to be treated.

---

66. *Supra*, pp. 13, 28, 29.

67. *Supra*, p. 29.

68. *Supra*, pp. 20-21.

69. *Supra*, p. 22.

70. *Supra*, p. 24.

71. *Supra*, p. 23.

72. *Supra*, p. 22.

73. *Supra*, p. 22.

74. *Supra*, pp. 22-23.

75. *Supra*, p. 23.

Evidence for the lack of agreement on methods of data acquisition, data use, and quality control is as follows: some nurses gather non-medical facts by non-scientific observation when opportunities arise,[76] whereas others are routinely sent to interview the parents with fact gathering in mind;[77] social workers are used as fact gatherers at some institutions and build their data into the medical chart;[78] whereas at other institutions social workers are restricted to a liaison function; doctors who profess to use para-medical data admit, when pressed, that the available data is poor quality;[79] doctors misjudge the family's ability to cope.[80].

A fifth issue relates to informed consent. Doctors who practice in neonatal intensive care obtain a sharply different perspective on informed consent than do lawyers who read the law reports. Doctors regard with suspicion and hostility the rule that a fully and freely informed parental consent must precede medical treatment.

Neonatal intensive care personnel treat the informed consent doctrine as a formality. In practice, the doctrine provides little substantive guidance for medical conduct. Where the neonatal team is of opinion that significant treatment is indicated, accepted practice requires the doctor to direct the parents towards that conclusion. The medical alternatives are explained fully to the parents only so long as they willingly accept the doctor's leadership.

Where the parents resist giving consent to treatment, doctors guide the parental decision by carefully selecting the information provided. The medical alternatives are narrowed. With strong, reluctant parents, the neonatal team may mount a campaign to convince. Parents who refuse outright may be subjected to legal action or coerced in other ways.

This is broadly similar to situations where the neonatal team is of opinion that treatment should be withheld. There is a difference, however, in that doctors feel less constrained by legal requirements to obtain an informed consent for withholding treatment. There is a broad consensus that doctors cannot be forced to treat personally; they are entitled to withdraw from the case.

---

76. *Supra*, pp. 25-26.

77. *Supra*, pp. 25-26.

78. *Supra*, pp. 25-26.

79. *Supra*, pp. 14, 25.

80. *Supra*, pp. 28-29.

Evidence for existence of this consensus is as follows: doctors are ignorant of the legal requirements of informed consent;[81] doctors describe the informed consent rules as "nonsense";[82] no consent is obtained to initiate or withdraw ventilation;[83] doctors conceal decisions to withdraw ventilation;[84] doctors assert that it is unfair to ask parents to make medical decisions;[85] doctors assert that parents are incapable of making medical decisions;[86] doctors fail to inform the parents of available lifesaving treatment;[87] information provided to the parents fails to present the medical alternatives objectively;[88] parents who disagree with the doctor's views get less objective information;[89] parents who resist giving consent are subjected to a campaign to convince by the neonatal team;[90] doctors refuse to treat even where the parents so request;[91] doctors assert that they cannot be forced to operate.[92]

A final dilemma concerns the care properly to be provided to a child whom the doctors decide not to treat. There is a general agreement that the child should be fed, kept warm and have his fluids managed.[93] A consensus exists that nothing further should be done for him. No antibiotics should be administered. No minor surgery should be performed. No resuscitation should be attempted.[94]

The research failed to document any consensus about more active forms of euthanasia for defective children who will not be treated.

---

81. No doctor surveyed could state with confidence what the informed consent doctrine required.

82. As in the following comment by a neurologist: '...informed consent; it's nonsense really. How can you say to a mother and dad who are used to living with this baby, 'well now, here's the story' ".

83. *Supra*, pp. 15, 16, 18.

84. *Supra*, pp. 16, 18.

85. *Supra*, pp. 14, 16, 21.

86. *Supra*, pp. 14, 19, 21.

87. *Supra*, p. 12.

88. *Supra*, pp. 21, 32.

89. *Supra*, p. 29.

90. *Supra*, p. 30.

91. *Supra*, pp. 28, 29.

92. *Supra*, p. 20.

93. *Supra*, p. 33.

94. *Supra*, pp. 33, 34.

While some units tolerate the administration of increasing dosages of painkillers with the intent of hastening death, no common practices, discoverable by existing research, appear to have developed. This is consistent with a similar lack of accord which characterizes the literature.[95]

95. See, for example, D.J. Roy, "Defective Babies: Quality of Life, The Measure of Care?" in D.J. Roy (ed.), *Medical Wisdom and Ethics in the Treatment of Severely Defective Newborn and Young Children*. Montreal: Eden Press, 1978; W.H. Baughman, J.C. Bruha and F.J. Gould, *Euthanasia: Criminal, Tort, Constitutional and Legislative Considerations* (1973), 48 Notre Dame Lawyer 1203; H. Baunemann, *Life Devoid of Value?* (1976), 115 C.M.A.J. 1086, R.E. Cooke, M.D., *Whose Suffering?* (1972), 80 J. Pediatrics 906; J.M. Freeman, *Is there a Right to Die Quickly?* (1972), 80 J. Pediatrics 904; Y. Kamisar, *Some Non-Religious Views Against Proposed "Mercy Killing" Legislation* (1958), 42 Minn. L. Rev. 969; Statement of W.W. Sackett, M.D., Member of the House of Representatives of the State of Florida, *Death with Dignity*, Part 1 — Washington, D.C., August 7, 1972.

CHAPTER TWO

LEGAL ASPECTS

CHAPTER TWO

LEGAL ASPECTS

I. DECISION MAKING AUTHORITY

1. Initiating Treatment

(a) Duty of Disclosure

How awful life would be were there no freedom from unwanted meddling with one's body. All civilized societies jealously protect the right to bodily integrity. In Canada, the human person is inviolable;[1] gratuitous interference with the body is not tolerated.

To ensure that the right to bodily integrity has teeth Canadian law requires consent or specific legal authority for all medical interference with the human person.[2] As Chief Justice Laskin stated: "The underlying principle is the right of a patient to decide what, if anything, should be done with his own body".[3] Non-consensual medical inter-

---

1. *Civil Code of Lower Canada* (1866), art. 19, as amended S.Q. 1971, c. 84, s. 2: "The human person is inviolable. No one may cause harm to the person of another without his consent or without being authorized by law to do so"; *Re Eve* (1979), 10 R.F.L. (2d) 317, 328, (P.E.I.S.C. Fam. Div.), (McQuaid, J.) revd. on other grounds (1980), 74 A.P.R. 97 (P.E.I.C.A.); "One of these rights is the inviolability of their persons from involuntary trespass" (on appeal to S.C.C.).

2. *Parmley* v. *Parmley*, [1945] S.C.R. 635, 645-6: "The right of a patient, when consulting a professional man in the practice of his profession ... is ... to determine what, if any, operation or treatment shall be proceeded with".

3. *Hopp* v. *Lepp* (1980), 13 C.C.L.T. 66, 73 (S.C.C.). See also *Reibl* v. *Hughes* (1980), 14 C.C.L.T. 1, 12-13 (S.C.C.). Chief Justice Laskin was echoing the famous dictum of Mr. Justice Cardozo in *Schloendorff* v. *Soc. of N.Y. Hosp.*, 211 N.Y. 125, 129; 105 N.E. 92, 93 (1914), overruled on other grounds, *Bing* v. *Thunig* 143 N.E. (2d) 3 (N.Y. 1957): "Every human being of adult years and sound mind has a right to determine what shall be done with his own body". In *Matter of Erickson* v. *Dilgard*, 44 Misc. (2d) 27, 28, 252 N.Y.S. (2d) 705, 706 (Sup. Ct. 1962) the Court said: "it is the individual who is the subject of a medical decision who has the final say". So too, in *Rutherford* v. *U.S.*, 438 F. Supp. 1287, 1299 (D. 1977), revd. 442 U.S. 544, 99 S.Ct. 2370 (1978): it is "incontrovertible that a patient has a strong interest in being free from non-consensual invasion of his bodily integrity"; and *Eichner* v. *Dillon*, 426 N.Y.S. (2d)

vention is strenuously resisted by Canada's legal system; it gives rise to civil responsibility for the torts of battery and trespass,[4] and criminal responsibility for assault.[5]

In order to promote the rights to bodily integrity and individual self-determination Canadian courts have imposed a corresponding duty upon the medical profession. It is a duty of disclosure. Mere consent of the patient to medical intervention, by itself, will not protect doctors from civil responsibility. The patient's consent must be informed, in the sense that the doctor must disclose to the patient details of the proposed procedure sufficient to enable a reasonable person, in the patient's position, to decide intelligently whether to consent. This means that the doctor

> should answer any specific questions posed by the patient as to the risks involved and should, without being questioned, disclose to him the nature of the proposed operation, its gravity, any material risks and any special or unusual risks attendant upon the performance of the operation.[6]

517, 536 (App. Div. 1980), affd. (*sub. nom. Matter of Storar*) 438 N.Y.S. (2d) 266, 420 N.E. (2d) 64 (1981): "There exists a solid line of case authority recognizing the undeniable right of a terminally ill but competent individual to refuse medical care, even if it will inexorably result in death". See also *Union Pacific Ry.* v. *Botsford*, 141 U.S. 250, 251, 11 S.Ct. 1000, 35 L. Ed. 734 (1980); *Matter of Melideo*, 88 Misc. (2d) 974, 975, 390 N.Y.S. (2d) 523, 524 (Sup. Ct. 1976); *Long Island Jewish-Hillside Med. Center* v. *Levitt*, 73 Misc. (2d) 395, 397, 342 N.Y.S. (2d) 356, 359 (Sup. Ct. 1973); *Matter of Nemser*, 51 Misc. (2d) 616, 273 N.Y.S. (2d) 624 (Supt. Ct. 1966); *Satz* v. *Perlmutter*, 379 So. (2d) 359 (Fla. Sup. Ct. 1980); *Superintendent of Belchertown State School* v. *Saikewicz*, 370 N.E. (2d) 417 (Mass. 1977); *Lane* v. *Candura*, 376 N.E. (2d) 1232, 1236 (Mass. App. Ct. 1978); *Matter of Osborne*, 294 A. (2d) 372 (D.C. 1972); *Matter of Estate of Brooks*, 32 Ill. (2d) 361, 205 N.E. (2d) 435; *Palm Springs Gen. Hosp.* v. *Martinez*, Civ. No. 71-12687 (Dade County Cir. Ct. July 2, 1977); *Matter of Yetter*, 62 Pa. D. & C. (2d) 619; See also Note, "Last Rights: Hawaii's Law on the Right to Choice of Therapy for Dying Patients", 1 Hawaii L. Rev. 144, 153-157; Note, "The Tragic Choice: Termination of Care for Patients in a Permanent Vegetative State" (1977), 51 N.Y.U.L. Rev. 285, 306-308; Bryn, "Compulsory Life-saving Treatment for the Competent Adult", 44 Fordham L. Rev. 1, 2-16.

4. *Marshall* v. *Curry*, [1933] 3 D.L.R. 260 (N.S.S.C.); *Murray* v. *McMurchy*, [1949] 2 D.L.R. 442 (B.C.S.C.); *Schweizer* v. *Central Hosp. et al.* (1974), 6 O.R. (2d) 606 (H.C.J.). In *Kelly* v. *Hazlett* (1976), 15 O.R. (2d) 290, 312-13, 1 C.C.L.T. 1, 27 (H.C.J.), Morden J. suggested a wider operation of the action in battery. If the basic nature and character of the treatment differs from that consented to or if a risk not disclosed, though collateral, nevertheless is material, battery would be available. This view was disapproved of in *Reibl* v. *Hughes* (1980), 14 C.C.L.T. 1, 12-13 (S.C.C.): battery should be confined to cases where there is no consent at all, or where treatment goes beyond that consented.

5. *Criminal Code*, R.S.C. 1970, c. C-34, s. 244, as amended.

6. *Hopp* v. *Lepp* (1980), 13 C.C.L.T. 66, 87 (S.C.C.).

The duty of disclosure rises and falls with the circumstances of the particular patient. The courts accept that certain patients, because of emotional factors, may be unable to cope with facts relevant to recommended treatment. In such a case a doctor would be justified in withholding or generalizing information where, with less emotional patients, he would be required to be more specific.[7] The intellectual capacity of a patient may suggest that the patient could not accept certain information without so obviously distorting it as to make the patient incapable of any rational choice at all.[8] A particular patient may waive aside any duty of disclosure and submit to the risks of treatment, whatever they may be.[9] The impact of full disclosure on a particular patient may suggest that full disclosure is medically unwarranted.[10] While these exceptions are judicially recognized, the current of medical law is running towards full disclosure. "It should not be for the physician to decide that the patient will be unable to make a choice", said Chief Justice Laskin. "A Surgeon is better advised to give the warning".[11] While extenuating circumstances justifying non-disclosure exist, the courts will treat reference to them with suspicion.

Additionally, the patient's consent must be voluntary. The doctors cannot mount an attack on the patient's will to induce consent. Nor can a valid consent be obtained while the patient is stupefied by drugs or anaesthetics. In *Beausoleil* v. *Soeurs de la Charité*[12] consent was vitiated where, thirty minutes prior to the operation, an anaesthetist visited the sedated patient for the first time and, through persistence, convinced her over her objections to have a spinal anaesthetic. In *Kelly* v. *Hazlett*[13] the court made clear that doctors labour under an onus to prove affirmatively voluntariness of consent.

If the doctor fails in his duty of disclosure he will be civilly liable to the patient for all damages caused, including damage caused by non-negligent medical treatment. Liability for non-negligent treatment arises if the court can say that a reasonable person, in the patient's

---

7. *Reibl* v. *Hughes* (1980), 14 C.C.L.T. 1, 17 (S.C.C.).

8. *Smith* v. *Auckland Hosp. Bd.*, [1964] N.Z.L.R. 241, 250-1, affd. [1965] N.Z.L.R. 191, cited approvingly in *Male* v. *Hopmans*, [1967] 2 O.R. 457, 64 D.L.R. (2d) 105 (C.A.).

9. *Reibl* v. *Hughes* (1980), 14 C.C.L.T. 1, 17 (S.C.C.); *Smith* v. *Auckland Hosp. Bd.*, *supra*, note 8.

10. *Reibl* v. *Hughes* (1980), 14 C.C.L.T. 1, 18 (S.C.C.).

11. *Hopp* v. *Lepp* (1980), 13 C.C.L.T. 66, 85 (S.C.C.).

12. *Beausoleil* v. *Communauté des Soeurs de la Charité de la Providence et al.* (1964), 53 D.L.R. (2d) 65 (Que. C.A.).

13. *Kelly* v. *Hazlett* (1976), 15 O.R. (2d) 290, 1 C.C.L.T. 1 (H.C.).

circumstances, would have refused to consent to the procedure had proper disclosure been made.[14]

(b) Criminal Law

A requirement for consent also arises from criminal law. All intentional applications of force to the person of another without consent constitute criminal assault.[15] Thus, all medical interference with the body of another is unlawful unless justified by consent or legal authority.[16] This includes such medical procedures as taking x-rays[17] or prescribing medication.[18]

Consent in the criminal context differs from consent relevant to civil liability. Both criminal and civil liability require that consent be referable to the medical act performed; consent to some other act, or fraudulent misrepresentation as to any material component of the treatment, will nullify consent.[19] However, obligations arising at criminal law imply no further duty of disclosure. Breach of a duty to inform gives rise to civil responsibility only.[20]

---

14. *Reibl* v. *Hughes* (1980), 14 C.C.L.T. 1, 22 (S.C.C.): "In saying that the test is based on the decision that a reasonable person in the patient's position would have made, I should make it clear that the patient's particular concerns must also be reasonably based ... for example, fears which are not related to the material risks which should have been but were not disclosed would not be causative factors. However, economic considerations could reasonably go to causation where, for example, the loss of an eye as a result of non-disclosure of a material risk brings about the loss of a job for which good eyesight is required. In short, although account must be taken of a patient's particular position ... it must be objectively assessed in terms of reasonableness".

15. *Criminal Code*, R.S.C. 1970, c. C-34, s. 244, as amended.

16. *Laporte* v. *Laganière* (1972), 18 C.R.N.S. 357, 361 (Que. Q.B.).

17. *Id.*

18. *R.* v. *Harley* (1830), 4 Car. & P. 369, 172 E.R. 744; *R.* v. *Dale* (1852), 6 Cox C.C. 14.

19. *Criminal: Bolduc and Bird* v. *The Queen* (1967), 63 D.L.R. (2d) 82 (S.C.C.); *Civil: Murray* v. *McMurchy*, [1949] 2 D.L.R. 442 (B.C.S.C.) (consent to caesarian section; doctor sterilizes patient; liable for trespass); *Schweizer* v. *Central Hosp.* (1974), 6 O.R. (2d) 606, 53 D.L.R. (3d) 494 (H.C.J.) (consent to operation on toe, doctor operates on back, liable for trespass); *Hobbs* v. *Kizer*, 236 F. 681 (U.S.C.A., 8th Cir., 1916) (civil fraud as to nature of operation performed vitiates consent).

20. Law Reform Commission of Canada, *Medical Treatment and Criminal Law* (1980), p. 66: "the Commission's recommendation amounts to this: failure to inform the patient of all the possible consequences would not obviate the patient's freely given consent for purposes of the criminal law, even though such failure may still attract civil liability".

The consent requirement at criminal law is qualified by an important statutory defence.[21] Section 45 of the *Criminal Code* protects everyone performing surgical operations for the benefit of a patient from criminal responsibility if

(a) the operation is performed with reasonable care and skill and

(b) it is reasonable to perform the operation, having regard to the state of health of the person at the time the operation is performed and to all the circumstances of the case.[22]

Section 45 is available to everyone; it is not limited to the hospital setting. The essential ingredients of the defence are performance with reasonable care and skill, and reasonableness of the procedure having regard to the health of the patient and the circumstances of the case. Although the operation must be for the "benefit" of the patient, benefit is widely conceived. It extends to non-therapeutic socio-economic benefits such as contraceptive sterilization.[23]

(c) Consent Legislation

Quite obviously newborns cannot consent to medical treatments. Consent must come from a legally authorized substitute. At common law parents are the natural guardians of their children[24] and thus have full power over their persons.[25] This includes authority to consent to

---

21. In *Cataford* v. *Moreau*, [1978] C.S. 933, 936, 7 C.C.L.T. 241, 253 Chief Justice Deschênes treated s. 45 of the *Criminal Code* as a defence, although this has been challenged in the law journals: See Somerville, *Medical Interventions and the Criminal Law: Lawful or Excusable Wounding?* (1980), 26 McGill L.J. 82, 96.

22. *Criminal Code*, R.S.C. 1970, c. C-34, s. 45.

23. In *Cataford* v. *Moreau*, [1978] C.S. 993, 7 C.C.L.T. 241 Chief Justice Deschenes said: "Dans le présent cas, compte tenu de l'âge des parties, du nombre de leurs enfants, de leur situation économique et sociale, il fait peu de doute que 'toutes les autres circonstances de l'espèce', pour citer le langage de l'article 45 C. cr., conduiraient à la conclusion que l'intervention a été pratiquée 'pour le bien' de la demanderesse". However, in *Re Eve* (1980), 27 N. & P.E.I.R. 97 (P.E.I.C.A.) (on appeal to S.C.C.), MacDonald J. would exclude application of s. 45 to non-therapeutic substituted consent cases. Mr. Justice MacDonald said, p. 125: "In my opinion this section is only intended to apply to cases where consent can be given by the person involved or in cases of emergency or necessity".

24. Co. Litt. 88b, 1 Bl. Comm. 46; *Ex. p. Hopkins*, 3 P. Wms. 152 (control of father absolute); *Hopper* v. *Steeves* (1899), 34 N.B.R. 591, 594 (C.A.) *per* Barker J: "The guardian by nature is the father, and on his death the mother, and this guardianship extends only to the custody of the person. The guardianship by nurture, which only occurs when the infant is without any other guardian, belongs exclusively to the parents, first to the father and then to the mother".

25. *Ex p. Bond*, 8 L.T. 252; *Hopper* v. *Steeves* (1899), 34 N.B.R. 591 (C.A.); *In re Flynn* (1848), 2 De G. & Sin. 457. At common law the father had the absolute right to care

medical treatment.[26] Although the permissible consent to treatment for minor children is limited to medical procedures which are not detrimental,[27] there is no requirement that the procedure actually benefit the child. It is sufficient if it is for the benefit of a third party.[28] However, the parents cannot consent to medically ineffective and harmful treatment. If they do certain administrative officials are justified in interfering with parental custody under the Child Welfare Acts.[29]

Provincial legislation dovetails with this law in important respects. Ontario[30] and New Brunswick[31] require written consent to "surgical

---

and control of his children. However, the absolute right of the father has been eroded so that *In Re McGrath*, [1893] 1 Ch. 143, 148 (1892), the Court of Appeal held: "The dominant matter for the consideration of the courts is the welfare of the child"; see also *J. v. C.*, [1970] A.C. 668, 697 (H.L.) *per* Lord Guest: "in my view the law administered by the Chancery Court as representing the Queen as parens patriae never required that the father's wishes should prevail over the welfare of the infant ... The father's wishes were to be considered but only as one of the factors as bearing on child's welfare. The father had no 'right' as such to the care and control of his infant children". In *DeLaurier v. Jackson*, [1934] S.C.R. 149 an issue arose as to a parent's right to determine the religious faith in which his child is to be educated. Mr. Justice Hughes said (at p. 158): "In equity a principle was early established that the court might control or ignore the parental right ... when judicially satisfied that the welfare of the child required that the parental right be suspended or superseded". Also note that in Ontario and the Yukon Territories the father and mother of an infant are now "equally entitled to the custody of the child": *Children's Law Reform Act*, R.S.O. 1980, c. 68, s. 20(1), as amended by S.O. 1982, c. 20, s. 1; *Children's Act*, Bill 19, 4th Sess., 25th Leg. Y.T., 1984, s. 63(1).

26. *Bonner* v. *Moran*, 126 F. (2d) 121 (C.A., D.C. 1941) (jury to be instructed that consent of parent necessary to medical procedure on a minor for the benefit of third party).

27. See generally Dickens, *The Use of Children in Medical Experimentation* (1975), 43 Medico-Legal Journal 166. American courts stretch the concept of what is or is not detrimental, in order to allow organ donation by a minor child to a sibling. In these cases the courts have found a "psychological benefit" to the donor child in keeping his sibling alive, and thus justified parental consent to the donation. *Strunk* v. *Strunk*, 445 S.W. (2d) 145 (Ky. C.A. 1969); *Hart* v. *Brown*, 289 A. (2d) 386 (Conn. 1972).

28. *Bonner* v. *Moran*, 126 F. (2d) 121 (U.S.C.A., D.C. 1941).

29. *Custody of a Minor*, 393 N.E. (2d) 836 (Mass. 1979) (parents compelled by the court to consent to chemotherapy for child suffering from leukemia); *Re D*, [1976] 1 All E.R. 326 (Fam. D.) (the court refused to authorize the sterilization of a mentally incompetent girl who was ward of the court. The Court held, (p. 335), "the frustration and resentment of realizing .... what had happened could be devastating ... This operation is neither medically indicated nor necessary, and ... it would not be in D's best interest for it to be performed").

30. R.R.O. 1980, Reg. 865, s. 50(b) under the *Public Hospitals Act*, R.S.O. 1980, c. 410, as amended.

31. N.B. Reg. 66-47, s. 40(1)(c), as amended, under the *Public Hospitals Act*, R.S.N.B. 1973, c. P-23.

operations" on patients under sixteen from a parent, guardian or next of kin. If an attending physician or hospital administrator in Ontario thinks consent in writing should precede "diagnostic testing" or "treatment", the parent, guardian or next of kin must sign for a child under 16.[31a] Quebec allows for effective consent by minors over the age of fourteen. However the parents or guardian must be informed if the minor is to be sheltered for more than 12 hours, or requires extended treatment.[32] Written consent from the patient or a legally qualified representative is required for all care provided to persons in hospital[33] and for all surgical operations.[34] In Saskatchewan written consent from a parent or guardian must be obtained prior to "surgical operations" on minors under eighteen.[35] Manitoba requires written consent for all surgical operations performed on patients in private hospitals.[36]

In New Brunswick, the law respecting consent to medical treatment of persons who have attained the age of majority applies in all respects to minors who have attained the age of 16 years in the same manner as if they had attained the age of majority.[37] In addition minors under 16 may validly consent to treatment if in the opinion of two legally qualified medical practitioners,

---

31a. R.R.O. 1980, Reg. 865, s. 50(b) under the *Public Hospitals Act*, R.S.O. 1980, c. 410.

32. *Public Health Protection Act*, R.S.Q., c. P-35, s. 42. If consent cannot be obtained or is refused, a judge of the Superior Court may authorize care or treatment in the child's best interests.

33. R.S.Q. 1981, c. S-5, r.1 under the *Health Services and Social Services Act*, R.S.Q., c. S-5, s. 58.

34. *Id.*

35. Sask. Reg. 331/79 under the *Hospital Standard Act*, R.S.S. 1978, c. H-10, s. 55. See also Man. R. Reg. 1971, Reg. P130-R1, s. 6 under the *Private Hospitals Act*, R.S.M. 1970, c. 206, C.C.S.M., c. P130; N.B. Reg. 47/66, as amended, under the *Public Hospitals Act*, R.S.N.B. 1973, c. P-23, s. 40.

36. Man. R. Reg. 1970, Reg. P130-R1 under the *Private Hospitals Act*, R.S.M. 1970, c. 206, C.C.S.M., c. P130.

37. *Medical Consent of Minors Act*, R.S.N.B., c. M-6.1, as amended, s. 2. However, medical treatment is defined by the statute (s. 1) as,
   (a) surgical and dental treatment,
   (b) any procedure undertaken for the purpose of diagnosis,
   (c) any procedure undertaken for the purpose of preventing any disease or ailment, and
   (d) any procedure that is ancillary to any treatment as it applies to that treatment.
   This narrow definition means that a minor would not be able to give effective consent to non-surgical treatment (as opposed to diagnosis or prevention), of a disease or ailment.

(a) the minor is capable of understanding the nature and conse-
      quences of a medical treatment and,
(b) the medical treatment and procedure to be used is in the best
      interests of the minor and his continuing health and well
      being.[37a]

If the minor does meet these criteria, the parents must consent
to surgical operation.[37b]

In British Columbia, an infant 16 or older may validly consent to
medical treatment as if he were of full age.[37c] However, this applies
only where the attending doctor makes a reasonable effort to obtain
parent or guardian's consent. Additionally, the attending doctor must
obtain a second opinion in writing, which confirms that treatment serves
the best interests of the infant.[37d]

The general rule, thus — with various statutory additions — is
that parents must give informed consent to all medical procedures on
their minor children. To this general rule there are exceptions. The
Canadian Medical Association's *Code of Ethics* requires a doctor to
"render such therapy as he believes to be in the patient's interests" if
the patient is unable to consent and an agent is unavailable.[37e] This
amounts to a virtual legal duty for the physician because the torts
system has scrupulous regard for documents such as the *Code of Ethics*
in articulating the scope of the doctor's duty to take care. In the same
vein the common law excuses doctors from civil responsibility for non-
consensual treatment if their conduct is justified by necessitous circumstances. In order to be embraced by the emergency doctrine the
circumstances must be urgent; immediate action must be required. It
must be unreasonable to postpone the procedure to a later date. There
must be a threat to life or health. The treatment must be reasonably
necessary for the preservation of life or health.[38] If, however, the patient

---

37a. *Medical Consent of Minors Act*, S.N.B. 1976, c. M-6.1, as amended, s. 3(1). Where
       the consent of parent or guardian is necessary and is refused or not available, any
       person may apply to the court for an order dispensing with consent (s. 4.).

37b. N.B. Reg. 66-47, as amended by N.B. Reg. 79-66, under the *Public Hospitals Act*,
       R.S.N.B. 1973, c. P-23.

37c. *Infants Act*, R.S.B.C. 1979, c. 196, s. 16(1).

37d. *Infants Act*, R.S.B.C. 1979, c. 196, s. 16(4).

37e. Canadian Medical Association, *Code of Ethics* (September 1982), "Responsibilities
       to the Patient", s. 14. See also *infra*, note 143.

38.   *Murray* v. *McMurchy*, [1949] 2 D.L.R. 442, 444-5 (B.C.S.C.); *Marshall* v. *Curry*,
       [1933] 3 D.L.R. 260, 267, 268, 271, 275 (N.S.S.C.); *Parmley* v. *Parmley*, [1945] 4
       D.L.R. 81, 84 (S.C.C.). See also *Rogers* v. *Lumbermans Mutual Casualty Co.* 119
       So. (2d) 649, 650 (La. App. 1960).

expressly or impliedly has refused consent, the emergency doctrine is exhausted; non-consensual treatment remains actionable in that case.[39] The doctrine is identical in the civilian legal system of Quebec.[40]

Similarly, necessitous circumstances excuse actions otherwise giving rise to criminal responsibility.[41] However, Canadian courts grudgingly admit the necessity doctrine in criminal law and confine it within a narrow compass. There must be an urgent situation of clear and imminent peril where compliance with the law is demonstrably impossible.[42]

Notwithstanding this cold reception by Canadian courts, academic writers are confident that emergencies justify a doctor in performing treatment on a patient who is unconscious or otherwise unable to consent.[43] There is equal confidence — and indeed the point seems difficult to refute — that this excuse is at an end if the patient is competent to consent and refuses.[44] Non-consensual treatment for life threatening situations is more easily justified under s. 45 of the *Criminal Code*. Section 45, however, has a limited scope; procedures other than "surgical operations" are not authorized by s. 45. They must be justified, if at all, by the common law necessity doctrine.

Provincial legislation extends the necessity doctrine in certain situations. Ontario dispenses with the consent requirement for "surgical operations" where delay caused by obtaining consent would endanger the patient.[45] In Quebec, "anaesthetic or surgical procedures" without

---

39. *Mulloy* v. *Hop Sang*, [1935] 1 W.W.R. 714 (Alta. C.A.) (refusal of consent in emergency circumstances gives rise to liability in battery and trespass); *Allan* v. *New Mount Sinai Hosp.* (1980), 11 C.C.L.T. 299 (Ont. H.C.J.) (refusal of consent in non-emergency circumstances gives rise to liability in battery).

40. *Parnell* v. *Springle* (1899), 5 R.J. 74; *Caron* v. *Gagnon* (1930), 68 C.S. 155. However, it was suggested in one lower court decision that an adult, competent patient could not refuse life saving medical treatment: see C.S. (Mtl.) 500-05-001336-765, 23 jan. 1976 (Barrette, J.); A. Mayrand, *L'Inviolabilité de la personne humaine* (1975), pp. 48-9, no. 40. This contradicts principles saturating the entire infrastructure of medical law and cannot be considered correct.

41. The common law defence of necessity is preserved by section 7(3) of the *Criminal Code*, R.S.C. 1970, c. C-34.

42. *Morgentaler* v. *The Queen*, [1976] 1 S.C.R. 616, 678; *R.* v. *Gilkes* (1978), 8 C.R. (3d) 159, 166 (Ont. Prov. Ct.) "The essence of the necessity plea is that the accused could have complied with the letter of the law but did not do so because the harm or evil resulting therefrom would be incommensurately greater than the harm or evil resulting from non-compliance".

43. Stephen, *Digest*, Article 311.

44. G. Williams, *Criminal Law: The General Part*, (2d ed. 1961), p. 732.

45. R.R.O. 1980, Reg. 865, s. 50 under the *Public Hospitals Act*, R.S.O. 1980, c. 410.

consent are authorized if the physician first certifies in writing that delay could be prejudicial to the patient.[46] If a minor is in danger of death, parental consent is not required for "care or treatment".[47] New Brunswick dispenses with the requirement for consent where treatment is "necessary in an emergency to meet imminent risk to the minor's life or health".[48]

With the exception of New Brunswick, the statutes are incomplete. Some apply only to surgical operations; others are restricted to public hospitals; still others require the doctor first to fill out forms, notwithstanding the presence of an emergency. Small wonder, then, that various law reform commissions have wrestled arduously with this problem.[49]

Because the statutes circumscribe a narrow compass, the common law emergency doctrine remains of paramount importance where initiation of treatment without consent is at issue. That doctrine, as modified by the legislation, becomes problematic when tested against routine practices of Canadian neonatal units. The reality of neonatal practice is that doctors retain decisional authority to initiate treatment as against parents. In some cases treatment is simply commenced without consent; in others doctors are highly selective in providing information to the parents in order to influence consent; in still others doctors resort to

---

46. R.R.Q. 1981, c. S-5, r. 1, s. 66 under the *Health Services and Social Services Act*, R.S.Q., c. S-5.

47. *Public Health Protection Act*, R.S.Q., c. P-35, s. 43.

48. The New Brunswick Act is based on the Model Act of the Uniform Law Conference: See *Medical Consent of Minors Act*, 1975 Proc. of the 57th Annual Meeting of the Uniform Law Conferences of Canada, 162; *Medical Consent of Minors Act*, S.N.B. 1976, c. M-6.1, s. 3(2). This overlaps with N.B. Reg. 66-47, s. 40(2) as amended, under the *Public Hospitals Act*, R.S.N.B., 1973, c. P-23, which authorizes emergency treatment but requires a written statement of the doctor. Section 55(2) of the *Hospital Standards Regulations, 1980*, Sask. Reg. 331/79, does not provide specific authority to dispense with consent. However, it superadds a requirement to the common law emergency doctrine: "Where a state of emergency exists and a surgeon proceeds with an operation without consent, the surgeon shall sign a statement that in his opinion a state of emergency exists and that it would therefore be inadvisable for the operation to be delayed ... pending ... consent ... and that statement shall become part of the patient's health record."

49. *Saskatchewan*: Tentative proposals for a Consent of Minors to Health Care Act, L.R.C. Sask., Nov. 1978; *Ontario*: Options on Medical Consent, Ont. Interministerial Committee on Medical Consent, Sept. 1979; *Alberta*: Report of the Institute of Law Research and Reform on the Consent of Minors to Health Care, Dec. 1975; *British Columbia*: The Medical Consent of Minors, 12th Report of the Royal Commission on Family and Children's Law, Aug. 1975; *Canada*: L.R.C. Canada, *Euthanasia, Aiding Suicide, and Cessation of Treatment* (1983).

moral and peer pressure to persuade parents to consent. Various justifications are offered for these practices. Certain decisions must be made speedily. The interdisciplinary nature of medical opinion in serious neonatal cases frequently resists non-technical summation in the form of yes or no options. In some cases parents are overwrought emotionally by the shock of having given birth to a damaged child. In others, the parents adamantly refuse consent to treat their deformed child in hopes that it will die.

In cases where the newborn's condition urgently requires treatment for the preservation of life or health medical procedures responsive to that compelling necessity will be justifiable without parental consent by the common law emergency doctrine. If however, the parents specifically refuse consent, common law justification is at an end. Neonatologists can only rely on the statutes.

It is doubtful that Ontario's legislation provides doctors with any greater authority than does the common law. The regulations[50] provide for non-consensual treatment only where "the surgeon believes that delay caused by obtaining the consent [of a parent, guardian or next of kin] would endanger the life ...". If there is no question of delay caused by obtaining the parents' consent, the statute is exhausted. It does not go on to give the doctor authority to override parental refusal. The statute deals only with delay caused by unavailability; if a doctor desires to encroach on parental refusal, administrative or judicial authority must be invoked to interfere with the parents' legal control over the child.[51] In Ontario, responsibility to protect the child against parental withholding of treatment lies with the judicial or administrative arms of the state, not with the medical profession.

That position characterizes certain other provincial legislation currently on the books or proposed. In New Brunswick, emergencies

---

50. R.R.O. 1980, Reg. 865, s. 50 under the *Public Hospitals Act*, R.S.O. 1980, c. 410.

51. Administrative authority derives from the *Child Welfare Act*, R.S.O. 1980, c. 66, s. 21. A "child in need of protection" is defined at s. 19(1)(b)(ix), (xi) as including children needing medical treatment or whose health is endangered. Various officials can seize a child in need of protection under s. 21(1). A court hearing is then necessary to authorize consent to medical treatment. Judicial authority derives from the wardship jurisdiction in the High Court: see generally *Everleigh on Domestic Relations* (6th ed., 1951), p. 600-1.

At time of writing, Bill 77, *Child and Family Services Act, 1984*, 4th Sess., 32nd Leg. Ont. 33 Eliz. II, 1984, had received first reading (May 18, 1984). Bill 77 is intended to be an extensive revision and consolidation of the statutes relating to children's services. It will expand the definitions of "child in need of protection" and "child's best interests". S. 209 of Bill 77 will repeal the *Child Welfare Act*. The law in Ontario will be analyzed in this chapter as presently contained in the *Child Welfare Act*, with reference to corresponding or differing - provisions contained in Bill 77.

justify non-consensual treatment if the parent is unavailable.[52] If the parents are available and refuse to consent, an application must be made to a judge of the Court of Queen's Bench for an order dispensing with consent.[53] If the Court is satisfied that withholding medical treatment would endanger the life or seriously impair the health of the minor, the court may by order dispense with consent.[54] Alberta's Draft Act is identical.[55]

Quebec has taken a different approach. A hospital or physician must provide treatment to every person in danger of death; parental consent for emergency treatment of minors is not required.[56] Ontario's Draft Act goes even further. A health care provider may treat without consent in an emergency if delay would place the patient in imminent and serious danger.[57] The point to notice is that unlike the common law and other provincial legislation, both statutes justify the medical profession in overriding a parent's refusal to consent to life saving treatment for a minor child in a life threatening emergency.

Saskatchewan's Draft Act also justifies non-consensual emergency treatment of minors without court or administrative authority.[58] However, the Saskatchewan proposal adds an interesting twist. Anyone, including the parents, may apply to the Court for an order prohibiting health care. Where the judge is satisfied that health care is not in the interests of the recipient's continuing "health and well being", he shall prohibit the health care.[59] Under this proposal a parent could object to treatment for quality of life reasons. The statutory phrase "well being", as contrasted with "health", is wide enough to enable the court to adjudicate the application on these grounds.

---

52. *Medical Consent of Minors Act*, S.N.B. 1976, c. M-6.1, s. 3(2).

53. *Medical Consent of Minors Act*, S.N.B. 1976, c. M-6.1, s. 4(1).

54. *Medical Consent of Minors Act*, S.N.B. 1976, c. M-6.1, s. 4(2).

55. Proposed *Minors Consent to Health Care Act*, s. 5, Report of the Institute of Law Research and Reform on the Consent of Minors to Health Care, December, 1975. See also Bill 35, *infra*, note 71, s. 6.

56. Nor does the imperative form of the obligation to treat seem to leave room for a parental refusal of consent to be effective: *Public Health Protection Act*, R.S.Q., c. P-35, s. 43. However, R.R.Q. 1981, c. S-5, r.1, s. 58 is more ambiguous, under which a hospital may refuse treatment "unless it be an emergency case". That leaves open the question whether a hospital may treat if consent is expressly refused by a parent of a minor child.

57. *Health Care Services Consent Act*, s. 13, Ont. Interministerial Committee on Medical Consent, Dec. 1979.

58. Law Reform Commission of Saskatchewan, *Tentative Proposals for a Consent of Minors to Health care Act*, Nov. 1978, s. 6.

59. *Id.*, s. 5.

(d) Impact on Neonatal Practice

To summarize broadly the impact of the consent rule on neonatal practice: Canadian doctors are justified in initiating non-consensual treatment for damaged newborns in response to life threatening emergencies if the parents are unavailable or incompetent to consent. If the parents are available and able to consent, doctors must obtain their consent prior to treatment (except in Quebec). Initiation of treatment without consent, or over a parent's refusal, in this situation, makes the doctor liable to civil actions for battery and trespass. Although the spectre of criminal prosecution for assault is raised, a s. 45 defence is probably (but not certainly) available. A criminal court would have to accept that parental refusal to consent makes it reasonable for the doctor to perform the operation in view of the baby's health and circumstances of the case.

In the usual case, parents will have consented to "all treatment necessary", or to "any form of treatment by the medical staff" on admission to the hospital.[60] It is doubtful that this consent covers procedures beyond nursing care. Common law requires that consent be referable to a particular treatment, because the doctor must disclose to the patient the nature of the proposed operation and its specific risks.[61] Blanket consent to treatment is legally insufficient. The common law rule is buttressed by provincial statutes with respect to surgical operations and certain other procedures.[62] General consent, in any event, is revoked by the patient's veto of specific treatment.

Where the parents consent to particular treatment for their damaged baby questions arise about the scope of the doctor's duty to make disclosure. Neonatal practice does not square with the legal requirement that a fully informed and freely given parental consent to treatment be obtained in all cases. No doubt many parents are overwrought emotionally when first told that their baby is severely damaged.[63] The Courts recognize that the doctor's duty of disclosure may vary accordingly. Doctors are entitled to consider that parents are at their wits end in deciding what information to disclose. Yet it is hard to see how this justifies selective, biased presentation of information calculated to influence consent in any case. It is even more

---

60. See ch. I, *supra*, fn. 31.

61. *Hopp* v. *Lepp* (1980), 13 C.C.L.T. 66, 87 (S.C.C.).

62. *Supra*, notes 30-37.

63. See Freeston, *An Enquiry into the Effect of a Spina Bifida Child Upon Family Life* (1971), 13 Develop. Med. Child Neurol. 456; Hare, Laurence, Payne, Rawnsley, *Spina Bifida Cystica and Family Stress*, [1956] Brit. Med. J. 757.

difficult to conceive why the neonatologist should be entitled to mount a systematic campaign of moral and peer pressure to induce consent. Provision of selective, biased information runs counter to the doctor's duty to disclose all facts that a reasonable person in the parents' position would want to know to make an intelligent decision. It would render a doctor civilly liable for all damage caused.

Furthermore, aggressive strategies to induce consent infects voluntariness. This may vitiate any consent thereby obtained. If consent is nullified for duress, the doctor becomes subject to liability for trespass, battery and criminal assault.

Failure to adhere to the consent requirements specified in provincial legislation renders a doctor liable to charges of professional misconduct under various provincial medical statutes.[64] So does provision of treatment against the parents' expressed wishes.[65] Parents, as other members of the public, are entitled to initiate complaints of professional misconduct,[66] thereby triggering the discipline machinery of the College of Physicians and Surgeons.

Is specific legal justification for non-consensual life saving treatment given by s. 197 of the *Criminal Code*? That section provides:

197(1)   Everyone is under a legal duty

(c)   to provide necessaries of life to a person under his charge if that person

(i)   is unable, by reason of detention, age, illness, insanity or other cause to withdraw himself from that charge ...

There is a clear and consistent line of authority that "necessaries of life" include medical treatment.[67]

The difficulty here is one of being able to say that a hospitalized child is "under the charge" of the attending doctor. Legal guardianship

---

64. Under s. 60(3)(c) of the *Health Disciplines Act*, R.S.O. 1980, c. 196 as amended, a member of the College may be found guilty of professional misconduct as defined in the regulations. Section 27(20) of R.R.O. 1980, Reg. 448 under the *Health Disciplines Act* defines professional misconduct as "contravening while engaged in the practice of medicine any ... provincial ... law ... designed to protect the public health".

65. S. 27(10) of R.R.O. 1980, Reg. 448 under the *Health Disciplines Act*, R.S.O. 1980, c. 196 as amended, defines professional misconduct as "failure to carry out the terms of an agreement with a patient".

66. *Health Disciplines Act*, R.S.O. 1980, c. 196, s. 58(1).

67. *R.* v. *Brown* (1893), 1 Ter. L.R. 475 (N.W.T.C.A.); *R.* v. *Brooks* (1902), 5 C.C.C. 372 (B.C.S.C.); *R.* v. *Lewis* (1903), 7 C.C.C. 261 (Ont. C.A.); *R.* v. *Morby* (1882), 8 Q.B. 571; *Oakey* v. *Jackson* (1914), 1 K.B. 217; *R.* v. *Senior* (1899), 1 Q.B. 283.

of the child rests with the parents by nature and nurture.[68] Parental guardianship includes discretion to judge what medical procedures are warranted. Exercise of that discretion in a particular way — as if the parents refuse consent to treatment — doesn't destroy the guardianship in the sense that the child thereby becomes "under the charge" of the doctor. It may be that unreasonable refusal to consent entitles the doctor to commence proceedings to interfere with the parents' guardianship, but until the guardianship is interfered with by competent authority the parents' right to refuse medical intervention for their child remains intact.[69] However, if the parents are unavailable, the position may well be different. In *R. v. Jones*[70] a woman was convicted of manslaughter for failure to provide proper medical attention to a child left in her care temporarily by the parents. This is sufficiently similar to the situation where the parents leave their child in hospital, as to attract liability under s. 197.

(e) Parents Refusing to Consent

Doctors faced with an unreasonable refusal of parental consent to treat a seriously ill child have two options: (1) they can engage the machinery of the Child Welfare Commissions, (2) they can engage the reserve power of the Court under its *parens patriae* jurisdiction.

(i) Child Welfare Statutes

Provincial Child Welfare Commissions have authority with respect to children in need of protection. The statutory definition of "child in need of protection" is reasonably uniform throughout the provinces. All the statutes capture deformed newborns whose parents refuse to consent to life saving treatment. Ontario defines a child in need of protection as a child whose guardian "neglects or refuses to provide or obtain proper medical, surgical or other recognized remedial care

---

68. *Supra*, notes 24-25.

69. The Law Reform Commission of Canada, *Medical Treatment and Criminal Law* (1980), p. 22 suggested that "hospitals, doctors, nurses and others who contract to care for someone who is helpless because of illness, insanity, or age, do have a duty to provide necessaries [within the meaning of s. 197(1) *Criminal Code*]". As a general proposition, this is correct. The cases make clear that being "under the charge" is a question of fact and does not require the supervention of control in law: see *Chattaway's case* (1924), 17 C.A.R. 7, 8; *R. v. Valade* (1915), 26 C.C.C. 233, 235 (Que. K.B.). However, the presence of an infant in a hospital, *simpliciter*, is not sufficient to place that infant "under the charge" of the hospital if his parents are there, protesting administration of treatment.

70. *R. v. Jones* (1902), 19 Cox C.C. 678.

or treatment necessary for the child's health or well being". The definition also embraces a child whose guardian refuses to allow treatment "recommended" by a doctor[71] and "a child whose life may be endangered by the conduct of the person in whose charge the child is".[72] Quebec approaches the matter differently. The *Youth Protection Act* not only defines parental duties; it also confers upon a child the right to receive health services according to his personal requirements.[73] Procedures are created which give substance to that right where infringed.

Under the statutes, various officials having reasonable and probable grounds to believe a child is in need of protection may seize and detain the child, or obtain an order to bring him before the court.[74]

---

71. *Family and Child Services Act*, S.P.E.I. 1981, c. 12, s. 1(2)(f); *Child Welfare Act*, R.S.O. 1980, c. 66, s. 19(1)(b)(ix) [but see Bill 77, *supra*, note 51, s. 38(2)(e),(h) does not mention recommendation by a doctor].

    See also Bill 35, *Child Welfare Act*, 2nd Sess. 20th Leg. Alta. 33 Eliz. II, 1984, s. 1(2)(c). At time of writing, Bill 35 had received first reading (April 18, 1984). Section 112 of Bill 35, if enacted, will repeal the Alberta *Child Welfare Act*, R.S.A. 1980, c. C-8. The law in Alberta will be referred to in this chapter as presently contained in the *Child Welfare Act*, with references to corresponding -or differing - provisions contained in Bill 35.

72. *Child Welfare Act*, R.S.O. 1980, c. 66, s. 19(1)(b)(ix) [*cf.* Bill 77, *supra*, note 51, s. 38(2) does not contain exactly equivalent provisions, although paras. (a), (b) refer to "physical harm".] As mentioned in the text, the statutes are quite similar, but certain variations are recorded in what follows: *Child Welfare Act*, R.S.A. 1980, c. C-8, as amended, s. 6(e)(x),(xii). Section 6(e)(i) includes in the definition of neglected child "a child who is not being properly cared for" [*cf.* Bill 35, *supra*, note 71, s. 1(2)(c) which refers to failure by the guardian to provide "necessities of life" which include "essential medical, surgical, or other remedial treatment that has been recommended by a physician"]; *Family and Child Services Act*, S.B.C. 1980, c. 11, s. 1 defines a child as needing protection if he is "abused or neglected so that his safety or well being is endangered", or if he is "deprived of necessary medical attention"; the *Child Welfare Act*, S.M. 1974, c. 30, C.C.S.M., c. C-80, s. 16 (c), (g); *Child and Family Services and Family Relations Act*, S.N.B. 1980, c. C-2.1, s. 31(1); the *Child Welfare Act, 1972*, S.N. 1972, No. 37, s. 2 as amended by S.N. 1981, c. 54, s. 2; *Children's Services Act*, S.N.S. 1976, c. 8, s. 2(m)(iv), (vii); *Family and Child Services Act*, S.P.E.I. 1981, c. 12, s 1(2)(b); *The Family Services Act*, R.S.S. 1978, c. F-7, s. 15(d), (e); *Child Welfare Ordinance*, R.O.N.W.T. 1974, c. C-3, s. 14(1)(k); *Children's Act*, Bill 19, 4th sess. 25th Leg. Y.T. 1984, s. 118(1).

73. *Youth Protection Act*, R.S.Q., c. P-34.1, ss. 8, 38.

74. *Child Welfare Act*, R.S.A. 1980, c. C-8, s. 7(1),(2) [Bill 35, *supra*, note 71, s. 17(9)]; *Family and Child Services Act*, S.P.E.I. 1981, c. 12, s. 15(2). The child may also be removed from his parents: *Child Welfare Act.*, R.S.A. 1980, c. C-8, s. 8(1) [Bill 35, *supra*, note 71, s. 19(1) allows the director to retain custody of the child for up to 2 days before obtaining a supervision order from the court]; *Family and Child Services Act*, S.B.C. 1980, c. 11, s. 9(1), (2), (3); *The Child Welfare Act*, S.M. 1974, c. 30, C.C.S.M., c. C-80, s. 17(2); *Child and Family Services and Family Relations*

Ontario and the Yukon Territory do not clothe the official with power to authorize medical treatment. Curial jurisdiction must be invoked first.[75] In Quebec the official may recommend treatment as a voluntary measure without judicial approval, but he must advise the parents of their right to refuse the measure. If they refuse, the Director must apply to the court.[76] The remaining provinces and territories authorize apprehending officials to consent to emergency care without parental or judicial approval.[77] Variations in the statutory language granting this power become important because some statutes grant considerably more power than others. For example, the Northwest Territories only gives power to authorize treatment "necessary to preserve the life of the child",[78] whereas in Alberta, the official may consent to any medical care he "considers necessary".[79] The latter provision is substantially wider.

In those provinces where Child Welfare officials must apply to court for judicial approval prior to authorizing medical treatment the procedure may be cumbersome and slow. A hearing must be held to

---

Act, S.N.B. 1980, c. C-2.1, s. 32(1); *The Child Welfare Act, 1972*, S.N. 1972, No. 37, s. 11(1) as amended; *Children's Services Act*, S.N.S. 1976, c. 8, s. 45(1); *Child Welfare Act*, R.S.O. 1980, c. 66, s. 21 [Bill 77, *supra*, note 51, s. 41]; *Family and Child Services Act*, S.P.E.I. 1981, c. 12, s. 16(2); *Youth Protection Act*, R.S.Q., c. P-34.1, s. 33 as amended; the *Family Services Act*, R.S.S. 1978, c. F-7, s. 20; *Child Welfare Ordinance*, R.O.N.W.T. 1974, c. C-3, s. 16 as amended; *Children's Act*, Bill 19, 4th sess. 25th Leg. Y.T. 1984, s. 121(1),(3).

75. *Child Welfare Act*, R.S.O. 1980, c. 66, s. 21(1) [but see Bill 77, *supra*, note 51, s. 41(8) which allows a child protection worker to consent to a medical examination]; *Children's Act*, Bill 19, 4th Sess. 25th Leg. Y.T. 1984, s. 183(1).

76. *Youth Protection Act*, R.S.Q., c. P-34.1, ss. 52, 54(e), (g) as amended by S.Q. 1984, c. 4, ss. 27, 28, 33.

77. *Child Welfare Act*, R.S.A. 1980, c. C-8, s. 9(1) [Bill 35, *supra*, note 71, s. 20(1)]; *Family and Child Services Act*, S.B.C. 1980, c. 11, s. 10(1)(b); the *Child Welfare Act*, S.M. 1974, c. 30, C.C.S.M., c. C-80, s. 21(1), (2); the *Child Welfare Act, 1972*, S.N. 1972, No. 37, s. 11 (5), (6) as amended; *Children's Services Act*, S.N.S. 1976, c. 8, s. 45(3); the *Family Services Act*, R.S.S. 1978, c. F-7, s. 43(3); *Child Welfare Ordinance*, R.O.N.W.T. 1974, c. C-3, s. 42; *Child and Family Services and Family Relations Act*, S.N.B. 1980, c. C-2.1, s. 32(2)(b).

78. *Child Welfare Ordinance*, R.O.N.W.T. 1974, c. C-3, s. 42.

79. *Child Welfare Act*, R.S.A. 1980, c. C-8, s. 9(1)(b) [*cf.* Bill 35, *supra*, note 71, s. 20(1) which provides that the director may consent to treatment recommended by two or more doctors. However, under s. 20(2), where the reason for apprehending the child is that the child's guardian refused to consent to essential treatment, the director must apply to the court for an order authorizing the treatment].

determine whether a child is in need of protection.[80] Proper notice must be served on the parents. If notice requirements are not complied with the court is utterly without jurisdiction under the statutes.[81] Ontario requires "reasonable notice" prior to the hearing.[82] Prince Edward Island provides that 5 days' notice must be given.[82a] Ontario allows the court to dispense with notice if delay might endanger the health of the child.[83] Prince Edward Island, by contrast, provides for abridging the notice requirement where "service of a notice ... cannot reasonably be effected ...".[84]

Where the Court finds the child to be a child in need of protection the court may make the child a ward of a children's aid society or a

---

80. In Ontario the hearing must be held "as soon as practicable or within 5 days of apprehension" of the child: *Child Welfare Act*, R.S.O. 1980, c. 66, s. 27(1) [Bill 77, *supra*, note 51, s. 43(1)]. See also *Family and Child Services Act*, S.P.E.I. 1981, c. 12, s. 19(b).

81. *Forsyth* v. *C.A.S. Kingston*, [1963] 1 O.R. 49 (H.C.J.) (trial judge found to have exceeded his jurisdiction when granting a temporary custody order under the *Child Welfare Act* without first complying with the notice requirements in the statute); *Re Kociuba* (1971), 18 R.F.L. 286 (Ont. H.C.J.) (plaintiff granted *habeas corpus* where it was held provincial court judge exceeded jurisdiction by ordering custody without first complying with notice requirement).

82. *Child Welfare Act*, R.S.O. 1980, c. 66, s. 28(6) [*cf.* Bill 77, *supra*, note 51, s. 40(3) which does not contain the word "reasonable"].

82a. *Family and Child Services Act*, S.P.E.I. 1981, c. 12, s. 27(1). See also Alberta Bill 35, *supra*, note 71, s. 21.

83. *Child Welfare Act*, R.S.O. 1980, c. 66, s. 28(10) [Bill 77, *supra*, note 51, s. 40(7)].

84. *Family and Child Services Act*, S.P.E.I. 1981, c. 12, s. 28.

crown ward.[85] If this happens the Children's Aid Society[86] or the
Crown,[87] as the case may be, becomes the child's legal guardian. They

---

85. In Alberta and Prince Edward Island, there are provisions for making a child a
temporary or permanent ward of the Crown. There are no provisions for making
the child a ward of the Children's Aid Society, although the society may be given
custody of the Crown wards. *Child Welfare Act*, R.S.A. 1980, c. C-8, ss. 16, 18 *[cf.*
Bill 35, *supra*, note 71, ss. 29, 32, which empowers the court to appoint a "Children's
Guardian"]; *Family and Child Services Act*, S.P.E.I. 1981, c. 12, ss. 3(2), 34(2).

In British Columbia, Manitoba, Newfoundland and the Territories, the relevant
sections provide that the child can be committed temporarily or permanently to the
care and custody of a Children's Aid Society or other child care agency or resource,
or of a director or superintendent of the society: *Family and Child Services Act*,
S.B.C. 1980, c. 11, s. 16(1); *The Child Welfare Act*, S.M. 1974, c. 30, s. 27(1) as
amended, C.C.S.M., c. C-80, s. 27(1); *The Child Welfare Act, 1972*, S.N. 1972, No.
37, s. 15(1) as amended; *Children's Services Act*, S.N.S. 1976, c. 8, s. 49(1); *Children's Act*, Bill 19, 4th sess. 25th Leg. Y.T. 1984, ss. 110(1), 128(2),(3); *Child Welfare
Ordinance*, R.O.N.W.T. 1974, c. C-3, ss. 19(d), 21(2) as amended.

In New Brunswick and Saskatchewan the relevant sections provide that the
child can be committed to the care and custody of the Minister of Social Services
on a temporary or permanent basis. In New Brunswick the permanent committal
is accomplished by a guardianship order. *Child and Family Services and Family
Relations Act*, S.N.B. 1980, c. C-2.1, ss. 55, 56; *The Family Services Act*, R.S.S.
1978, c. F-7, s. 29.

In Ontario the child can be made a temporary or permanent ward of the Crown
or of the Children's Aid Society. *Child Welfare Act*, R.S.O. 1980, c. 66, s. 30(1) [Bill
77, *supra*, note 51, s. 54(1)].

In Quebec there is no provision for making the child a ward. Rather, specific
powers are given to the court to order compulsory foster care. *Youth Protection
Act*, R.S.Q., c. P-34.1, s. 62. See also, *supra*, note 76.

86. In all the provinces and territories, excepting Quebec, once a child is committed to
the care and custody, or made a ward of a particular person or agency, that person
or agency then acts as the legal guardian of the child. *Child Welfare Act*, R.S.A.
1980, c. C-8, s. 24 [Bill 35, *supra*, note 71, ss. 29(1), 32(1)]; *Family and Child Service
Act*, S.B.C. 1980, c. 11, s. 14; *The Child Welfare Act*, S.M. 1974, c. 30, s. 1(x), 27(1)
as amended, C.C.S.M., c. C-80, ss. 1(x), 27(1); *Child and Family Services and
Family Relations Act*, S.N.B. 1980, c. C-2.1, s. 56; *The Child Welfare Act, 1972*,
S.N. 1972, No. 37, s. 2(i); *Children's Services Act*, S.N.S. 1976, c. 8, s. 51; *Child
Welfare Act*, R.S.O. 1980, c. 66, ss. 40(1), 41 [*cf.* Bill 77, *supra*, note 51, s. 60(2)
which confers upon the society the "rights and responsibilities of a parent for the
purposes of the child's care, custody and control", but does not speak of a "legal
guardian"]; *Family and Child Services Act*, S.P.E.I. 1981, c. 12, s. 37(1); *The Family
Services Act*, R.S.S. 1978, c. F-7, s. 43; *Child Welfare Ordinance*, R.O.N.W.T. 1974,
c. C-3, ss. 24(2), 25(2); *Children's Act*, Bill 19, 4th sess. 25th Leg. Y.T. 1984, s.
138(1).

In Quebec, the *Youth Protection Act*, R.S.Q., c. P-34.1, s. 91(b) as amended,
gives the court the power to withdraw the exercise of certain rights of parental
authority.

87. *Child Welfare Act*, R.S.O. 1980, c. 66, s. 40(1) [*cf.* Bill 77, *supra*, note 51, s. 60(1)
under which the Crown does not act as "legal guardian", but rather has "the rights

thus acquire the right to consent to medical treatment for the child over the objections of the natural parents. Canadian courts have used this power to order life-saving treatment for damaged babies, despite parental objections.[88]

In deciding whether to transfer legal guardianship to the Children's Aid Society or the Crown, the Court must be guided by "the best interests of the child"[89] as statutorily defined. This raises an intri-

---

and responsibilities of a parent ... including the right to give or refuse consent to medical treatment ... where a parent's consent would ... otherwise be required."].

88. See *The Ottawa Citizen*, Jan. 23, 1977, p. 90 (decision of Judge Morris Genest of Family Division of the Ontario Provincial Court, Middlesex Co.); *Re S.D.*, [1983] 3 W.W.R. 618 (B.C.S.C.).

89. Manitoba, New Brunswick, Ontario, and Prince Edward Island and the Yukon Territory require the courts to consider the best interests of the child as defined by statute. *The Child Welfare Act*, S.M. 1974, c. 30, as amended, C.C.S.M., c. C-80, s. 27(1); *Child and Family Services and Family Relations Act*, S.N.B. 1980, c. C-2.1, s. 53(2); *Child Welfare Act*, R.S.O. 1980, c. 66, s. 30(1) [Bill 77, *supra*, note 51, ss. 38(3), 54(1)]; *Family and Child Services Act*, S.P.E.I. 1981, c. 12, ss. 1(1)(d), 2; *Children's Act*, Bill 17, 4th Sess. 25th Leg. Y.T. 1984, s. 132(1).

Alberta and Newfoundland require the courts to consider "the public interests and the interest of the child found to be neglected". *Child Welfare Act*, R.S.A. 1980, c. C-8, ss. 16, 18 [*cf.* Bill 35, *supra*, note 71, in which the format is substantially altered. S. 2, for example, sets down a number of criteria, including the interests of the child and society, which must be considered by any authority acting pursuant to the proposed *Act*]; *The Child Welfare Act, 1972*, S.N. 1972, No. 37, s. 15 as amended.

Nova Scotia provides that when the court makes an order for return of children to parents under "friendly supervision", it should consider the "best interests of the child". However, there is no similar requirement when a court makes a custody order: *Children's Services Act*, S.N.S. 1976, c. 8, s. 49(1)(c). However, in *Colchester C.A.S.* v. *Maguire* (1979), 9 C.P.C. 220, 228, the Nova Scotia Supreme Court considered "the best interests" of the child when deciding whether to award custody to the C.A.S.

In Saskatchewan there are no specific considerations required by statute when the Court makes a decision in respect to wardship. However, the sections dealing with the extension, termination or transfer of wardship require the court to consider the "best interests" of the child: *The Family Services Act*, R.S.S. 1978, c. F-7, ss. 46, 47. Also see *Beeching* v. *Eaton* (1979), 10 R.F.L. (2d) 129 (Sask. Q.B.); *Re E.* (1980), 4 W.W.R. 296 (Sask. Prov. Ct.) which suggest the court in fact considers the best interests of the child when deciding whether to award custody or wardship to the C.A.S. .

In Quebec, decisions of all authorities under the statute must be in "the interests of the child and respect of his rights": *Youth Protection Act*, R.S.Q., c. P-34.1, s. 3 as amended by S.Q. 1984, c. 4, s. 4.

In British Columbia, the "safety and well being of the child shall be the paramount considerations": *Family and Child Service Act*, S.B.C. 1980, c. 11, s. 2.

In the Northwest Territories there are no specific considerations enumerated in the statute.

guing problem: "best interests" is defined to mean the "best interests of the child in the circumstances having regard ... to ... the mental ... and physical needs of the child and the appropriate care or treatment ... to meet such needs."[90] What is "appropriate treatment" for a grossly deformed newborn who has no chance for a life of acceptable quality? Can it ever be in such a child's "best interests" that all care, except food, warmth and fluid management be withheld, as is the practice in most neonatal centres?

These are questions of utmost importance. Curial and administrative power to order lifesaving medical treatment for grossly deformed newborns over parental objections occur only in situations where the answers are affirmative. If aggressive medical intervention for a particular child is not "appropriate care" or is not in the child's "best interests", there is no judicial or administrative power under the Child Welfare laws to interfere with a parents' refusal to consent to treatment.

What do the austere phrases "appropriate care" and "best interests" mean? That is a question of considerable difficulty. One promising line of inquiry lies in considering the meaning acquired by the phrase "appropriate treatment" in negligence law. Generally speaking, medical treatment will be considered to be appropriate, in the sense of being non-negligent, when it can be shown to be in accordance with approved and customary medical practice. "If a physician's conduct complies with

---

90. New Brunswick, Ontario and Prince Edward Island provide statutory definitions of "best interests of child", which are all essentially the same.
   Child and Family Services and Family Relations Act, S.N.B. 1980, c. C-2.1, s. 1(a): "best interests of the child" means the best interests of the child under the circumstances taking into consideration
      the mental, emotional and physical health of the child and his need for appropriate care or treatment, or both.
   Child Welfare Act, R.S.O. 1980, c. 66, s. 1(b) [Bill 77, *supra*, note 51, s. 38(3) nos. 1, 12]: "best interests of the child" means the best interests of the child in the circumstances having regard, in addition to all other relevant considerations, to
      (i) the mental, emotional and physical needs of the child and the appropriate care or treatment, or both, to meet such needs,
      (viii) any risk to the child of returning the child to or allowing the child to remain in the care of his or her parent.
   Family and Child Services Act, S.P.E.I. 1981, c. 12, s. 1(d): "best interests of the child means the best interests of the child under the circumstances, having regard, in addition to all other relevant considerations, to
      (ii) the mental, emotional and physical health of the child including any special needs for care and treatment.
   See also *Children's Act*, Bill 19, 4th Sess. 25th Leg. Y.T. 1984, s. 132(1)(i),(j).

the customary practices of his profession he is virtually assured of being exonerated when something goes wrong".[91]

The reasons why customary practices are considered "approved" are compelling. Custom is endowed with a moral quality — a sense of rightness — because it comports with society's expectations. Custom is good evidence that a reasonable standard of conduct has been met. Measuring "appropriateness" by reference to custom allows the professions to develop a sense of responsible autonomy.[92] The professions are better placed than courts to develop reasonable standards of professional conduct. Courts see the problems of a particular profession infrequently. They do not have the whole context before them; they deal with fragmented minutiae. Peer review bodies see professional problems over and over again. They are highly expert. Problems are seen in context.

While customary practice is formidable evidence that the practice is "appropriate", it is not conclusive. Courts will scrutinize all the evidence, medical and otherwise, to determine the appropriateness of medical conduct in the circumstances.[93] Curial interference with customary practice is much more likely if the practice "is demonstrably unsafe or dangerous",[94] or if "the so-called standard practice related to something which was not essentially conduct requiring special medical skill and training for a proper understanding".[95] Superimposition of judicial standards on customary practice makes sense in these circumstances, if sparingly used. Otherwise, progress would be stifled. The medical profession would be permitted to insulate itself from civil responsibility; expert witnesses would usurp the fact finding function of courts.[96]

---

91. Linden, *The Negligent Doctor* (1973), 11 Osg. Hall L.J. 31, 32.

92. Linden, *Custom in Negligence Law* (1968), 11 Can. Bar J. 151, 152-5.

93. *White* v. *Turner* (1981), 31 O.R. (2d) 773, 790, 15 C.C.L.T. 81, 120 O.L.R. (3d) 269 (H.C.J.) *per* Linden J.: "it is now open to the courts ... to participate in the process of evaluating the information disclosed and to find it wanting in appropriate cases, even if the medical profession disagrees"; *Anderson* v. *Chasney*, [1949] 4 D.L.R. 71, 85-86 (Man. C.A.) per Coyne J.A.: "If a practitioner refuses to take an obvious precaution, he cannot exonerate himself by showing that others also neglect to take it"; *Crits* v. *Sylvester* (1956), 1 D.L.R. (2d) 502,514 (Ont. C.A.): "Even if it had been established that what was done by the anaesthesist was in accordance with standard practice, such evidence is not necessarily taken as conclusive on an issue of negligence ..."; *Penner* v. *Theobold* (1962), 35 D.L.R. (2d) 700, 712 (Man. C.A.): "it is the courts and not the particular profession concerned which decide whether negligence is established in a particular case".

94. *Gent and Gent* v. *Wilson*, [1956] O.R. 257, 265 (C.A.).

95. *Crits* v. *Sylvester* (1956), 1 D.L.R. (2d) 502, 514 (Ont. C.A.).

96. Linden, *Custom in Negligence Law* (1968), 11 Can. Bar J. 151, 152-5.

Evidence of neonatal practice is therefore highly relevant to courts faced with a Child Welfare application to approve treatment for which parents have refused consent. If neonatologists routinely treat actively similar cases, proof of this would be a compelling, although not conclusive, indication that treatment is appropriate, and in the child's best interests. Such evidence would gain relevance in proportion to proof that treatment resulted in a life of acceptable quality.

In cases where evidence cannot show that treatment produces life of acceptable quality — where despite aggressive medical interventions the child has poor chances for cognition, mobility or social integration — evidence of medical custom loses its cogency. In such a case, understanding of the child's best interests and appropriate treatment does not require special medical skill or training. The question whether life of poor quality is better than death is ethical, not medical. The court is as well placed as the medical profession to say whether the child's best interests are served by being "maintained in limbo, by aggressive interventions, in a sterile room, by machines controlled by strangers", when his parents desire that he be allowed to die quickly in peace.[97]

A second approach to the interpretation of appropriate care and best interests lies in consideration of the duty to preserve life created by the *Criminal Code*. Under s. 197 of the *Code* that duty is discharged by providing necessaries of life in various circumstances. A consistent line of authority holds that necessaries include medical treatment.[98] Some of these cases take a broad view, embracing within necessary medical treatment "such necessaries as tend to preserve life".[99] These cases prompted the Federal Law Reform Commission to conclude that the medical care required under s. 197 includes *"anything* necessary for the prevention, cure or alleviation of disease or disorder that threatens life ...".[100]

This view is unsubtle, and overstates the true position discernible from the decided cases. The precedents do not require *anything* neces-

---

97. Steel, *The Right to Die: New Options in California*, 93 Christian Century July-December 1976, as quoted in Comment, "North Carolina's Natural Death Act: Confronting Death with Dignity", 14 Wake Forest L. Rev. 771.

98. *R.* v. *Senior*, [1899] 1 Q.B. 283; *R.* v. *Brooks* (1902), 5 C.C.C. 372 (B.C.S.C.); *R.* v. *Lewis* (1903), 7 C.C.C. 261 (Ont. C.A.); *R.* v. *Morby* (1882), 15 Cox C.C. 35.

99. *R.* v. *Brooks* (1902), 5 C.C.C. 372 (B.C.S.C.); *cf. R.* v. *Sydney* (1912), 20 C.C.C. 376 (Sask. S.C.) "such things as are essential to preserve life".

100. L.R.C.C., *Medical Treatment and Criminal Law* (1980), p. 23. The emphasis is ours.

sary to alleviate life threatening disease. In *R. v. Lewis* the Ontario Court of Appeal held that "necessaries" include medical aid "when it is reasonable and proper that it should be procured".[101] That position was specifically endorsed in *R. v. Elder.* " [N]ecessaries", said the Manitoba Court of Appeal, "include medical treatment in cases where ordinary prudent persons would obtain them".[102] In the earlier case of *R. v. Senior* the court was clear to point out that "neglect is ... the omission of such steps as a reasonable parent would take, such as are usually taken in the ordinary experience of mankind ...".[103] Finally, the Court of King's Bench stated in *Oakey v. Jackson*:[104] "A refusal to allow an operation is not necessarily such a failure to provide adequate medical aid as to amount to willful neglect ... . The justices in deciding that question must take into consideration the nature of the operation and the reasonableness of the parents' refusal to permit it". In *Barber v. Superior Court of California* the Court considered a murder charge brought against two doctors who acceded to requests of the family to discontinue life support equipment and intravenous tubes from a patient in a persistent vegetative state. "There is no duty to continue [life sustaining machinery]" said Mr. Justice Compton, "once it has become futile in the opinion of qualified medical personnel".[104a] The Court concluded that the omission to continue treatment under the circumstances, though intentional and with knowledge that the patient would die, "was not an unlawful failure to perform a legal duty".[104b]

So far from creating a *per se* rule, the precedents take pains to point out that reasonable measures only must be taken, measures of which the community would approve. The criminal law thus squares nicely with the reasonableness limitation to the duty to provide medical treatment suggested by the negligence cases. Both lines of authority bring customary practices of parents and the medical profession very much into prominence.

There is therefore every reason to think that a court asked to approve medical treatment for a seriously defective newborn over parental objections is perfectly entitled to consider quality of life under the Child Welfare statutes. That is what most parents do. A court is not bound to follow this custom — it could rule to protect the sanctity

---

101. *R. v. Lewis* (1903), 7 C.C.C. 261 (Ont. C.A.).

102. *R. v. Elder* (1925), 44 C.C.C. 75 (Man. C.A.).

103. *R. v. Senior*, [1899] 1 Q.B. 283.

104. *Oakey v. Jackson*, [1914] 1 K.B. 216.

104a. *Barber v. Superior Court of California*, 195 Cal. R. 484, 491 (Ct. App. 1983).

104b. *Id.*, p. 494.

of life at all costs. But neither is the court obliged to disregard this custom. In every other situation where the courts have been asked to rule on "reasonableness" and "appropriateness" customary practice has offered a sure guide. Thus it appears that compelling reasons would be required to convince the courts to upset customary practices of neonatal units.

(ii) Parens Patriae

The Superior courts retain an inherent common law jurisdiction to protect those who cannot protect themselves. The jurisdiction is equity's way of implementing the Crown's responsibility, as *parens patriae*. It derives from feudal incidents of knight's service tenure.[105] The *parens patriae* jurisdiction claimed by Chancery is implemented by the institution of wardship, which is "essentially a parental jurisdiction". The main considerations prompting its exercise are "the benefit or welfare of the child". The Court of Chancery is responsible to do "what under the circumstances a wise parent acting for the true interests of the child would or ought to do".[106] Precise limits for the jurisdiction cannot be stated in advance. The court may stretch out its arm in whatever direction is required to protect the welfare of its ward.[107]

---

105. On the death of a tenant by knight's service or grand serjeanty tenure leaving a male heir under age 21 or a female heir under age 14, the lord had wardship both of person and lands of the heir. This entitled the lord to the rents and profits of the fief. It also entitled him to the right to arrange the ward's marriage, for which he would receive profit for the arrangement. These rights were subject to a duty to maintain and educate the ward according to his station: see generally, Holdsworth, *A History of English Law*, 648; Lowe and White, *Wards of Court*, London: Butterworths, 1979, ch. I; Cross, *Wards of Court* (1967), 83 L.Q.R. 200. A special court, the Court of Wards, was established to administer the collection and supervision of wardship revenues. The tenurial institution of wardship was abolished by the *Statutes of Tenures* 12 Charles II, c. 24 (1660) with the abolition of Knight's Service tenure. The Court of Wards suffered the same fate: see generally Bell, *The Court of Wards and Liveries* (1953). After this date, the Court of Chancery claimed on the Crown's behalf a power as *parens patriae* to supervise all infants within its allegiance, whether or not they were heirs to landed property: *Falkland v. Bertie* (1698), 2 Vern. 333, 342, 23 E.R. 814: "In this court there were several things that belonged to the King as *Pater Patriae* and fell under the care and direction of this Court, as ... *[inter alia]* infants ... and afterwards such of them as were of profit and advantage to the King were removed to the Court of Wards by the statute; but upon the dissolution of that Court came back again to the Chancery"; and see Lowe and White, *Wards of Court* (1979), p. 2.

106. *R. v. Gyngall*, [1893] 2 Q.B. 232, 248; see also *Re McGrath*, [1893] 1 Ch. 143, 147-50; *J. v. C.*, [1970] A.C. 668.

107. *Wellesley v. Wellesley*, [1828] 2 Bli. N.S. 124, 142-3, 4 E.R. 1078, 1085; but see *Re X*, [1975] 1 All E.R. 697 (Fam. D.), (wardship, order to prevent publication of book said to be psychologically damaging to ward refused on grounds such an order would unduly restrict freedom of press).

Once the wardship is operative " [n]o important step in the child's life can be taken without the court's consent."[108] The great and overriding consideration prompting exercise of modern wardship's jurisdiction is "the welfare of [this] child ... The court must act in her best interests".[109] Curial power may be used to authorize[110] or refuse[111] medical intervention on behalf of a ward, whether requested by the legal guardian or medical profession.

It is now beyond question that Canadian courts retain a common law wardship jurisdiction coextensive with that enjoyed by English tribunals.[112] It is a jurisdiction existing side by side with various statutory regimes for the protection of incompetents,[113] but which is "confined to gaps in the legislation and to judicial review".[113a] Under the Judicature Acts, the jurisdiction is exercised by the Superior Courts.[114] In some provinces, statute provides that wardship power may also be exercised by unified family courts.[115]

---

108. *Re S*, [1967] 1 All E.R. 202, 209 (Ch. D.).

109. *Re D*, [1976] 1 All E.R. 326, 333 (Fam. D.).

110. *Re L*, [1968] 1 All E.R. 20 (C.A.) (blood tests to determine ward's paternity ordered); *Re Eve* (1980), 74 A.P.R. 97, 27 N. & P.E.I.R. 97 (P.E.I.C.A.) (on appeal to S.C.C.) (application by parent for non-therapeutic sterilization of adult retarded ward granted).

111. *Re D*, [1976] 1 All E.R. 326 (Fam. D.).

112. Some doubt formerly existed. See Robinson, "Custody and Access" in 2 *Studies in Canadian Family Law* (da Costa, ed. 1972), 543, 552-3: "In Canada, however, the courts have apparently never adopted this practice [wardship] and indeed, it may be argued that the legislatures, by enacting comprehensive legislation dealing with custody, have precluded the development of this remedy at this time". A vigorous dissent from this view is found in Stone, *Jurisdiction over Guardianship and Custody of Children in Canada and in England* (1979), 17 Alta. L. Rev. 532, 538-41. The point is now settled in favour of the jurisdiction: see *Re Eve* (1980), 74 A.P.R. 97, 126 per McDonald J.A., 137-8 per Campbell J.A., 111 per Lange J.A. (P.E.I.C.A.); *Beason v. Director of Child Welfare*, [1982] 2 S.C.R. 716; *Re S.D.*, [1983] 3 W.W.R. 613 (B.C.).

113. *Re Eve* (1980), 74 A.P.R. 97, 139, 27 N. & P.E.I.R. 97, 139 (P.E.I.C.A.) (on appeal to S.C.C.).

113a. *Beason v. Director of Child Welfare*, [1982] 2 S.C.R. 716, 724; *A. v. Liverpool City Council*, [1981] 2 All E.R. 385, 388-89 (H.L.) *per* Lord Wilberforce: "The court's general inherent power is always available to fill gaps or to supplement the powers of the local authority; what it will not do (except by way of judicial review where appropriate) is to supervise the exercise of discretion within the field committed by statute to the local authority".

114. *E.g. Judicature Act*, R.S.O. 1980, c. 223 as amended, s. 18(1): "... the Supreme Court and every judge shall give to the plaintiff such and the same relief as ought to have been given by the Court of Chancery ...".

115. *E.g. Unified Family Court Act*, R.S.O. 1980, c. 515, s. 4(3): "The Court has and may exercise the same *parens patriae* powers as the Supreme Court in respect of any matter before it".

In *Re S.D.* the British Columbia Supreme Court resorted to its parens patriae power to order a shunt revision for a profoundly handicapped child over the objection of the child's parents, supported by the infant's pediatric neurologist. Mr. Justice McKenzie formulated this test

> 'The Court must decide what its ward would choose if he were in a position to make a sound judgment'. ... The decision can only be made in the context of the disabled person viewing the worthwhileness or otherwise of his life in its own context of a disabled person.[115a]

Although the cases repeat *ad nauseam* that the ward's "best interests" are the governing criteria of the jurisdiction, it is possible to take this too literally. Suppose, for example, a child is born to parents of low intelligence, poor psychological adaptation, in dire economic circumstances and already encumbered with more children than they can handle. A stranger desiring and able to give the child a superior home applies under the wardship jurisdiction to ask the court for custody.[116] Can it be denied that in at least some cases the application is in the child's "best interests"? That no court would agree — largely because of parent-centered considerations — demonstrates how incomplete and misleading singleminded concentration on the "best interests" criteria can be.

In fact, all the reported cases introduce into common law wardship jurisdiction other criteria of decision making. Most of these are not child-centered factors; they concern other parties interested in the child's activities. In *Re D.*[117] the mother of a retarded eleven year old girl feared that her daughter might become pregnant. The mother, a fifty one years old widow, worked full time. The prospect of raising D's child - assuming D. could not do so herself - tormented her. She therefore arranged to have D. sterilized. In a wardship application to prohibit sterilization brought by certain professionals interested in D. the court said: "Mrs. B.'s [the mother's] concern, however, cannot be disregarded".[118] However, on the view that the matter was premature; that the means chosen (hysterectomy) were too intrusive and irreversible, that in all likelihood D could herself decide in time, permission to operate was withheld. The point to notice is that interests other than the child's figured prominently in the decision formula. In *Re L.* the ques-

---

115a. *In re S.D.*, [1983] 3 W.W.R. 618, 631-2 (B.C.S.C.).

116. The example was suggested by Mr. Justice Cross: see his *Wards of Court* (1967), 83 L.Q.R. 200, 205-6.

117. [1976] 1 All E.R. 326 (Fam. D.).

118. *Id.*, p. 334.

tion was whether wardship jurisdiction could be invoked to order non-therapeutic blood tests on an infant to determine paternity. Lord Denning held that the blood tests were "in the best interests, not only of the child *but of all the three adults*".[119] In *Re X*[120], the Court accepted that publication of a book detailing scandalous sexual practices of X's father would be psychologically harmful to X. It would cause her "substantial injury ... grave ... injury to her emotional psychological health".[121] Counsel supporting publication said that freedom of the press was more important. In ordering publication Roskill L.J. noted that "the court is required to do a difficult balancing act".[122] Interests other than those pertaining to the child must be considered in the exercise of wardship jurisdiction. It is not correct to say, Lord Justice Roskill noted, "that in every case where a minor's interests are involved, those interests are always paramount and must prevail".[123] In *Rogers* v. *Commissioner of the Department of Mental Health*, the Court enumerated six factors judicial authorities must consider in arriving at a substituted consent to the medical treatment for incompetent patients. One of these was "the impact of the decision on the ward's family".[123a]

The most important case in this series is the decision of the Prince Edward Island Court of Appeal in *Re Eve*.[124] In that case the widowed mother of a severely retarded adult woman applied to court for authority to sterilize her daughter by tubal ligation. The Court took the view that *Re D.* was distinguishable in that D. had potential to marry; Eve had not.[125] Mr. Justice MacDonald stressed the necessity that the applicant demonstrate that the real object of the application was protection of the ward, not advancement of some parent-centered interest. Sterilization was approved on the view that without permanent contraception the mother would restrict Eve's activities. Eve's "environment will become a guarded environment and the loss to 'Eve' in terms of her social options and her relative freedom would cause substantial injuries ...".[126] Once again, despite the impressive ward-centered

---

119. *Re L.*, [1968] 1 All E.R. 20, 27 (C.A.).

120. [1975] 1 All E.R. 697 (Fam. D.).

121. *Id.*, p. 702.

122. *Id.*, p. 706.

123. *Id.*

123a. *Rogers* v. *Commissioner of the Department of Mental Health*, 458 N.E. (2d) 308, 319, 52 U.S.L.W. 2357, 2358 (Mass. 1983).

124. (1980), 74 A.P.R. 97, 27 N. & P.E.I.R. 97 (P.E.I.C.A.) (on appeal to S.C.C.).

125. *Id.*, p. 109-110.

126. *Id.*, p. 142 per Campbell, J.A..

language, it is clear that third party conveniences and considerations prominently entered the decisional formula.

Once engaged, wardship jurisdiction may be used to override a parent's refusal of consent to treatment.[126a] This proposition follows logically from the lack of limits on the court's jurisdiction,[127] and the object of protecting the ward's welfare.[128] How else could a court respond when faced with a parent's unreasonable refusal to consent to necessary life saving treatment for an infant ward? In *Re L.*, Lord Justice Willmer said that where the court "is exercising the ancient parental jurisdiction it is for the judge and not for guardian *ad litem*, to decide whether the child is to be subjected to a blood test or indeed to any other form of medical examination".[129] Although controversial, wardship power has been used at least twice in Canada to order blood transfusions for children of Jehovah's Witnesses over their parents' objections.[130]

The great advantage of common law wardship is that it is not encrusted with statutory formalities or technicalities. The court's jurisdiction can be speedily engaged. The child may be separately represented. There are no time limits specified nor any necessity to waive them; there is no limit to the court's power or procedure. This is the kind of flexibility which could provide useful machinery for resolving disputes if coupled with serious understanding of the problems neonatal units face.

Apart from procedure, it is important to notice that the decided cases take a broad view of the child's best interest. "Best interests"

126a. *Re S.D.*, [1983] 3 W.W.R. 618 (B.C.S.C.).

127. *Re X*, [1975] 1 All E.R. 697, 705 (Fam. D.): "I would agree with counsel for the plaintiff that no limits to that jurisdiction have yet been drawn and it is not necessary to consider then what (if any) limits there are to that jurisdiction".

128. But see *Re Eve* (1980), 74 A.P.R. 97, 128, 27 N. & P.E.I.R. 97, 128 (P.E.I.C.A.) (on appeal to S.C.C.). Mr. Justice McDonald outlined the factors which a court would consider in authorizing non therapeutic sterilization. He included this: "The parent or guardian of the person must agree that sterilization is a desirable course of action". This is *obiter* on two counts. Firstly, the parent did not object in *Re Eve*. Secondly, and more importantly, the case involved a non-therapeutic procedure. If the parents unreasonably refuse consent to necessary therapeutic procedures, the statement could not serve as authority.

129. *Re L.*, [1968] 1 All E.R. 20, 32 (C.A.).

130. One case was reported in How, *Religion, Medicine and the Law* (1960), 3 Can. Bar. J. 365, 409; the second case occurred in Quebec and was the subject of the unreported judgment Que. Sup. Ct. No. 05-001338-75, 12 Jan. 1976, referred to in S.R. Magnet, *The Right to Emergency Assistance in the Province of Quebec* (1980), 40 R. du B. 373, 413-414 n. 154. This latter was based, at least in part, on the statutory provisions of the *Public Health Protection Act*, S.Q. 1972, c. 42. See also *Pentland v. Pentland and Rombaugh* (1979), 5 R.F.L. (2d) 65 (Ont. H.C.J.).

is robustly conceived; it includes the child's social, emotional,[131] psychological[132] and physical[133] well being. The concept can be related to the interests of the third parties[134] and the overriding public interest.[135] This wide ranging view enables a court to consider arguments based on quality of life. Court action, under wardship jurisdiction, can thus investigate whether in particular cases of severe birth defects - cases where the infant is condemned to a vegetative institutional existence - the child's interests are best served by withholding aggressive medical intervention. Where doctors and parents disagree on that issue, wardship jurisdiction appears to be an attractive means of dispute resolution.

2. Withholding Treatment

(a) Right to Refuse Treatment

The rights to bodily integrity and self-determination are fundamental in medical law. They are the inspiration by which the legal system articulates its vision of human dignity in situations where the propriety of medical treatment is challenged. These broad principles excite more precise legal rules as to consent, confidentiality and various special excuses from civil and criminal responsibility for doctors.

Bodily integrity and self-determination require that everyone has a right to give informed consent to proposed medical procedures. Equally, the principles imply that everyone is entitled to refuse medical treatment, no matter how beneficially intended or how unreasonable may appear the refusal. This is a position our law has embraced in various contexts.[136] Nevertheless, difficulties arise where the refusal

---

131. *Re Eve* (1980), 74 A.P.R. 97, 142, 27 N. & P.E.I.R. 97, 142 (P.E.I.C.A.).

132. *Re X*, [1975] 1 All E.R. 697, 702 (Fam. D.).

133. *Re D*, [1976] 1 All E.R. 326 (Fam. D.).

134. *Supra*, notes 89-104b.

135. *Re X*, [1975] 1 All E.R. 697, 704 (Fam. D.); *Re Eve* (1980), 74 A.P.R. 97, 127, 27 N. & P.E.I.R. 97, 127 (P.E.I.C.A.) (on appeal to S.C.C.).

136. A general statement of the law is found in *Pollock on Torts* (14th ed.), p. 124: "Force to the person is rendered lawful by consent in such matters as surgical operations ... Taking out a man's tooth without his consent would be an aggravated assault and battery. With consent it is lawfully done every day". By implication a person has the right to refuse to consent to treatment: *Masney* v. *Carter-Halls-Aldinger Co.*, [1929] 3 W.W.R. 741 (Sask. K.B.) (plaintiff refused to consent to a necessary operation. Although the plaintiff's refusal was "unreasonable" and led to permanent brain damage, doctors could not intervene); *Mulloy* v. *Hop Sang*, [1935] 1 W.W.R. 714 (Alta. S.C. App. Div.) (patient refused to consent to amputation of his hand even though operation necessary to preserve his life. Doctor

comes from a surrogate, as if the patient be a minor, incompetent or newborn.

(b) Surrogate Refusal

Minority and incompetency do not destroy substantive rights. Infant entitlement to property is nonetheless a right, even if it must be exercised through the representation of the infant's natural or legal guardian.[137] Newborns are entitled to bodily integrity, despite the necessity of a surrogate to protect the right. Incompetents can receive (non therapeutic) treatment, notwithstanding that consent must be given by a guardian.[138] Minors are entitled to refuse unwanted or harmful treatment although a surrogate must refuse for them.[139]

Surrogate refusal of life saving treatment for newborns makes unqualified application of the principles stated less credible for several reasons. First, decisions for passive euthanasia chafe against inherent state interests. Civilized societies have high regard for the preservation of life. This is reflected by laws destroying legal capacity to

---

proceeded to amputate in spite of refusal; was successfully sued by patient for trespass). *Marshall* v. *Curry*, [1933] 3 D.L.R. 260, 276 (N.S.S.C.): "... in the ordinary course where there is an opportunity to obtain the consent of the patient, it must be had. A person's body must be held inviolate and immune from invasion by surgeon's knife, if an operation is not consented to ... If an operation is forbidden by the patient, consent is not to be implied". Foll'd *Parmley* v. *Parmley & Yule*, [1945] 4 D.L.R. 81 (S.C.C.); *Murray* v. *McMurchy*, [1949] 2 D.L.R. 442 (B.C.S.C.); *Hopp* v. *Lepp* (1980), 13 C.C.L.T. 66, 73 (S.C.C.): "The underlying principle [of informed consent] is the right of a patient to decide what, if anything, should be done with his body"; *Reibl* v. *Hughes* (1980), 14 C.C.L.T. 1, 13 (S.C.C.): "battery in respect of surgical or other medical treatment should be confined to cases where ... there has been no consent at all ..."; *Laporte* v. *Laganière* (1972), 18 C.R.N.S. 357 (Que. Q.B.) (absent specific statutory authority, any medical interference with body of another constitutes assault; no statutory authority in *Criminal Code* to authorize removal of bullet for evidentiary purposes where general anaesthetic required).

137. In Quebec the institutions differ. Parental authority derives from the *Que. Civil Code* (1980), art. 646. Tutorship is a civilian institution analogous to legal guardianship. Tutors have control over the property and person of their pupils, as do legal guardians: see *Civil Code of Lower Canada* (1866), art. 290. Parental powers and duties are provided for in the *Que. Civil Code* (1980), art. 647 as follows: "The father and mother have the rights and duties of custody, supervision and education of their children. They must maintain their children".

138. *Re Eve* (1980), 74 A.P.R. 97, 138, 27 N. & P.E.I.R. 97, 138 (P.E.I.C.A.) (on appeal to S.C.C.): "the court is competent in its parens patriae jurisdiction to authorize non-therapeutic tubal ligation [for an adult incompetent]."

139. *Re D*, [1976] 1 All E.R. 326 (Fam. D.).

consent to infliction of death;[141] and state power to discourage irrational and wanton acts of self destruction which violate fundamental norms of society.[142] The state is equally interested in maintaining the ethical integrity of the medical profession.[143] Government premised on consent of the governed is threatened when doctors are compelled or allowed to violate basic ethical norms. State interests are equally engaged when

---

141. *Criminal Code*, R.S.C. 1970, c. C-34, s. 14.

142. *Pentland* v. *Pentland and Rombaugh* (1979), 5 R.F.L. (2d) 65 (Ont. H.C.J.) (Court has inherent power to declare child to be in need of protection for purposes of providing life saving treatment, which child has expressly refused, even if child is over 16 and thus beyond reach of Child Welfare Act). See in particular *Eichner* v. *Dillon*, 426 N.Y.S. (2d) 517, 537 (App. Div. 1980), affd. (*sub nom. Matter of Storar*) 438 N.Y.S. (2d) 266, 420 N.E. (2d) 64 (1981).

143. *Health Disciplines Act*, R.S.O. 1980, c. 196, s. 60(3)(c) provides that a member of the College of Physicians and Surgeons of Ontario can be found guilty of "professional misconduct as defined in the regulations". By R.R.O. 1980, Reg. 448, s. 27, professional misconduct is defined as "21. failure to maintain the standard of practice of the profession" and "32. conduct ... that ... would reasonably be regarded by members as disgraceful, dishonourable or unprofessional".

The "standards of practice of the profession" are laid out in the C.M.A. The College of Physicians and Surgeons of Ontario, By-law No. 1, s. 25 (Dec. 1975) provides that there "shall be a Code of Ethics which shall be the Code of Ethics adopted from time to time by resolution of the Council." The Council by resolution adopted the C.M.A. *Code* of June, 1978, although at time of writing it had not adopted the more recent *Code* of September, 1982. However, the two *Codes* do not differ in the provisions cited in this Chapter.

As a result of the above provisions, the *Code of Ethics* is incorporated into the *Health Disciplines Act*, creating a statutory duty on doctors to practise medicine in an ethical fashion.

This statutory duty can be expanded to an obligation in tort if it can be shown that the statutory obligation is so intertwined with the provision for the security of others that it would be an "unjust" reproach to the ordinary prudent man to suppose he would do such a thing in the teeth of the ordinance": Thayer, *Public Wrong and Private Action* (1914), 27 Harv. L. Rev. 317, 326.

In the fact of a statutory duty and a possible tortious obligation to practise medicine in an ethical fashion, the state is unlikely to impose liability on a doctor who fulfills these obligations. For example, a doctor is ethically bound by the Hippocratic Oath not to reveal the contents of his conversations with his patients. At the same time it is well recognized that in the common law province the doctor-patient relationship is not privileged: S. Schiff, *Evidence in the Litigation Process* (2d ed., 1983), pp. 1019-20; *Wheeler* v. *Le Marchant* (1881), 17 Ch. D. 675. As a result the doctor could be forced to reveal these conversations or risk charges of contempt of court. The courts, however, have recognized the doctor's dilemma, and in the absence of strong public policy concerns have refused to force the doctor to reveal these conversations: *Dembie* v. *Dembie* (1963), 21 R.F.L. 46, 49 (Ont. H.C.J.). Schiff (*supra*, this note) makes reference to a more relaxed approach which appears to be developing toward privilege within a number of professional relationships.

large number of doctors are exposed to civil and criminal responsibility for complying with accepted practices of the medical profession.

A second difficulty with surrogate refusal of life-saving treatment emanates from statutory duties to preserve life. The newborns' parents or guardian are required to provide him with necessaries of life, including medical care.[144] Doctors undertaking to treat must continue if failure to do so may be dangerous to life or health.[145] In Quebec, everyone must furnish life saving aid - including medical treatment[146] - to a person whose life is imperilled.[147] Under the Child Welfare Acts everyone has a duty to report to various officials children in need of medical treatment.[148]

A third difficulty relates to the fiduciary nature of a guardian's responsibilities. Everything practicable must be done to promote the

---

144. *Criminal Code*, R.S.C. 1970, c. C-34, s. 197(1)(a).

145. *Criminal Code*, R.S.C. 1970, c. C-34, ss. 199, 202(1)(b), 207; *R.* v. *Kitching and Adams* (1976), 32 C.C.C. (2d) 159 (Man. C.A.); *R.* v. *Instan* (1893), 1 Q.B. 950; 11 *Hals.* (4th), p. 15, para. 9. Civil liability may follow by proximity of relationship or on the reliance theory: see generally Linden, *Canadian Tort Law* (1977), p. 278ff; *Zelenko* v. *Gimbel Brothers*, 287 N.Y.S. 134 (Sup. Ct. 1935).

146. See S.R. Magnet, *The Right to Emergency Medical Assistance in Quebec* (1980), 40 R. du B. 373, 398ff.

147. *Charter of Human Rights and Freedoms*, R.S.Q., c. C-12, s. 2.

148. In Alberta, British Columbia and Newfoundland, there is a duty to report information tending to show a child is "neglected" or "in need of protection". Failure to report this information is an offence under the statute: *Child Welfare Act*, R.S.A. 1980, c. C-18, ss. 35(1), 39 [Bill 35, *supra*, note 712, s. 3]; *Children's Service Act*, S.N.S. 1976, c. 8, s. 77 [see amendment proposed in Bill 48, *An Act to Amend Chapter 8 of the Acts of 1976, the Children's Services Act*, 3rd Sess. 53rd Gen. Ass. N.S. 33 Eliz. II, 1984. s. 3 (first reading March 28, 1984)]; *The Child Welfare Act, 1972*, S.N. 1972, No. 37, s. 49 as amended by S.N. 1974, c. 100, s. 4, S.N. 1981, c. 54, s. 6; *Family and Child Service Act*, S.B.C. 1980, c. 11, s. 7(4).
In Prince Edward Island, Manitoba, Quebec and Saskatchewan, there is a duty to report information relevant to neglect. However, failure to do so does not constitute an offence: *Family and Child Services Act*, S.P.E.I. 1981, c. 12, s. 14; *Child Welfare Act*, S.M. 1974, c. 30, C.C.S.M., c. C-80, s. 36; *Youth Protection Act*, R.S.Q., c. P-34.1, s. 39; *The Family Services Act*, R.S.S. 1978, c. F-7, s. 16.
In New Brunswick and Ontario, there is a positive duty on everyone to report information relevant to a child in need of protection. Failure of a "professional" to report constitutes an offence: *Child and Family Services and Family Relations Act*, S.N.B. 1980, c. C-2.1, s. 30; *Child Welfare Act*, R.S.O. 1980, c. 66, ss. 49, 94(1)(f)(ii) [Bill 77, *supra*, note 51, s. 69].
In the Northwest Territories and Yukon Territory, there is no positive duty to report. The Yukon *Children's Act*, Bill 19, 4th Sess., 25th Leg. Ass. Y.T., s. 117(1) provides only that a person "may report".

infant's health.[149] Decisions which intend the child's speedy death are difficult to reconcile with this obligation.

Bodily integrity and self determination imply that a surrogate is entitled to refuse treatment. That this should conflict with other high principles of the legal system associated with the worth of life is hardly surprising. Medical technology has outstripped the law's settled assumptions about the commencement and termination of life. Medical advances have added urgency to the abortion controversy. The steady glow of preconceived ideas about the beginning of life pales in the paramount lustre radiating from medical understanding about fetal viability. So too, new medical comprehension challenges current superstitions about when life ends.

Growth in medical discernment has prompted reformulation of various common law doctrines. In *Re Warwicker, McLeod* v. *Toronto General Trusts*,[150] the Ontario High Court accepted expert medical evidence that death occurs with the cessation of respiratory and cardiac functions. That rule was applied to determine which of two drowning victims had survived the other for testamentary purposes. Suppose that identical facts occur today. Mechanical ventilators are used to maintain respiration and heart beat. No doctor now seriously believes that artificially maintained breathing and circulation, by themselves, indicate life. There must also be brain function.[151] Can the law blindly

---

149. The parent is the guardian by nature of the child. See *Hopper* v. *Steeves* (1899), 34 N.B.R. 591 (C.A.): "The guardian by nature is the father, and on his death the mother, and this guardianship extends only to the custody of the person". As such, the parent or guardian of the child has certain obligations towards the child as well as certain rights. *In Re Flynn* (1848), 2 DeG. & Sm. 457, 474-75, 64 E.R. 205, 212, Vice Chancellor Knight Bruce said: "The acknowledged rights of a father with respect to the custody and guardianship of his infant children are conferred by the law, it may be with a view to the performance by him of duties towards the children, and, in a sense, on condition of performing those duties; but there is great difficulty in closely defining them". The Court went on to say that it would only interfere where "the father has so conducted himself, or has shown himself to be a person of such a description ... as to render it not merely better for the children, but essential to their safety or to their welfare, in some serious and important respect". Thus, common law makes clear that the absolute rights of the parent are subject to, or conditional upon, the provision of some minimal level of care. The Child Protection statutes vastly extend the scope of parental duties, as guardian, to provide for the child's health.

150. *Re Warwicker, McLeod et al.* v. *Toronto General Trusts Corp.* (1936), 3 D.L.R. 368 (Ont. H.C.J.).

151. The courts agree: see *R.* v. *Kitching and Adams*, [1976] 6 W.W.R. 697 (Man. C.A.). So does at least one legislature: see *The Vital Statistics Act*, S.M. 1982-83-84, c. 58, C.C.S.M., c. V-60, s. 2. So does the Law Reform Commission of Canada, *Criteria for the Determination of Death*, Report no. 15 (1981).

follow precedent based on superstition? The answer, of course, is no. To be credible, the law must adjust to new scientific rationality. Thus, it is hardly surprising that law reform commissions, legislatures and courts have reformulated common law doctrine to take account of medical developments with respect to brain death.[152]

It is equally necessary to rethink legal institutions relevant to passive euthanasia of severely damaged newborns in light of modern pediatric medicine. The reality in neonatal units is that doctors retain ultimate decisional authority when withholding treatment is perceived as medically indicated. Doctors do not inform parents of all treatment alternatives. Parents are not consulted about decisions to initiate or discontinue life saving ventilation. Doctors refuse to operate in the face of some parental requests. Selective, biased presentation of medical information is used to control parental choice. Typically, parental involvement rises in proportion to concord with the doctors' views. Where clear divergence of opinion exists, final decisional authority is retained by the medical team.

These practices abrase against current law on two fronts. First, it must be questioned whether anyone, doctor or parent, can lawfully withhold life saving treatment from a baby. Second, doubt exists whether the medical profession legally can usurp the surrogate's decisional role with respect to refusing treatment.

(c) Legality of Passive Euthanasia

The *Criminal Code* at s. 197 requires parents to provide medical treatment to minor children. Parents failing to do so are criminally responsible if the child's life or health is endangered.[153] While the *Code* is categorical, case law makes clear that the duty is not absolute. The treatment required is *appropriate* treatment, such treatment as *reasonably* would be provided in the circumstances.[154] The duty imposed by the *Code* is buttressed by civil obligations sounding in contract and tort. The doctor owes a duty of security to the baby. Thus, the central question lies beyond the terse phrasing of the *Code*. The Court must consider whether provision of medical treatment to a severely damaged newborn is appropriate. While this determination is for the court, expert

---

152. *Id.*

153. *Criminal Code*, R.S.C. 1970, c. C-34, s. 197(2)(a)(ii). This is now almost certainly a *mens rea* offence, requiring intent or recklessness to put the child's health at risk (the *mens rea*) as well as failure to provide the treatment (the *actus reus*): *R.* v. *Sheppard*, [1980] 3 W.L.R. 960 (H.L.).

154. *Supra*, notes 91-104 b.

medical evidence is relevant. The evidence will be found to run both ways, but a useful example of the latitude courts have in deciding this question appears from the following statement by Dr. Searle in the *British Medical Journal* for 1977:

> In cases where curative medicine has nothing more to offer it is accepted as good medical practice to see that patients die in comfort and with dignity. Furthermore, it is also accepted that when a patient's life is merely being prolonged by the sophistication of intensive care, with no prospect of restoring health, those techniques should be withdrawn.[155]

The Canadian Medical Association's *Code of Ethics* supports the general thrust of this position by recognizing that an ethical physician "will allow death to occur with dignity and comfort when death of the body appears to be inevitable".[155a] However, the C.M.A. has gone one significant step further. In 1974, the governing body passed a resolution, against the advice of its legal defence arm, which recognized the ethical acceptability of entering a "no resuscitation" order on a patient's file in some conditions of "ill-health". "Ill-health" was used in contrast to "impending inevitable death" and, thus, implies conditions of ill-health where death is not inevitable.[155b] The Canadian Medical Association thus appears to recognize that it is proper to withhold treatment from salvageable newborns in certain cases. If the "appropriateness" criteria is taken seriously, it becomes clear that the courts have considerable latitude to bring the law into line with current neonatal practice.

Under s. 199 of the *Criminal Code*:

> Everyone who undertakes to do an act is under a legal duty to do it if an omission to do the act is or may be dangerous to life.

---

155. Searle, *Life with Spina Bifida*, [1977] Brit. Med. J. 1670. Most of the relevant American cases are decided on the basis of evidence of this kind. See *Severns* v. *Wilmington Medical Center*, 421 A. (2d) 1334, 1338 (Del. Sup. Ct., 1980).

155a. C.M.A. *Code of Ethics* (September 1982), "Responsibilities to the Patient", art. 18.

155b. See C.M.A., Council on Community Health, General Council, 1974, p. 84, resolution 37: "Be it resolved that the C.M.A. recognize that there are conditions of ill-health and impending inevitable death where an order on the order sheet by the attending doctor of 'no resuscitation' is appropriate and ethically acceptable. Carried". Recognizing that legal liability could attach to a doctor giving effect to this resolution, the C.M.A. sought the advice of a joint C.M.A./C.B.A. Committee and of the Medical Protective Association. These sources advised the withdrawal of the resolution for legal reasons. The Council ignored this advice and reaffirmed their position the following year. A representative of the C.M.A. summed up the Association's attitude in a telephone interview with the author's research assistant: "The law be damned".

Some would argue that the section is relevant to a doctor undertaking treatment of a newborn.[156] If the doctor discontinues treatment on realizing that passive euthanasia is indicated, he breaches a duty imposed by law[157] for the purpose of criminal negligence. This is defined at s. 202.

Everyone is criminally negligent who

(b) in omitting to do anything that it is his duty to do, shows wanton or reckless disregard for the lives or safety of other persons.

Causality is established by s. 207.[158] If criminal negligence causes death, criminal responsibility follows.[159]

This rigorous logic overlooks the crucial question: what did the doctor undertake to do? Here again the court has a choice. The court may determine that the doctor undertook to provide appropriate treatment in accordance with the standard practices of his profession. Alternatively, it can hold that he undertook to preserve life by all extraordinary means. The first option leaves wide room for the court to accommodate current neonatal practice.[159a] American Courts have boldly

---

156. Swardon and Himel, *Legal Opinion on Position Paper: Withholding Treatment* (1979), 24 Can. J. Psychiatry 81, 82: "the court may impose a legal duty on a physician to undertake an act the omission of which would be dangerous to life". See also Robertson, *Involuntary Euthanasia of Defective Newborns: A Legal Analysis* (1975), 27 Stan. L. Rev. 215, 229-30.

157. Equally, it is sufficient if the duty arises by contract: see *R*. v. *Mary Nicholls* (1875), 13 Cox C.C. 74, 76: "if a person who has chosen to take charge of a helpless creature lets it die by wicked negligence, that person is guilty of manslaughter ... wicked negligence ... is ... a wicked mind in the sense that she was reckless and careless whether the creature died or not"; *R*. v. *Chattaway* (1922), 17 Cr. App. R. 7; *R*. v. *Marriott* (1838), 8 Car. & P. 425, 433, 173 E.R. 559, 563 (for jury to say whether prisoner "by way of contract, in some way or other [had] taken upon him" care of helpless person; if prisoner broke contract he becomes criminally responsible); *R*. v. *Instan* (1893), 17 Cox C.C. 602, 603.

158. But see *St. Germain* v. *The Queen*, [1976] C.A. 185 (Que.).

159. *Criminal Code*, R.S.C. 1970, c. C-34, s. 203.

159a. This view is upheld in a recent decision of the Leicester Crown Court in England: see *Acquittal of Paediatrician Charged after Death of Infant with Downs Syndrome* (1981), 2 The Lancet 1101.
In this case a doctor was acquitted on charges of attempted murder resulting from his compliance with parental wishes to withhold treatment from a mongoloid baby. However, the case was decided on the narrow fact that the prosecution failed to show that the withholding of treatment was the cause of death. In a second case, a doctor decided not to ventilate a very premature baby. An unsigned letter to the College of Physicians and Surgeons complained that the baby was left crying for two hours in a hospital corridor. An investigation by the College concluded that the doctor was not negligent, although the College recognized that the deci-

occupied this ground by finding that doctors have no duty to provide treatment which is "ineffective" ... futile ... [or] useless ... in the opinion of qualified medical personnel.[159b]

This latitude is equally apparent with respect to the general duty to report to officialdom children in need of protection. The question must be asked whether severely damaged newborns not receiving active treatment are in need of protection. They are in need of protection only to the extent that active treatment is appropriate and in their "best interests". Since "appropriateness" and "best interests" are matters for the court, the judges have flexible legal materials with which to manoeuvre the law into conformity with pediatric medicine.

American Courts, for the past several years, have been asked to wrestle with these problems. The reported decisions are among the most remarkable achievements in the history of jurisprudence. They merit close attention.

(i) Comatose Incompetency

The first significant decision provoked widespread public attention and international debate. In *Karen Ann Quinlan's* case,[160] a twenty-two year old girl ceased breathing for two 15 minute periods. The result was devastating. She fell into an unresponsive coma, thus losing awareness of anyone or anything around her. All cognitive functioning was destroyed. Karen was in a "chronic persistent vegetative state".[161]

Karen's father petitioned the court under a guardianship statute for permission to remove the mechanical respirator which maintained her breathing. The doctors objected that this action would conflict with their professional judgment.[162] The New Jersey Supreme Court held that the right of privacy, constitutionally enshrined in the penumbra of specific Bill of Rights guarantees, "is broad enough to encompass a patient's decision to decline medical treatment under certain circumstances ... The State's interest [in the sanctity of life] *contra* weakens and the individual's right to privacy grows as the degree of bodily

---

sion to place an infant on a life support system is "a dilemma — a medical, moral and ethical dilemma:" see *The Citizen* (Ottawa), Nov. 18, 1981, p. 48. Thus, the proposition stated in the text cannot be considered to have been authoritatively decided.

159b. *Barber* v. *Sup. Ct. of Calif.*, 195 Cal. R. 484, 491 (Ct. App. 1983).

160. *Matter of Quinlan*, 70 N.J. 10, 355 A. (2d) 647 (1976).

161. *Id.*, p. 654.

162. *Id.*, p. 663.

invasion increases and the prognosis dims."[163] In Karen's case, the personal right of privacy surpassed the state's interests in preservation of life. Very great intrusion was required to maintain life; the prognosis was very poor. That entitled Karen to refuse further treatment.

Karen, of course, could not refuse herself. The question then arose whether Karen's father, by asserting Karen's right of privacy on her behalf, could refuse for her. The court agreed that he could. "[H]er right of privacy ... should not be discarded solely on the basis that her condition prevents her conscious exercise of the choice. The only practical way to prevent destruction of the right is to permit the guardian and the family of Karen to render their best judgment ... as to whether she would exercise it in these circumstances."[164]

It is important to notice that the court requires the exercise of surrogate judgment to be subjective. As far as possible the surrogate must determine what the unconscious patient would have done. There is a limit. The exercise of substituted judgment must not offend "the common moral judgment of the community".[165]

The *Quinlan* court considered appropriate procedural controls on the exercise of surrogate choice. Court approval of the surrogate's decision would be generally inappropriate "not only because that would be a gratuitous encroachment on the medical profession's field of competence, but because it would be impossibly cumbersome".[166] Rather, the Court required Karen's guardian, family and doctors to conclude that Karen's comatose condition would not improve. The hospital's ethics committee had to agree with that determination. If the committee agreed, life support could be withdrawn with immunity from all civil and criminal liability.

Quinlan's case stands for the proposition that a comatose patient in a chronic vegetative state is entitled to refuse life saving treatment by surrogate action. In every subsequent case dealing with comatose chronically vegetative persons, the right first articulated in *Quinlan* has been upheld.[167] The basis of the decisions is narrow. The courts

---

163. *Id.*, p. 663-4.

164. *Id.*, p. 664.

165. *Id.*, p. 665.

166. *Id.*, p. 669.

167. *Matter of Young*, Calif. Supr. Ct., Orange Co., Sept. 11, 1979, No. A-100863 (Sumner, J.), digested in 48 U.S.L.W. 2238 (patient described as "in a stable and hopeless medical circumstance" as a result of car accident. Application by conservator to have breathing device turned off. The court held, "People have the right to refuse medical treatment and the right to terminate medical procedures that have been

do not assume in them any broad jurisdiction to adjudicate quality of life. Rather, they deal with life in the comatose, non-cognitive, vegetative state. Under these decisions, state interests in the preservation of life lose all cogency where tested against surrogate asserted rights to bodily integrity and self determination when cognition is irrevocably lost.

To some, the ultimate horror lies in being "maintained in limbo, by aggressive interventions, in a sterile room, by machines controlled by strangers".[168] The *Quinlan* line of authority makes clear that this horror does not have to be endured. A surrogate has power to release vegetative life from mechanical purgatory.

(ii) Poor Quality of Life

Much more difficult is the situation where a surrogate declines life saving treatment on behalf of an incompetent who is neither comatose nor vegetative. This problem has come before the courts in several different contexts, and produced diverse results. In *Superintendent of Belchertown State School* v. *Saikewicz*[169] the Massachusetts Supreme

---

initiated on their behalf ... A conservatee does not lose this right when a conservator is appointed, and if she believes it to be in the best interests of the conservatee, a conservator can assert this right on behalf of the conservatee"); *Matter of Dinnerstein*, 380 N.E. (2d) 134 (Mass. Ap. Ct. 1978) (patient of advanced age "in an essentially vegetative state", irreversibly and terminally ill; the Court held that in these circumstances the law did not prohibit a course of medical treatment, excluding attempts at resuscitation in the event of cardiac or respiratory arrest); *Eichner* v. *Dillon*, 426 N.Y.S. (2d) 517 (App. Div. 1980), affd. (*sub nom. Matter of Storar*) 438 N.Y.S. (2d) 266, 420 N.E. (2d) 363 (1981) (priest brought proceeding to have religious brother who was in "chronic vegetative state", declared incompetent and to obtain judicial approval for withdrawal of extraordinary life sustaining measures, consisting of respirator. Although case was decided on the basis of a specific statement of intent by the patient before becoming comatose, the Court went on to discuss the situation where there is no express intention. In these cases the courts approve the approach taken in *Quinlan; Severns* v. *Wilmington Medical Center*, 421 A. (2d) 1334 (Del. 1980) (husband of comatose wife brought action in which he sought appointment as guardian of her person and to request the removal of life sustaining supports. The court held (at p. 1347), "a person in a coma is helpless — she cannot invoke her own rights, including those that may be essential to her well-being ... Under such circumstances, the Court of Chancery, in our opinion, may recognize the right of a guardian of the person to vicariously assert the constitutional right of a comatose ward to accept medical care or refuse it"); *Matter of Colyer*, 660 P. (2d) 738 (Sup. Ct. Wash. 1983); *Barber* v. *Sup. Ct. of Calif.*, 195 Cal. R. 484 (Ct. App. 1983).

168. *Supra*, note 97 and accompanying text.

169. *Superintendent of Belchertown State School* v. *Saikewicz*, 370 N.E. (2d) 417 (Mass. 1977).

Judicial Court considered the report of a guardian *ad litem* about a sixty-seven year old leukemia sufferer, which recommended withholding life extending chemotherapy. Saikewicz was profoundly retarded; his I.Q. was ten, his mental age two years and eight months. He could not communicate verbally. Apart from leukemia, his health was generally good, and he was ambulatory.

Chemotherapy has painful adverse side effects. In *Saikewicz's* case, it was said to have a 30-40 percent chance of producing a remission for 2 to 13 months, *but no chance of producing a complete cure.*

The *Saikewicz* Court initially followed the path blazed in *Quinlan*. Competent persons have the right to refuse treatment; the right must be balanced against state interests in preservation of life; the right is not lost because incompetency supervenes; it may be exercised by substitution. At that point, the *Saikewicz* Court took a new departure into then uncharted waters. The State, it held, had responsibility as *parens patriae* to protect the best interests of incompetent persons.[170] The "best interests" of incompetents is flexible, depending not on what the reasonable man or the mass of competent persons would do, but on the "singular situation viewed from the unique perspective of the person called on to make the decision".[171] "[T]he goal is to determine with as much accuracy as possible the wants and needs of the individual involved".[172]

This heightened subjectivity is partly fictitious, because it is of course impossible to know what a person with the mental age of two wants. Who among us can interpret the desires of two year olds in respect of things they cannot understand? The Court thought that Saikewicz would experience fear precipitated by the pain and disorientation that chemotherapy causes - "fear without the understanding from which these patients draw strength". Would Saikewicz desire to exchange his fear, pain and disorientation for a possible 12 months more of life? How can we say with any confidence what a two year old mentality would choose with respect to this devil's bargain?

What the *Saikewicz* Court has done is to create an ingenious fiction behind which to accommodate quality of life arguments. A quality of life perspective saturates the judgment. The court surveys current medical ethics to conclude that current medical ethics disdains the "use of extraordinary means of prolonging life...when...it becomes apparent

---

170. *Id.*, p. 427.

171. *Id.*, p. 428.

172. *Id.*, p. 430.

that there is no hope for the recovery of the patient. Recovery should not be defined simply as the ability to remain alive; it should mean life without intolerable suffering".

Life of acceptable quality. Life without intolerable suffering. This is the axis on which the *Saikewicz* reasons revolve. To forestall sliding down the slippery slope which a quality of life perspective invites, the court neatly reverses the focus. Any attempt to equate "the value of life with any measure of the quality of life", is "firmly rejected".[173] In order to accommodate quality of life decisional criteria while at the same time rejecting quality of life as measure of the value of life, the court took an ingenious turn. Mr. Justic Liacos stretches the subjective test of decision beyond anything hitherto known in jurisprudence - stretches it, that is, to the breaking point. Quality of life is something assessed by the incompetent; "quality of life should be understood as a reference to the continuing state of pain and disorientation precipitated by the chemotherapy treatments". The decision to withhold chemotherapy from Saikewicz thus becomes something "based on a regard for his actual ... preferences".[174]

The judgment of the *Saikewicz* court is elegant and convincing - to a point. It cannot, however, be taken completely at face value. To the extent that the Court requires determining the preferences of a person unable to communicate, having a mental age of two, it is asking the impossible. None of us speaking the language of the law knows or could know what those preferences are, just as none of us knows what it feels like to be dead. The Court requires the surrogate to "don the mental mantle of the incompetent", to act on "the same motives and considerations as would have moved him".[175] We ask: how?

The only possible way to comply with the Court's test is to introduce a measure of objectivity - to ask, what would Saikewicz choose were he lucid for a moment?[176] How would he then weigh lengthening

---

173. *Id.*, p. 432.

174. *Id.*

175. *Id.*, p. 431. See also *Custody of a Minor*, 379 N.E. (2d) 1053, 1065 (Mass. App. Ct. 1978), where the Court reaffirmed this approach.

176. Apparently, the Supreme Judicial Court appreciates this difficulty and agrees with the assessment stated in the text. This is how we interpret this important passage from the subsequent decision of the Court in *Custody of a Minor*, 379 N.E. (2d) 1053, 1065 (Mass. App. Ct. 1978):

"In a case like this one, involving a child who is incompetent by reason of his tender years, we think that the substituted judgment doctrine is consistent with the best interests of the child test. It is true that, when applying the 'best interests' test, the inquiry is essentially objective in nature, and the decisions are made not by, but on behalf of the child. Nevertheless, the best

by painful treatments his unfortunate situation against withholding aggressive, disagreeable intervention? In proportion to the introduction of this objective element, the *Saikewicz* Court tolerates pure quality of life factors in the decisional balance.

If it is difficult to see how the surrogate can "don the mental mantle" of an adult incompetent, it is impossible to understand how to do this in the case of a deformed newborn. What are the preferences of a newborn? He has no life history from which one can infer his desires. He has never had relationships. His personality is indistinct. He has not formed a subjective consciousness. How can we don his mental mantle to second guess his actual preferences?

The logic of the *Saikewicz* court snaps as applied to this case. Even the Massachusetts Supreme Judicial Court appears to recognize that this is so, for, in the second *Chad Green* case the court equated a child's preferences with objective criteria. In considering whether parents, as surrogates, could refuse chemotherapy for their three year old boy, Chief Justice Hennessey said: "In the case of a child, however, the substituted judgment doctrine and the 'best interests of the child' test are essentially co-extensive, involving examination of the same criteria and application of the same basic reasoning".[177]

Joseph Saikewicz was a hopeless case. His illness was terminal; with or without treatment he would die quickly. This raises a question whether the judgment is confined to hopeless terminal cases. Can the court authorize surrogate refusal of life-saving treatment from a severely damaged child whom treatment would merely save but not improve? The California Court of Appeal shed light on the question *In Re Phillip B.*[178] This case concerned a twelve year old Down's Syndrome[179] child suffering from a correctable congenital heart defect. If left unrepaired

---

interests analysis, like that of the substituted judgment doctrine, requires a court to focus on the various factors unique to the situation of the individual for whom it must act. As a practical matter, the criteria to be examined and the basic applicable reasoning are the same".

Moreover, in *Matter of Spring*, 405 N.E. (2d) 115, 120 (Mass. 1980), the Court emphasized that Saikewicz was "suffering from an incurably fatal disease. The treatments in question were intrusive and were life prolonging rather than life saving; there was no prospect of a cure, or even of recovery of competence".

177. *Custody of a Minor*, 393 N.E. (2d) 836 (Mass. 1979).

178. *In Re Phillip B.*, 92 Cal. App. (3d) 796, 156 Cal. R. 48 (1979).

179. Down's Syndrome or mongolism is associated with chromosomal abnormality, usually trisomy or chromosome 21. It produces moderate to severe mental retardation, a flattened skull and nose and widened space between the first and second digits of the hands and feet.

the poorly functioning heart would damage Phillip's lungs to the point where he would be unable to oxygenate blood. This would cause a lessening of physical functioning initially, followed by severe incapacitation and death. Surgery would significantly increase Phillip's life span. Phillip's doctors recommended surgery; his parents refused their consent.

The California court followed a similar logical path as that first cut by the *Quinlan* and *Saikewicz* courts. A constitutionally protected right of privacy extends to certain aspects of the family; it protects parental choice to raise their children as they think best; the right has to be balanced against state interest, as *parens patriae*, in the sanctity of life; the underlying consideration is whether medical treatment will serve the child's "best interests". The evidence suggested Phillip would be at greater risk than the normal 5-10% risk of mortality from the surgery because of his mongolism and vascular deformity. On that view, the court upheld the parents' refusal. In so doing, Mr. Justice Caldecott outlined the factors relevant to consider in such cases:

> The state should examine the seriousness of the harm the child is suffering or the substantial likelihood that he will suffer serious harm; the evaluation for the treatment by the medical profession; the risks involved in medically treating the child; and the expressed preferences of the child.[180]

By including "the evaluation for the treatment by the medical profession", the court appears to introduce quality of life factors - the anticipated outcome of treatment - to be tested against state interest in the sanctity of life. In *Phillip B.'s* case, it is difficult to resist the conclusion that Phillip's mental deficit, which the surgery could not improve, was the decisive factor influencing the parents and court to withhold life saving treatment.[181]

Saikewicz and *Phillip B.* may thus be interpreted as authorities which authorize quality of life factors to be weighed in the balance where passive euthanasia is at issue. By this reading, subject to procedural controls discussed below, parents would be entitled to refuse life saving treatment for a deformed child who had poor prognosis for

---

180. *In Re Phillip B.*, 92 Cal. App. (3d) 796, 156 Cal. R. 48, 51 (1979).

181. See Annas, *Denying the Rights of the Retarded: The Phillip Becker Case* (1979), 9 Hastings Center Report 18, 19, who recounts more of the evidence than does the report. According to Professor Annas, the parents'
"primary reason for refusing consent was that they do not want Phillip to outlive them. They believe that geriatric care in this country is terrible and that Phillip will not be well cared for after they die. 'His qualify of life would be poor in such a place,' and 'life in and of itself is not what it's all about.' "

development. That decision would have to be respected by the medical profession, subject to court approval where good faith or the child's "best interests" were called into question.

There is another, equally plausible interpretation of the cases which must be considered. This is that *Saikewicz* is limited to withholding aggressive intervention in the hopelessly terminal case; the act of dying does not have to be painfully prolonged. On this view, *In Re Phillip B.* is wrongly decided.[181a] It is "an arbitrary decision based on a vague standard ... a beacon cautioning us that courts too make mistakes".[182]

Indeed, this is how the Massachusetts Supreme Judicial Court views its *Saikewicz* decision. In *Custody of a Minor*[183] the parents of a twenty month old leukemia child refused consent for chemotherapy treatment. They were concerned about adverse side effects caused by chemotherapy, and therefore preferred to treat with laetrile.[184] According to the medical evidence, chemotherapy offered the only known medically effective treatment for the child's disease; he had responded well to initial treatment. On these findings, the Court readily distinguished *Saikewicz*:

> ... this form of treatment is not 'extraordinary' in the sense that it promises merely to prolong life where there is no hope of recovery. Contrast *Superintendent of Belchertown State School* v. *Saikewicz* ... chemotherapy now offers certain types of leukemia patients a substantial hope of cure.[185]

181a. This view gains strength in light of the most recent development in the Phillip Becker case. Although the court recognized the right of the parents to refuse treatment on Phillip's behalf, the same court has since awarded guardianship of Phillip to an interested couple in spite of the parents' objections. One of the factors considered in the award was the willingness of the applicants to "give the issue of surgery upon the child the most careful and searching consideration possible", the implication being that the applicant would be willing to consent to the surgery: 50 U.S.L.W. 2133 (1981).

However, this does not necessarily imply that the only case where treatment can be withheld is that of the hopelessly terminal patient as some have interpreted the ruling in *Saikewicz*. There appears to be an intermediate category between the hopelessly terminal case and the quality of life experienced by an otherwise healthy mongoloid child. In such intermediate cases, the courts may well sanction refusal of treatment, based on quality of life considerations.

182. Annas, *Denying the Rights of the Retarded: The Phillip Becker Case* (1979), 9 Hastings Center Report 18, 20.

183. *Custody of a Minor*, 379 N.E. (2d) 1053 (Mass. App. Ct. 1978).

184. See the further proceedings where this evidence appears: *Custody of a Minor*, 393 N.E. (2d) 836 (Mass. 1979).

185. *Custody of a Minor*, 379 N.E. (2d) 1053, 1064 (Mass. App. Ct. 1978).

...

[T]he State has an interest in the preservation of life. In stressing the importance of this interest we recognized in *Superintendent of Belchertown State School* v. *Saikewicz*, that there is a 'substantial distinction in the State's insistence that human life be saved where the affliction is curable, ... [and] the State's interest where ... the issue is not whether, but for how long, and at what cost to the individual that life may be briefly extended.[186]

Custody of a Minor interprets *Saikewicz* as a hopeless terminal case where prolonging life briefly by painful means could not elevate the State's interest in life above the privacy interests of the patient. It does not interpret *Saikewicz* as holding that the patient's interest in being freed from a life of poor quality outweighs state interest in preservation of life. Yet neither does *Custody of a Minor* decide that a patient's interest in being released from poor quality cannot outweigh state interest in the sanctity of life. *Custody of a Minor* does not deal with a child having poor prognosis for development or with a life of poor quality at all. It concerns a normal child who had "a substantial hope for cure".[187]

This last question - whether a surrogate can lawfully reject life saving treatment for a child facing poor developmental prospects - is a problem best dealt with by returning to general principles. There are four basic considerations the courts will consider: parental rights, state responsibility to protect life, bodily integrity and the child's welfare. American law accepts that there is a private area of family life which the State cannot enter.[188] The parents, as natural guardians of their child, are autonomous; as long as they do not disregard the child's welfare or trespass unduly on state interests in preserving life, their decisions must be respected.[189]

The child equally has a right to privacy and bodily integrity. "[T]he State must recognize the dignity and worth of an incompetent person and offer to that person the same panoply of rights and choices it recognizes in competent persons".[190] Thus, minors have the right to refuse

---

186. *Id.*, pp. 1063, 1066.

187. *Id.*, p. 1067. Similarly, in *Re Phillip B.*, 92 Cal. App. (3d) 796, 156 Cal. R. 48 (1979), the potential for development was excellent save for the factor of mongolism. It is unreasonable to refuse treatment for mongolism alone; there is nothing about mongolism touching the poor quality of life contemplated by the court in *Saikewicz*.

188. *Prince* v. *Massachusetts*, 321 U.S. 158, 166, 64 S. Ct. 438, 88 L. Ed. 645 (1949).

189. *Wisconson* v. *Yoder*, 406 U.S. 205, 234, 92 S. Ct. 1520, 32 L. Ed. 15 (1972).

190. *Superintendent of Belchertown State School* v. *Saikewicz*, 370 N.E. (2d) 417, 428 (Mass. 1977).

treatment by the substituted judgment doctrine so long as their surrogate choice does not violate fundamental norms of the community, or unduly interfere with State interests in the preservation of life.

Subject to the State's interest in the sanctity of life, discussed below, basic principles thus suggest that in a proper case, parents are competent to refuse life saving treatment for a defective newborn whose prognosis for development is exceptionally poor. The parents' right to refuse rests on the principle of parental autonomy, and the surrogate's ability to assert the child's independent rights to bodily integrity and privacy. Although withholding treatment must be in the child's best interests, the parents have a degree of latitude in assessing these rights. As the New York Court of Appeal said in *Matter of Hofbauer*,

> The court cannot assume the role of a surrogate parent and establish as the objective criteria with which to evaluate a parent's decision its own judgment as to the exact method or degree of medical treatment which should be provided...the court's inquiry should be whether the parents, once having sought accredited medical assistance and having been made aware of the possibility of cure if a certain mode of treatment is undertaken, have provided for their child a treatment which is recommended by their physician and which has not been totally rejected by all responsible medical authority.[191]

These conclusions are of course subject to the overriding state interest in the preservation of life. That interest, as has been demonstrated above, is not absolute. It will yield to a surrogate's refusal of life saving treatment for a hopeless, comatose patient in a vegetative state. It will also yield to a surrogate's refusal of painful life - prolonging treatment for terminally ill incompetents. It must now be asked whether the state's interest in the preservation of life will yield to a surrogate's refusal of life saving treatment for a severely damaged child with poor developmental possibilities, but who is neither comatose nor terminally ill.

There are two contrary lines of authority relevant to that question. The first group of cases suggests that the State's interest in preservation of life overrides surrogate refusal of life saving treatment for a viable child with poor developmental potential. In *Maine Medical Center* v. *Houle*[192] the court considered the case of a damaged baby

---

191. *Matter of Hofbauer*, 47 N.Y. (2d) 648, 411 N.Y.S. (2d) 416, 393 N.E. (2d) 1009 (App. Div. 1979) (parental decision to reject chemotherapy in preference to lactrile treatment for their child afflicted with Hodgkins's disease upheld).

192. *Maine Medical Center* v. *Houle*, Maine Superior Ct., Cumberland, No. 74-145, Feb. 14, 1974.

born without a left eye or ear canal, a malformed left thumb and a trachael esophagea fistula. The latter deficit prevented ingestion of food, necessitating tube feeding, and allowed fluids to enter the lungs, leading to pneumonia and other complications. There was a certainty of some brain damage. The baby's father refused consent to surgical repair of the trachea, and directed the doctor to stop tube feeding. Further developmental problems led the attending physician to form the opinion that all life support measures should be withdrawn. In neglect proceedings, the court authorized the guardian *ad litem* to consent to surgical repair of the trachea and to take other treatment measures as medically required. "[A]t the moment of live birth", said the court, "there does exist a human being entitled to...the right to life". If the doctor formed the opinion that life itself could not be preserved, life support could be withdrawn. "However, the doctor's qualitative evaluation of the value of life to be preserved is not legally within the scope of his expertise ... the issue ... is not the ... quality of life to be preserved, but the medical feasibility of the proposed treatment compared with the almost certain risk of death should treatment be withheld".[193] In *Matter of Storar*[194] the New York Court of Appeals followed suit. In this case a fifty-two year old incompetent, having a mental age of eighteen months, suffered from terminal bladder cancer. As a result of his condition he experienced blood loss through lesions in his bladder, and thus required blood transfusions. After initial transfusions, Storar's mother, as guardian, refused consent to continue because Storar found the procedure disagreeable. This decision implied an earlier death, although death was certain to come soon in any event. On application by the Medical Center, the court overrode the mother's decision, and ordered the transfusions to be maintained. "[A] court should not allow an incompetent to bleed to death because someone, even someone as close as a parent or sibling, feels that this is best for one with an incurable disease".[195] In so holding, the Court narrowed its own *Hofbauer* ruling to require treatment if the only other alternative is death. If alternative life saving treatments are available, the parents have latitude of choice between various procedures. However, "the courts may not permit a parent to deny a child all treatment for a condition which threatens his life".[196]

It is hard to see that *Houle* is other than a decision *per incuriam*. No cases whatsoever are cited in the reasons; neither are any statutes.

---

193. *Id.*, p. 4.
194. *Matter of Storar*, 438 N.Y.S. (2d) 266, 420 N.E. (2d) 64 (1981).
195. *Id.*, at 275-76, 420 N.E. (2d) at 73.
196. *Id.* at 275, 420 N.E. (2d) at 73.

Mr. Justice Roberts does not explore fundamental principles or competing interests. The judgment appears to be knee jerk reaction to the proposition that life is sanctified at all costs. *Storar* is hardly better reasoned. Although Mr. Justice Wachtler cites five cases in support of the view that a parent "may not deprive a child of life saving treatment",[197] the cases he cites do not support that broad proposition. Nor do any of these cases require the taking of extraordinary measures to salvage a child who, although viable, has no potential for development. *Matter of Sampson*[198] involved court ordered cosmetic surgery to repair a facial disfigurement. The parents objected to the surgery on religious grounds, because blood might be required. The case did not present a choice between death and a life of poor quality; it presented a choice between life of good quality and life of better quality. Neither did *Matter of Vasko*[199] present the court with a choice between death and a life of poor quality. This case involved an otherwise normal child suffering from a malignant tumor. The parent's failure, on religious grounds, to consent to surgery, meant certain death, whereas the recommended procedure implied a complete cure. *Matter of Santos* v. *Goldstein*[200] concerned parental objection, on religious grounds, to transfuse a normal child during surgery. *Custody of a Minor*[201] dealt with treatment alternatives for a child with a "substantial chance for cure", who, if cured, would have no deficits and could lead a normal life. *Matter of Hofbauer*[202] considered therapeutic alternatives in respect of a treatable disease, which would invariably be fatal if left unattended. The Court upheld the parent's choice of therapy as reasonable.

The *Storar* Court has thus based its decision on quicksand. The authorities are silent on the question whether parents may refuse life saving treatment for a child with no developmental potential. Nor does the *Storar* Court examine important relevant principles, such as the right to privacy, sanctity of life, and self determination. Moreover, there was no reason for the court to make such a broad ruling. *Storar* was a terminal case; he had a life expectancy of between three and six

---

197. *Id.*

198. *Matter of Sampson*, 65 Misc. (2d) 658, 317 N.Y.S. (2d) 641 (Fam. Ct. 1970), affd. 37 A.D. (2d) 668, 323 N.Y.S. (2d) 253 (1971), affd. 29 N.Y. (2d) 900, 278 N.E. (2d) 918 (1972).

199. *Matter of Vasko*, 238 App. Div. 128, 263 N.Y.S. 552 (1933).

200. *Matter of Santos* v. *Goldstein*, 16 App. Div. (2d) 755, 227 N.Y.S. (2d) 450 (1962).

201. *Custody of a Minor*, 379 N.E. (2d) 1053 (Mass. App. Ct. 1978).

202. *Matter of Hofbauer*, 47 N.Y. (2d) 648, 411 N.Y.S. (2d) 416, 393 N.E. (2d) 1009 (App. Div. 1979).

months whether or not transfused.[203] The Court's broad ruling requiring life saving treatment in all non-terminal cases, thus, is only a gratuitous *obiter*. In our submission, therefore, these cases cannot be considered authoritative on the question whether poor quality life must be preserved at all costs.

The second line of authority suggests that poor developmental potential, alone, can be a sufficient reason to uphold a surrogate's refusal of extraordinary intervention. These authorities include some of the masterpieces of medical jurisprudence. In *Superintendent of Belchertown State School* v. *Saikewicz* the Court expressly addressed the question whether aggressive intervention was required to maintain life when the result of intervention, at best, would salvage a life of exceptionally poor quality. Mr. Justice Liacos said:

> The current state of medical ethics in this area is expressed by one commentator who states that: 'we should not use extraordinary means of prolonging life or its semblance when, after careful consideration, consultation and the application of the most well conceived therapy it becomes apparent that there is no hope for the recovery of the patient. Recovery should not be defined simply as the ability to remain alive, it should mean life without intolerable suffering'.

> Our decision in this case is consistent with the current medical ethics in this area.[203a]

Further articulation of this idea came from the *Dinnerstein* Court. Treatment should be provided where there was a reasonable expectation of effecting relief from the "condition" being treated, said Mr. Justice Armstrong. Treatment was not required where it offered no hope of "a return towards a normal, functioning, integrated existence". The Court noted that all of the cases where the right to refuse treatment was overridden by compelling State interests involved:

> the availability of a treatment offering hope of restoration to normal, integrated, functioning, cognitive existence.[203b]

It follows that where no reasonable expectation exists for a damaged newborn to obtain an integrated, functioning, cognitive existence, the surrogate is entitled to refuse extraordinary intervention. The cases

---

203. *Matter of Storar*, 438 N.Y.S. (2d) 266, 271, 420 N.E. (2d) 64, 69 (1981): The Court does indicate that if the blood transfusions are given, the quality of Storar's life during the 3-6 month period would be improved. However, that is a different matter. It adds no weight to the broad ruling that life must be preserved at all costs regardless of quality.

203a. 370 N.E. (2d) 417, 424 (Mass. 1977).

203b. *Matter of Dinnerstein*, 380 N.E. (2d) 134, 138 (Mass. App. Ct. 1978).

make clear that the baby's family are to be left a degree of latitude in reaching their momentous decision. As Mr. Justice Armstrong said in a *Matter of Spring*, there is no doubt about "the importance the law attaches to the role of the family as next-of-kin in evaluating the appropriateness of treatment in the circumstances of a particular case".[203c]

How should the law decide whether the family has acted responsibly within the margin of appreciation committed to it? Some commentators have suggested a distinction between "ordinary" versus "extraordinary" treatment - ordinary care being obligatory while extraordinary care being optional.[203d] Although one Canadian court has been persuaded to follow the example of certain American colleagues in employing this conceptual framework,[203e] it is doubtful whether the distinction enhances the case law, or has staying power.[203f] Better analytical tools emanate from the California Court of Appeal, building on the work of the President's Commission for the Study of Ethical Problems in Medicine. In *Barber* v. *Superior Court of California*, the Court rejected using the "ordinary/extraordinary" framework because "the use of these terms begs the question". Rather, the Court proposed to determine

> "whether the proposed treatment is proportionate or disproportionate in terms of the benefits to be gained versus the burdens caused. Under this approach, proportionate treatment is that which, in the view of the patient, has at least a reasonable chance of providing benefits to the patient, which benefits outweigh the burdens attendant to the treatment. Thus, even if a proposed course of treatment might be extremely painful or intrusive, it would still be proportionate treatment if the prognosis was for complete cure or significant improvement in the patient's condition. On the other hand, a treatment course which is only minimally painful or intrusive may nonetheless be considered disproportionate to the potential benefits if the prognosis is virtually hopeless for any significant improvement in condition".[203g]

203c. *Matter of Spring*, 399 N.E. (2d) 493, 503 (Mass. App. Ct. 1979) revd. on other grounds 405 N.E. (2d) 115 (Mass. 1980).

203d. McCartney, *The Development of the Doctrine of Ordinary and Extraordinary Means of Preserving Life in Catholic Moral Theology Before The Karen Quinlan Case* (1980), 47 Linacre Q. 215.

203e. In *Re S.D.*, [1983] 3 W.W.R. 597, 618 (B.C. Prov. Ct.), revd. [1983] 3 W.W.R. 618 (B.C.S.C.).

203f. See generally, President's Commission for the Study of Ethical Problems of Medicine and Biomedical and Behavioural Research, *Deciding to Forego Life Sustaining Treatment: A Report on the Ethical, Medical and Legal Issues in Treatment Decisions* (1983), p. 82 ff.

203g. 195 Cal. R. 484, 491 (Ct. App. 1983).

These cases are exhaustive in their exploration of fundamental principles, medical ethics, and relevant authorities. They radiate an aura of authority which is convincing. If they are to be considered wrong, it is difficult to discern the fault. In our submission, these rulings must be taken as authoritative on the proposition that parents have a realm of autonomy to decide to withhold treatment from a viable child with poor developmental potential.

(iii) Indeterminate Cases

The most difficult - and most common - type of case experienced in neonatal units relates to medical uncertainties. In many instances, despite the poor prognosis for development attributed to a damaged child, doubt remains. Notwithstanding the ambiguity displayed by the case, the doctor must decide whether to commence treatment. This decision implies two terrifying consequences. If treatment is withheld, a life that may otherwise have developed normally is destroyed. If treatment is initiated, the child may survive in a comatose, vegetative state, but without mechanical life support. The opportunity for passive euthanasia is lost.

This is the dilemma presented by cases of low birth weight babies suffering from respiratory distress. Techniques used to assess the developmental potential of these neonates are unreliable. In one third of extreme asphyxiation cases, newborns, unlike adults, recover completely, even if spontaneous respiration is absent for thirty minutes. Two thirds, however, suffer severe damage, destroying, in many cases, all capacity for socialization and self-awareness.[204]

The dilemma doctors face in indeterminate cases turns a spotlight on the concept of *passive* euthanasia. What is the difference between passive and active euthanasia - between allowing to die and killing? Some neonatal units use standardized criteria to decide which cases to treat. This artificially removes the indeterminacy, with the result that some salvageable children are lost. Is it not unsubtle in the indeterminate case invariably to withhold treatment with a view to avoiding the issue? Would it not be more consistent with a sanctity of life ethic to treat all indeterminate cases, thereby removing the uncertainty?

---

204. Steiner and Neligan, *Perinatal Cardiac Arrest: Quality of Survivors* (1975), 50 Archives of Disease in Childhood 696; Scott, *Outcome of Very Severe Birth Asphyxia* (1976), 51 Archives of Disease in Childhood 712; Chance, *The Severely Handicapped Newborn: A Physician's Perspective* (1980), 1 Health Law in Canada 34. But see also, *Most low weight preemies grow normally, study finds,* Globe and Mail (Toronto), 6/1/82, p. 15 which suggests 85% of children studied developed normally.

Babies that can develop are thereby salvaged. Those which cannot develop challenge the settled assumption that life can never be destroyed. This approach casts a heavy burden on those who favor *passive* euthanasia, but are opposed to infanticide, to explain why.[205]

Ethical arguments that revolve around a quality of life axis take comfort in distinguishing between active and passive euthanasia. " '[K]illing' and 'allowing to die' are not morally equivalent".[206] This proposition may be true, and if so, would be relevant to the hopeless terminal case. A terminal patient may be allowed to die: his suffering does not have to be extended briefly by painful means.[207] Killing him, however, requires a justification which quality of life arguments do not supply.

Is the distinction relevant to indeterminate cases? It is hard to see how the distinction between passive and active euthanasia assists decisions about uncertain cases. It is at once too broad and too narrow; too broad because passive euthanasia of the indeterminate case is gruesome. At least some of the babies admitted to neonatal units for severe asphyxiation have potential for development. Should not life with potential be allowed to live? The distinction is too narrow because it blurs focus on a crucial issue. When it is certain that life has no potential, and the option of allowing to die has passed, the grim question must be asked: should the law criminalize infanticide in all cases? Or is justice better served by allowing the parents this latitude in cases where it is certain no developmental potential exists?

It seems clear that actively killing a child - no matter how severely deformed - is punishable as murder in our law.[208] A beneficent purpose is irrelevant. The common law offers no leeway to the intent to kill "no matter how kindly the motive".[209] Nor is consent of the victim or his parents an excuse.[210]

---

205. This is the position of Dr. Lorber: see his "The Doctor's Duty to Patients and Parents in Profoundly Handicapping Conditions" in *Medical Wisdom and Ethics in the Treatment of Severely Defective Newborn and Young Children* (D. Roy ed. 1978), p. 21. We return to this question in chapters 3 and 4.

206. E.W. Keyserlinyk, *Sanctity of Life or Quality of Life*. Ottawa: Law Reform Commission of Canada, 1979, p. 132.

207. This is the only category of case Mr. Keyserlinyk seriously considers.

208. *Criminal Code*, R.S.C. 1970, c. C-34, s. 212(a)(i): "Culpable homicide is murder (a) where a person who causes the death of a human being (i) means to cause his death ...".

209. *State* v. *Ehlers*, 98 N.J.L. 236, 119 A. 15, 7 (1922).

210. *Criminal Code*, R.S.C. 1970, c. C-34, s. 14.

In order for the crime of murder to be committed, the victim must be a "human being".[211] A child does not become a human being until it has completely proceeded, in a living state, from its mother's body.[212] This leads to the rather anomalous position that a child who has not completely proceeded from its mother may be deprived of life with impunity for murder, although a question remains whether this would constitute illegal abortion.[213]

That question has recently become of importance because the development of intrauterine diagnostic techniques, particularly amniocentesis, has been remarkable. Recent articles in the medical journals have reported several cases where intrauterine diagnosis of Down's Syndrome was made for only one of two fetal twins.[213a] A procedure has been developed to insert a needle into the heart of the anomalous twin and draw off a quantity of blood. Assuming the procedure is successful, cardiac activity in the affected twin ceases; the mother will deliver a living normal twin and a stillborn anomalous twin at term.[213b] If this procedure is to be performed lawfully in Canada, abortion laws will require amendment.[213c]

Glanville Williams has taken the view that English law did not account a "monster" as a person, and as such "a creature that is clearly a monster...could lawfully be put to a merciful death".[214] This view is based on a considerable misinterpretation of Bracton's manuscript. Bracton asserted that an infant monster could not be heir to landed property. The reason for this is that the monster "utters a roar when it ought to utter a cry" - that is, the monster springs from the union

---

211. *Criminal Code*, R.S.C. 1970, c. C-34, s. 212.

212. *Criminal Code*, R.S.C. 1970, c. C-34, s. 206(1).

213. Abortion is defined by s. 251 of the *Criminal Code* as procuring "a miscarriage". "Miscarriage" is defined in the medical books as "loss of the products of conception from the uterus before the fetus is viable": *Dorlands Illustrated Medical Dictionary* (25th ed.), p. 971. The law books have a different definition. "Procuring miscarriage" is the act of destroying the foetus or unborn offspring, at any time before birth: *Chitty on Medical Jurisprudence*, p. 410.

213a. See Kerengi and Chitkara, *Selective Birth in Twin Pregnancy with Discordancy for Down's Syndrome* (1981), 304 New England Journal of Medicine 1525 and notes 2-6 of that article.

213b. Kerengi and Chitkara, *supra*, note 213a, reported on this procedure recently. In advance of the procedure they obtained "confirmation from a court of law of the parents' right to consent on behalf of the normal fetus".

213c. See *supra*, note 213

214. G. Williams, *The Sanctity of Life and the Criminal Law* (1970), p. 333.

of man and beast.[215] Bracton accounts monsters along with bastards, changelings and stillborn children as a class that cannot inherit. Blackstone understood Bracton's reference well. In referring to the passage in the manuscript he adds a gloss that "[a] monster which bears the resemblance of the *brute creation*" cannot be heir to landed property. The reason, says Blackstone, is "too shocking" to discuss.[216] It seems clear that it is the monster's illegitimacy, rather than his lack of juristic personality, which disinherits him. Killing a monster, therefore, would be punishable as murder in the same way as would killing a bastard or changeling.

The euthanasia societies are uneasy about including defective children within the embrace of recommended legislation. The English Bill of 1936 would have restricted the right to euthanasia to patients over twenty-one suffering from an incurable and fatal disease.[217] The American society originally included a provision for involuntary euthanasia of defective newborns.[218] A bill containing this provision was introduced into the Nebraska legislature in 1937.[219] The bill was defeated, and no further attempt to introduce a bill having such a clause has been made in America or England since.[220] This has prompted one commentator to describe legislative proposals for involuntary euthanasia of defective newborns as "politically insignificant".[221] Be that as

---

215. Bracton, *Rerum Britannicarum Medi Aevi Scriptores* (Rolls Series), p. 459 (f. 438 a, b), Kraus Reprint Ltd. 1964. See also: Co. Litt. f. 7b.

There is, of course, a long mythical tradition of monsters having human and animal characteristics, such as centaurs, sphinxs, minotaurs, griffins and wyverns. One line of this tradition characterized monsters as the offspring of union between man and beast. For example, see Sir John Maundeville, *The Voiage and traivaile of Sir John Maundeville* (1400, repr. 1839), V. 47: "A monster is a thing disformed azen Kynde both of Man or of Beast", and Edward Topsell, *The History of Fourefooted Beasts* (1607), p. 337: "A horse-keeper which broght ... an infant, or rather a monster, which he had got upon a Mare".

216. *Blackstone's Commentaries* VII, p. 246 (1st U.S.A. Ed.).

217. 182 Law Times 412 (1936).

218. See Gurney, *Is There a Right to Die? — A Study of the Law of Euthanasia* (1972), 3 Cumberland - Sanford L. Rev. 235, 248.

219. L.B. 135, 52d Sess., Neb. Leg. (1937).

220. Euthanasia legislation was introduced in Florida and Wisconsin in 1970. Neither had provisions for involuntary euthanasia: see H.B. 3184, Fla. Leg. (1970); S.B. 670, S.B. 715, Wis. Leg. (1971). These are similar to the English Act introduced in 1969 in the House of Lords. All the bills failed. The statutes are discussed in Broughman, Bruke, Gould, *Euthanasia: Criminal, Tort, Constitutional and Legislative Considerations* (1972-73), 48 Notre Dame Lawyer 1202, 1352ff.

221. G. Williams, *The Sanctity of Life and the Criminal Law* (1970), p. 350.

it may, the significant case load of severely asphyxiated newborns admitted to neonatal intensive care raises profound and searching questions whether such a provision is not preferable to withholding treatment from all such cases, as is currently practised by some neonatal units.

(d) Procedure

Difficulty has arisen in American courts with respect to the procedure properly required for decisions to withhold life saving treatment. Can a surrogate, clothed with authority as parent or legal guardian, refuse life saving treatment without more? Does he need approval of the hospital's ethics committee? Does the State's interest in preservation of life make mandatory a State presence in the form of courts or administrative officials?

The apparent procedural difficulty cuts deeper. Doctors who withhold life saving treatment are exposed to civil and criminal liability. The doctor is caught on the horns of a dilemma; if he treats over a refusal, he is gored by a risk of liability for battery and criminal assault. If he respects a refusal, he is punctured by liability for various homicides and failure to provide necessaries.

This dilemma has prompted many American doctors to refuse to comply with a surrogate's request to withhold treatment in any case unless granted immunity from civil and criminal liability by prior court order.[222] Joseph Quinlan had to go to court to compel doctors to cease further life support for his comatose, vegetative daughter. In adjudicating Joseph Quinlan's petition, the New Jersey Court took a dim view of any requirement for prior court approval.

> We consider that a practice of applying to a court to confirm such decisions would generally be inappropriate, not only because that would be a gratuitous encroachment upon the medical profession's field of competence, but because it would be impossibly cumbersome.[223]

In so stating, the Court was clear that access to the courts in justiciable controversies was not foreclosed; "we speak rather of a general practice and procedure".[224] The Court thus left open to the surrogate an avenue of redress if the doctors unreasonably refused to comply with his instructions.

---

222. See, *e.g.*, *Severns* v. *Wilmington Medical Center*, 421 A. (2d) 1334, 1338 (Del. 1980).

223. *Matter of Quinlan*, 355 A. (2d) 647, 669 (N.J. 1976).

224. *Id.*

At that point, the New Jersey Court did something other courts have been unable to accept. It authorized the appointment of Karen's father as guardian, but refused to decide whether he could authoritatively decline further life support. Rather, the Court required him to obtain the concurrence of the attending physician, the hospital's ethics committee and the "family" (left undefined) that no reasonable prospect existed for Karen to return to cognitive life. Upon completion of that procedure, life support could be withdrawn.

In Massachusetts, the courts have been critical of delegating "ultimate" decision-making responsibility to non-curial bodies.[225] In *Superintendent of Belchertown State School* v. *Saikewicz* the Supreme Judicial Court held that "[w]hen a court is properly presented with the legal question, whether treatment may be withheld, it must decide that question and not delegate it to some private person or group".[226] The *Saikewicz* Court rejected any procedure which refused to answer questions properly asked, leaving "ultimate" decisional power to others.

The Massachusetts decisions "should not be taken to establish any requirement for prior judicial approval".[227] The judgments only require courts to respond to questions presented. Failure of parents or doctors to obtain judicial authorization for withholding treatment does not, by itself, imply any kind of liability in Massachusetts.

If prior court approval is not sought, the Massachusetts Court indicates that ethics committees may have a role to play. The finding of such committees would be highly persuasive to a court presented, after the fact, with a question whether withholding treatment in a particular case gave rise to liability.[228] However, ethics committee proceedings are not a requirement.[229] If medical decisions are made responsibly and in good faith, they are immune from (civil) liability.

---

225. *Superintendent of Belchertown State School* v. *Saikewicz*, 370 N.E. (2d) 417, 434 (Mass. 1977):
> "We take a dim view of any attempt to shift the ultimate decision-making responsibility away from the duly established courts of proper jurisdiction to any committee, panel or group, ad hoc or permanent. Thus, we reject the approach adopted by the New Jersey Supreme Court in the *Quinlan* case of entrusting the decision whether to continue artificial life support to the patient's guardian, family, attending doctors, and hospital 'ethics committee'."

This was reaffirmed in *Matter of Spring*, 405 N.E. (2d) 115, 120 (Mass. 1980).

226. *Matter of Spring*, 405 N.E. (2d) 115, 122 (Mass, 1980).

227. *Id.*, p. 120.

228. *Superintendent of Belchertown State School* v. *Saikewicz*, 370 N.E. (2d) 417, 434 (Mass. 1977).

229. *Id.*: "We do not believe that this option should be transformed by us into a required procedure".

The value of seeking ethics committee approval is that the committee's concurrence with the medical decision is "highly persuasive on issues of good faith and good medical practice".[230]

The decisions do not foreclose the possibility of obtaining prior court approval. If court authorization is given the doctor will be immune from liability "because the standard for determining whether treatment was called for is the same after the event as before".[231] Liability could follow only if the doctor is negligent in implementing the court's order.[232]

In *Matter of Dinnerstein*, the Massachusetts Appeals Division tried to narrow freedom to act without prior judicial approval to cases where the patient is irreversibly ill. Only terminal cases are "peculiarly within the competence of the medical profession".[233] If the case presents a "significant treatment choice or election" or if there is "some reasonable expectation of effecting a permanent or temporary cure", the Appeals Court would require prior judicial approval of withholding treatment.[234]

It is doubtful that freedom to act without court approval can be thus taken away. In *Matter of Spring* the Supreme Judicial Court agreed with the result in *Dinnerstein*. However, the Supreme Judicial Court was careful to point out that *Dinnerstein's* case involved a vegetative, terminally ill person. On that basis the Supreme Judicial Court upheld the result in *Dinnerstein*, but did so "[w]ithout approving all that is said in the opinion of the Appeals Court".[235]

The question whether prior judicial authorization is mandatory before termination of life support has also arisen in New York. In *Eichner* v. *Dillon* the Appellate Division held that "societal interests" in termination of life support were "so great" that it was necessary for the courts "to intervene and examine each case on an *individual* patient-to-patient basis".[236] The court went on to lay down extensive procedures, making mandatory the following steps prior to removal of life support: (1) certification by the attending doctor that the patient is terminally ill and in a chronic vegetative coma; (2) confirmation of the

---

230. *Matter of Spring*, 405 N.E. (2d) 115, 122 (Mass. 1980).

231. *Id.*

232. *Id.*

233. *Matter of Dinnerstein*, 380 N.E. (2d) 134, 139 (Mass. App. Ct. 1978).

234. *Id.*, pp. 138-9.

235. *Matter of Spring*, 405 N.E. (2d) 115, 120 (Mass. 1980).

236. *Eichner* v. *Dillon*, 426 N.Y.S. (2d) 517, 550 (App. Div. 1980), affd. (*sub. nom. Matter of Storar*) 438 N.Y.S. (2d) 266, 420 N.E. (2d) 64 (1981).

prognosis by a majority of the appropriate hospital committee, or, if none exists, by a specially appointed committee; (3) commencement of proceedings; (4) notice to the Attorney General and appropriate District Attorney; (5) appointment of a guardian *ad litem* for the patient.[237]

The Appellate Division based its requirement of prior judicial approval on the *Saikewicz* case. Mr. Justice Mollen said:

> We agree with the *Saikewicz* court that the neutral presence of the law is necessary to weigh these factors, and, thus, judicial intervention is required before any life-support system can be withdrawn.[238]

It is apparent that this is a considerable misinterpretation of *Saikewicz*, at least insofar as that decision has been explained by the Massachusetts Supreme Judicial Court in *Matter of Spring*. Mr. Justice Cardamone, in a stinging dissent in the *Storar* case, was highly critical of the Appellate Division's procedures. The procedures, he said, are "practical nonsense because judges have no extraordinary insight enabling them to measure the 'quality of life'.[239] On further appeal to the New York Court of Appeals, the result in *Eichner* was approved, but the procedures omitted. "It is not inappropriate for those charged with the care of incompetent persons to apply to the courts for a ruling on the propriety of conduct which might seriously affect their charges", said Mr. Justice Wachtler. "We emphasize, however, that any such procedure is optional". After some vacillation, thus, New York has fallen into line with Massachusetts.[240]

The Washington Supreme Court has added an interesting development to this body of law. In *Matter of Colyer*, the Court agreed that

---

237. *Id.*

238. *Id.*

239. *Matter of Storar*, 434 N.Y.S. (2d) 46, 47 (App. Div. 1980), affd. 438 N.Y.S. (2d) 266, 420 N.E. (2d) 64 (1981).

240. In Delaware, the question has not been put to the courts squarely. In *Severns* v. *Wilmington Medical Center*, 421 A. (2d) 1334, 1339 (Del. 1980), the question was whether the Court of Chancery "may ... grant the relief sought". The Court was not asked, nor did it answer, the question whether the petitioner *must* apply to court. Hence, the Court's ruling that an evidentiary hearing must be held prior to ruling on the issue whether life support could be withdrawn cannot be taken to establish any requirement to apply to court prior to termination of life support. However, if the surrogate chose to apply to a Delaware court, then an evidentiary hearing must be held to establish an appropriate factual record.

Interestingly, the Supreme Judicial Court of Massachusetts recently took a different approach in a case where the patient was not terminally ill. In *Rogers* v. *Comm'r of the Dep't of Mental Health*, 458 N.E. (2d) 308, 318 (1983), the Court ruled that "if a patient is declared incompetent, a court must make the original

a decision to terminate life sustaining treatment does not necessarily require judicial intervention.[240a]

In *Colyer*, the Court was critical of utilizing ethics committees because, as Mr. Justice Brachtenbach reasoned, these committees are "amorphous", "use ... non-medical personnel to reach a medical decision", and are characterized by "bureaucratic intermeddling".[240b] The Court proposed an alternative, a "prognosis board". This would be a committee of two doctors who have an understanding of the patient's condition, plus the attending physician. In the case of a comatose patient in a permanent vegetative state "these physicians should agree there is no reasonable medical probability that the patient will return to a sapient state". If there is disagreement, a court decision would be required utilizing a "clear and convincing evidence" standard.

Dicta in *Colyer* stated that a court ruling would be required to withhold treatment from a person who has always been incompetent, as his wishes are unknown. In *Re Hamlin*, that situation arose. Mr. Justice Brachtenbach narrowed the judiciary's role. Where the patient had no family, the Court must appoint a guardian to represent the patient. Reversing his *dicta* in *Colyer*, Justice Brachtenbach held that the court need not make or approve the guardian's decision.[240c]

The problem of appropriate procedures is by no means solved, but the courts are groping towards a coherent position. The results in *Saikewicz*, *Spring* and *Eichner* come to this: prior court approval is not necessary, but if the court is asked for its opinion on a proposed course of action, that opinion must be given. The court's opinion is

---

substituted judgment treatment decision and should approve a substituted judgment treatment plan." In *Rogers* the seven plaintiffs were all patients of a state psychiatric hospital, who had not been declared incompetent. The plaintiffs successfully challenged the hospital's practice of sedating patients without consent, using antipsychotic drugs. The hospital argued that the practice was necessary to prevent the patients from committing violence against themselves and others, and to preserve security and discipline within the institution. It was not argued that the antipsychotic drugs were administered as treatment to combat a life-threatening condition. The use of antipsychotic drugs is itself controversial because of negative side effects. All these factors appear to have been relevant in leading the Court to rule in favour of mandatory court intervention and supervision, a position apparently different from the one it expounded in *Saikewicz* and *Matter of Spring*.

240a. The Court reaffirmed that point in *In re Hamlin* 689 P. (2d) 1372, 1378 (Wash. 1984). See also: *John F. Kennedy Memorial Hospital Inc.* v. *Bludworth* 452 So. (2d) 921 (Fla. 1984).

240b. *Matter of Colyer*, 660 P. (2d) 738, 749 (Wash. 1983).

240c. It should be noted that *Hamlin* is a case of a patient in a persistent vegetative state, not a case of indeterminate prognosis, or poor quality prognosis.

conclusive as to any after-the-fact question of liability, unless the court order is executed without due care or good faith. If prior court approval is not sought, the opinion of an ethics or prognosis committee, while not required, may be helpful to establish due care and good faith, if subsequently called into question.

This is an eminently sensible course of decisions. It allows latitude to the surrogate and doctor to act speedily and alone, if the case so requires. If time allows, and if thought desirable, the doctors and parents may await the ruling of an ethics committee or court. They are not required to shoulder the terrible responsibility for life and death alone, unaided and ignorant of the legal consequences.

It is hard to see how *Dinnerstein* can be correct in restricting this procedural flexibility to comatose, vegetative patients, while requiring prior court approval for every other case. The reasoning of the *Dinnerstein* court is that the hopelessly comatose patient presents a question peculiarly within the competence of the medical profession - "what measures are appropriate to ease the imminent passing of an irreversibly, terminally ill patient in light of the patient's history and condition and the wishes of her family".[241] Why is that question for the medical profession while the appropriate treatment of a viable baby having no developmental prospects is for the courts? The only reason we can think of is that the court would never authorize withholding treatment in the latter case. If this be the true explanation of *Dinnerstein* it cannot be regarded as authoritative. Under disguise of creating procedures, the court attempted to answer an important substantive question: whether passive euthanasia on grounds of poor developmental potential is lawful. This question was not before the Court. Mrs. Dinnerstein was without developmental potential; she was irreversibly, terminally ill and in a vegetative state.

(e) Conclusions in an American Perspective

Can a surrogate refuse life saving medical treatment for a seriously deformed newborn? That question is too broad - obscuring in its embrasive sweep the fine details which legal wisdom requires to operate. It is not unlike asking "how big is a fish?".

The classes of cases need to be broken apart - distinguished into more discrete problems. The relevant questions follow, with tentative answers attempted where gleanings from the cases allow.

Can a surrogate refuse treatment for a deformed newborn in a comatose, chronically vegetative state? The answer is yes. Quality of

---

241. *Matter of Dinnerstein*, 380 N.E. (2d) 134, 139 (Mass. App. Ct. 1978).

life does not have to be adjudicated in such cases; state interests in the preservation of life shrink to insignificance where the surrogate asserts, on behalf of the comatose vegetative individual, a right to bodily integrity and self-determination.

Can a surrogate refuse treatment for a life of poor quality or poor developmental potential? The answer appears to be yes, but this conclusion stems from principle and extensive interpretation of the cases, rather than a hard ruling of a court asked to meet this issue head on. In deciding whether the life is of sufficiently poor quality or lacking in potential for development, the parents have a margin of appreciation. Unless their decision is unreasonable in the sense that no rational person could have come to that result, the courts will allow the parents' decision to stand.[241a] The courts test the question of rationality on four basic considerations: parental rights, state responsibility to protect life, bodily integrity and the child's welfare - and attempt to ascertain whether the proposed treatment is proportionate in terms of the benefits to be gained versus the burdens caused.

Indeterminate cases are opaque as to legal requirements. The issue has not come squarely before the courts. On principle, one would think that all indeterminate cases must be treated to remove the indeterminacy. If that is so, the prohibition on infanticide needs to be reconsidered. If the law constrains medicine to adopt protocols which insure that large number of comatose incompetents and cases without potential for development will survive, the infanticide prohibition comes into sharp focus. An unthinking acceptance of this rule is inconsistent with the law's treatment of similar cases when presented with the opportunity for passive euthanasia. Unless ethics can draw a clear distinction between active and passive euthanasia, the arguments in favour of relaxing the infanticide prohibition take on added importance.

Recourse to the courts is not required before the surrogate makes an authoritative decision. The surrogate has a margin of appreciation to decide; if the surrogate's decision is unreasonable, in the sense that no rational person could have so decided, the courts may interfere. The opinion of an ethics or prognosis committee is not required to validate the surrogate's decision, but it will be useful to determine rationality of the decision if subsequently called in to question. Prior court approval

---

241a. Cf. *John F. Kennedy Memorial Hospital* v. *Bludworth* 452 So. (2d) 921 (Fla. 1984) where the standard recognized was "good faith". It may be that this standard is slightly different from the reasonableness standard, in that one could act in subjective good faith, but be, by objective standards, unreasonable. Thus, there is some question as to the scope of the parent's primary decisional power before a challenge to their decision could be successfully brought in court.

is similarly not necessary. Nevertheless, if the court is asked for its opinion on a proposed course of action, that opinion must be given and it will be authoritative.

(f) Application to Canada

Many of the American cases gather strength from constitutional rights which find no equivalents in other common law jurisdictions. The *Quinlan*[242] case is based exclusively on a constitutionally protected right to privacy which entitles a person by himself, or through a surrogate, to refuse medical treatment. *Custody of a Minor*[243] recognizes as relevant to parental autonomy the existence of "a private realm of family life which the State cannot enter". Other courts have followed this lead in creating a constitutional axis around which surrogate refusal of treatment decisions revolve.[244]

Canadian Constitutional Law as yet knows no theory of the right of privacy as does its American counterpart. This is hardly surprising, since entrenchment of fundamental freedoms in Canada's Constitution is recent. Entrenchment of Charter-protected freedoms may be highly relevant to surrogate refusal of life saving treatment for defective newborns. Section 7 of the *Canadian Charter of Rights and Freedoms* enshrines "the right to life, liberty and security of the person and the right not to be deprived thereof except in accordance with the principles of fundamental justice". The cases so far are split as to whether s. 7 may be given a substantive as well as procedural interpretation.[245]

Section 7 certainly invites elaboration of the substantive rights to life and security of the person. The key point to notice is that the section is conjunctive: it embraces both "the right to life, liberty and security of the person" *and*, the right not to be deprived thereof except in accordance with procedural regularity. The first right stands by itself, without any procedural limitations. A court could well conclude that the right to "life" or the right to "security of the person" is relevant in the sense foreseen in the American cases.

Relevant as well is s. 12 of the *Charter*, which provides protections against "cruel and unusual punishment". One Canadian court has been

242. *Matter of Quinlan*, 355 A. (2d) 646 (N.J. 1976).

243. *Custody of a Minor*, 393 N.E. (2d) 836 (Mass. 1979).

244. *Superintendent of Belchertown State School* v. *Saikewicz*, 370 N.E. (2d) 417, 424 (Mass. 1977); *Matter of Spring*, 405 N.E. (2d) 115, 119 (Mass. 1980); *Severns* v. *Wilmington Medical Center*, 421 A. (2d) 1334, 1347 (Del. 1980).

245. The relevant cases are collected in J.E. Magnet, *Constitutional Law of Canada* (1985), Vol. II, Part V, 6(a).

persuaded that a proposed shunt revision, in the case of a severely brain damaged patient, without cognitive awareness, and in a persistent vegetative state would constitute cruel and unusual punishment.[245a] This ruling is interesting more for the impact the submission made on the court, than for a reasoned judgment expounding constitutional principles. The court merely states the constitutional result, without more.

The constitutional foundation is not the exclusive basis for American legal developments. They stand equally on the common law.[246] In some cases, the ruling of the court rests exclusively on the common law. In *Eichner* the court refused to consider the "disputed" constitutional question because "the relief granted ... is adequately supported by common law principles".[247] To date, the United States Supreme Court has consistently refused to review the constitutional foundation of these cases, although many certiorari petitions have been presented.

Insofar as the American cases proceed from a common law right to refuse treatment they are perfectly consistent with the law as expounded in other common law jurisdictions, particularly in Canada. It is very old Canadian law that a person has the right to refuse unwanted medical intervention.[248] It is equally settled law that this right may be exercised by a surrogate.[249] In truth, the entire theory of substituted consent elaborated in the American cases is based on old English common law precedents never disputed in a Canadian court.[250] That being so, Canadian courts presented with these questions will enjoy the rich common law fruit developed by the labours of their American brethren.

245a. *Re S.D.*, [1983] 3 W.W.R. 597, 613 (B.C. Prov. Ct.), revd. on other grounds, [1983] 3 W.W.R. 618 (B.C.S.C.).

246. *Superintendent of Belchertown State School* v. *Saikewicz*, 370 N.E. (2d) 417, 424 (Mass. 1977); *Matter of Spring*, 405 N.E. (2d) 115, 119 (Mass. 1980); *Severns* v. *Wilmingtom Medical Center*, 421 A. (2d) 1334, 1340 (Del. 1980).

247. *Matter of Storar*, 438 N.Y.S. (2d) 266, 273, 420 N.E. (2d) 64, 70 (1981).

248. *Supra*, note 136.

249. *Re Eve* (1980), 27 N. & P.E.I.R. 97 (P.E.I.C.A.); *Re D*, [1976] 1 All E.R. 326 (Fam. D.) (on appeal to S.C.C.).

250. In *Superintendent of Belchertown State School* v. *Saikewicz*, 370 N.E. (2d) 417 (Mass. 1977), the Court relied on *Ex. p. Whitbread* (1816), 35 E.R. 878 as authority for the substituted judgment doctrine. In *Ex. p. Whitbread* the Court held that in the case of a lunatic, "the court will not refuse to do for the benefit of the lunatic that which it is probable the lunatic himself would have done". The case was subsequently followed in *Re Evans* (1882), 21 Ch D. 299 and *In Re Darling* (1888), 39 Ch. D. 210.

In England, the courts are moving in similar directions.[251] In *In re B.*, a mongoloid child was suffering from a life-threatening intestinal blockage. Surgery could repair the intestines; failure to perform the surgery meant certain death by starvation. The parents refused consent to the intestinal operation on the basis that it was in the best interests of the child that she be allowed to die, rather than live a life of poor quality.

The doctors brought suit for permission to operate. In granting permission, the Court of Appeal recognized that there may be cases where "the future is so certain and where the life of the child is so bound to be full of pain and suffering" that withholding treatment would be approved.[252] The Court also recognized that the parents had a margin of appreciation to make the treatment decision by ruling that "great weight ought to be given to views of parents".[253]

In the Court's opinion, this was not a proper case to withhold treatment, primarily because no evidence has proved that the child's life would be intolerable.[254] In such a case, the Court held it was justified in overruling parental wishes and ordering treatment. The baby's rights took precedence; the Court's "first and paramount consideration [was] the welfare of this unhappy little baby".[255]

In Re B. makes clear in British law that the parents have a realm of autonomy to decide what is in the "best interests" of their child. Parental decisions are subject to reversal in the courts where it appears that their decision is without any reasonable foundation. To the extent, therefore, that the crucial questions relevant to passive euthanasia have arisen in English courts, the decisions are consistent with the American decisions.

This body of law has been considered by two British Columbia courts, with results that are reconcilable with British and American developments. The cases concern the same child, S.D. Although the second case is a petition for judicial review of the first, there was *de novo* finding of facts by the reviewing court. The findings of fact in

---

251. *In re B.*, [1981] 1 W.L.R. 1421 (C.A.).

252. *Id.*, p. 1424.

253. *Id.*, p. 1422.

254. *Id.*, p. 1424: "The evidence in this case only goes to show that if the operation takes place and is successful then the child may live the normal span of a mongoloid child, with the handicaps and defects and life of a mongol child, and it is not for this court to say that life of that description ought to be extinguished."

255. *Id.*

each court differ markedly - so markedly that the cases must be considered as two separate cases. Essentially, the factual differences mean that the two courts did not address the same problem.

In the Provincial Court, Judge Byrne described a severely damaged child who was "well-cared for and loved" by his parents.[255a] Judge Byrne found S. to be in a persistent vegetative state, with no reflex movement, without cognitive awareness, suffering from severe brain damage, and without the capacity to progress in the cognitive sense.[255b] A shunt revision was proposed to relieve accumulated hydrocephalus. Judge Byrne found that if the shunt revision were refused, "S will probably die in the near future" whereas "revisions of the shunt will greatly prolong his life".[255c]

Judge Byrne considered certain paramedical factors. Her Honour found that it was very difficult for the parents to care for S., partly because feeding and physiotherapy required eleven to twelve hours daily.[255d] Even visiting S. posed difficulties.[255e] Judge Byrne found that S. required 24-hour per day care, "and to have him return home would adversely affect the other members of [the] family.[255f]

On these facts, Judge Byrne distinguished *In Re B*. According to Judge Byrne, the operation requested for B "may" result in improvement. S., by contrast, had already had two operations. His parents adopted a "let's see" attitude 7 years ago. Now his diagnosis and prognosis are known and hopeless.[255g]

Judge Byrne adopted an ordinary/extraordinary conceptual framework. She found that the shunt was a life support system, and that the proposed shunt revision was extraordinary surgical intervention. She found "as a fact" that the proposed shunt revision would constitute cruel and unusual treatment of S. Therefore, S. was returned to his parents under the *Family and Child Service Act*, with the knowledge that they would refuse to consent to the shunt revision.

In the Supreme Court of British Columbia Mr. Justice McKenzie found the parents' decision unreasonable - "their minds are firmly made

---

255a. *Re S.D.*, [1983] 3 W.W.R. 597, 607, 618 (B.C. Prov. Ct.).

255b. *Id.*, p. 610-11.

255c. *Id.*, p. 610.

255d. *Id.*, p. 600.

255e. *Id.*, p. 602.

255f. *Id.*

255g. *Id.*, p. 613.

up and closed shut". On the evidence, Mr. Justice McKenzie found that "S. exhibits a degree of adaptive behaviour";[255h] "he will be a candidate for toilet training";[255i] if the operation is performed, there is no reason why S. would not have a normal life as a mentally retarded child";[255j] "a real possibility exists that [S. will not die, and] that his life will go indefinitely but in pain and progressive deterioration."[255k]

Mr. Justice McKenzie did not accept Judge Byrne's finding that this was a case of severe proved damage where the future is certain. Rather, he held, adopting the words of Templeton L.J. in *Re B.*, that " 'the life of this child is still so imponderable that it would be wrong for her to be condemned to die' ".[255l] In other words, Mr. Justice McKenzie held that S. was not a case of persistent vegetative existence; he was an indeterminate case.

We have noted above that the persistent vegetative case (Judge Byrne's finding) is dealt with by different rules of law and different ethical precepts from the indeterminate case (Judge McKenzie's finding). It is therefore not surprising that in the *S.D.* cases, the Courts came to different results: Judge Byrne approved withholding surgery, Justice McKenzie ordered the surgery. These different holdings can be rationalized on appreciation of the facts proved in evidence.

Mr. Justice McKenzie held that "this Court could not sanction the termination of a life except for the most coercive reason".[255m] As in *In Re B.*, the clear implication is that the court's *parens patriae* jurisdiction is sufficiently broad to approve a substituted judgment to withhold treatment in an appropriate case. It is tempting to conclude that had Mr. Justice McKenzie shared the findings of Judge Byrne below that S. was in a persistent vegetative state, he would have approved Judge Byrne's ruling allowing the parents to make a substituted refusal of life saving medical treatment. If the *S.D.* cases are appreciated in this light, their broad thrust channels Canadian law in the main current of its more fully elaborated American cousin.

255h. *Re S.D.*, [1983] 3 W.W.R. 618, 632 (B.C.S.C.).

255i. *Id.*, p. 624.

255j. *Id.*

255k. *Id.*, p. 632.

255l. *Id.*, p. 633.

255m. *Id.*, p. 629.

II. DECISION MAKING PROCEDURE

1. Medical Usurpation of Surrogate's Right to Withhold Treatment

Parents do not always have the choice to decline life saving treatment. Doctors sometimes make that decision for them. As Chapter One amply demonstrates, where doctors conclude treatment is improper, they retain decisional authority. Three mechanisms are employed: (1) doctors use their control over the flow of medical information to the parents to shape the parents' views; (2) coordinated interchanges between neonatal staff and parents influence the parents; (3) doctors refuse outright to treat and advise the parents to seek care elsewhere.

It is impossible to see that the law tolerates any of these practices. It is very old law that doctor-patient relationships are contractual.[256] The initial contact between doctor and patient satisfies all of the substantive requirements (parties capable, consent, an object, cause or consideration) for the validity of a contract required by both legal systems in Canada.[257] Failure to disclose to parents that available life saving treatment is being withheld from their baby is actionable as a breach of contract. The doctor undertakes to use due care and skill to serve his patient's interests.[258] If this does not include informing him about available life saving treatment, it is hard to see that any contractual obligation exists.

The doctor must also comply with legal duties of care imposed by the torts system. Take the very case cited in the research. The doctor says: "I'm sorry. Your child was just too small to make it...it just didn't have what it took to live", knowing full well that this is untrue. The baby is viable, but lacks developmental potential.[259] Is not this a deliberate misrepresentation calculated to deceive - in other words fraud? In *Derry* v. *Peek*,[260] the House of Lords made clear that an untrue statement made knowingly or recklessly, which is intended to be and in fact is relied upon, is actionable as deceit.

---

256. *Everard* v. *Hopkins* (1615), 2 Bulst. 332, 80 E.R. 1164; *Slater* v. *Baker* (1767), 2 Wils. 359, 95 E.R. 860.

257. *Civil Code of Lower Canada* (1866), art. 984, and see generally J.E. Magnet, *Liability of a Hospital for the Negligent Acts of Professionals* (1978), 3 C.C.L.T. 135, 138.

258. *Davy* v. *Morrison*, [1932] O.R. 1, 6 (C.A.).

259. *Supra*, ch. 1, p. 15.

260. *Derry* v. *Peek* (1889), 14 App. Cas. 337 (H.L.).

The informed consent doctrine is relevant to deliberate withholding of medical information. "Patients have a right to know what risks are involved in foregoing certain surgery or other treatment," said Chief Justice Laskin.[261] Doctors have a corresponding duty to disclose these risks to the patient or his surrogate. This means that doctors must disclose the "probable risks ... that ... would reasonably be expected to affect the patient's decision ... not to submit to a proposed operation or treatment."[262] The scope of the duty of disclosure is a matter that "must be decided in relation to the circumstances of each particular case".[263] It would be relevant if the parents waived "aside any question of risks"[264] indicating that they were quite prepared to defer to the doctor's judgment, whatever it might be. It would be equally relevant if the emotional condition of the parents suggested that they were unable to cope with germane facts. That would entitle the doctor to withhold or generalize "information as to which he would otherwise be required to be more specific".[265]

The crucial difficulty with controlling this kind of fraudulent medical conduct by recourse to civil actions relates to assessment of damages. Canadian law is clear that damages for fatal accidents resulting from negligence are limited to pecuniary losses. With respect to the loss of a child, all that courts can award is "the loss in dollars and cents, the pecuniary loss to the parents". The courts "must not allow the parents anything for solatium or loss due to their great affection for the child".[266] The pecuniary loss resulting from death of a newborn child is nil. As Mr. Justice Gillis says in *Alaffe* v. *Kennedy*: "in the case of a baby in arms it appears impossible to demonstrate reasonable expectation of pecuniary benefit".[267]

Canadian law allows exemplary damages where the defendant's conduct is fraudulent or malicious.[268] These often amount to cold comfort.

---

261. *Reibl* v. *Hughes* (1980), 14 C.C.L.T. 1, 17 (S.C.C.).

262. *Hopp* v. *Lepp* (1980), 13 C.C.L.T. 66, 85 (S.C.C.).

263. *Id.*, p. 87.

264. *Reibl* v. *Hughes* (1980), 14 C.C.L.T. 1, 17 (S.C.C.).

265. *Id.*

266. *Vale* v. *R.J. Yohn Construction Co. Ltd.* (1970), 12 D.L.R. (3d) 465; [1970] 3 O.R. 137 (C.A.). This action is statutory as are the limitations on its application: see, *e.g.*, *Fatal Injuries Act*, R.S.N.S. 1967, c. 100; *Family Law Reform Act*, R.S.O. 1980, c. 152, s. 60.

267. *Alaffe* v. *Kennedy* (1973), 40 D.L.R. (3d) 429, 437 (N.S.S.C.).

268. *McKenzie* v. *Bank of Montreal* (1975), 7 O.R. (2d) 521 (H.C.J.); *Unrau* v. *Barrowman* (1966), 59 D.L.R. (2d) 168 (Sask. Q.B.); *Gouzenko* v. *Lefolii*, [1967] 2 O.R. 262, 63 D.L.R. (2d) 217 (C.A.).

In a case where the defendant's conduct was characterized by the trial judge as "barbarous, cruel, heartless, verging on the criminal, pure maliciousness" and in which extensive damage was caused, only $300 was awarded as exemplary damages.[269] In any event, if the defendant is punished criminally for the same act, exemplary damages are unavailable, no matter how much the court may disapprove of defendant's conduct.[270]

The restriction of damages to pecuniary loss for the death of children has been sharply criticized by American courts. "Barbarous", said Mr. Justice Smith in describing the origins of the doctrine. "A reproach to justice". The doctrine proceeds from "one of the darkest chapters in the history of childhood".[271] Because of this criticism, American courts have boldly refashioned assessment of damages for fatal injuries to children to recognize "that a deceased child has a value to other members of the family as a part of the family unit and that a child's death represents substantial injury to the familial relationship".[272]

Certain jurisdictions, with Ontario in the lead, have extended the damages recoverable beyond pecuniary loss to include such matters as "loss of guidance, care and companionship that the complainant might reasonably have expected to receive from the injured person if the injury had not occurred".[272a] This section applies equally to fatal as to non-fatal injuries; each is to be assessed on the same basis. In *Mason v. Peters*, the Ontario Court of Appeal interpreted this statutory language as according "greater recognition to the interest in family relations and ... aimed at repairing certain losses which may not fall within the pecuniary loss category".[272b] However, the Court held that damages recoverable are limited to guidance, care and companionship; "grief, sorrow and mental anguish ... remain non-recoverable".[272c] This

---

269. *Unrau* v. *Barrowman* (1966), 59 D.L.R. (2d) 168 (Sask. Q.B.).

270. *Amos* v. *Vawter* (1969), 6 D.L.R. (3d) 234 (B.C.S.C.) (defendants stole and wrecked plaintiff's car; defendants convicted of theft; plaintiff not entitled to an award of exemplary damages); *Natonson* v. *Lexier*, [1939] 3 W.W.R. 289 (Sask. K.B.); *Loomis* v. *Rohan* (1974), 46 D.L.R. (3d) 423 (B.C.S.C.) (plaintiff shot four times by defendant and rendered paraplegic; no punitive damages allowed); *Radovskis* v. *Tomm* (1957), 9 D.L.R. (2d) 751 (Man. Q.B.) (defendant brutally raped a five-year old child; no punitive damages permitted because the defendant already jailed for the offence).

271. *Wycko* v. *Gnodtke*, 105 N.W. (2d) 118 (Mich. 1960).

272. *Bedgood* v. *Madalin*, 600 S.W. (2d) 773, 778 (Tex. 1980).

272a. *Family Law Reform Act*, R.S.O. 1980, c. 152, s. 60(2)(d), replacing *Fatal Accidents Act*, R.S.O. 1970, c. 164.

272b. *Mason* v. *Peters* (1983), 39 O.R. (2d) 27, 34, 36 (C.A.).

272c. *Id.*, p. 39.

restriction may limit severely the utility of the statutory reform for controlling medical conduct of the kind described. The parents' principal complaint centers in emotional distress. It is unlikely that the courts would approve large damage awards for the loss of companionship of a severely deformed newborn child with limited or no cognitive capacities.

The criminal law takes a dim view of doctors who refuse to treat. Section 199 of the *Criminal Code* creates a specific duty on persons undertaking acts to continue if failure to do the act may be dangerous to life. This is certainly relevant to doctors who undertake the treatment of a damaged child. Breach of this duty triggers the criminal negligence sections of the *Code*[273] and, if death results, constitutes unlawful homicide.[274] Section 200 penalizes every one who abandons a child under ten years such that its life or health is likely to be endangered.[275] Defences otherwise available to doctors in respect of crimes would not be available in a refusal to treat situation.[276] Section 45 offers no excuse because that section is relevant to the *performance* of "surgical operations" only; it is not relevant where any treatment - surgical or otherwise - is withheld. Nor does it seem likely that the doctor could plead that his actions were in accordance with good medical practice, and thus fell within the scope of the acts he undertook to do. The C.M.A. *Code of Ethics* requires a doctor who "has accepted professional responsibility for an acutely ill patient [to] continue to provide his services ... until he has arranged for the services of another suitable physician". The doctor is equally required to "ensure that his conduct in the practice of his profession is above reproach".[277] Failure to comply with these ethical standards gives rise to discipline by provincial Colleges of Physicians and Surgeons.[278] Certainly, lying to the patient is not

---

273. *Criminal Code*, R.S.C. 1970, c. C-34, s. 202(1)(b).

274. *Criminal Code*, R.S.C. 1970, c. C-34, s. 205(5)(b).

275. This can certainly be relevant to withholding treatment. In *R* v. *Hammond* (1913), 22 C.C.C. 120 (Sask. C.A.), a prematurely born child was left outside on a pile of straw. The resulting death sustained a charge of murder.

276. However, to prosecute the offences referred to in the text successfully, it is necessary to establish a causal connection between death and the refusal: see *R.* v. *St. Germain*, [1976] C.A. 185 (Que.).

277. C.M.A. *Code of Ethics* (September 1982), "Responsibilities to the Patient", arts. 15, 3.

278. As outlined *supra*, note 143, the College of Physicians and Surgeons of Ontario, pursuant to By-law 1, s. 25 (Dec. 1975), adopted by resolution of the Council the identical provisions contained in the C.M.A. *Code* of June, 1978. A member of the College may be disciplined under the *Health Disciplines Act*, R.S.O. 1980, c. 196, s. 60(3)(c) for professional misconduct as defined in the *Regulations*. R.R.O. 1980,

above reproach. Nor is any act which gives rise to actions for deceit and fraudulent misrepresentation. If the medical profession requires a doctor, under pain of discipline, to continue on the case, how can that doctor assert, for the purposes of the *Criminal Code*, s. 199, that he undertook to do something else? The result is that any refusal to treat causing death, to which parents have not consented, brings the full weight of the criminal law to bear upon the guilty doctor. Lying to the patient or withholding information about available treatment give rise to civil liability and professional discipline.

If a doctor is faced with an unreasonable request to treat a particular child, what is he to do? Take the very case cited in the research. A mother "begs" for treatment of her child. The doctor refuses because he perceives the baby's condition and the mother's social advantages to be poor.[279] How does the law react?

Withholding treatment over a parent's demand to treat lies beyond the lawful discretion of the medical profession. The parents are entitled to demand continuity in life sustaining treatment; it is not for the doctor to force the option of passive euthanasia upon them. This result is perfectly consistent with basic principles of medical law. A high regard for self determination requires that parents be permitted to save and raise their severely damaged baby, even if the medical profession is contrarily minded. Is not contravention of this principle the reason why we are revolted by the previously cited case of the doctor refusing to treat the child with the leaky meningocele, although his mother begged for treatment?

If, contrary to the parents, the doctor thinks that treatment cuts against the child's best interests, the law does not allow him to take matters into his own hands. Neither does it leave him without recourse. In the same way as the law allows invocation of judicial or administrative power to treat over a refusal, so too this option is available to authorize withholding of treatment over the parents' objections. The doctor may invoke administrative power under the Child Welfare statutes or the wardship jurisdiction of the court to vindicate his perception of the child's welfare.[280] These proceedings would be mandatory for

---

Reg. 448, s. 27 defines professional misconduct as "failure to maintain the standard of practice of the profession", which must be taken to incorporate a Code of Ethics adopted by resolution of the profession's governing body.

279. *Supra*, ch. 1, p. 28-29.

280. *Re D.*, [1976] 1 All E.R. 326 (Fam. D.) offers a precedent for this procedure. In that case the parent desired treatment (albeit of a non-therapeutic nature). The doctor was opposed to treatment. The doctor applied to court to compel compliance with his views. He succeeded. In *Re S.D.*, [1983] 3 W.W.R. 597 (revd. on other

doctors wanting to act against the parent's wishes because it is necessary to interfere with the parent's power, as legal guardian, to determine the extent of medical treatment for their child.[281]

A final possibility is that the parents are unavailable or incompetent to accept or reject the doctor's recommendation to withhold treatment. In such cases the doctor would be justified in withholding treatment in accordance with good medical practice and the best interests of the child. This follows from the implied scope of his undertaking. Although it would not be necessary to place the case before an ethics or prognosis committee, or the court for prior approval, the practice is desirable. If this procedure were followed it would add weight to the doctor's assertion of due care and good faith, if subsequently challenged.

2. Duty to Consult

A team approach to medicine is essential to neonatal intensive care. Serious pediatric cases once thought untreatable can be successfully treated by the inter-disciplinary approach practised in the units. Meningomylocele, for example, produces deficiencies in urological, neurological and orthopedic functioning. A urologist would not be competent to treat meningomylocele, but, as a member of the neonatal team, he could illuminate for other doctors whether the urological system was repairable, and describe the expected quality of the child's life from a urological point of view. Neurological and orthopedic data would be separately assessed by pediatric neurologists and orthopods. The neonatologist collates, assembles, and discusses all the data with participating members. Proper decision making thus follows a team approach.

Early negligence cases found it difficult to conceive that the doctor laboured under any duty to consult his colleagues. If a doctor uses "a reasonable degree of skill and care" in his treatment of the patient, said Mr. Justice Wright, "he has discharged his duty".[282] He is not obliged to refer the case to a specialist.

---

grounds, [1983] 3 W.W.R. 618 (B.C.S.C.)), the British Columbia Provincial Court found as a fact that some treatments may unconstitutionally constitute cruel and unusual treatment, and be controllable on that doctrine.

281. See *supra*, notes 74-79. Most child welfare statutes give administrative officials power to order treatment without court intervention. Wardship jurisdiction requires court intervention.

282. *Jarvis* v. *Internat'l Nickel Co.* (1929), 63 O.L.R. 564, 571 (H.C.J.).

Developments in modern medicine have required a change in that position. Medical practice has become increasingly specialized; the rule now, rather than the exception, is for doctors to concentrate their skills in one area of medicine only. Medicine is increasingly inhabited by practitioners whose knowledge is vast in depth, but confined within a narrow compass. As the C.M.A. *Code of Ethics* makes clear, a doctor must "recognize [his] limitations and the special skills of others in the ... treatment of disease".[283] An important result produced by this restructuring of the medical profession is that academic writers,[284] courts[285] and legislatures[286] have expounded a duty to consult in cases where specialist skills, lying outside the doctor's field of expertise, are required.

The common law duty to consult is flexible and variable. It rises and falls with the circumstances of the case, and has additional regard to the organization of the particular medical discipline. A duty to consult may arise out of inexperience, as if an intern does not take the caution of "seeking verification" of a difficult diagnosis.[287] It may equally arise when a general practitioner is "unable to diagnose the cause of a rapidly deteriorating condition".[288] A duty to consult, in fine, proceeds from the general obligation of physicians to use due care. A doctor must thus consult "when a prudent practitioner would deem it advisable".[289]

---

283. C.M.A. *Code of Ethics* (September 1982), art. III.

284. Linden, *The Negligent Doctor* (1973), 11 Osg. Hall L.J. 31, 37; Sherman, *The Standard of Care in Malpractice Cases* (1966), 4 Osg. Hall L.J. 222; E. Picard, *Legal Liability of Doctors and Hospitals in Canada* (1978). The duty to consult in the United States is roughly equivalent. See generally, Hirsh, "Duty to Consult and Refer", 1977, *Legal Medicine Annual* 249; Savage, *As a Family Practitioner Must You Consult With Other Specialists?* (1979), 7 Legal Aspects of Medical Practice 35. Also, in *King* v. *Flamm*, 442 S.W. (2d) 679 (Tex. Sup. Ct. 1969), Mr. Justice Walker said: "If there is expert testimony fairly supporting the conclusion that a reasonably careful and prudent general practitioner would have sought consultation under the same or similar circumstances, the trier of fact is entitled to find that the defendant was negligent in failing to do so".

285. *Vail* v. *MacDonald*, [1976] 2 S.C.R. 825, 832: "failure to consult a cardio-vascular specialist when he was unable to diagnose the cause of the rapidly deteriorating condition of the respondent's leg, constituted a breach of duty to the respondent ...".

286. *Public Hospitals Act*, R.S.O. 1980, c. 410, s. 31(3).

287. *Fraser* v. *Vancouver General Hospital*, [1952] 2 S.C.R. 36 (the Court held that the intern "failed, not it may conceded in reading the plate incorrectly but in not being more acutely sensitive to the grave symptoms that stood out before him and in not exercising caution against his inexperience, in not seeking verification").

288. *Vail* v. *MacDonald*, [1976] 2 S.C.R. 825, 832.

289. Linden, *The Negligent Doctor* (1973), 11 Osgoode Hall L.J. 31, 39.

The courts have been astute to recognize a duty to consult when the care required relates to a well defined medical specialty. The reason is that, in addition to the ready availability of specialist expertise, the specialities tend to be highly technical, well organized, and thus constitute separate disciplines in their own right. The specialist has skill which others do not. The obligation to use due care implies that this skill be made available. This is precisely why Mr. Justice Walsh found negligence where the diagnosis of a fracture by a general practitioner was delayed for a time through his misreading of the x-ray: "c'est parce qu'il n'avait pas assez l'expérience dans cette spécialité, et en ce cas il fut quelque peu imprudent en ne les montrant pas à un spécialiste en radiographie ou à un orthopédiste".[290]

The duty to consult emanates from the obligation to use due care. For this reason, evidence of accepted medical practice is highly persuasive to establish the duty, and equally relevant to questions whether it has been breached. This turns a spotlight on practices in neonatal units. The intensive care nursery is created to reap the benefits of interdisciplinary medicine. Consultation between different specialists is the inspiration behind the neonatal concept. Neonatologists have designed neonatal medicine on an interdisciplinary footing. Consultation has proven to be the central ingredient of the phenomenal medical success which neonatal units enjoy. All neonatologists are agreed that failure to consult in appropriate cases impairs the integrity of neonatal medicine. "It is a problem"[291] needing correction. Against this background, it is hard to conceive of any situation in the intensive care nursery involving multiple system anomalies where approved practice does not require consultation. Failure to consult in these cases would thus give rise to civil actions for all damage caused.

In Ontario, the duty to consult has been overlaid by statute in a limited range of cases. Where the chief of medical staff or department head becomes aware of serious problems relating to diagnosis, care or treatment of a patient "he shall ... discuss ... the patient ... with the attending physician".[292] If satisfactory changes in treatment are not made, the chief must remove the attending doctor from the case. Failure to comply with this obligation triggers the tortious liability of the responsible medical officer.[293]

---

290. *Daoust* v. *The Queen*, [1969] 2 Ex. R. 129, 146.

291. *Supra*, ch. 1, p. 20.

292. *Public Hospitals Act*, R.S.O. 1980, c. 410, s. 31(3).

293. See *supra*, note 143.

This statutory obligation underlines the responsibility of Ontario's six chief neonatologists to supervise their staff to insure that serious problems in diagnosis, care and treatment are avoided. Suppose the chief becomes aware that certain members of the neonatal team routinely fail to consult with their colleagues in cases of multiple system anomalies? Is not the chief then aware that serious problems in treatment exist? it is hard to see how the answer can be negative in a unit whose *raison d'être* is the creation of a collegial approach to pediatric medicine.

Various statutory instruments and internal by-laws of medical governing bodies impose a duty to consult in appropriate cases. As mentioned, the C.M.A. *Code of Ethics* requires the doctor to recognize his limitations and the special skills of others in provision of treatment.[294] The *Code* goes on to require the doctor to recommend additional opinions and services to the patient when indicated,[295] and "to request the opinion of an appropriate confrere acceptable to the patient when diagnosis or treatment is difficult or obscure".[296] If a doctor's opinion is requested, the *Code* requires him "to report in detail his finding and recommendations to the attending physician".[297]

The C.M.A. *Code* has been adopted by by-law of most provincial Colleges of Physicians and Surgeons.[298] Breach of the *Code's* prescriptions, thus, activates the discipline machinery of the Colleges. As explained earlier, in Ontario, s. 60(3)(c) of the *Health Disciplines Act*[299] allows a member of the College to be found guilty of professional misconduct as defined in the *Regulations*. By the Regulations, professional misconduct is defined as "21. failure to maintain the standard of practice of the profession" and "32. conduct ... that ... would reasonably be regarded by members as ... unprofessional". These sections must be taken to incorporate a Code of Ethics, such as the C.M.A. *Code*, which is adopted by resolution of the profession's governing body.

---

294. C.M.A. *Code of Ethics* (September 1982), art. III.

295. *Id.*, "Responsibilities to the Patient", art. 4.

296. *Id.*, "Responsibilities to the Profession", art. 15.

297. *Id.*

298. As outlined *supra*, note 143, the Ontario College had not adopted the 1982 *Code* at the time of writing, but rather continued with the 1978 *Code*. Similarly in Manitoba, the College adopted the C.M.A. *Code* (1978) by annexation as Sched. E. to By-law 1 (July 1981); the 1982 *Code* had not been adopted at time of writing. However, as stated in note 143, the two C.M.A. *Codes* are the same in respect to the provisions referred to in this chapter.

299. *Health Disciplines Act*, R.S.O. 1980, c. 196 as amended. See also *supra*, note 143 and accompanying text.

Contravention of the *Code* thus gives rise to discipline by the College. Discipline proceedings may be initiated by complaint of a member of the public or a member of the College.[300]

A final source of the duty to consult is the by-laws of many hospitals. In most provinces, hospital by-laws must be approved by the Minister of Health, and thus constitute statute law.[301] As such, breach of hospital by-law may add additional weight to an allegation of negligence in the tort system. In Ontario, the *Health Disciplines Act* specifically includes contravention of hospital by-laws within the definition of "professional misconduct".[302] Any breach of hospital by-law thus

---

300. *Health Disciplines Act*, R.S.O. 1980, c. 196, s. 58.

301. In Alberta, British Columbia, Nova Scotia, Prince Edward Island and Saskatchewan the hospital by-laws must be approved by the Minister of Health: *Hospitals Act*, R.S.A. 1980, c. H-11, s. 32(2); *Hospital Act*, R.S.B.C. 1979, c. 176, s. 28(1)(c); *Hospitals Act*, R.S.N.S. 1967, c. 249 as amended, s. 5(3); *Hospitals Act*, R.S.P.E.I. 1974, c. H-11, s. 7(3); *The Hospitals Standards Act*, R.S.S. 1978, c. H-10, s. 22(1). In New Brunswick and Ontario the hospital by-laws must be approved by the Lieutenant Governor in Council: *Public Hospitals Act*, R.S.N.B., c. P-23, s. 9(2); *Public Hospitals Act*, R.S.O. 1980, c. 410, as amended, s. 9(3). In Manitoba the hospital by-laws must be approved by the Manitoba Health Services Commission established under *The Health Services Insurance Act*, S.M. 1979, c. 81, C.C.S.M., c. H-35 (which in s. 5 provides that "[t]he Commission is an agent of Her Majesty in right of Manitoba"): *The Hospitals Act*, R.S.M. 1970, c. H-120, C.C.S.M., c. H-120, s. 5(4). In Quebec, by-laws come into force upon approval by the board of directors: *An Act Respecting Health Services and Social Services*, R.S.Q., c. S-5, s. 114. Section 76 of the same Act provides that the powers of the hospital are exercised by the board of directors provided that the hospital has received written authorization to that effect from the Minister. Newfoundland is the only province with no provision for approval of hospital by-laws.

302. R.R.O. 1980, Reg. 448, s. 27(10), under the *Health Disciplines Act*, R.S.O. 1980, c. 196. In the other provinces there is no specific provision which includes breach of hospital by-laws within a definition of professional misconduct. However, New Brunswick is the only province that does not have a statutory provision for the discipline of doctors displaying unprofessional conduct. The remaining provinces use general language which could readily include breach of hospital by-laws. See the *Medical Professions Act*, R.S.A. 1980, c. M-12, s. 34(1) ("... unbecoming conduct ... is a question of fact ...."); *Medical Practitioners Act*, R.S.B.C. 1979, c. 254, s. 51(3); *The Medical Act*, R.S.M. 1970, c. M-90, C.C.S.M., c. M-90, s. 36(1); *The Medical Act, 1974*, S.N. 1974, No. 119, s. 25; *The Medical Act*, S.N.S. 1969, c. 15, s. 1(i); *Medical Act*, R.S.P.E.I. 1974, c. M-8, s. 33; *The Medical Profession Act, 1981*, S.S. 1981, c. M-10.1, s. 46.

In Quebec the *Professional Code*, R.S.Q., c. C-26, s. 87 provides for the adoption of a code of ethics which must contain provisions determining which acts are derogating to the dignity of the profession.

raises the spectre of discipline by the College of Physicians and Surgeons.[303]

The by-laws of the Ottawa Civic Hospital[304] provide a good example of the way in which the duty to consult arises in this context. Under s. 10.2.4, each staff doctor must "request a consultation whenever the medical welfare of his patient requires it ...". The section goes on to require consultation "as may be demanded by departmental rules ...". By s. 15.5.1, "the chief of each department ... shall organize the work of his department and establish ... such procedures as are necessary". Would it not be desirable for the chief of neonatology at the Ottawa Civic Hospital to establish departmental rules requiring consultation in appropriate cases of multiple system anomalies? Is not this the whole point of the considerable investment made in the highly specialized neonatal units?

A member of the medical staff who contravenes provisions of the hospital by-law or a departmental rule thereunder is subject to immediate informal discipline by the departmental chief as provided under the *Public Hospitals Act*, R.S.O. 1980, c. 410.[305] Sanctions include temporary suspension of all staff privileges pending a hearing. The doctor has the right to a hearing before the Board of Trustees, and, if dissatisfied there, may appeal to the Hospital Appeal Board.[306]

It seems clear that the only effective way to control doctors who refuse to respect normal consultation procedure is through informal administrative discipline by the hospital's governing organs. The departmental chief and other hospital personnel are close to the scene; they are the people who know what and where the problems are. In

---

303. All provinces, with the exception of New Brunswick, have statutory provisions for the discipline of doctors displaying unprofessional conduct. In Alberta, British Columbia, Manitoba, Saskatchewan and Ontario the disciplinary body is the College of Physicians and Surgeons. See *Medical Professions Act*, R.S.A. 1980, c. M-12, s. 34(2); *Medical Practitioners Act*, R.S.B.C. 1979, c. 254, s. 51(3); *The Medical Act*, R.S.M. 1970, c. M-90, C.C.S.M., c. M-90, s. 36(1); *Health Disciplines Act*, R.S.O. 1980, c. 196, s. 60(2); *The Medical Profession Act, 1981*, S.S. 1980-81, c. M-10.1, s. 43. In Newfoundland, Nova Scotia and Prince Edward Island discipline is dealt with by Provincial Medical Boards or Councils. See *The Medical Act, 1974*, S.N. 1974, No. 119, s. 25; *The Medical Act*, S.N.S. 1969, c. 15, ss. 27(1), 30, 30A; *Medical Act*, R.S.P.E.I. 1974, c. M-8, s. 33(1), (2). In Quebec there is a Discipline Committee appointed by a professional and medical corporation under the *Professional Code*, R.S.Q., c. C-26, s. 116.

304. Ottawa Civic Hospital, By-Law (March 1982).

305. *Id.*, s. 23.2.

306. *Id.*, s. 23.2-23.3.

order for discipline machinery to improve the quality of neonatal care, it is crucial that hospital agencies take their responsibilities seriously. This implies detailed review and supervision of departmental procedures and personnel. It also implies continuing research to insure that departmental routines are functioning at optimal levels in light of medical knowledge. It would be helpful if operating procedures were articulated as standards in the departmental rules, and continuously revised in light of mandatory reseach. Ultimate curial control would enter only if the hospital were negligent in implementing an appropriate review and supervision mechanism, or failed in its research obligations.[307]

3. Duty to refer

The legal materials described above equally pertain to creation of a duty to refer. A duty to refer is particularly relevant to the situation where a severely damaged child is delivered in a hospital which has no neonatal unit. The baby needs treatment which the hospital is not competent to give; the treatment is readily available elsewhere and specialized transport is provided on request. Delivery facilities should take care to heed the warning of the Canadian Medical Protective Association: "Do only work for which you are trained; refer work you cannot or should not do to someone else".[308]

Non-specialized delivery facilities routinely refer serious pediatric cases to the intensive care nursery.[309] However, a problem has developed because the obstetrician and parents sometimes opt for passive euthanasia without resorting to assessment by a neonatal unit. If passive euthanasia becomes an option, is referral to neonatal intensive care required in every case?

To answer this question one must concentrate attention on the obligation of parents and doctors to provide the baby with appropriate medical treatment, having regard to the child's best interests. Certain clear cases of congenital anomalies would lie within the competence of delivering facilities to diagnose. Anencephaly is an example. Medical

---

307. In fact, the by-laws provide for review of standards and operations governing organs. Under s. 5.2.3 of the Ottawa Civil By-Law (March 1982) the Joint Conference Committee is required to "discuss the broad concepts and philosophies of the Hospital". Under s. 6.8, the Medical Advisory Committee must be "informed and consulted on matters affecting patient care". Should not these agencies discuss and plan for appropriate hospital policy with respect to passive euthanasia of defective newborns? Would it not make sense for the result of their discussions to be articulated in rules and procedures of the neonatal unit? See *infra* , ch. IV.

308. Canadian Medical Protective Association, *Annual Report* (1976), p. 13.

309. *Supra*, ch. 1, p. 10.

opinion is unanimous that the anencephalic child's condition is incompatible with life. Referral to neonatal care would be pointless, but would add to the burden placed on the parents. In such a case, the birth facility, in concert with the parents, would be competent to opt for passive euthanasia.

Where doubt or controversy exists about the appropriate course of medical action, legal institutions require referral to neonatal intensive care. The duty to refer stands out in bold relief. The birth facility lacks readily available diagnostic expertise; the medical profession has differentiated a specialist facility and distinctive transport for these purposes; the standard practice of the profession is to refer. It is difficult to appreciate how an unspecialized facility, which failed to refer an ambiguous case to a neonatal unit, could demonstrate that it took due care if challenged. Since the duty to refer is imposed by law, an omission to refer appropriate cases may attract criminal sanctions under the criminal negligence sections of the *Criminal Code*.[310]

---

310. *Criminal Code*, R.S.C. 1979, c. C-34, ss. 202-4.

III. USE OF PARAMEDICAL DATA

All legal institutions relevant to decisions for passive euthanasia concentrate attention on the need to protect the patient's best interests. The C.M.A. *Code of Ethics*, enforceable through the torts system,[311] and discipline machinery of the hospital[312] and College of Physicians and Surgeons[313] requires the physician to "[c]onsider first the well-being of the patient".[314] The parents jeopardize natural guardianship of their child if they do not have regard to his best interests.[315] The doctor has a civil duty to use due care for the baby's security.[316] The *Criminal Code* requires the parents to provide the baby with appropriate medical treatment.[317] Doctors performing surgical operations have a special s. 45 defense, only if the operation is for the "benefit" of the patient.[318]

The principle that the patient's best interests be supreme in all contexts saturates the infrastructure of medical law. This raises an important question with respect to neonatal decisional procedure. Paramedical factors routinely influence decisions about medical treatment in the intensive care nursery. Some of these factors go beyond the immediate concerns of the child and have regard to the interests of the parents; others are centered on the welfare of third parties and society at large. Can the consideration of paramedical data be squared with the requirement that decisions about the child's medical care promote the *child's* best interests?

1. Doctor's Use of Paramedical Data

Neonatologists routinely use paramedical data in medical decision making, and for a very good reason. Paramedical facts are often critical to assessment of the child's potential for improvement. If a particular condition is repairable, but needs constant attention which is unavail-

---

311. *Supra*, note 143. See also Linden, *The Negligent Doctor* (1973), 11 Osg. Hall L.J. 31.

312. For example Ottawa Civil Hospital By-Law (March 1982) s. 9.3.24 requires the physician to give an undertaking that he shall "maintain acceptable ethical standards".

313. See *supra*, text at notes 298-99.

314. C.M.A. *Code of Ethics* (September 1982), art. I.

315. *Supra*, note 85.

316. *Supra*, text pp. 30-31.

317. *Criminal Code*, R.S.C. 1970, c. C-34, s. 197(1)(a). See also *supra*, notes 71-73.

318. *Criminal Code*, R.S.C. 1970, c. C-34, s. 45.

able, this must necessarily influence the overall prognosis, just as would the unavailability of life saving medicines.

It is also true that doctors who limit their practice to specialized branches of pediatrics learn to distinguish situations which are conducive to development from those which are not. This is why a consensus has developed that unwed parents, mentally retarded parents, poor economic means, and so forth are factors weighing against treatment.

Data of this type presents two difficulties. First, any data used must be justifiable in terms of relevance and reliability. Lack of systematic research into paramedical data impairs justification of its relevance. It remains to be demonstrated as a scientific proposition, as opposed to gossip, that a single mother desperately wanting her damaged child weighs on the debit side of the child's assessment. Secondly, most paramedical data amassed by neonatal units tends to be of poor quality. There is no systematic method of data collection or quality control. Lack of research into gathering methods and quality control weakens any assertion that paramedical facts are reliable. It is not farfetched to suppose that the doctor's civil obligation to use due care requires more sophisticated methods of data gathering and quality control. This might well imply a research obligation on those units routinely including paramedical criteria in their assessments.

In any event, it is not for the doctor to decide that treatment should be withheld. The ultimate decision lies with the parents subject to administrative and court intervention. Paramedical data, if relevant and reliable, may be used by the doctor to assist in making his assessment, but the doctor's assessment, and any controversial grounds on which it is based, must be disclosed to the parents.[319] The doctor's duty of disclosure certainly requires that the parents are entitled to know that facts about them or their environment have weighed heavily in the doctor's evaluation. Poor environmental criteria bearing on the child's potential for development must be considered to be a specific risk of submitting to or foregoing treatment which the informed consent doctrine requires to be disclosed.

2. Parent's Use of Paramedical Data

Parents have wide latitude to make determinations concerning their child's welfare. It is only when their decision is patently unreasonable that courts interfere. Courts "treat the exercise of parental prerogative with great deference".[320] The parents are allowed a degree

---

319. See *supra*, text at notes 6-11.

320. *Custody of a Minor*, 393 N.E. (2d) 836 (Mass. 1979).

of autonomy; courts "act cautiously" in deciding to suspend or supersede parental rights.[321]

Prima facie, it is difficult to see how the parents can consider their own situation as a factor suggesting passive euthanasia is in their child's best interests. However, closer analysis is required. Someone must determine what medical treatment is indicated to promote the child's best interests. Our law leaves this decision to the parents, unless good faith or reasonableness is challenged. Even so, judicial investigation of the parent's good faith and reasonableness is limited. As Mr. Justice Jasen said, the court investigates only whether the parents have adopted a course of treatment "recommended by their physician and which has not been totally rejected by all responsible medical authority".[322]

Doctors consistently find relevant to the child's prognosis for development paramedical criteria relating to the parent's age, marital status, intelligence, psychological adaptation, economic resources and number of other children. Assume for the moment that no problems exist with the relevance and reliability of these factors in assessing developmental potential. The paramedical criteria have passed scientific scrutiny as to relevance properly assisting neonatal assessment. If, as assumed, the factors bear significantly on the specific risks of submitting to or foregoing treatment, they must be disclosed to the parents and taken into account in their decision.

This analysis is predicated on the assumption that potential for development is a relevant criterion in determining whether active intervention is medically indicated. Suppose that the assumption proves false and the courts require life saving intervention for all viable children, even if potential for development is absent. Would this eventuality suggest that paramedical factors are inappropriate to consider or that they have less legal validity than do medical factors in the eyes of the law?

If courts prohibit withholding treatment on grounds of poor developmental potential, then medical viability becomes the *only* relevant criteria. Paramedical factors could not lawfully be considered in assessing the child's suitability for treatment. However, neither could medical factors, other than viability, such as existence in a vegetative state. This indicates a further equivalence between medical and paramedical criteria for purposes of determining "best interests": no discernible legal principle or set of facts appears to distinguish them.

---

321. *DeLaurier* v. *Jackson*, [1934] S.C.R. 149, 157.

322. *Matter of Hofbauer*, 47 N.Y. (2d) 648, 393 N.E. (2d) 1009 (1979).

There are many different kinds of paramedical data. The different types cannot be reduced to a common denominator. Facts such as parental intelligence and psychological adaptation are considered relevant because they bear on the child's potential for development. Other criteria may not relate to developmental assessments. The ability of the parents to have additional children or the effect which the addition of a deformed child would have on the family stands on a different footing. These facts are not centered on the child's interests but on the interests or convenience of others. Can paramedical data of this kind lawfully be considered in the decision whether treatment is warranted?

3. Curial or Administrative Use of Paramedical Data

Courts and Child Welfare Officials have no authority to interfere unless the parent's guardianship is challenged. Once curial or administrative authority is invoked, their power is circumscribed by statute. Parental decisions about the child's medical care can be varied only if they are shown to cut against the child's "best interests" as statutorily defined.

Three provinces provide statutory definitions of "best interests of the child". All include paramedical criteria. Ontario, New Brunswick and Newfoundland instruct statutory appointees to consider, in addition to the child's "physical" needs, the child's "mental" and "emotional" needs and "the appropriate care or treatment, or both, to meet such needs".[323] The decision maker is also to consider "the child's opportunity to have a parent-child relationship and to be a wanted and needed member within a family structure".[324] Finally, the authority must weigh the "merits of any plan" proposed by the child welfare agency against the merits of leaving the child in the care of his parents.[325] New Bruns-

---

323. *Child Welfare Act*, R.S.O. 1980, c. 66, s. 1(b)(i) [Bill 77, *supra*, note 51, s. 38(3)(1)]; *Child and Family Services and Family Relations Act*, S.N.B. 1980, c. C-2.1, s. 1; *The Child Welfare Act, 1972*, S.N. 1972, No. 37, s. 2 as amended by S.N. 1981, c. 54, s. 2.

324. *Child Welfare Act*, R.S.O. 1980, c. 66, s. 1(b)(ii) [Bill 77 *supra*, note 51, s. 38(3)(6)]. New Brunswick differs slightly, requiring the courts to consider "the love, affection and ties that exist between the child and each person to whom the child's custody is granted ...". This is distinct from the child's opportunity for such a relationship. The New Brunswick statute concentrates on existing relationships: *Child and Family Services and Family Relations Act*, S.N.B. 1980, c. C-2.1, s. 1. See also Alberta Bill 35, *supra*, note 71, s. 2(e).

325. *Child Welfare Act*, R.S.O. 1980, c. 66, s. 1(b)(v) [Bill 77 *supra*, note 51, s. 38(3), nos. (9), (12)], *Child and Family Services and Family Relations Act*, S.N.B. 1980, c. C-2.1, s. 1. See also Alberta Bill 35, *supra*, note 71, s. 2(f)(ii), (iii).

wick superadds a further criterion: "the need to provide a secure environment that would permit the child to become a useful and productive member of society".[326] In provinces that do not legislate detailed definitions of "best interests" it is probable that the above criteria are incorporated by implication.[327]

These statutory criteria make clear that courts and administrative officials must include paramedical criteria relating to the child's emotional security in the family and potential for social integration in any decision whether to interfere with the parents' chosen course of medical action. They equally add weight to the entitlement of parents to consider para-medical factors, since any review of parental decisions will take these criteria into account. This in turn impacts favourably on the use of para-medical factors by doctors in making their initial assessment of the child.

It is important to underline that statutorily approved paramedical factors are circumscribed within a narrow compass. They are centered on the child's emotional development, family security and potential for social integration. The statutes do not provide for consideration of interests or convenience of third parties, such as effects on siblings or parental ability to have additional children, although at least one American decision suggests such factors are appropriately factored into the decisional formula. In *Rogers* v. *Commissioner of Mental Health*, Mr. Justice Abrams included "the impact of the decision on the Ward's family" as one of six factors which had to be considered in arriving at a substituted judgment decision.[328] It is doubtful if this criterion could ever achieve paramount importance, given the sharp tilt of medical law towards the best interests of the patient. In jurisdictions with statutory definitions of "best interests" the statutory list may be viewed as a complete code, thus chilling further the possibility to amend judicially the list by addition of factors related to others.

In cases where common law *parens patriae* jurisdiction has been invoked, the courts resort to a broader spectrum of interests to weigh in the decisional balance. Most of these include paramedical data about

---

326. *Child and Family Services and Family Relations Act*, S.N.B. 1980, c. C-2.1, s. 1.

327. E. Driedger, *The Construction of Statutes* (2d ed. 1983) p. 158: "Law outside the statute under consideration may not be relevant; but it may always be looked at and if it is relevant it may have a bearing on the construction of the statute." Thus, it would be relevant in interpreting the undefined general phrase, "best interests", to look to Child Welfare statutes in other jurisdictions *in pari materia*, where specific definitions are provided.

328. *Rogers* v. *Commissioner of Mental Health*, 458 N.E. (2d) 308, 319 (Mass. 1983).

the child. The Courts are "required to do a difficult balancing act". While child centered concerns stand out in bold relief, it is "obvious that far reaching limitations ... on the exercise of [wardship] jurisdiction exist".[328a] In some cases child centered concerns conflict with state or third party interests. In others, the courts take "a more flexible view of the best interests of the ward".[329]

Paramedical facts of various kinds may thus be relevant to cases adjudicated under the *parens patriae* power. This does not mean that such facts are or tend to be important. Relevance must be distinguished from weight. While considerable lip service is paid to recitation of paramedical data proved in evidence, it is the rare case where such facts tilt the balance.

Family centered concerns are factors with which many courts have had to wrestle. Family interests are considered in a variety of contexts. There is the class of cases where family anguish is pleaded.[330] Another class of cases takes into account deeply held personal or religious views of the parents.[331] A surprising class of cases has regard to family convenience.[332] Finally, a distinct class of cases holds that parental wishes are significant.[333] Courts consider expressed wishes of the parents without looking beyond the expression to the foundation upon which the wishes are formed. In *Custody of a Minor*, Chief Justice Hennessey said that the parents' rights are not "chiefly to be consid-

---

328a. *Re X*, [1975] 1 All E.R. 697, 706 (Fam. D.).

329. *Superintendent of Belchertown State School* v. *Saikewicz*, 370 N.E. (2d) 417, 428 (Mass. 1977).

330. *Eichner* v. *Dillon*, 426 N.Y.S. (2d) 517, 534 (App. Div. 1980), affd. (*sub nom. Matter of Storar*, 438 N.Y.S. (2d) 266, 420 N.E. (2d) 64 (1981): "in circumstances such as those at bar ... the anguished family ... demand a solution having the sanction of law".

331. *Matter of Storar*, 438 N.Y.S. (2d) 266, 275, 420 N.E. (2d) 64, 73 (1981).

332. *Re D*, [1976] 1 All E.R. 326, 331 (Fam. D.) (possibility the family may have to raise the ward's child); *Re L*, [1968] 1 All E.R. 20, 27 (C.A.) (parent's desire to have paternity established); *Re S.*, [1967] 1 All E.R. 202, 208 (Ch.) (whether psychological assessment should be ordered; parental convenience weighed in the balance).

333. *Re S.D.*, [1983] 3 W.W.R. 613, 632 (B.C.): "I respect and have given anxious consideration to the views of the parents"; *Matter of Spring*, 399 N.E. (2d) 493, 503 (Mass. App. Ct. 1979): "The [trial] judge did not err in giving deference to the decision of the family", and at p. 499: "It is evident that we are dealing with a close-knit family unit ... . In such circumstances the decision of the family ... is of particular importance ... as a factor lending added weight to the patient's interest in privacy and personal dignity". See also *Re Eve* (1980), 27 N. & P.E.I.R. 97, 128 (P.E.I.C.A.) (on appeal to S.C.C.).

ered" because "the paramount duty is to the welfare of the child".[334] This indicates that parental interests are relevant, but are to be accorded less weight.

The interests of third parties and the community at large can be a source of paramedical facts, although one would have thought that these operate in a narrow range. The *Spring* judgment was clear that "the interests of third persons"[335] are relevant to decisions to refuse treatment; other courts have particularized further situations in which these take on weight. The paradigm situation where third party interests become relevant is where a refusal of life saving treatment impacts adversely on the support of third party dependants.[336] Courts have recognized that such interests can dampen the force of the right to bodily integrity, whether asserted directly or by a surrogate.

Finally, no act can shock the public conscience without producing reactions from the legal system. All legal rules are ultimately intertwined with the collective assessment of societal morality and interests. The *Quinlan* court explicitly recognized curial responsibility to examine "underlying human values" so that the fearful decision for life or death will be responsive "to the common moral judgment of the community at large".[337] The cases have recognized that community interests may rise above child welfare.[338] Whether this be viewed as including social factors in assessing best interests[339] or a necessity to test the child's welfare against societal interests[340] is immaterial. Community interests which have weighed in the decisional balance where treatment is at issue include whether the ward "would be

---

334. *Custody of a Minor*, 379 N.E. (2d) 1053, 1063 (Mass. App. Ct. 1979).

335. *Matter of Spring*, 405 N.E. (2d) 115 (Mass. 1980).

336. *Eichner* v. *Dillon*, 426 N.Y.S. (2d) 517, 537 (App. Div. 1980), affd. (*sub nom. Matter of Storar*) 438 N.Y.S. (2d) 266, 420 N.E. (2d) 64 (1981): "The interests of the State are also strongly indicated where the patient is responsible for support of minor children and where refusal to accept treatment threatens to bring about their 'abandonment' "; *In re Osborne*, 294 A. (2d) 372 (D.C. 1972) (refusal of life saving treatment by competent adult upheld where provisions were made for children).

337. *Matter of Quinlan*, 355 A. (2d) 647, 665, 70 N.J. 10 (1976).

338. *Re X*, [1975] 1 All E.R. 697, 704 (Fam. D.) (publication of book causing "grave" injury to child's psychological health allowed in interests of free press).

339. The Courts have done this: see *e.g.*, *Re Eve* (1981), 27 N. & P.E.I.R. 97, 128 (P.E.I.C.A.) (on appeal to S.C.C.): " 'injury' must be taken in its social ... or economic interests". So has one legislature: see *Child and Family Services and Family Relations Act*, S.N.B. 1980, c. C02.1, s. 1.

340. *Re X*, [1975] 1 All E.R. 697, 704 (Fam. D.).

unable...to maintain herself", would "have to enter an institution",[341] or would have social options and "social interests" severely diminished.[342]

In sum, paramedical data lawfully can be included in neonatal assessments and neonatal decision making. There are limits to this broad proposition. Methods of fact gathering and quality control will have to withstand curial scrutiny in light of the obligation to take due care. Relevance and reliability must be justified affirmatively, if challenged. Not all categories of paramedical facts can withstand this test. In any event, it would be the rare case where significant weight lawfully would be attributed to paramedical criteria in neonatal decision making.

---

341. *Re D.*, [1976] 1 All E.R. 326, 331 (Fam. D.).

342. *Re Eve* (1981), 27 N. & P.E.I.R. 97, 142 (P.E.I.C.A.) (on appeal to S.C.C.).

IV. INTERIM CARE

1. Lethal Drugs

Active euthanasia is unlawful. There is no excuse in law to kill by administration of a deadly drug, no matter how kindly the motive. Administration of a lethal dosage of morphine by a person who means to cause death is murder.[343]

It is equally murder if lethal dosages are administered drop by drop or dose by dose. If the cumulative effect is deadly, superaddition of intent attracts criminal sanction. This brings certain conduct cited in the research very much into prominence. A nurse says: "we kept increasing the medication ... essentially we knew we were poisoning the child".[344] This is a common phenomenon in pediatrics. Can the practice be justified in law?

The answer is no, the practice can never be justified in such a clear case. But such clear cases are rare. The drug is administered on doctor's orders. Those orders are issued *at least* in part to relieve pain. So there is a more ambiguous intention - an intent to relieve pain, with the understood effect of hastening death. Does the complexity of the mental element change the legal result?

Glanville Williams has taken the view that there is a difference. "The excuse" for administration of the drug, he argues, "rests upon the doctrine of necessity". Necessitous circumstances exist because there is at this junction no way of relieving pain without ending life.[345]

The point is debatable because the *mens rea* necessary to support a charge of murder is knowledge or recklessness that the act will cause death.[346] The intent to ameliorate pain certainly complicates the mental picture of the doctor or nurse, but the requisite knowledge is present. Test the proposition in this way. A fireman is piteously, mortally burned at a fire. His suffering is dreadful. Death must come soon, certainly

---

343. *Criminal Code*, R.S.C. 1970, c. C-34, s. 212; see also *supra*, text at notes 208-216.

344. *Supra*, ch. 1, p. 35.

345. G. Williams, *The Sanctity of Life and the Criminal Law* (1970), p. 324.

346. *Leary* v. *The Queen* (1977), 74 D.L.R. (3d) 103, 116 (S.C.C.) *per* Dickson J. dissenting on other grounds: "mental state basic to criminal liability consists in ... either (a) an intention ... or (b) foresight or realization on the part of the person that his conduct will probably cause or may cause the *actus reus* together with assumption of or indifference to a risk, which in all of the circumstances is substantial or unjustifiable"; *R.* v. *City of Sault Ste-Marie* (1978), 85 D.L.R. (3d) 161, 181 (S.C.C.) *per* Dickson J.: "*mens rea* [consists] of some positive state of mind such as intent, knowledge or recklessness".

before transport to hospital. A faithful friend, to end the suffering, and at the fireman's request, bludgeons him. Is not this murder? Why should it make a difference if, instead of a confrere, a doctor knowingly administers a lethal dose of morphine to relieve pain? What difference is there if the fireman is transported to hospital where, again to the relieve pain, increasing dosages of morphine are administered, in the knowledge that death will be caused or accelerated? Is it not true that all of these examples exhibit "foresight or realization ... that [the] conduct will probably cause [death]"?[347]

Professor Williams' argument is elegant. He justifies the administration of increasing doses of pain killers by an analogy to surgical operations. His point is that "every surgical operation involves some risk that the patient may die under the anaesthetic", but the operation remains lawful nevertheless. A great benefit to health may justify a slight risk of harm. An immense benefit can justify a great risk. As the doses increase, so does the risk, but so also does the benefit. It is artificial to stigmatize the final dose as murder, when all others are lawful.[348]

The argument has force, but rests on erroneous assumptions. Professor Williams assumes that the doctor is dealing in risks. He is not. The doctor knows that his treatment will cause death: "essentially we knew we were poisoning the child". So there is a difference. On Professor Williams' hypothesis the *mens rea* is absent; in reality it is present. This distinction in fact makes all the difference to the legal result, because a risk/benefit calculus is legally insufficient to constitute *mens rea*, whereas knowledge and foresight coincide precisely with the requisite intent.[349]

---

347. *Leary* v. *The Queen, supra* note 346.

348. G. Williams, *The Sanctity of Life and the Criminal Law* (1970), p. 323.

349. Apparently Mr. Justice Devlin in the Dr. Adams murder trial would have shifted the debate onto the axis of causation: "no act is murder which does not cause death ... 'Cause' means nothing philosophical or technical or scientific. It means what you ... as a jury ... would regard in a common sense way as the cause ... [T]he proper medical treatment that is administered and that has an incidental effect of determining the exact moment of death is not the cause of death in any sensible use of the term". See G. Williams, *The Sanctity of Life and the Criminal Law* (1958), p. 289. It would appear that the threads of several legal ideas are interwoven in Mr. Justice Devlin's remarks. It is not clear what the final fabric portends. This is not suprising as the remarks were an oral address to a jury. If, however, Mr. Justice Devlin meant to articulate the proposition that the acceleration of death by medical treatment is not a cause of death such as to incur criminal liability, he is clearly wrong. See *Criminal Code*, R.S.C. 1970, c. C-34, s. 209, which provides: "Where a person causes bodily injury ... that results in death, he causes the death ...

2. Lethal Omissions

A second important issue relates to the level of care that may be withheld, once a decision for passive euthanasia has been made. Canadian units generally withhold all care except food, warmth and fluid management. In America, cases have been reported of withholding all food and water in order to starve the child.[350]

The criminal law is wary about penalizing omissions. An omission to act will not attract the criminal sanction unless there is a duty to do the act omitted.[351] The duty can arise by law, but it may equally have a source in contract or proximity of relationship. Thus, if a person has a duty to feed, care for, or treat a defective newborn, any omission to discharge those duties, with fatal results, constitutes the *actus reus* of various homicides. If there is legally relevant knowledge or foresight that death would be the probable consequence of the omission, the person responsible may be convicted of murder or manslaughter.

Various statutory duties, previously discussed, require the parents to obtain necessary medical treatment for minor children.[352] Doctors are required to provide necessary treatment to patients "under their charge", and to continue to treat patients whose care they have undertaken.[353] The broad outlines of a duty to support criminal liability for omissions are thus present; it remains to be seen how the finer detail is relevant to interim care in the intensive care nursery.

It has been previously demonstrated that the duty to provide medical treatment is not a duty *per se*. Rather, it is a duty to provide the appropriate treatment.[354] To some extent, this makes medical practice in neonatal units self-justifying in the eye of the law, as it is difficult to stigmatize as inappropriate the actions of a doctor who follows the accepted routines of his profession. Nevertheless, there are limits. Medical conduct which shocks the community's conscience cannot escape legal scrutiny, no matter how widely practised.

---

notwithstanding that the effect of the bodily injury is only to accelerate his death from a disease or disorder arising from some other cause".

350. See "Allegedly left to die, Siamese twins saved," *Globe and Mail* (Toronto), May 18, 1981, p. 12.

351. *Kenny's Outlines of Criminal Law* (J.W. Cecil Turner ed., 19th ed. 1966), pp. 19-20; Cross and Jones, *Introduction to Criminal Law* (R. Card ed., 9th ed. 1980), pp. 26-7; see generally Skegg, *The Termination of Life Support Measures and the Law of Murder* (1978), 41 Mod. L. Rev. 423.

352. See text at notes 144, 146, 149, 153.

353. See text at notes 145, 146.

354. See text at notes 100-104 b, 154 ff., and note 159 ff.

Withholding minor surgery in appropriate cases, thus, is almost certainly justifiable. So is the entry of a "no resuscitation" order on the patient's medical chart.[355] More difficult is the withholding of antibiotic drugs to combat infection. The problem arises because antibiotics, by combatting a fever, would tend to make the patient more comfortable. The common morality of the community[356] would find it hard to accept that the decision for passive euthanasia should increase suffering, even temporarily. This raises doubts about whether withholding antibiotic drugs is "appropriate", even though administration of the drug is inconsistent with the decision for passive euthanasia.

Withholding food is very difficult to justify, even if passive euthanasia otherwise is lawful. It is apparently painful for the baby; gruesome and degrading for the attending nurses and shocking to public morality. The duty to provide food to children, in any event, is legally distinguishable from the duty to provide medical treatment. While the cases view withholding "inappropriate medical treatment" understandingly, we know of no case that tolerates starving children in any circumstance.

The issue of withholding food arises in various situations. A common occurrence in pediatric practice is duodenal atresia - a blockage in the intestinal tract which prevents digestion of food.[357] Relatively minor surgery can correct the feeding difficulty, and the question is thus presented whether the surgery should be performed on a child having other severe anomalies. In 1974 a mongoloid child born at the John Hopkins Hospital with intestinal obstruction starved to death eleven days after the decision was made to withhold corrective surgery. The case became a cause célèbre and produced profound negative comment.[358] In important ways the commentary is misdirected at the practice of withholding surgery. The real point of criticism is that the case was inappropriate for passive euthanasia. The child's potential for development, with surgery, was good. Mongolism, by itself, cannot justify a conclusion that developmental potential, such as would justify passive euthanasia, is absent. However, if in addition to duodenal atre-

---

355. *Severns* v. *Wilmington Medical Center*, 425 A. (2d) 156 (Del. Ch. 1980).

356. This is reflected in the legal doctrine of public policy. The doctrine is relevant to the scope of the duty at common law and under various statutes.

357. See generally Girvan and Stephens, *Congenital Intrinsic Duodenal Obstruction* (1974), 9 J. Pediatric Surgery 883.

358. See *e.g.*, McCormick, *To Save or Let Die* (1974), 299 Journal of the American Medical Association 172; Gustafson, *Mongolism, Parental Desires and the Right to Life* (1973), 16 Perspectives in Biology and Medicine 529.

sia the child has no developmental potential, it is hard to see how corrective intestinal surgery is "appropriate", assuming other forms of aggressive treatment are not.

Withholding tube feeding is a common practice in the "hopes that those who are not treated should not live long".[359] Tube feeding is a means of introducing high caloric value into the stomach by means of a conduit inserted through the nasal passages into the esophagus. It is appropriate for cases where normal feeding through the mouth and intravenous feeding are unavailable for reasons of vascular deficiency, unconsciousness or otherwise. Finally, there are cases where normal ingestion of food and water through the mouth is denied for no reason other than acceleration of death.[360]

It is difficult in these cases to extend legal precision further than the juridical concept of appropriate care. Appropriate care is a concept that oscillates between accepted medical practice and aroused public conscience. Where doubt exists, one must remember that parents are allowed a degree of autonomy in deciding about their child's welfare; courts are slow to upset the awesome decision parents are called upon to make. With the legal definition of "appropriate care" in mind, it is difficult to see how the legal system could tolerate withholding normal ingestion of food and water in order to hasten death by starvation. The prospect is too macabre. By contrast, if the law requires correction of duodenal atresia in the case that has no developmental potential, juridical form is carried to a fare-thee-well. The common law system cannot be more precise than that. Further distinction must come from ethics. We turn to this in the next chapter.

---

359. See Lorber, "The Doctors Duty to Patients and Parents in Profoundly Handicapping Conditions" in *Medical Wisdom and Ethics in the Treatment of Severely Defective Newborn and Young Children* (D. Roy ed. 1978), p. 21.

360. See "Allegedly left to die; Siamese twins saved", *The Globe and Mail* (Toronto), May 18, 1981, p. 12: "a hospital worker defied an alleged request from their father, a doctor, that they be denied food and water".

CHAPTER THREE

DELIBERATE DEATH IN THE INTENSIVE CARE NURSERY: AN ETHICAL ANALYSIS

CHAPTER THREE

DELIBERATE DEATH IN THE INTENSIVE CARE NURSERY: AN ETHICAL ANALYSIS

I. INTRODUCTION

Our previous discussion considered the medical-legal implications of infanticide in the intensive care nursery. We have not yet concentrated attention on the ethics of what ought to be done. This chapter identifies the ethical parameters of neonatal practise; analyses these practices for conformity to the guiding ethical tenets of Anglo-American society; and sketches a model of ethically acceptable deliberate death in the intensive care nursery.

The success of this undertaking depends on the clarity and acceptability of the ethical concepts adduced. It depends also on our ability to relate these concepts to medical practices. For these reasons we preface our presentation of the issues raised by neonatal care with a brief discussion of ethical systems and their implications for newborn intensive care.

Although we mention other frameworks, our primary focus is on teleological and deontological ethical theory. These approaches are most commonly encountered in western democracies. They constitute the greater part of the justificatory structure appealed to in neonatal decision making.

II. ETHICAL THEORIES

To say that human behaviour in social context is subject to different kinds of evaluations would be to utter the obvious. To attempt to enunciate these evaluations individually, perhaps under legal, ethical, religious, medical, or sociological headings would be to stretch the limits of patience. What is not obvious is that each approach contains internal theoretical differences. These differences lead the sociologist and theologian, for example, to weigh the same data differently, and direct them to distinct, even antagonistic conclusions. This is important to ethics; for when all is said and done, we demand of any evaluation of human behaviour not simply that it work but that it be ethically correct. The theoretical differences between ethical approaches, therefore, cut deeper than classification. They eventuate in conflicts between what is and what is not acceptable in a given situation. Any hope of resolving such conflicts is predicated on clear understanding of the respective ethically distinct approaches.

Ethical approaches divide into four main types:[1] teleological or goal-directed; deontological, or rule-focussed; agapistic, or love-centred; and religious, or belief-derived. Anglo-American society, while not unaware of the agapistic and religious approaches, favours the teleological and deontological in its social and legal practise.[2] Accordingly, we focus on these.

---

1. For a good discussion of types of ethical theories, see R.B. Brandt, *Ethical Theory: The Problems of Normative and Critical Ethics* (Englewood Cliffs, N.J.: Prentice-Hall, 1959); and W.K. Frankena, *Ethics* (Englewood Cliffs, N.J.: Prentice-Hall, 1963). A classical but more traditional account is found in C.D. Broad, *Five Types of Ethical Theory* (N.Y.: Harcourt, Brace & Co., 1934).

2. Very little has been written about the ethical basis of the law in specific contexts. For a useful first glance, however, see Edgar Bodenheimer, *Jurisprudence: The Philosophy and the Method of the Law* (Cambridge, 1967); Ronald Dworkin, *Taking Rights Seriously* (Harvard University Press, 1977); H.L.A. Hart, *The Concept of Law*, (Oxford, 1961); John Rawls, *A Theory of Justice* (Harvard University Press, 1971); and S.F. Cohen, *Ethical Systems and Legal Ideals* (Westport, Conn.: Greenwood, 1976). These represent contemporary booklength works on a general theoretical level. A somewhat more practice-oriented analysis of the relevance of ethics with respect to the present topic is to be found in W.H. Baughman, J.C. Bruha and F.J. Gould, "Euthanasia: Criminal, Tort, Constitutional and Legislative Considerations" (1973), 48 *Notre Dame Lawyer* 1207-60 *passim*; and still more to the point in T.S. Ellis, III, "Letting Defective Babies Die: Who decides?" (1982), 7 *American Journal of Law and Medicine* 393-423. In both of these analyses, however, as in all other cases, the ethics is entirely secondary.

The most important teleological ethical system is *utilitarianism*.[3] Utilitarianism is best delineated in terms of its fundamental principle, the principle of utility: that act is right which, all other things being equal, produces or is likely to produce the greatest amount of good for the greatest number of people. The principle leaves open the nature of the good aimed at and the structure of justification for various actions done to accomplish the desired end.

This gives rise to a variety of approaches within utilitarianism itself. *Hedonistic* utilitarianism presents pleasure as the ultimate good. *Ideal* utilitarianism focuses on abstract values like equality and understanding.[4] Certain utilitarian systems determine utility on a case-by-case basis. These are *act-orientated* approaches. *Rule-orientated* approaches evaluate the utility of actions by conformity to general rules of conduct; utility of the rules is separately justified in terms of the ultimate good.

One might be tempted to dismiss these differences between utilitarian systems as pragmatically useless, of interest only to taxonomically inclined theoreticians. The temptation might soften on realization that precisely these differences in theory may lead to differences in practise. The question whether euthanasia is ethically appropriate in a specific instance may be answered in one way by hedonistic utilitarian and another by an ideal one. Rule as opposed to act utilitarianism may in turn lead to still different conclusions. The opportunity for pragmatic conflict on the basis of theoretical divergence is therefore great.

The governing thesis of the deontological approach is that the individual person is of ultimate and incommensurable value. Action must be evaluated by how well it preserves the autonomy of the individuals involved and safeguards their respective rights, not by any end aimed at or produced. While the Roman adage, "Fiat iustitia, ruat coeli !" (let justice be done, though the heavens fall !) would be putting the point too strongly, it does capture the thrust of the deontological position. It is the interplay and balance of rights that is here important - of rights as anchored in the autonomous individual person - and anything that violates these rights or produces an imbalance is morally objectionable, even though very important ends be at stake.

---

3. The classical statements of utilitarianism are given by Jeremy Bentham in *The Principles of Morals and Legislation* (1789), and J.S. Mill in *Utilitarianism* (1863). For a modern version, see R.B. Brandt, *A Theory of the Good and the Right* (Oxford, 1979).

4. *Cf*. Frankena, *supra*, note 1.

The reasons for adopting one ethical system over another are not entirely academic. Each approach has strengths and weaknesses. Utilitarianism has a quantitative outlook that allows for the introduction of cost-effectiveness considerations and of social and familial considerations that transcend the individual himself. From a pragmatic standpoint, that counts for a great deal. In principle it allows us to construct a decision-making framework of weighted parameters, independent of subjective variables, which may be implemented in practice.

Nevertheless, in that very calculative feature lies a shortcoming of utilitarianism. In focussing on the ultimate quantity of social good, utiliarianism allows, at least in principle, the dilution of individual rights in the name of the greater good. It operates on the maxim that the end justifies the means. That maxim seems inherently inimical to the absolute value Anglo-American society places on the individual person. Hence society's simultaneous acceptance of the deontological approach as a separate underpinning for its laws. Western law evaluates a given action by its respect for existing individual rights, and their interplay, not in terms of utility. In this way the law safeguards the autonomy of individuals at the price of those very cost-benefit considerations of ultimate outcome and social return that make utilitarianism so attractive as a decision-making tool.

Medical decision-making exhibits certain utilitarian tendencies. This creates conflict with the rights-oriented deontological approach. Medical decision-making incorporates a peculiar blend of the ideal and the pragmatic and is frequently drawn towards both ethical poles in an inconsistent fashion.

III. DECISION-MAKING

Neonatal decision-making involves many actors: healthcare professionals - principally physicians and nurses; the family, next of kin, or other interested parties; and the judiciary.[5] The level, nature and degree of input into the process by each of the actors varies greatly, as does the power that each wields.

1. Decision-Making Power

(a) The Parents

Legal theory invests parents with primary decisional power in the intensive care nursery.[7] In exceptional cases, parents can be overruled by the judiciary; but only under very special circumstances and for closely circumscribed reasons,[8] such as neglect or abuse of their responsibilities to protect their child's welfare.[9] Abuse aside, however, parental decisional power is deemed supreme.

Parental power has been defended on five considerations: (i) propinquity,[10] (ii) assumption of best interest,[11] (iii) obligation of care,[12] (iv) social cohesion,[13] and (v) the sanctity of the family.[14] We consider each in turn.

---

5. This is not to say that others may not be involved, either as resource persons or as legally interested parties. An example would be field or administrative personnel, attached to child welfare agencies. However, where other parties have standing, they usually fall under one of the rubrics mentioned, either naturally or by convention. Child welfare officials, for example, are assimilable to the judiciary, as instruments of state policy.

7. See chapter two, *supra*, section (I)(1)(c).

8. The powers of the judiciary in this respect are generally grounded in the *parens patriae* doctrine and its various implications: see chapter two, section (I)(1)(e)(ii). Each Province of Canada has detailed legislation dealing with the question of under what circumstances the judiciary may intervene: see chapter two, section (I)(1)(e)(i).

9. As was found to be the case, for example, by McKenzie, J., in *In the Matter of Stephen Dawson*, [1983] 3 W.W.R. 613 (B.C.).

10. See *cf. Hopper* v. *Steeves* (1899), 34 N.B.R. 591 (C.A.): "The guardian by *nature* is the father, and on his death the mother" (emphasis added). See also *Re Agar-Ellis* (1883), 24 Ch. 137.

11. *Cf. Child and Family Services and Family Relations Act*, S.N.B. 1980, c. C.2.1, s. 1.

12. *Cf. In re Flynn* (1848), De G. & Sm. 457; *Hepson* v. *Maat*, [1957] S.C.R. 606.

13. *Cf. Custody of a Minor*, 393 N.E. (2d) 876 (Mass. 1979).

14. *Cf.* Carson Strong, "The Neonatologist's Duty to Patient and Parent", *Hastings Centre Report* 14:4, 13. For a somewhat different analysis, see Ellis, *op. cit.*; and Natalie Abrams, "Defective New-borns: A Framework for a Case Analyses", *The Westminster Institute Review*, 2:2 (Winter, 1983) pp. 3-7.

(i) Propinquity can be understood in two ways: natural or congenital, and conventional. Natural propinquity arises from closeness in virtue of biological parenthood; conventional propinquity arises from closeness in virtue of adoption. Only the former concerns us here. The need to make decisions about radically defective neonates occurs within the immediate temporal context of birth, not after lengthy adoption procedures have run their course. Although conceivable, initiation of adoption is unlikely in such cases.

The argument from propinquity considers that natural biology binds consanguinally related individuals, particularly parents and children.[15] That bond puts parents in a unique position of proxy power. No similar claim exists because only the parents are responsible for the existence of the child. Even the state - so the reasoning continues - if and when it overrides parental power, does so on the fiction that it is parent in a still more fundamental sense *parens patriae*, parent of the country as a whole.[16]

The biological facts relevant to the propinquity argument are indisputable. The difficulty is that no ethical inference follows. Biological facts, like any other facts, are ethically neutral. It is the manner in which facts relate to social and personal interaction that embues them with ethical significance. How the fact of biological parenthood functions in the social context in general, and how it manifests itself in personal interaction in particular, determines whether it has ethical import, and if so, of what sort. Ethical rights and obligations - in this case, decision-making power - are not inherent, without more, in biological facts.

Nor are these additional considerations merely theoretical. Appreciation of the social context is reflected in ordinary practice. We need merely consider the case of adoption. If biological parenthood implied proxy decisional power, others could not have or acquire it because convention cannot alter facts of biology. One might, of course, say that in adoption cases biologically grounded power is transferred to the adoptive parents: that a special ethical status is created for them through this act of transfer. That concession, however, posits a distinction between biological and ethical status even in the case of the natural parents, because only on assumption of such a distinction can the ethical

---

15. *Cf. Hopper* v. *Steeves* (1899), 34 N.B.R. 591 (C.A.) "The guardian *by nature* is the father, and on his death the mother ..." (emphasis added). The concept of "natural guardianship" is here basic.

16. See note 9, *supra*, where McKenzie, J. explicitly refers to this at 6.

status be transferred. As an attempt at justifying the special ethical status of parents, therefore, the argument from propinquity fails.

(ii) The best interests argument is based on implication of an emotional bond of overwhelming depth and strength. Because of that bond, so it is said, parents have the best interests of their offspring at heart and, therefore, stand before all others to assume the proxy decision-maker's role.

From a purely pragmatic standpoint, this reasoning is attractive. We know that most parents do have beneficent emotional involvement and do take their children's best interests to heart. That this is not universal, however, sufficiently appears from the gruesome statistics detailing child negligence and the battered child syndrome.[17] The assumed best interests argument thus fails in its generality, and is open to rebuttal in individual cases. Precisely because of the child abuse phenomena, best interest should be proved in each case. One might also argue that there is no inevitability about parents fulfilling the best-interest role; it is culture-bound and a function of conditioning. It therefore fails to establish the naturalness of the parental right/obligation that is claimed.

These, however, are picayune cavils.

The important point can be put in general ethical terms. The fact of a best-interest concern, like that of consanguinal relation, is ethically neutral. By itself, it does not imply proxy decisional power. If it did, then not only parents, but anyone else who could demonstrate a best interest concern should be able to lay claims to such authority. This is clearly wrong. In order to give rise to an ethical implication, whether that be the right/obligation of proxy decision-making power or anything else, the fact of best interest concern must be related to some other *ethically* significant fact - a fact that carries the basis of decision-making authority within it. This does not mean that the criterion of best interest is not a relevant, even crucial component in the ultimate grounding of decisional authority. Combined with that other ethical fact - or facts - it may well be. But it does imply that assumed best interests is insufficient, ethically, to ground decisional power.

(iii) The argument from obligation of care focuses on the fact that parents, by virtue of procreating and allowing the pregnancy to proceed uninterruptedly, voluntarily assume an obligation of care for the neonate.[18] That obligation extends beyond providing necessaries of life;

---

17. *Cf.* Selwyn M. Smith, *The Battered Child Syndrome* (London: Butterworths, 1975).

18. For a fuller discussion, see E.-H.W. Kluge, *The Practice of Death* (Yale University Press, 1975) pp. 97 *et passim.*

it includes safeguarding the neonate's legal status as a person. From this two consequences flow: The first grounds decision-making power in the assumed obligation to administer rights; the second grounds it in the preconditions necessary to fulfil this obligation.

The argument assumes that the neonate is a person with rights like any other: life, autonomy, health-care, and so on. Obviously a newborn cannot himself exercise these rights. Unless they are exercised for him, they will be lost. Therefore, newborns require surrogate decision-makers. Those who assume the obligation of care for the neonate *qua* person also assume the obligation to act as surrogate decision-maker to protect the child's rights. Not to act in that way is dereliction in the exercise of a voluntarily assumed duty of care.

The second leg of the argument gathers strength from the principle of impossibility: One cannot have an obligation to do that which is impossible. To look after the rights of the neonate without proxy decision-making authority is impossible. If parents are without authority to make surrogate decisions, the obligation of care would be impossible to fulfill. This is sufficient to couple decision-making authority to the obligation of care as a necessary precondition. On this argument, decisional authority follows as an ethical implication from parenthood.

(iv) The argument from social cohesion grounds parental decision-making authority differently, but just as successfully. It, too, begins with the premise that the neonate is a person.[21] He is a member of the family into which he is born and also of society at large. Certain rights derive from his social existence:[22] life, a certain quality of life, and health care among them. Society fulfils these rights through its agencies and ultimately through delegated individuals. A meaningful guarantee of the neonate's rights requires identifiable individuals to exercise society's corresponding obligations. Society delegates its responsibility to protect the neonate's rights to the parents. It recognizes the

---

21. This would be denied by those who, like Michael Tooley, "A Defense of Abortion and Infanticide," in Joel Feinberg, ed., *The Problem of Abortion* (Belmont, Calif., 1973) argue that the neonate is not a person until quite some time after birth. See also S.I. Benn, "Infanticide and Respect for Persons", in Feinberg, *op. cit.*, and A.R. Jonsen, R.H. Phibbs, W.W. Tooley, M.J. Garlan, "Critical Issues in Newborn Intensive Care: A Conference Report and Policy Proposal," *Pediatrics* 55; 6 (June 1965) pp. 756-68 at 758.

22. This does not mean that the rights are functions of existence itself. They arise out of the context of social existence and interaction but are not circumscribed or defined by them. For a closer analysis see E.-H.W. Kluge, "Rights as Emergent Entities: Naturalism Revisited", forthcoming in *Proceedings of the 10th Inter-American Congress of Philosophy* in Tallahassee, Florida, 1981.

overwhelming likelihood that parents have the best interests of their progeny at heart; consequently it confirms the social institution of the family unit as an autonomous body, where the obligation of care for the children is concentrated in the parents. As we have already seen, that obligation logically entails correlative decision-making authority as a necessary precondition. Social confirmation carries with it a corresponding transfer of the surrogate decision-making power which otherwise belongs to society: of the power that logically belongs to society in virtue of its obligations to each individual member.

This argument is buttressed by the ethical principle of best action.[23] Normally parents are in a better position than anyone else to determine what is in the best interests of the neonate. Consequently it is they who, being best placed to perform the relevant actions, should have the appropriate power.

(v) The argument from the sanctity of the family is more diffuse. Its general thrust is as follows: The family, as a social unit, is not merely sacred in itself but that sacredness also finds reflection in the fact that its continued existence as a social institution is necessary for the existence of society. The family is a unit characterized by close interactions and relations among its members on a variety of levels. The functional integrity of the unit therefore requires that problems arising within it be solved within it. This implies that those who chart its destiny be allowed to come to grips with tragedy without external interference so as to be able to redefine and restructure the destiny of the unit in a way that is fair to all. The precondition for this, where the tragedy is the birth of a radically deformed child, is that the parents have the right/obligation of proxy decision-making for infantile members of the unit. To deny parents that power is to deny them the right to adjust to tragedy in a meaningful fashion. It is to strip them of their autonomy and make them subject to the dictates of external, emotionally unaffected, emotionally uninvolved agencies. A tragic accident of fate must not be compounded by destroying the family unit itself through interference with its autonomy.[24]

---

23. See p. 51 *infra*.

24. The core of this reasoning resides in the Anglo-American notion of family autonomy which finds judicial reflection in the fact that interference with the exercise of parental authority may occur only for closely circumscribed reasons. The ultimate danger with this notion is that it tends to foster a proprietary view of children. *Cf. Prince v. Massachussetts*, 321 U.S. 158, 166, 64 S. Ct. 438, 88 L.Ed. 645 (1949); *Wisconsin v. Yoder*, 406 U.S. 205, 234, 92 S. Ct. 1520, 32 L.Ed. 15 (1972). See also *Custody of a Minor*, 393 N.E. (2d) 836 (Mass., 1979) which recognizes "a private realm of family life which the State cannot enter."

The general tone of this reasoning involves three separate strands: one based on sacredness of the family unit, another centering in social necessity, and a third concentrating on the ethics of group interaction. Not all of these carry equal weight. From a purely ethical standpoint the claim of sacredness is irrelevant. It has a purely religious nature without inherent ethical content; and while quite probably convincing to those who share a religious viewpoint incorporating this notion, it will hardly be persuasive to those of a different mind.[25]

Ethically, then, the claim of sacredness cannot be used to ground the thesis of parental authority. Neither can the claim of social necessity. Social necessity is a utilitarian consideration that, ethically, cannot be supported in its generality. Its factual basis - the thesis that parental decision-making authority is necessary to the survival of society - can also be questioned. There are cultures in which family units, if they exist at all in the sense that is here at issue, do not have such lines of authority but proceed by communal decision-making. Even aside from this, the whole train of reasoning immediately calls forth the question whether, ethically speaking, the continuation of our society in its present form is important. If that survival is possible only on the basis of a condition which cannot be defended on independent ethical grounds, then its prospective disappearance cannot itself be heralded as supplying that ground. If its survival is contingent on the continued existence of a type of family unit whose ethical structure is in question, then neither the continued existence of that form of society nor the structure of that type of family unit can be defended by pointing to the existence of that interrelation. To do so is to beg the question.

But of course there are good and sufficient grounds for insisting on that line of authority: grounds that fall within an extended meaning of 'sacredness of the family' - and this takes us to the third strand of the argument: ethics of group interaction. The group interaction that we find in families is characteristic of groups that, as a whole, are charged with the obligation of taking care of and looking after the best interests of its members where some of the members are incompetent. No one can be obliged to do the impossible. No one can be obliged to fulfill a task if the means for fulfilling it are denied him.

The reasoning goes further and changes focus. Decision-making within groups of this sort must proceed on the basis of a balancing of rights. The rights of *all* members must be considered by those who have the task of making the decisions. The very nature of the group

---

25. Fundamentally different religious views such as the Buddhistic will be here implicated.

- the fact that it includes incompetents - entails that the considerations of these rights can occur only if the decision-makers have the authority to advance and by proxy act on them. The extent of that authority, however, cannot reasonably be curtailed if the balancing of rights involved is to be just and fair and exercised in a responsible fashion. Consequently full proxy decision-making authority must belong to the parents. As long as that authority is exercised in strict accordance with the ethical principles governing the balancing of rights, neither the fact nor the use of that power can be attacked.

A balancing of rights, however, is just that: a balancing. It must take into account the fact that no right is absolute in its extent. Not even the right to life. All rights are subject to limitation by the competing rights of others. This implies limits to the claims of any given individual acting by himself or through a proxy. As long as that balancing process is carried out fairly, there is no ethically acceptable reason for outside intervention. This is the core of the argument from the sacredness of the family when stripped of its non-ethical components. It reduces to the claim that although the institution of the family is a social phenomenon and although the basis of parental power ethically lies in the *de facto* delegation from the state in virtue of its institutional recognition of the family unit as the means of fulfilling its obligation, parental exercise of that power cannot be interfered with unless the condition on which it is granted is violated. That condition is that the power be exercised in a fair and just fashion through a balancing of rights within the unit. Therefore, so long as that condition is met, the exercise of that power may not be overruled.

These three arguments - obligation of care, social cohesion and sacredness of the family - ultimately ground the primacy of parental power. Although these arguments initially appear counter-intuitive, that counts for very little. Intuition is a psychological phenomenon that is a very poor guide in matters of ethics. If it were otherwise, ethical problems would not exist.

(b) The Judiciary

Parental decisional authority derives from the social institution of the family unit. Society's acceptance of the family unit as its agent results in delegation of power, transfer and recognition of an obligation of care, and a concomitant right of decision-making. Society's delegation is conditional, and may be rescinded when the conditions are violated. That is why - and when - the parents must bow to the higher authority of the judiciary.

This does not mean that the judiciary can interfere with parental authority simply because it is derivative. A just and overwhelming cause is required because of the nature of the case. Delegation to the family occurs on the presumption that in this way the rights of new members will be most effectively guaranteed and their best interests protected. On occasion, this does not occur because of the absence of the bond,[26] cognitive and/or emotive incompetence, or a sheer lack of ethical sensibility. We are too well aware of cases where proxy power is treated as a dispositionary right over the neonate rather than an obligation to exercise his rights for him. In these cases society, acting through the court system, must step in and revoke the delegation of authority. Revoke, not overrule: since the ethical basis of parental authority does not exist in these cases, the delegation of power cannot ethically be upheld.

The authority of the state, as exercised through the judiciary, is ethically basic. That does not mean that it is exercised prior in time. Given the continuous and *de facto* delegation to parents, the exercise of judicial power must await parental misconduct; consequently it will be posterior in time. Still, the possibility for judicial intervention must always exist. To fail to provide for it in the legal structure would be to abandon society's ultimate obligations to its most vulnerable members.

It would be misleading to foster the impression that the role of the judiciary can be defended only from a deontological standpoint. In view of the pragmatically oriented current of utilitarianism that pervades so much of bio-medical decision-making, it is important to note that similar conclusions can be reached from a utilitarian standpoint. Unless some mechanism like judicial intervention existed, the normal and smooth operation of society would be threatened in crisis contexts such as this. To be sure, the existence of such mechanisms constitutes a threat of state intervention into the family setting, and that might itself be thought to contravene utility. That intrusion, however, is heavily circumscribed and would occur only in situations where the normal family mechanisms were unable to produce a solution acceptable to the remainder of society. In other words, the disutility in not providing such a mechanism would exceed the immediate family setting and would affect all of society with disquieting results. There

---

26. For present purposes the question whether the origin of this "bonding" is genetic or psychological may be ignored. The bond also may be said to arise in adoption cases either psychologically or by convention. These, however, are complications that need not concern us here.

would be no general, consistent rule of behaviour to effect a smooth solution. There would always remain the threat that individual interests would result in a burden for all.

That is to say, social utility is best served by having consistent rules of behaviour applicable to all individuals in the same way under similar circumstances.[27] The principle of justice familiar from the deontological context can be defended as a utility-maximizing rule of behaviour on a utilitarian footing. In practical terms this means that the rights of individuals must be safeguarded, notwithstanding incompetency. This implies a need for surrogate decision-makers within the utilitarian context. These, in turn, demand an agency which monitors their operation: an agency that has the power of intervention should misadministration occur. That agency is the judiciary of the state. Once again, however, its actual interference will be rather infrequent. Its supervenient function will come into play only when the principle of justice in its utilitarian interpretation is violated on a specific occasion. While the mechanism of intervention must exist, it may be involved only upon demonstrated need.[28]

It is clear, then, that both utilitarian and deontological approaches, despite their fundamental valuational differences, provide solid support for ultimate judicial power. Suffice it to say that what may be perceived as being only a theoretical and idle difference becomes pragmatic and has profound implications when it comes to determining the criteria for neonatal decision-making.[29]

(c) The Physician

In Chapter One we detailed how physicians, whether primary care, specialist or neonatologist, make final determinations for deliberate death. Directly or indirectly, overtly or covertly, by simple statement or through parental manipulation, physicians decide what will happen.

Can this practice be ethically defended? Four justifications are commonly advanced: (i) for want of proper education and training, parents cannot understand technical medical data relevant to neonatal

---

27. *Cf.* Brandt, *Ethical Theory, supra,* note 1, pp. 253-8 and 396-405. See also Stephen Toulmin, *An Examination of the Place of Reason in Ethics* (Cambridge, 1950). Brandt has a good bibliography.

28. The onus therefore will always be on the state.

29. This becomes especially important when right-of-access questions are raised in the context of the larger issue whether a given treatment for a radically defective neonate would be ordinary or extraordinary treatment. See Chapter IV, *infra.*

decision-making;[30] (ii) because of personal involvement, parents are emotionally incapable of rational action even assuming they understand the facts of the case;[31] (iii) physicians have a special duty, arising from their role as physician, to make such decisions for parents;[32] (iv) emergencies present no alternative: a decision must be made fast, consultation cannot take place, the decisional burden falls to the physician as leader of the medical team.[33]

From an ethical standpoint, not all of these claims carry equal weight nor are they equally persuasive. The reasoning under (i) assumes that medical data or its significance cannot be understood without medical training. This is doubtful on the facts. While average parents may not understand raw, uninterpreted medical data in jargonistic language, this does not imply they cannot do so when information is appropriately presented and explained. The legal doctrine of informed consent would be absurd were it otherwise.[34] Our experience with informed consent is that reasonable people do understand and react rationally to medical data when appropriately presented and explained. Nothing in the medical data relating to newborn intensive care is uniquely opaque. The underlying error here is confusing inability to understand data without appropriate explanation, with inability to understand *tout court*.

Even were the assumption of non comprehension correct, the ethical implication does not follow that decisional power passes to the physi-

---

30. See J. Shaw, "Dilemmas of 'Informed Consent' in Children", (1973), *New England Journal of Medicine* 885.

31. *Cf.* Ellis, *supra*, note 2 at 414. See also Nielsen, "A Longitudinal Study of Psychological Aspects of Myelomeningocele" (1980), 21 *Scandinavian Journal of Psychology* 45-54; Mandelbaum and Wheeler, "The Meaning of a Defective Child to Parents" (1960), *Social Casework* 360; Goodman, "Continuing Treatment of Parents with Congenitally Defective Infants", *Social Work* 9:1 (1964) at 92.

32. *Cf.* E.-H.W. Kluge, *The Ethics of Deliberate Death* (Kennikat, 1981) at 92.

33. This may in part be derived from the judgment in *Schloendorff* v. *New York Hospital* 211 N.Y. 125, 127, 129 N.E. 92, 93 (1914). Emergency situations are always exceptions in ethics. For fuller treatment see *infra* p. 163. See also B.B. Shapiro, "Legal Aspects of Unauthorized but Necessary Emergency Treatment" (1963), *Law Society of Upper Canada Special Lectures* 255; *Medical Treatment and Criminal Law*, Working Paper 26 of the Law Reform Commission of Canada (Ottawa, 1980) at 43, 73 *et passim*.

34. For the Canadian Law, see *supra*, chapter II. See also F.J. Ingelfinger, "Informed (But Uneducated) Consent", *New England Journal of Medicine* 287 (Aug. 31, 1972) at 465 f.; for a bioethical analysis, see Tom L. Beauchamp and James F. Childress, *Principles of Bio-Medical Ethics* (Oxford, 1974) Chapter 3, and Paul Ramsey, *The Patient as Person* (Yale University Press, 1979) Chapter I.

cian.[35] Apart from emergencies, the state in its *parens patriae* role would be ethically more appropriate, as we have seen.

Which brings us to (ii) - alleged inability of the parents to act rationally due to emotional turmoil. Again, the reasoning rests on doubtful facts. Nothing in our survey suggests overwhelming parental irrationality as claimed. In any event, incompetence should never be assumed as a general principle. Even if we assume emotionally grounded parental incompetence, the ethical inference of physician decision-making authority does not follow. As we have shown, the ethically appropriate decision-maker is the judiciary as agent of the State. The individual physician has no mandate to shroud himself in the mantle of the State.

Finally, certain statistical studies conclude that physicians have greater-than-average fear of death[36] and that physicians often view the death of a non-senescent patient as a personal failure. This suggests that the intensive care nursery produces intense emotional strain for physicians, a conclusion supported by our survey.[37] If the principle of emotional disqualification underlying (ii) were applied consistently, it would require that physicians should be the last to be involved.

Before leaving (i) and (ii), a word about ethically competent decision-making in general. Such competence is not something that can be analysed simply in terms of technical, conceptual awareness and emotional equilibrium. It involves four, not two parameters: understanding, reasoning ability, will and emotion. A person can be considered ethically competent if and only if he is capable of understanding the relevant data and grasping the appropriate ethical principles when properly explained; can identify appropriate goals of action on the basis of these and determine acceptable ways of attaining them; is sufficiently free from coercive and biasing influences to be able to adhere to these goals and follow the course of action selected; and can disengage himself enough from his emotional involvement to be able to do all this without introducing an ethically (reasonably) unjustifiable skew into the whole procedure. None of this implies that emotions - even intense and deeply felt ones - may not be present; nor does it entail

---

35. *Cf.* Ellis, *supra*, note 2 at p. 415.

36. *Cf.* Marya Mannes, *Last Rights* (New York, 1974) at 26 f. For a general philosophical discussion of the fear of death, see Douglas N. Walton, *On Defining Death* (McGill-Queens, 1979) Chapter 11, which also contains a good bibliography. For statistical sociometric analyses, see Diana Crane, *The Sanctity of Social Life* (New York: Russell Sage Foundation, 1975).

37. *Supra*, chapter I, p. 36-37.

that the data necessary for the decision process must be couched at a professional level. All that follows is that the individual must be capable of grasping the relevant data, appreciate their import, and convert that appreciation into rational and acceptable action. The *a priori* assumption must always be that these conditions are met. Any denial here goes to incompetence. Since that affects the autonomy of the individual *qua* person, it must always be proved.

Argument (iii), the professional role approach, grounds the physician's decision-making right/obligation in the nature and traditions of the medical profession. It is argued that the physician's activity requires that he make such decisions more frequently than anyone else. From his greater experience, the physician is better qualified to decide than parents. It is also said that neonatal decision-making focuses on medical facts and data: this uniquely falls into the physician's professional domain. The conclusion drawn is that the physician is best qualified to act as decision-maker.[37a]

The argument is less than compelling. Medical tradition is of historical interest and import. While it has legal significance, ethically it has none. Ethical inferences based on tradition are invalid because of the attempt to derive an *ought* from an *is* - a statement of ethical right/obligation from the mere description of a state of affairs. That is impossible. The fact that a certain state of affairs obtains - even that it has obtained for millennia - leaves entirely open whether it ought to obtain in the first place. Slavery is a good example. So is religious discrimination.

Nor is the problem resolved by the fact that physicians make intensive care decisions more frequently than do parents. Even if experience leads to expertise, that is insufficient. We still need a separate, ethical premise to effect the transition from what is to what ought to be. One

---

37a. See Alexander M. Capron, "A Functional Approach to Informed Consent" (1974), 123 *University of Pennsylvania Law Review* 364-71, reprinted in Thomas A. Mappes and Jane S. Zembaty, *Biomedical Ethics* (McGraw-Hill, 1981) at 76. See also the opinion in *Canterbury* v. *Spence* 464 F. (1972). A classic discussion of the paternalistic approach here involved is found in Gerald Dworkin, "Paternalism", *The Monist* 56 no. 1. A reply is found in Bernard Gert and C.M. Culver, "Paternalistic Behaviour", *Philosophy and Public Affairs* 6:1 (Fall 1976). See also Rosemary Carter, "Justifying Paternalism", *Canadian Journal of Philosophy* 7 (1977) 133-45; Douglas Husak, "Paternalism and Autonomy", *Philosophy and Public Affairs* 10 (1980-81) 27-46; Donald VanDeVeer, "The Contractual Argument for Withholding Medical Information", *Philosophy and Public Affairs* 9 (1978-80) 198-205; Robert Young, "Autonomy and Paternalism" *Canadian Journal of Philosophy* 8 (1982) 47-66; James Woodward, "Paternalism and Justification", *Canadian Journal of Philosophy*, 8 (1982) 67-89.

might argue that frequency of decision-making establishes right of decision-making independently of initial authority, or that expertise in decision-making confers independent right of decision-making. However, not only are both premises doubtful as principles, they are certainly unacceptable in this particular instance.

One way of avoiding this difficulty is to insist that inductively acquired expertise provides authority because no one is so well placed to make the right decision, either ethically or medically. Reflection reveals this defense to be unsuccessful. The mere frequency of an action - the fact that it is done over and over again - does not guarantee its ethical correctness. *A fortiori*, therefore, one cannot establish a claim of ethical expertise based on induction. Both the correctness of the act and ethical expertise based on it have to be established on independent grounds.

Not only parents, but physicians themselves have raised doubts about the ethical acceptability of decisions made by physicians in the intensive care nursery.[38] This view is buttressed by hard statistical data which reveals that the frequency and the predictable patterns of these decisions reflect no more than established patterns of professional practice in a given locale into which the individual has become acculturated as a matter of peer pressure and training. Professional pressure ensures that the newer physicians learn to do like the old - or at least the established. Inductively acquired expertise, therefore, instead of reflecting increasing ethical competence, merely reflects acculturation into the medical profession. The thrust of these considerations is particularly telling in light of statistical data about the process of medical decision-making in various types of settings.[39] These show that physicians' decision-making are determined by the customs and attitudes of the institutes of their schooling, their religious outlook, the area of their specialization and their current institutional affiliation. Consequently while it may be fair to say that frequent encounter with this type of problem and the fact of frequent decision-making do sensitize the physicians to the technical, psychological and professional problems that arise in this area and inure them to what is considered acceptable in the particular medical sub-culture in which they function, this does not license an inference to ethical expertise. In short, the inductively acquired expertise is more likely to be an expertise with respect to sub-cultural conformity than of ethical correctness.

---

38. See pp. 14, 27, *supra*.

39. *Cf.* Crane, *supra*, note 36. Especially Part II chapters 6-8.

However, even if the claim of inductively grounded ethical expertise be granted, no right/obligation of neonatal decision-making is thereby implied for the physician. The sole inference would be of a physician's obligation to benefit parents not only with medical, but also ethical advice. No expert, simply because he is an expert, acquires decision-making authority.

It could be argued that this reasoning misses the important point. The physician's role is to deal with these matters. Decision-making authority belongs to him by virtue of his profession.

Is this really true? No doubt professionals are more competent than non-professionals in matters within their expertise. However, two further consideration are a propos. First, unless the professional is a professional ethicist, his expertise is technical, not ethical. Second, the inference involves a confusion of meta-professional and professional authority.

The first point is self evident. The second goes to the heart of the issue. Professional expertise is relevant to decision-making in matters of professional skill and judgment. These include identification of possible goals, the distinction between reasonable and unreasonable goals, and the analysis of optimal means to attain these goals. However, whether a particular goal ought to be aimed at in the first instance - as opposed to technical feasibility - is not something that lies within the mandate of the professional qua professional. Additional authority would be required. Nor is it an area into which the professional may venture simply because of his technical expertise.[40] The critical distinction is between decisions made within the domain of the profession, and decisions about the profession. Neonatal decisions certainly draw on professional expertise for clarification of medical options. Nevertheless, the crux of these decisions is not how best to maximize life by medical means. It is whether, given poor prognosis with all medical options, life is worth living. This falls outside of medical expertise.

A particular decision may be made because it appears to be the only reasonable one. Judgments of reasonableness, however, involve more than technical criteria. They involve meta-professional considerations drawn from beyond the context of medical facts. Only after the decision has been made does professional expertise come into play to attain the chosen goal. The right of choice as to how best to attain the desired goal does not include the right to decide whether profes-

---

40. The whole notion of informed consent to treatment is here implicated. The question to be settled is not one of technical feasibility and/or advisability, but whether the patient or his agent wishes it, for whatever reasons.

sional services ought to be employed in the first instance, or to what end.

The judgment of reasonableness finds its ethical base not in technical expertise but in legitimate authority to prolong or terminate life saving measures. The fallacy of expertise[41] seriously undermines the notion of personal autonomy and the concept of informed consent. It is at war with the rationale underlying surrogate decision-making.[42] It is no more acceptable for being hallowed in practice.

This analysis does not stand unopposed. Commentators argue that diminishing the importance of medical competence reduces medical ethics to an "engineering model",[43] and that it compromises the ethical integrity of the physician. The claimants reason thus: Medicine is a monopoly.[44] Monopolies are granted on the assumption that only through them are the needs of society best met. In the case of medicine, the assumption is that the monopoly best safeguards the body politic's right to proper health care. The physician is accordingly in a special position. He owes an obligation of service. An unreasonable barrier of parental authority interferes with his discharge of this obligation. If the physician lets himself be bound by parental decisions which he believes are medically contra-indicated, he becomes ethically guilty for allowing a wrong decision to be put into practise. By acceding to parental decisions he knows to be medically mistaken, he allows the neonate's right to health care to be compromised. The physician's integrity is at stake. He has no choice but to arrogate decisional power to himself.

What is the strength of this reasoning? To be sure, medicine is a professional monopoly and physicians are experts. Yet more is involved than merely medical considerations. Social, psychological, financial and

---

41. For a different expression of this in the nursing context, see Dan W. Brock, "The Nurse-Patient Relationship" in Mappes & Zembaty, *supra* note 37a at 92.

42. I.e., the technical expert would always, or at least most of the time, be in a position to overrule the patient/decision-maker. Legal rejection of this is well established. Ethically, the whole body of literature dealing with paternalism is here relevant. See Charles H. Montange, "Informed Consent and the Dying Patient" (1974), 83 *Yale Law Journal* 1632-64. The reader is also referred to the Bibliography put out by the Hastings Centre for Society Ethics and the Life Sciences, Hastings-on-Hudson, New York, for an up-to-date listing.

43. Robert M. Veatch, "Models for Ethical Medicine in a Revolutionary Age" (1972), 2 *Hastings Centre Report* 5-7. See also Bruce Miller and Howard Brody, "Contracting the Principles of Medical Ethics", *Westminster Institute Review* 2:3 (Spring 1983) pp. 11-13.

44. For a more extended discussion of this notion, see E.-H.W. Kluge, "The Profession of Nursing and the Right to Strike", *The Westminster Review* 2:1 (Fall 1982) at 5.

ethical parameters are relevant. These have nothing to do with the monopolistic status of the profession. Medical facts are merely one parameter among a series of others. A professional obligation of service is not a professional right, nor an obligation to impose.

The point can be sharpened in the neonatal context. Suppose a physician encounters a situation where, in his judgment as a professional, the wrong parental proxy decision is made. Even though the decision goes against his medical judgment and even though in his opinion it violates the neonate's right of access to health care, he may not overrule or disregard the decision of the parents. To be sure a physician need not stand idly by or simply do what he is asked. He may challenge the decision. But if his challenge is as a professional, his objection must be confined to technical medical aspects of the situation, to the feasibility of what is decided or to the availability of access. If, in his judgment, the parental decision is a violation of the neonate's rights, the physician is entitled to complain as a citizen asked to participate in a wrong. These challenges must be addressed to the proper authorities, the judicial and administrative arms of the state.

Let us recall that the neonatal context is one of proxy decision-making and that the proxy decision-maker must approach the problem in the spirit of administering rights. The power to do so may be removed from the proxy, but not on the basis of greater medical expertise, or of an external obligation *on someone else* to provide a service. It can be removed only upon ethical malfeasance in the proxy administration of rights. However, neither the fact that the parents are insufficiently aware of alternatives nor the fact that they are unsophisticated amounts to ethical malfeasance. Instead it entails an obligation on their part to seek out the relevant data, to be open to them and for the physician to provide data in a usable fashion. If the parents deliberately ignore his attempts, deliberately refuse to take the data into account or otherwise make their decision in an unreasonable fashion, then they would be guilty of malfeasance. Then the physician has the duty to take appropriate action.

The fact that medical data are not treated as decisive is not necessarily an indication of malfeasance. Access to and use of health care services is a right, not an obligation. It is perfectly conceivable that for good and sufficient reasons the proxy decision-makers may decide that the ethically appropriate course of action is not to exercise the right on that occasion. The proxy decision-making matrix, after all, is quite complex and is beset by many problems. The neonate cannot reasonably be said to have wishes or desires about how his rights are to be exercised. This implies an obligatory use of the objective standard of the reasonable person, not automatic insistence on the right. Furthermore, the proxy decision-maker must play several roles at once. The neonate does not exist in isolation. He exists in a familial and social setting where his rights compete with those of others. The parental decision-maker must not only administer the neonate's rights in a surrogate fashion but must also engage in a balancing act which pays due regard to the rights of all concerned, including the parents. The physician in his professional role is not sufficiently well-placed to evaluate all of these parameters. This is why he may merely challenge, and why his challenge must take the form we said. While in the eyes of some this may "reduce" medicine to the status of other professions and medical ethics to an "engineering model", it leaves the moral integrity of the physician intact.

Emergency situations (iv) are ethically different. Time is of the essence. A decision must be made. Parents may not be available. There may be no time for extended explanation.

Three situations require distinction, each with different ethical characteristics: (1) situations foreseen in the course of prenatal care, but which require speed in the actions necessary; (2) situations where the crisis, although unexpected, was reasonably foreseeable;[45] and (3) situations where the crisis is neither common nor a significant possibility in the circumstances.

Only the last two are emergencies in the full sense of that term, and only in these does the question of special authority for the physician arise. In cases of genuine and unexpected emergency, the decision immediately falls to the physician on the principle of possibility; only he can make an appropriate response in time. That argument holds only for the third case. In the second, although the particular situation could not have been predicted, it belongs to an array of possible scenarios each one of which might reasonably have been foreseen. It would therefore be incumbent on the physician to acquaint the parents-to-be with these possibilities[46] and to elicit from them a decision on how to

---

45. The reasonable person standard is formally recognized in *Reibl* v. *Hughes* for competent decision-making. It is only fair that the standards should be the same for proxy-decision-making. See Kluge, *The Ethics*, 109 ff. See also Montange, *op. cit.* 1649 ff.; Michael T. Sullivan, "The Dying Person: His Plight and His Right", 8 *New England Law Review* 197, 210 ff.; Baughman, *supra*, note 2.

46. It will be apparent that an ethical solution to the problem of radically defective neonates requires explicit recognition of the fact that a great deal of the difficulties that arise could be avoided by proper prenatal counselling. Discussion of this, however, transcends our present scope.

proceed, in the event the situation occurs. Most emergencies in neonatology fall under this rule.

This may mean that expectant parents consider a series of disheartening scenarios in order to provide guidelines. Failure to raise these possibilities deprives parents of the opportunity to exercise their legitimate authority. The material facts of the specific situation when it occurs may qualify the precise nature of the parent's decision or of its implementation. In an emergency, and to that degree, the physician will be the final decision-maker after all. Nevertheless, any changes must occur within the guidelines provided by the parents. The physician has no right to alter or contravene them.

In a foreseeable emergency (situation 2), as otherwise, the physician has no special ethical status. A foreseeable emergency does not confer on him an authority which overrules that of the parents. The only emergency in which this might occur is the third situation.

Emergencies that are neither common nor reasonably foreseeable (situation 3) are subject to three elements of constraint. The physician may have the parents' general views for other cases. These views, insofar as relevant, should be considered as guidelines for the physician's decision. Second, guidelines may have been established by the neonatal unit. These guidelines must be followed when parental directives developed in other contexts offer no help. Third, where neither parental nor institutional guidelines are applicable, the physician must be guided by the objective standard of the reasonable person. His personal preferences and predilections may not enter the picture.

Frequently what appears to be an emergency situation of the third type is not really that at all. It is the result of a failure to engage in the consultative process we have described. It is also of concern that variations in emergency decisions made under the third rubric are not necessarily the result of adjustments to fact but of an institutional failure to establish guidelines.

While emergency situations of the unforeseen variety occur, they are exceedingly rare. When they do occur contemporary medical techniques often allow the neonate to be stabilized until an ethically acceptable decisional procedure can be initiated. In some cases this will entail that stabilization processes which were initiated be discontinued. This calls for an investigation of the ethics of start/stop treatment vs. no start at all. We consider this later.

(d) The Nurse

For legal theory, nurses are subordinate in neonatal decision-making. They are confined to purveying information to physicians about the parents and the condition of the neonate. Nurses are expected to execute decisions of physicians and to act as a buffer between physicians and the family. Nurses have no strong decisional voice and they never have the final say.

Is this ethically correct? In light of our analysis of physicians, we could scarcely advocate overriding decisional power to nurses. Nevertheless, of all players in the intensive care nursery, nurses have the greatest appreciation of the daily implications of the situation. Because nurses deal with the neonate continuously they can evaluate cogently what a specific decision entails in terms of care.

The medical facts relevant to neonatal decision-making go beyond data provided by the physician. Data of a pragmatic medical nature are also relevant. Parents need data that focus on the nature and implications of care to make competent and informed surrogate decisions. Parents ought, therefore, to hear the nurse's voice, alongside that of the physician.

This view differs from the role usually assigned to nurses. Yet ethically, the nurse's subordinate position is indefensible if it results in the suppression of information relevant to the parents, as decision-makers.

2. Decision-Making Parameters

From decision-making authority we turn to decision-making parameters. There are two major rubrics: data and values. Each has its own particular sub-categories: ethical, medical and para-medical in the context of data; religious and non-religious in the context of values. We begin with an ethical analysis of the use of data.

(a) Data

It is important to distinguish two factors: relevance and weight. Certain types of data are ethically irrelevant. Their use is unacceptable. Alternatively, there may be data which common wisdom rejects, but which are ethically relevant.

The other factor to be considered is weight. Data may be ethically relevant in a specific context. That fact does not determine the weight to be attached in the decision process. Nor can there be a presumption that all relevant data carry equal weight - or, for that matter, that similar data carry the same weight under all circumstances. Weighting must be determined on the basis of the specifics of the case. The operative principle here is the principle of relevant difference. Relevant difference allows for a distinction in weighting depending on the variables of the actual situation, without contradiction at the level of principle.

(i) Ethical Data

Ethical data, as opposed to ethically relevant data, are data of pure ethics that govern any and all considerations in the present context. There are three important ethical data: personhood, justice and fairness.

Unless the neonate is a person, the complex of issues that focus on whether to provide medical care and how, is rendered nugatory. Is the neonate a person?

The preceding chapter has amply demonstrated that this question is more frequently ignored than raised. It is assumed that any offspring of human parents is a human being and therefore a person. The identification of humanity and personhood is ethically suspect. Humanity is a biological concept defined in terms of genetic make-up.[47] Personhood is ethical. "Person" implies a self-aware rational being, or a being having potential to so develop without undergoing a fundamental change in his nature or constitution.[48]

The material basis of awareness resides in the brain. A neonate is a person only if his cerebral development can progress so that the cerebral centres scientifically identifiable as the basis for self-awareness are present. This provides medically useful criteria for determining the ethical fact of personhood.[49] Anencephalic infants, for example, have no potential for cerebral development necessary to self awareness and as such are not 'persons'. They cannot therefore have surrogates. The ethical problems we have grappled with relevant to surrogate decision making are not implicated.

---

47. See Kluge, *The Ethics*, Chapter Four, and "Human and Persons Normative Concepts in Contemporary Biomedical Decision-Making", invited paper for the *Symposium on Human and Person*, sponsored by the Law Reform Commission of Canada and the Centre for Bioethics, Montreal, May 10-11, 1979; and "St. Thomas, Abortion and Euthanasia", *Philosophy Research Archives* (1981). See also H.T. Engelhardt, Jr., "On the Bounds of Freedom", *Connecticut Medicine* 41 (January 1976).

48. *Cf.* Kluge, *The Ethics loc.cit.*

49. For a fuller discussion of the critical role played by medical data in this context, see E.-H.W. Kluge, "Cerebral Death", *Theoretical Medicine* 5 (1984) 209-31.

Another ethical set of data focuses on the interplay of rights and obligations that exists in the neonatal setting. Let us assume that the defective neonate is in fact a person and that surrogate decision-making is therefore *a propos*. Anglo-American law presupposes that the rights of the individual take precedence over mere utility. Nevertheless, no right is absolute. All rights must be evaluated with respect to rank and weight vis-a-vis the competing rights of others. The more fundamental the right, the higher it ranks.[50] The right to life, and hence the right of access to health care, is usually considered fundamental.[51] When these rights compete with others that are not as fundamental, they outrank the latter. In practical terms, within a deontological setting, no defective neonate may be denied access to the necessaries of life[52] merely because another would be inconvenienced financially or by curtailment of his life-style.

All this presents no problem. Problems arise when equally ranked rights of different individual conflict, and competition for limited resources results. It is here that weight comes in. Weight can be assigned to rights of equal rank on the basis of the principle of possibility. If the likelihood of successful outcome upon medical intervention in one case is greater than in another, or more pointedly still, if it is possible to save one but not the other, or, still more acutely, if there is expected significant improvement in the quality of life of the one upon intervention, but none in the other, then the principle entails that the latter right, even though equal in rank, has lesser weight.

This problem has ramifications beyond neonatal intensive care. Contemporary hospitals are settings where allocation of resources is exclusive. What is given to the one must be taken from the other - not perhaps in the same medical area, but withheld nevertheless.[53] Allocation of resources to defective neonates must be ethically justified knowing that ultimately we withhold resources from individuals who

---

50. *Cf.* Kluge, *The Ethics*, pp. 120 ff.

51. For a different analysis, see S.I. Benn, in Joel Feinberg, *op. cit.* at 99.

52. For the interpretation of "Necessaries of Life" as inclusive of medical treatment, see *R.* v. *Brooks*, 9 Brit. Col. L.R. 13 at 18; *R.* v. *Lewis* (1903), 60 L.R. 132, 20 W.R. 566, 7 C.C.C. 261 (C.A.) See also E.-H.W. Kluge, "Euthanasia of Radically Defective Neonates: Some Statutory Considerations", (1980), 6 *Dalhousie Law Journal* 238.

53. In other words, the individual allocation must be evaluated in terms of the macro-allocation parameters. See Jonsen *et. al.*, at 761, 763, etc. On the problem of allocation, see Richard Trubo, *An Act of Mercy: Euthanasia Today* (Nash, 1973) at 153; Eliot Slater, "Health Service or Sickness Service", *British Medical Journal* 4 (Dec. 18, 1971).

also have a claim. Their claim is not to specific resources, but to general hospital resources which, having been allocated to the intensive care nursery, are no longer available elsewhere.

Any decision allocating resources to defective newborns must be justified against the competing claims of others. The fact that allocation is resource intensive and may well constitute the apportionment of more than a fair share must be considered. Rights of equal rank must be weighted not only on the principle of possibility, but also on the basis of equity and justice.

This immediately raises the question what constitutes a just and fair share from an ethical point of view.[54] When the apportionment of goods and services to an individual detracts significantly from available resources so as to interfere with access to health care by others it exceeds the bounds of fairness. However, not all claims to access are legitimate or of equal importance. The treatment of hangnails for the masses does not weigh as heavily as that of a liver-condition of the few. Furthermore, the fact that not all individuals start from the same level of health is relevant. Some are congenitally handicapped, as indeed in some of the cases under discussion, and through no fault of their own require a disproportionately large disbursement of medical resources to reach even that basic level of health common to society. The principle of justice suggests that allowances be made for such cases and the notion of fairness adjusted appropriately.[55]

This is crucially important for the radically defective neonate. Any adjustment in the notion of fairness must start from the position that no neonate is responsible for the health condition in which he finds himself. Since negative health is a handicap, and the function of social institutions is to ensure justice in the treatment of its members, it follows that the handicap must be allowed for on a proportional basis in the weighting of rights to resources. Such an adjustment is deontologically motivated, not the result of utilitarian consideration.

This perspective brings questions of fairness into focus in terms even that utilitarians can appreciate. Defective neonates require a proportionally large allocation of resources. The allocatory shift must not reach such a degree as to interfere unfairly with the right of access to health care by other members of society. The health-status of others

---

54. For a theoretical discussion with a different slant, see Rawls, *op. cit.* See also E.-H.W. Kluge, "The Calculus of Discrimination: Discriminatory Resource Allocation for an Aging Population" forthcoming in *Proceedings of the Conference on Ethics and Aging*, U.B.C. 1984.

55. For more see *infra*. See also Beauchamp and Childress, *supra*, note 34, Chapter 6.

may not be lowered below that of the neonate in receipt of the proportionally adjusted allocation.[56] A balance must be struck where no one, because of utilitarian or institutional considerations *predictably* ends up in a position of advantage. Such a denouement would violate the principles of equity and justice.

Our discussion implies that the allocation of resources to neonatal intensive care, at the macro level, has regard to the availability of health resources in overall social context; not only the quality of life of radically defective neonates but of all others. The same principle introduces an ethical limit on resource-allocation for a particular neonate. That limit depends on availability of intensive care resources. In addition to expected quality of life, possibility of desired result, etc., neonatal decision-makers may ethically take account of this resource based limit.

It is important to appreciate that our discussion does not reduce to a utilitarian calculus. We are concerned with the deontological balancing of rights.

(ii) Medical Data

Ethical principles are abstract; they require instantiation by particular facts in order to translate into practise. Many believe that medical facts are all important in the intensive care nursery. Medical facts, they reason, create the dilemma requiring a decision. This view accounts for the pre-eminent role played by physicians in the decision-making process.

Closer examination shows that single minded concentration on medical data in decision-making raises ethical problems. The assumption that we can recognize a medical fact, that medical data are hard and absolute, is open to challenge.[57] So is the conviction that medical facts are ethically decisive. Let us be more precise.

What are perceived as medical facts are conditioned by medical concepts of health and disease.[58] The perception of a state as positive

---

56. Furthermore, this must hold for every adult member of society.

57. *Cf.* Joel Feinberg, "Disease and Values", in J. Feinberg, *Doing and Deserving: Essays in the Theory of Responsibility*, (Princeton, 1970) pp. 253-5; H.T. Egelhardt, Jr., "Human Well-Being and Medicine: Some Basic Value Judgements in the Biomedical Sciences", in *Science, Ethics and Medicine*, ed. by H.T. Engelhardt, Jr. and Daniel Callahan (Hastings Center, 1976); Horatio Fabrega, "Concepts of Disease: Logical Features and Social Implications", *Perspectives in Biology and Medicine* 15 (1972) pp. 583-616.

58. See special issues of *Journal of Medicine and Philosophy* 1:3 (1978) on "Concepts of Health and Disease", and 5:2 (1980) on "Social and Cultural Perspectives on Disease". See also Ivan Illich, *Limits to Medicine* (1976) pp. 261-78.

or negative, as health or disease, is ineluctably connected with its perception as a medical phenomenon *tout court*. Medical concepts derive from medical culture.[59] The perception that a given phenomenon falls within the sphere of medical attention depends on the background of the physician, where he received his training, his religious affiliation and his institutional affiliation.[60] Each of these settings has its own characteristic notions which define the conceptual framework through which those who operate in that setting classify reality and perceive the world. Each conceptual framework, can be likened to a pair of irremovable glasses. Each conditions what is seen and thus determines how the world affects the individual who wears them. The physician is conditioned by his conceptual glasses, by his acquired conceptual framework. What he perceives, how he perceives - even whether he perceives data as relevant - are determined by it. The variables that exist here have immediate pragmatic import because they affect the decision process.

Culturally determined facts which vary with the physician's indi-vidually acquired conceptual framework form the medical basis of neonatal decision-making. That introduces variables into the procedure which, unless carefully appreciated and controlled, may invalidate the process. Given the nature of human interaction, it is difficult to see how this danger can be entirely avoided. Its omnipresent nature notwithstanding, it constitutes an ethical problem because of the unpredictable bias that it entails. Medical data are not hard. They are data-as-perceived, coloured by the concepts and values developed by the medical profession.

Medical evaluation involves an ineluctable element of prognosis.[61] The situation is described with an eye to what is possible and what is not. This involves a forecast of the success or failure of medical inter-vention. Forecasts of success of medical intervention are invariably adduced as hard medical data, and thus factored into the decisional process.

We can distinguish between two notions of success: the one act oriented, the other outcome-directed.[62] Each is associated with a differ-ent understanding of the role of the medical and technical feasibility of the action itself under the prevailing circumstances. It counts as

---

59. *Cf.* Crane, *supra*, note 36.

60. See note 59 *supra*.

61. The variations in the knowledge of individual physicians here play a fundamental role. For a tutioristic argument against euthanasia based on this, see D.N. Walton, *Brain Death* (Purdue Research Foundation, 1980), pp. 21 ff.

success the mere ability to initiate or continue the procedure or providing the service without doing harm to the patient. This conception goes hand-in-hand with the notion that the physician *qua* physician has the obligation to do all that it is possible to do under the circumstances, governed solely by the rule *primum non nocere.*[63]

In constrast to this, the outcome-oriented conception focuses on the question whether, under the circumstances, medical intervention will (or is likely to) bring about an improvement in health status. According to this conception, merely extending the patient's life-span cannot be considered success. If the price of continued existence is perpetuation of an experiential and/or functional level that was qualitatively unacceptable to begin with - indeed, as is often the case, a deterioration to mere biological existence acted upon with monomaniacal intensity - such activity can only be considered as doing harm to the individual, as inflicting the 'injury of continued existence'. Success in the outcome oriented conception is evaluated by quality-of-life parameters, and from that perspective more than continued existence is at stake.[64]

The distinction between these two conceptions is fraught with significance. Ethically speaking, the existence of this conceptual duality implies two distinct approaches to the same medical facts,[65] each explicitly subscribing to a success-oriented ethos, and yet each reaching essentially different prognoses - where the latter are presented as medical data on the basis of which the neonatological decision must be made.[66] It is not clear how this danger can be avoided - except by explicit identification of the conception of success employed. That, of course, carries its own pragmatic problems with it - not the least of these being that the physicians in question frequently are unaware of the very distinction, let alone how it enters their evaluation, analysis and presentation. However, unless some way is devised to alert the decision makers, the judgment based on the medical data may be askew from an ethical point of view.

---

62. For a caustic critique of traditional models, see Martin Shapiro, *Getting Doctored* (Kitchener, 1978).

63. I.e., "Above all, do no harm." *Cf.* Beauchamp and Childress, *supra*, note 34, Chapter 4.

64. For various discussions of this, see Marvin Kohl (ed.), *Infanticide and the Value of Life* (Prometheus, 1978), Chapter IV. See also *Euthanasia, Aiding Suicide and Cessation of Treatment*, Working Paper 28 of the Law Reform Commission of Canada (Ottawa, 1982) especially pp. 38 ff. and 58 ff.

65. See note 59 *supra*.

66. *Ibid.*

A prognosis of success implies that intervention does not harm the patient's quality of life. We have already indicated that quality of life projections are relevant data on which the surrogate may refuse treatment for the incompetent.[67] Quality-of-life considerations, including pain, nausea, mentation, personal functioning, the ability to socialize and sensory awareness are often presented in medical terms as though they were medical data. However, it is the evaluation of these by an individual that imbues them with ethical significance. Without that interpretative element these factors would be neutral, and would carry no weight. For this reason, quality of life considerations should not be presented purely as medical data. They ought to be introduced as they are, medical data interpreted according to a particular scale of values.

There remains a danger that parents will attribute undue significance to medical facts because of what is *not* said. The significance of a particular fact depends on its context. A failure to describe that context adequately is distortion of the data. It may give the impression that all the relevant factors are on the table, subject to no further conditions. A deliberate failure to disclose relevant data is the ethical equivalent of lying.[68]

Presentation of medical data must be complete, untouched by censorship. The limit is relevance; not all information is relevant to the decisional process. There is a correlation between gravity of implication and need to know - a correlation that will be intuitively appreciated by the reasonable person. Consequently an objective standard of complete disclosure must be followed, a standard which is grounded in the ethics of informed consent.[69]

To sum up: medical data, clearly, completely and appropriately presented and properly circumscribed as to bias and orientation, form the basis of all neonatal decision-making. Data must be presented to the best ability of the physician and in keeping with the level of sophistication of the surrogate decision-maker. The assumption that ethical weight inheres in medical data, determining of itself what ought to be done, is erroneous. Whatever weight medical data carry is a function of the valuational systems employed; a non-medical parameter. The best that medical data offer are preludes for making such evaluations.

---

67. See the opinion of Brachtenback, J., in *Matter of Bertha Colyer*, 660 P. 2d 738 (Sup. Ct. Wash., 1983).

68. *Cf.* Sissela Bok, *Lying: Moral Choices in Public and Private Life* (New York, 1978).

69. For a legal reflection, see *Reibl* v. *Hughes* (1980), 14 C.C.L.T. 1 (S.C.C.).

(iii) Paramedical Data

Paramedical data, including social, familial, legal and financial facts, are often important in the decisional process. Paramedical data are relevant because they are an integral part of the context the neonate inhabits. The important ethical question transcends relevance; it concerns the weight of paramedical facts in the decisional balance.

Paramedical factors pertain to assessment of quality of life. Man is a social animal. The quality of life he leads is partly determined by his ability to interact with others. If ability to interact is gravely impaired by health, quality of life is diminished. These considerations weigh against treatment that would prolong an existence incapable of significant interpersonal interaction. If the opportunity for acceptance and integration into the family is low or non-existent, that factor also weighs negatively from a quality of life perspective.

Paramedical data must be adduced with great caution. It is exceedingly difficult to judge how an individual neonate would react to his environment. The variations of personal reaction are wellnigh impossible to assess.

Paramedical considerations are *not* appropriate when adduced in a calculative way. To be sure, costs may be assessed from a utilitarian standpoint and quantified in decision-theoretical conflict matrices.[70] Nevertheless, from a deontological perspective, negative social, familial and financial considerations entail an obligation to ameliorate these conditions so that fundamental rights belonging to the neonate *qua* person can be met.

Deontological considerations need not eschew the use of paramedical data. The neonate exists in familial and social contexts. On both levels there are competing rights to personal autonomy and health care resources. Resources are limited. It is important to consider whether a reasonable person, in view of the quality of life that may be achieved, would exercise his right to medical care. Paramedical data of resource limitation play a crucial role here because quality of life is very much a function of just and fair distribution within the available. In a just society, neonates may not be disadvantaged in access to resources by accidents of birth. Society must provide social programmes and assistance to ensure that fairness and justice are preserved. Neither may

---

70. See Anthony Shaw, "Who Should Die and Who Should Decide?", in Kohl, *supra* note 64; M.C. Weinstein and W.B. Stason, "Foundations of Cost-Effectiveness Analysis for Health and Medical Practice," *New England Journal of Medicine* 296 (1972), 716-21. See also Ellis, *supra*, note 2.

families be penalized unfairly by what for them is also an accident of fate. Life-style and aspirations, rights and expectations must not be curtailed unfairly because of unfortunate happenstance which, given greater resources, the family would handle with equanimity.

One suggestion to prevent this unfair situation from developing is to permit infanticide for resource-poor families to preserve the rights of the family and its autonomy. The proposal is ethically unacceptable. We cannot punish the neonate for his bad luck of the draw in parents. The proper solution is to recognize that the burden of limited resources must be born by society as a whole. This does not mean that society should shoulder all the burden in every case. There are limits to neonatal expenditure. These influence the quality of life that may reasonably be expected. An ethically correct analysis of neonatal expenditure may suggest reassignment of priorities in expenditure categories in order to prevent unjustly penalizing neonate and family alike.[71]

(b) Values

The values held by participants in the decision-making process are critical to the outcome. It is easy to see why; they lend weight to raw data. Without them, data would be neutral, and would entail no obligation to act. One cannot get an "ought" from an "is".[72] What values are ethically justified in this context, and to what degree?

There are various valuational systems, both ethical and non-ethical. We have identified the former as usually represented by deontological and utilitarian approaches. The latter find focus in religious, aesthetic, psychological, and cultural beliefs. We have already considered the ethical system. Here we focus on the non-ethical. For the sake of expository convenience and in keeping with their actual predominance, we shall consider them under the rubrics of religious and non-religious values.

(i) Religious values

Assessment of religious values in surrogate decision contexts is as simple as it is negative. Religious values are entirely out of place.

---

71. For a somewhat different analysis, see Elizabeth Telfer, "Justice, Welfare and Health Care," *Journal of Medical Ethics* 2 (Sept. 1976) pp. 107-11; D.F. Beauchamp, "Public Health and Social Justice," *Inquiry*, 13:1 (March 1976) pp. 3-14; R. Sade, "Medical Care as a Right; A Refutation," *New England Journal of Medicine*, 285:1288-92 (1971); and Beauchamp and Childress, *supra* note 34, Chapter VI. See also Rawls, *supra*, note 2, Chapters II and V.

72. There is a plethora of analyses dealing with the relation of facts to obligations. For an introductory discussion, see Brandt, *Ethical Theory* Chapters 14 and 15; A.I. Melden (ed.), *Essays in Moral Philosophy* (Univ. of Washington Press, 1958).

In the case of the normal competent adult who becomes incompetent and requires surrogate administration of his rights, the expression of beliefs and opinions previously held are crucially relevant. To ignore or contravene these would constitute a grave violation of rights.[73] For the surrogate decision-maker to substitute his own convictions would be ethically unacceptable.[74]

The defective neonate differs. He has no religious beliefs, and hence no religious values. The religion of his parents, which may be some indication of the beliefs and values that he would come to hold, is not an unfailing indicator. His possible future views cannot serve as the basis of a decision in the here and now. The only other way in which religious values could enter would be from an objective standpoint. If it could be shown that the reasonable person would accept certain religious beliefs and values as correct, and would use them as determinants in his decision-making, then they would have a legitimate role to play. This is not the case. There is no objectively correct religion, no objective way of adjudicating competing claims. Different groups within society adhere to different religious beliefs and values without any suggestion of diminished competence. No particular set may be ascribed to the "reasonable person". These constitute imponderables. Consequently, it is ethically unacceptable to employ religious values when deciding for the neonate.

The ethical unacceptability of religious values is also revealed by state activity in its *parens patriae* role. Organized government is mandated to preserve the rights of the individual according to principles of equity and justice. The neonate is entitled to the state's protection. Different religions place different values on life and quality of life. Justice and equity demand that life and death decisions for neonates do not hang on the biological accident of parentage. To attach weight to the religious values of the parents, or of anyone in authority, would be to do just that. Justice and equity prohibit discrimination based on religious values. It is comforting to know that this conclusion accords well with the preponderance of cases that have reached the level of judicial determination. From an ethical standpoint, the ultimate question is whether the decision is ethically acceptable, not whether it conforms to particular religious values. Religious values may provoke ethically indefensible decisions. A state which disdains to interfere with such a decision out of misunderstood notions of family autonomy misjudges the ethics of the situation, and is derelict in its *parens patriae* role.

---

73. See note 62 *supra*.

74. See M.T. Sullivan, *op. cit.*

(ii) Non-religious values

Certain values may be grouped under philosophy of life considerations. For example, aesthetic values attached to human appearance influence the weight accorded a judgment of hideous deformity in the decisional balance.

Philosophy of life values go to quality of life, and as such their consideration is neither irrational nor unethical. A philosophy-of-life that does not value pleasure over pain, satisfaction over dissatisfaction and happiness over unhappiness is neither reasonable nor implementable in practise. Relevance admitted, a further question arises as to their orientation.

As previously established, the surrogate cannot orient himself to the neonate's philosophy of life. That leaves three choices: the subjective orientation of the surrogate himself, the standards of the medical profession, and the objective orientation of the "reasonable person". The first is ethically unacceptable for the same reasons as are religious values. The professional standard, *mutatis mutandis*, is equally subject to this critique, writ large. That leaves the reasonable person standard, to which we see no ethical objection.

IV. THE NATURE OF THE ACTION

We turn now to the nature of the action that concludes the decisional process. Ethically, negative decisions are most controversial. Negative decisions require that medical intervention cease, and the newborn be permitted to die. "Nature is allowed to take its course." Outright killing by the physician appears to be rare.

This action is justified on a distinction between killing and letting die, between active and passive euthanasia. The contention is also advanced that while treatment may be withheld without moral objection in the first instance, it would be unethical to stop treatment once initiated.

If the morality of these distinctions is untenable, the reasoning and choices based on them will require careful re-examination.

1. Active v. Passive Euthanasia

The distinction between killing and letting die, between active and passive euthanasia, figures prominently in medical and religious discussion of deliberate death.[75] On this distinction a failure to treat the defective newborn is adjudged acceptable; active termination is deemed murderous. The distinction itself is supported by three considerations: passive euthanasia lacks an intent-to-kill; it lacks causal determinancy; it leaves open the possibility of cure because death is not certain.[76]

The first argument assumes that whoever refrains from overt, physical action, from expending energy to alter the foreseen sequence of events, is content to let nature take its course. He does not "intend" the death of the neonate as the outcome. His relevant intent is to prevent the lengthening of suffering by artificial means. From an ethical standpoint, it is argued, this intent is laudatory, and exonerates the decision-maker from any blame.

---

75. See Kluge, *The Ethics*, Chapter 1.

76. There is a fourth attempt to establish the difference that is sometimes encountered. Active euthanasia, in contradistinction to passive, brutalizes the agent. However, so far from establishing an ethical difference, this reasoning simply assumes it and argues on the basis of that assumption that therefore active euthanasia is ethically objectionable. It harms the agent. To proceed thus, however, is to beg the central question. Furthermore, as should be clear by now and will be clearer in what follows, brutalization of the agent is not a difference in any case. Passive euthanasia may involve (or at least lead to) just as callous an attitude on part of the agent, as active euthanasia. In fact, probably more so, because it requires that the agent face with equanimity the dehumanized quality of life which has been described by Engelhardt as "the injury of continued existence".

The second argument concentrates on the absence of physical activity. No act, in the ethically relevant sense, has occurred. Since moral culpability attaches only to acts, *a fortiori* it cannot attach to a purely passive stance.[77]

The third argument builds on recent developments in deontic logic[78] and action theory.[79] It reasons that the point in time at which the action/non-action option is open to the decision-maker is one where various outcomes are possible, depending on what decision is made. Active killing excludes all but one possible outcome death. All possibility of recovery, miraculous or otherwise, is ruled out. Indeterminacy and possibility pervade non-intervention. Consequently, it is concluded, there is a moral difference.

The first argument ignores that death is the *raison d'être* of the position, not a happenstance by-product. The decision-maker opts for non-action precisely because he believes non-action will lead to death. If the surrogate expected non-intervention to result in continued existence of the neonate, he would feel morally obliged to interfere with procedures designed to improve quality of life. Only because he expects death to result does the surrogate refrain from action. The surrogate's intent inheres in his awareness of the impending death, and his decision not to interfere *in spite of* the expected death. Death is "intended", and is nonetheless so because the intent is executed by deliberate omission as opposed to action.

The second argument errs in identifying lack of causal determinancy with absence of action. What is ethically important about acts and omissions is the way they determine the course of events to a forseeable outcome, not the expenditure of energy. Omissions may exclude other possible outcomes to the same degree as acts. To refrain from acting is merely a peculiarity of implementation. The parameter of deliberate determination is what lends ethical significance. If blame attaches to deliberate determination of the course of events resulting in death, an omission calculated to bring death about does not alter the ethics of assessment. The claim fails to distinguish ethics from physics. It confuses the question 'does blame attach to the deliberate determination of a course of events' with the question, 'was energy

---

77. For a variant analysis, see Walton, *op. cit.* Chapter VII.

78. See Walton, *op. cit.*

79. See Lennart Aquist, "Modal Logic with Subjunctive Conditionals and Dispositional Predicates," *Journal of Symbolic Logic* 2:1-76 (1973); D.N. Walton, "Modal Logic and Agency", *Logique et Analyse* (1975) 69-75:103-111.

expended to bring about the result?' The argument from lack of causal determinancy fails.

The argument from exclusion of possibilities assumes that allowance for a remote possibility or an extraordinary turn in the established course of events alters the ethics of the decision. The decision not to interfere is based on an awareness of what is likely to happen. That awareness may include the belief that a miraculous turn of events is always possible; the decision not to act positively may, at least in part, be motivated by the desire not to exclude this possibility. Nevertheless, decision-making in the ethical context must follow standards of reasonableness, and must be in accord with the principle of best action. Miraculous events cannot and do not form part of the data-base of a decision maker. To stand by , knowing full well the likely outcome, is like watching a drowning child flounder without intervening. In each instance, nature will take its course. Barring the unforeseen and unforeseeable passage of a boat, the child will drown. Barring a miraculous turn of events, the neonate will die. To maintain that no moral gravamen attaches to non-treatment because the possibility of recovery is not ruled out is like saying that no gravamen attaches to watching the child drown because the possibility of a passing vessel is not actively excluded.

While the facts of the argument cannot be disputed, their ethical import can. If there had been no awareness of miraculous possibilities, each situation would immediately be judged as culpable. Awareness of a remote possibility does not alter this judgment, unless intangible, incalculable and irrational possibilities form a basis for rational action. We would not excuse the negligence of someone who ran out of gasoline, because his decision not to fill up was based on awareness that a miracle might fill it. The ethical judgment of omitting to intervene medically in hopes of a miracle is the same.

The three attempts to establish an ethical difference between a positive and a negative causal sense, therefore, fail. The distinction between active and passive euthanasia falls with them. What is ethically important is the act or omission which deliberately determines the course of events. This is not to say that the distinction lacks psychological significance. Its psychological impact is tremendous. But we must reject any claim of ethical import.

Our conclusion does not imply that active and passive euthanasia are ethically acceptable or unacceptable. We merely conclude that the ethical status of deliberately terminating neonatal life is independent of whether the means are active or passive.

2. Start/stop v. no start at all

Alea in acta est ! Caesar's pronouncement captures well the position of those many who maintain that once treatment has been initiated, an overriding obligation to continue obtains. The attitude underlies the view that one ought not initiate life-saving or supporting measures for neonates of doubtful viability until a positive prognosis obtains;[80] for once treatment is started, it would be unethical to stop. To initiate action and then to stop is said to prolong the suffering of the neonate in the first instance, only to abandon him later on. By treating the neonate, the physician has acquired or accepted the obligation to do all that is in his power to save or sustain the child's life. If the physician is not willing to accept that obligation, he ought not initiate treatment.

Our survey of medical practise suggests that this reasoning is persuasive in many neonatal units. It is a specific application of the widespread thesis that inception of medical intervention is *de facto* acceptance of the duty of care.[81]

Even if we grant that a general duty of care arises with inception of treatment, care is not synonymous with the unrelenting struggle to save life. The duty of care, initially expressed as an obligation to save or sustain life, may be transformed by circumstances into a duty to provide palliative treatment only. To act otherwise may be to abandon care for the monomaniacal exercise of professional expertise.

If inception entails duty, that duty must be considered in context. The quality of life that is expected to result from treatment is crucial. Procedures are initiated in the expectation they will produce a certain quality of life. When that expectation is not met, the *raison d'être* for treating dissolves. The obligation to continue vanishes with it. If this were not the case, we could imagine horrible scenarios where the neonate is subjected to incessant medical intervention although it produced nothing but suffering. No justification exists to posit an obligation to continue under these circumstances.

Every obligation must be discharged in accordance with the principle of best action. It must be predicated on the reasonably available facts and proceed within the boundaries of what is ethically acceptable *per se*, according to the best ability of the agent in question. When the

---

80. See Walton, *On Defining*, pp. 149 ff. See Chapter 1, *supra*, where this view is implemented by giving the newborn a 'trial of life'.

81. This seems to underlie Paul Ramsey's position in *The Patient as Person* (Yale University Press, 1970), especially Chapter 3. See also Hilda Regier, "Judge Rules ...," *Journal of Legal Medicine* 3:10 (Nov.-Dec., 1975) at 10.

situation changes, the ethical manifestation of the obligation changes too. The original choice may no longe. constitute the best action. Under different circumstances earlier choices may become unethical. Even if we assume inception of a given procedure constitutes *de facto* acceptance of an obligation of care, that obligation may change with circumstances; it is not a duty to perform particular actions forever, no matter what.

The contention that treatment must be continued, once begun, is ethically mistaken. We must not assume that the ethically relevant determinants of a neonatal decision are given at the outset, once and for all. That assumption may lead to the situation stigmatized as torture unto death - "the injury of continued existence."

It is mandatory to re-evaluate and reassess the situation constantly. When all hope for life of acceptable quality is destroyed, intervention should cease. In certain cases high regard for principles of self determination and autonomy may require the surrogate to opt for ending the belaboured existence as quickly and painlessly as possible.

These considerations have special significance for high-risk low birth-weight infants. One third of this population develops normally; two thirds fail to achieve an acceptable quality of life. Our discussion implies that - subject to an evaluation of feasibility, fairness and likelihood of improvement - all such infants should be treated aggressively in the expectation of future improvement. Subsequent re-evaluation will distinguish those neonates who have potential for development from those who have none. Principle suggests that where treatment is initiated in high hopes of success, but results only in unacceptable levels of suffering with no further expectation of improvement, life saving treatment ought to be discontinued. The indeterminancy has been removed. Suffering neonates, without potential for development, are entitled to a "fair and easy passage", with active assistance if necessary. This last point follows from our discussion which fails to find relevant distinction between active and passive euthanasia.

We may generalize for interim care. Interim care may be initiated only when there is reasonable expectation of a positive outcome with an acceptable quality of life. Interim care may not be initiated nor continued for its own sake, because such care is possible, or in the expectation of a miracle. Decisions must accord with the principle of best action.

It is sometimes difficult psychologically for parents to let their offspring go. This is manifest in a clinging to any shred of hope, with sublime disregard for the ethics of the situation. Physicians share a corresponding psychological inability to see death as anything but personal failure. The inability to accept death is buttressed by what is thought to be an ethical justification. It is perceived that to stop acting, when more could be done, is tantamount to a deliberate decision for death, morally equivalent to murder. As our previous discussion has shown, however, this mistakes the truth. The moral acceptability of decisions for death do not depend on deliberateness. Nor can it be gauged by whether more could be done. The decision must be evaluated by the reasonableness of continued action and the expectation for ensuing quality of life, in the context of resource-availability and the balancing of individual rights. There is no hard and fast answer that condemns or praises all decisions for death. Each case is unique.

3. The Team Approach: The Ethics of Shared Responsibility

In Chapter 1, we detailed how neonatal decision-making is a team process for doctors. The team model holds when the context is expanded to include parents and nursing staff. The result is a decision to which many have contributed. The question arises: who carries the ethical gravamen for the decision?

One might suggest that the ethical burden redounds to the executive in the team. This thesis has been defended on the basis of the master-servant relationship, and also on the bald assertion that executive power entails ultimate responsibility.

The master-servant relationship inaccurately characterizes the workings of modern medical teams. Among physicians a collegial, consultative relationship obtains. As we showed in Chapter 2, the theoretical position of the neonatologist as team leader is insufficient to attract the master-servant model. Perhaps with due allowances, that description helps to understand the relation between physician and nurse. Nurses follow orders. They do not participate in the decisional process as autonomous equals.

This description even of the nurse's role is dated. Nevertheless, were it correct, no ethical implication follows that the nurse is less of an autonomous moral agent. She has still the obligation to evaluate the aims and actions of the team prior to participating, and a further obligation to re-evaluate the situation on an ongoing basis. If she chooses to execute the tasks delegated to her, she endorses the relevant decision.[82] It follows that the nurse's lack of decisional power is not in itself

---

82. This follows from her position as an autonomous agent. According to the various recognized codes of Nursing Ethics, the nurse always may withdraw when her conscience so requires.

ethically exculpating. As a result of *de facto* endorsement, she equally bears the ethical burden of the decision.

Just as a subservient role does not exculpate the nurse, neither does consultative, non-executive participation exculpate other members of the team. To be sure, one individual does have the final say. Nevertheless, that fact must be weighed against the continued participation of team members, and its implication of *de facto* endorsement.

Is responsibility not lessened to some extent if the individual is not in an executive position? This brings us to the second line of reasoning: the claim that ethical responsibility inheres in executive position.

The ethically relevant questions are: did the participants understand the decision, and agree to it knowingly? Did they knowingly continue participation in the efforts of the team? Ethical responsibility adheres to the participants, commensurate with their degree of knowledge, competence and understanding of the decision's import, and voluntary agreement to participate in its implementation, not with their theoretical position in the decisional hierarchy.

We have assumed that the individual's contributive action is essential to the final outcome. Variations here may lessen the degree of moral responsibility. An individual whose contribution is less essential than that of another cannot be equally responsible with the latter, even though that individual's knowledge and expertise be greater. Professional competence and position on the one hand, and nature of contribution on the other, are the ethically relevant parameters when apportioning responsibility. Executive position is merely the reflection of a pragmatic or culturally necessary need to have an identifiable decision-maker.[83] It amounts to no more than an administrative idiosyncrasy. From an ethical standpoint, the fundamental fact of individual decision-making is all-decisive.

---

83. For other models of decision-making, see Alex C. Michalos, *Foundations of Decision-Making* (Ottawa: Canadian Library of Philosophy, 1978), Chapter II.

V. ETHICAL PRINCIPLES

Our discussion has considered various parameters of neonatal deci-sion-making. We have highlighted what is correct, and what is objec-tionable. We have tried to delineate the general ethical factors that ought to govern ethical dilemmas arising in the intensive care nursery. Although we have amplified on this initial sketch, we have not probed fundamental ethical principles, or their interrelations, which bear on the decision. A full treatment of this would belong to a treatise on theoretical ethics, and by that token transcends the present work. Nevertheless, it will be useful to explore deontologically oriented prin-ciples relevant to neonatal decision-making in a more comprehensive and coherent form. This will serve not only as a check against which to compare the preceding analyses. It will also function as a *vade mecum*: a guide to future decision-making.

Ethical problems in the intensive care nursery orbit around one central axis - surrogate administration of rights. The neonate is a person. In ethics, this implies autonomy. The neonate also exists in a social context. This implies relative equality in entitlement to rights. Newborn rights require proxy administration which concentrates on justice to the neonate and to the constellation of social forces in which he exists. The ethical problems we have detailed revolve around these consid-erations. Ethical dilemmas would be minimized if neonatal decision-makers have scrupulous regard to the respective rights and autonomy of *all* actors, particularly the neonate.

This brings us to the principles involved in balancing these rights, and to our promise to clarify. We may identify six principles relevant to balancing competing rights in newborn intensive care: the principles of autonomy, priority, impossibility, best action, relevant difference and justice.

1. *Principle of Autonomy*: **All persons have the right to self-deter-mination limited only by unjustified infringement of the rights of others.**

Any action which derogates from the autonomous status of a person or which treats individuals as objects instead of moral agents is ethi-cally unacceptable. Violation of this principle is apparent to the extent the neonate is treated as a research object to see how far a given method of treatment can be pushed; to the extent he is treated as an object of emotional succor and aid for parents, instead of as an indi-vidual in his own right; or where the decision for treatment is made solely on a cost/benefit basis.

The principle of autonomy is equally infringed by unjustified arrogation of decisional power by physician or judiciary. Parents are the ethically proper decision-maker. They are *in statu personae* for the neonate; they wear the mantle of their child's autonomy. Unjustified interference with parental decisions, paternalism, to put it bluntly[84] - violates the neonate's autonomy and his ethical status as a person.

There will be situations where, because of emotional, cognitive or psychological problems, parents are unable to exercise their child's autonomy in an ethically appropriate fashion. In these cases external arrogation of power is justified.[85] This is not a case of paternalism, but a situation where the proxy decisional authority (temporarily) has shifted. In all other cases, parental autonomy must be respected.

The principle of autonomy has further implications. Whoever the proxy decision-maker may be, he must not exercise rights as though they are duties. It is incorrect that failure to insist on the neonate's rights to life and medical care constitutes dereliction of duty. Ethically, rights differ from duties in that rights *may* be exercised at the discretion of the holder; duties *must* be performed: there is no discretion.

The surrogate decision-maker, in assuming the autonomy of the neonate *qua* person, must not forget that the neonate enjoys discretion to forego his right to medical care in appropriate circumstances. Refusal to countenance this possibility violates the neonate's autonomy. Autonomy entails the capacity to make genuine choices. Surrogates personally unable to bear this responsibility must pass the mantle of authority to others.

2. *Principle of Priority*: **Rights can be ranked according to priority. We identify priority of three kinds: logical, natural and voluntary.**

a. *Logical Priority: If a right can be exercised if and only if a particular condition is satisfied, then the right includes the right to bring about that condition, and the latter right is logically prior to and more fundamental than the former.*

This is particularly well illustrated in situations involving the balancing of rights, as with the rights to life and health care. The neonate's right

---

84. For an analysis of paternalism, see Gerald Dworkin, *et. al.*, *supra*, note 37a.

85. That arrogation, however, must follow the ethical lines indicated in the preceding discussion. Furthermore, it will be entirely natural because it really is nothing other than a response to what amounts to incompetence of the parents. To characterize it as external interference, therefore, as is frequently done - even as justified interference - is to put the point in a misleading fashion.

to health-care can be exercised only if he is alive. The right to life is a precondition for the right to health care, and hence more fundamental. The right to life takes precedence, not merely in the individual case but in all cases. The same principle applies to the right to attempt a certain quality of life.[86] The right to life takes precedence over all others in balancing the rights of neonate, family and society.

b. Natural Priority: Rights that arise out of the nature of the situation take precedence over conventional rights that are grounded in voluntary agreement.

The right to an equitable level of health care takes precedence over the right to elective medical procedures contracted for between physician and client. The right to medical services necessary for ensuring functional health status outranks the right to cosmetic treatment with no functional implications. In situations of conflict between fundamental neonatal rights and institutionally established rights of procedures having no other basis, the latter are outranked.

c. Voluntary Priority: Every competent person may voluntarily subordinate his prior or more basic rights to posterior or less basic rights.

This differs from the right to forego the exercise of a particular right altogether. It concerns the re-ordering of the ranking of rights. An individual may voluntarily restructure the order of his rights such that his right to life is outranked by the posterior right to a certain quality of life. In the neonatal context the surrogate has the right to reorder priorities in this way. It is here that parents, medical professionals and judiciary make many errors. Refusal to accept the reordering of rights in accordance with the dictates of reasonableness too often results in the injury of forced existence.

The principle of priority entails that, although there is an overall *a priori* structure which defines the interrelationship between rights, that structure is not absolute. It may be adjusted for good and sufficient reason.

---

86. "To attempt" - not to have. There is no right to a certain quality of life as such, any more than there is a right to health. There is a right to try to attain it, but no-one is blameable because it cannot be reached by certain members of society.

3. *Principle of Impossibility*: **A right which cannot be fulfilled under the circumstances is ineffective as a right. An obligation which cannot be met under the circumstances ceases to be an obligation. One is never obliged to demand or do the impossible.**

This principle ought to play an important role in the balancing process, even though it is not a ranking parameter. The right to life, for example, is paramount. Suppose that careful prognosis indicates the neonate faces agonizing death within six months no matter what is done.[87] Medicine can keep the neonate alive for a short while. There is no hope for a normal life span. Insistence on the neonate's right to life, thus, demands the impossible. At this juncture the principle of impossibility becomes relevant, and entails that the right to life is no longer effective. There is no ethical obligation to attempt or continue efforts that predictably will end in failure. All other rights take precedence by default.

4. *Principle of Best Action*: **He who has an obligation, has the ethical duty to discharge it in the best manner possible under the circumstances.**

This principle entails that the discharge of an obligation cannot be determined in advance, nor settled once and for all occasions. The manner in which an obligation ought to be discharged is determined by the practical parameters of the situation. The obligation will likely express itself in different ways on different occasions. The ethically responsible proxy should ascertain the best data relevant to each situation, and adopt the course of action most likely to satisfy the obligation in the best fashion. An acceptable procedure in one case is not so in another. What benefits the neonate in one case would contravene the principle of best action in another. The principle may render a particular right ineffective because all the routes that lead to the fulfillment of that right also lead to a deterioration of the status of the neonate.

This principle is sometimes called the Principle of Beneficence. That is a misnomer, and at the same time is too narrow. It is not an obligation to do good, but to do the best possible under the circumstances.

---

87. See Kluge, "Euthanasia of Radically Defective Neonates", for a case along these lines.

5. *Principle of Relevant Difference*: **A right is effective to the degree that nothing in the relevant situation contravenes the conditions on which it came into being.**

In neonatal decision-making this principle becomes relevant to ranking the rights of the family unit and of society. In some instances conditions creating the right to health care arise from actions over which the right holder had some degree of knowledge and control. For example, the need for increased medical services for a defective neonate may result from parental smoking, alcohol consumption, drug abuse or a foreseeable genetic condition. Although the neonate's rights must still be fulfilled, the right of parents to increased social assistance is reduced in proportion to their culpability in bringing about the defective state. Parents must bear a proportionately larger part of the burden. Reduced social assistance for parents is limited by the need to respect the rights of the neonate. Nevertheless, the general relation remains.

With respect to the neonate: his unusual position of need, which is not self-induced, marks out a relevant difference that increases his right to health care beyond the normal.

6. *Principle of Justice*: **A right is effective only to the degree that it promotes or preserves justice.**

The right to medical expenditure is limited.[88] Greater-than-average medical expenditure for a group requires justification since it interferes with competing rights-of-access to medical care. The principle of justice requires that allowance be made for the difference in starting positions in life that fate inflicts on defective newborns. If the right of the defective neonate to health care were the same as that of all other persons, his disadvantaged position would be perpetuated. That is unjust.

Are there limits to the increased resources which should be allocated to defective newborns? The answer is yes. The principle of justice requires that relevant adjustments should not themselves introduce injustice.

We have described the principles governing neonatal rights and corresponding obligations. None of these principles is unique to the neonatal context. The difference between neonates and others is that the parameters that hold for all manifest themselves in unique circumstances, not that special principles apply. We may go further. Any attempt to introduce special and unique ethical parameters in this

---

88. *Cf.* note 54 *supra*.

context is mistaken. The radically defective neonate is nothing more nor less than an incompetent person in need of an unusually high level of medical care. His claims must be evaluated and administered like those of all other persons.

VI. CONCLUSION

Commentators on the ethics of neonatal decision-making often ask: "Who has the right to make the decision?" We might rephrase: "Who has the obligation?" This avoids the plethora of problems centering in conflicts with professional power. It also brings the ethical basis of the issue into fuller focus. The situation requires surrogate decision-making. The central consideration is how best to administer the infant's rights.[89] If the neonate is a person, the administration of his rights must follow the same pattern as all surrogate decision-making. The sole difference is that no indication of subjective preference can be forthcoming.

The primary consideration can never be social utility. It must be the preservation and balance of rights according to the principle of best action. The obligation of decision-making falls to those who, more than any other, are responsible for the existence of the child and who, by virtue of proximity and acquaintance, are best able to evaluate the global state of affairs. This identifies the parents as the primary decision-makers.[90]

Parents should not make decisions on the basis of personal preference. They should use objective standards. Medical data will be crucial. These must be supplied in a manner understandable by and useful to the primary decision-makers, and without personal censorship on the part of the physician. The role of medical and nursing personnel is critical to developing and interpreting this data for parents.

Paramedical data are relevant because they supply deontic and ethical significance to facts otherwise purely clinical and neutral. Socio-economic, psychological and cultural data are equally significant. The surrogate decision is a quality-of-life decision, a decision as to whether exercise of the right to life would be reasonable under the circumstances. It must be evaluated in the context of competing rights of others and of limited resources. Such considerations are therefore appropriate. In resorting to these criteria, decision-makers should ensure that the evaluation process does not become a mechanical exercise of utilitarian calculus.

The surrogate must keep in mind that whereas the neonate's claim to health-care is great, it is not unlimited. Others also have rights. The principle of justice demands that apportionment of what initially seemed

---

89. If the infant is not a person, there is no problem. The ethical issue arises only in situations where personhood is present. See Kluge, "Infanticide."

90. *Matter of Colyer*, 660 P. 2d 738 (Sup. Ct. Wash., 1983).

fair, does not constitute reverse discrimination. The effect of this constraint is a functionally variable ceiling on the amount of neonatal expenditure.

It must always be remembered that the ethical justification of surrogate decision-making is the obligation to administer the rights of an incompetent. The wisdom distilled by several courts is therefore telling: "An incompetent's right to refuse treatment should be equal to a competent's right to do so." The rights to life and treatment must not be turned into duties. Once the decision to refuse has been made, the action that follows should not constitute *de facto* punishment of the incompetent. All palliative measures that are normally employed to ease passing should be utilized. The surrogate decision to refuse treatment is a quality-of-life decision. It is scarcely consistent with this to allow the infant to die of dehydration or starvation.[91] An ethically acceptable proceeding requires the administration of medicaments of an appropriate nature and in sufficiently large doses to make for "a fair and easy passage."[92]

---

91. *Cf.* Kluge, "Euthanasia", pp. 255-257.

92. Francis Bacon, *Advancement of Learning*, p. 163.

CHAPTER FOUR

GIVING THE HEMLOCK: A POLICY PROPOSAL

CHAPTER FOUR

GIVING THE HEMLOCK: A POLICY PROPOSAL

I. INTRODUCTION

Death is allowed, sometimes even hoped for, in the intensive care nursery. Actively or passively,[1] directly or indirectly,[2] deliberate death is an essential feature of newborn intensive care. Neonates are allowed to die for medical, ethical, even financial reasons.[3] There is no unanimity of criteria for deciding on death, for identifying those who will decide, or for the manner in which death occurs.[4] From a legal perspective, infanticide is a crime, though charges rarely are laid and convictions are even rarer. We have seen that deliberate neonatal death is not ethically objectionable in all cases. In some instances there may be an obligation to bring the death about.

These points, taken together, present a conflicted whole. Practice opposes law, law conflicts with ethics, ethics contravenes practice. This state of affairs is disagreeable from the standpoint of social practice and of social morality. Social practice is unacceptable if it violates ethi-

---

1. This is not an endorsement of the ethics of the distinction. See Chapter III, *supra*. T.S. Ellis, III, Letting Defective Babies Die: Who Decides?" (1982), 7 American Journal of Law and Medicine 398. Cf. Working Paper 28 of the Law Reform Commission of Canada, *Euthanasia, Aiding Suicide and Cessation of Treatment* (Ottawa, 1982), p. 8.

2. See 1 *supra*. See also E.-H.W. Kluge, *The Ethics of Deliberate Death* (National University Publications, 1981), pp. 14 f.

3. See 1 *supra*. See Chapter I, *supra*. Joseph Margolis, "Human Life: Its Worth and Bringing It to an End," in Marvin Kohl, ed., *Infanticide and the Value of Life* (Prometheus, 1978), p. 189. But see Karen Metzler, "If There's a Life, Make it Worth Living," *op. cit.*, at p. 172 ff.; T.S. Ellis, *op. cit.*, p. 421. An interesting discussion is found in E.W.D. Young, "Caring for Disabled Infants," *Hastings Center Report*, 13:4 (August 1983), 15-18.

4. Cf. Crane, *op. cit.*. See also Working Paper 28, p. 9.

cal principles, professional tradition notwithstanding. Laws which contribute to this situation are pernicious.

The present chapter aims to sketch a model for deliberate neonatal death circumscribed within ethically acceptable and pragmatically workable limits. Our model includes evaluative criteria, decision-making structures and a statutory amendment.

We divide our discussion into several parts. The first deals with the need for standardized criteria and procedures of implementation; the second details the parameters of decision-making and the criteria involved; the third considers who shall perform the act; and the fourth elucidates the precise nature of the act in question. We conclude with statutory proposals.

II. THE NEED FOR STANDARDIZED CRITERIA AND PROCEDURES

Standardized criteria and publicly known procedures are required by ethics, law and pragmatics.

1. Ethics

Our previous treatment of this topic has established that in some instances euthanatizing radically defective neonates is not merely permissible, but obligatory.[5] We argued that neonates are persons and, therefore, *ceteris paribus*, have the same rights as others. Quality-of-life criteria as well as the principles of autonomy, fairness, impossibility and best action were central to our argument. The danger exists that unless these ethical parameters are clearly identified and spelled out in a publicly accessible fashion and enshrined in statute law, ethical practice will remain piecemeal and haphazard. The point is not that there is something ethically magical or salutory about formal structures and regulations but that, absent an assumption of unfailing ethical insight by decision-makers and actors alike, it is highly likely that the individual idiosyncracies that distinguish individuals will continue to lead to differences in practice which in any other context would be branded as injustice. The ethical acceptability of deliberate neonatal death should not be compromised by personal preferences of individual decision-makers nor perverted by chance variations in implementation. Decision-making and action should not be allowed to diverge because of non-ethical variables like parental religious attitudes, preferences of individual health care practitioners, or vagaries of law enforcement.

Statutory revision is also mandated by a factual ethical parameter: the absence of ethical sophistication on the part of most actors in the neonatal drama. This absence is accounted for in part by the lack of ethical training that professionals as well as laymen receive — in other words, is a personal parameter — and in part is circumstantial. Not much can be done about the former except to provide guiding statutes. The latter can be remedied in a similar fashion. The sailor caught in a gale cannot begin to devise and acquire nautical techniques or the art of navigation. Indeed, he would be foolish were he to venture forth without being adequately prepared. Likewise here. Where time is of the essence, the decision-maker cannot begin to develop an ethical framework within which to arrive at a conclusion, or puzzle about the general acceptability of neonatal death. The prudent course of action

---

5. See Chapter 3, *supra*, esp. pp. 178, 182, 188.

is to come prepared with ethical guidelines that point the way. Statutory indications are the most readily usable and effective.[6]

The above concerns the ethics of what to do. Legislation should not ignore the decision-making process. The decision-maker exercises the rights of the incompetent in an objective fashion, providing a free and informed consent.[7] In the absence of statutory revision of existing laws, this cannot occur. The conditions of freedom are violated, and with it the principle of autonomy. If the radically defective neonate is a person in the full sense of the term, then the ethics of decision-making require that all options open to others be open to him, administered by his proxy. Any unjustified infringement is a violation of autonomy. We can neither agree with the Criminal Code as extant, nor assent to the Law Reform Commission's recommendations[8] "that the substance of the present provisions of the Criminal Code tending toward the preservation of life be retained," and "that these provisions be extended to apply also where there is a danger of permanent injury to a person's health."[9]

Moral reasoning requires that we go further. Thus, we advocate explicit legalization of passive *and* active euthanasia as a matter of ethical consistency. If suicide is open to the competent individual, as it is,[10] that right should equally be available to the incompetent. This

---

6. Cf. *Euthanasia, Aiding Suicide and Cessation of Treatment*, Report 20 of the Law Reform Commission of Canada (Ottawa, 1983), pp. 9 ff. While the substance of the report differs, the reasoning is the same. See also Ellis, *op. cit.*, at p. 417, especially note 99 for further references.

7. See L.R.C.C., note 1 *supra*, p. 8 ff., 24 ff. Again while we differ in our stance from that adopted by the Commission, the formal rationale is the same. See also *Matter of Colyer*, 660 P. 2d 738 (Sup. Ct. Wash., 1983).

8. Working Paper 28, p. 68.

9. *Medical Treatment and Criminal Law*, Working Paper 26, Law Reform Commission of Canada (Ottawa, 1980), p. 92.

10. This right finds its most obvious legal expression in the 1972 repeal of Section 225 of the Criminal Code of Canada. However, legal sanction of a particular attitude, state of affairs or action is not *eo ipso* a guarantee of its ethical acceptability. It is, therefore, important to note that the right to suicide can be defended from a purely ethical standpoint in at least three different ways: on the basis of the nature of rights, from the presupposition structure of rights, and on the basis of the right to self-determination.
    As to the first, everyone is perceived to have a right to life. Rights, however, differ fundamentally from duties in that whoever has a right may exercise it at his own discretion but need not do so - the choice is his; whereas whoever has a duty must fulfill it when called upon to do so, whether he will or not. It follows that persons deemed to have a right to life as opposed to a duty, have the option of not exercising it. However, an option is not an option if it is (made) in principle impossible for the individual to act on it. Therefore those modes of action that are integrally involved

implies that the surrogate have access to suicide as an option: suicide by agent. Without this, the rights of the incompetent are less than those of the competent, solely because of incompetence[11] — an ethically unjustifiable state of affairs.

2. Law

Statutory recognition of deliberate neonatal death — so it is argued —whether passively or actively imposed, would be too dangerous. It would open the door to misuse,[12] would ignore the uncertainties of human knowledge and the ever-changing face of medical sophistica-

---

in the choice of a certain option and which would allow the individual to effectuate his right, must be open to him. What that means in the present context is that since each person has a right to life and not a duty, he may choose not to exercise that right and hence adopt a course of action, active or passive, that would be an expression of that choice. He may commit suicide actively or passively so long as there are no legitimate supervenient rights on the part of others that would prevent it. (Cf. pp. 34 f *infra*.)

The last clause entrains the second chain of reasoning: the argument from the presupposition structure of rights. Rights can be ranked with respect to priority on the basis of the presupposition relations that obtain among them. For the present context, the operative component of this relation is that the existence of a logically posterior right entails the concomitant existence of the logically prior. Now, it is granted on all sides that, *ceteris paribus*, each competent individual has the right to self-determination: the right to decide how he will live. The right to decide *that* he will live is logically presupposed by the right to decide that he will live in a particular fashion. The latter is a particularization of the former and hence logically posterior to it. It follows that since persons have the right to decide how to live, they have also the right to decide whether to live, with all that this entails.

Finally, the right to suicide may be established on the basis of the right to self-determination. A right is non-existent if it is impossible in principle to exercise it. The options than make it a right rather than a duty must be real. This means that all actions that constitute options must be available to the individual who has the right (subject, of course, to the *ceteris paribus* clause above.) The most fundamental pair of options for a living being is whether to be or not to be. That is the most profound of all choices relating to self-determination. It follows that unless a supervenient rights clause is operative - and that cannot universally be the case, because that would turn the right into a duty - there will be situations in which each competent individual will have the option of choosing deliberate death: Suicide.

For a similar train of reasoning, see Tom L. Beauchamp, "What is Suicide", in Beauchamp and Perlin, eds. *Ethical Issues in Death and Dying* (Prentice Hall, 1978) *q.v.* for a bibliography.

11. *Matter of Colyer*, 660 P. 2d 738 (Sup. Ct. Wash., 1983).

12. Cf. Yale Kamisar, "Some Non-Religious Reasons Against Proposed Mercy-Killing Legislation" (1958), 42 *Minn. Law Rev.* which is a classic statement of the various dangers.

tion,[13] and above all would mark the beginning of a slide down a slippery slope to the legally sanctioned murder of groups deemed undesirable.[14]

We shall neither expand on these objections nor rebut them. We have done so elsewhere.[15] The fact that they are not found entirely persuasive, even within the legal context, is evidenced by the recommendation of the Law Reform Commission that passive euthanasia be decriminalized.[16] Instead, we will focus on some facts that are overlooked by objections and commentaries alike. Not only are extant laws against euthanasia rarely applied, the inspiration of the statutes that prohibit it contradicts the deontological spirit of the common law.[17]

Sections 197-199 and 202-205 of the Criminal Code state that everyone has the legal duty to provide the necessaries of life to a person under his charge if that person is incompetent or otherwise prevented from or incapable of providing them for himself. Case law interprets "necessaries of life" to include medical attention.[18] These sections amply cover radically defective neonates. However, courts do not require strict adherence to the letter of the law.[19] "Appropriate medical treatment" is the deciding parameter. 'Appropriateness' is determined by accepted medical practice.[20] This provides relief from the letter of the

---

13. Cf. Kluge, *The Ethics*, pp. 25-28.

14. See 12 *supra*. See also Kluge, *op. cit.*, pp. 54-59.

15. See Chapter III, *supra*; Kluge, *op. cit.*.

16. Cf. Report 30, pp. 23-28.

17. On lack of application, see Working Paper 28, pp. 8 ff. and especially 20-22.

18. Cf. Walkem, J. in *R.* v. *Brooks*, 9 Brit. Col. L.R. 13 at 18; see also E.-H.W. Kluge, "The Euthanasia of Radically Defective Neonates: Some Statutory Considerations" (1980), 6 *Dal. L.J.* 238.

19. See Chapter II. See also R.S. Duff and A.G.M. Campbell, "Moral Dilemmas in the Special Care Nursery," *New England Journal of Medicine*, 289 (Oct. 25, 1973), 890-894; and J. Lorber, "The Doctor's Duty to Patients and Parents in Profoundly Handicapped Conditions," in D.J. Roy, ed., *Medical Wisdom and Ethics in the Treatment of Severely Defective Newborn and Young Children* (Eden Press, 1978). See also, A.G.M. Campbell, "Which Infants Should Not Receive Interim Care?", *Archives of Disease of Childhood*, 57 (August 1982), 569-571. But see J.M. Freeman, "Ethics and the Decision-Making Process for Defective Children," in Roy, *op. cit.* For readily available albeit somewhat ambiguous Canadian mortality data, see *Vital Statistics* Vol. III, Mortality, which records 4345 perinatal deaths in 1979. If we accept Crane's statistics that 1-3% of pediatricians are willing actively to euthanatize a radically defective neonate, and allowing for variations in neonatal concentrations by centres and specialization allocation, we come upon an approximately figure of 210 deliberate neonatal deaths in 1979.

20. Which, of course, varies. But for particular types of situations the reader is referred to the records detailing death as due to anencephaly, trisomy 13, encephalomeningocele, severe perinatal trauma, and the like.

law. The statutory injunction thus can adjust to changes in circumstances, take idiosyncratic variations of situations into account, and preserve the individuality of the person from sacrifice at the altar of the common good.

Nevertheless, problems remain. The existence of these sections creates the possibility of prosecution. This has already happened in British Columbia, although the Deputy Minister intervened to abort the proceedings. This creates a chilling effect on the development of current neonatal practice along ethically acceptable lines.

Second, it may be doubted whether the case law can reflect what is appropriate. The situation has developed into a vicious circle. The law considers 'appropriate medical practice' that which is generally done in the medical community. However, medical practice, on these issues, has scrupulous regard to what is and what is not likely to result in prosecution. The law looks to medicine, and medicine looks to the law in precisely those cases which require guidance. If the law really wanted to determine what is medically appropriate and then determine the extent of liability and obligation, it would be faced with an insoluble problem. Both doctors and lawyers realize that current standard practice is out of step: not with respect to each other — in light of the scenario just sketched, agreement with each other is a foregone conclusion — but with the world of social reality and public understanding. The situation requires change, and that suggests legislative amendment.

Third, it may be seriously questioned whether the standard of appropriateness, as interpreted in case law, is consistent with similar standards in the informed consent doctrine. To be sure, the latter is not here the issue; but the two are closely related in one relevant respect: both cases pose the question what criteria are appropriate. Should standards be subjective, objective or professional? Recent court cases[23] considering informed consent opt for the objective reasonable person standard precisely because it is considered the appropriate one in matters involving medical action — or lack thereof. This stance, however, would seem to contradict the standard here in issue. The objective, reasonable person standard would retain the reality of an option in favour of death, active or passive; the appropriateness standard, developed in fear of the law, would emasculate that position.[24]

---

23. See our discussion of *Reibl* v. *Hughes* and *Hopp* v. *Lepp* in Chapter II.

24. See the California Supreme Court's recent (Jan. 18, 1984) rejection of Elizabeth Bouvia's request to be allowed to starve herself to death.

The extant statutes, even as interpreted, violate the deontological spirit of the common law. Respect for autonomy of the individual is the touchstone of the common law's deontological orientation. That respect manifests itself in the freedom of individuals to exercise self-determination so long as the rights of others are not infringed unjustifiably. While respect for persons inheres in the provisions mandating proxy decision-making for infants,[25] it is contradicted by the injunction that removes from the proxy decision-maker those options that are open to the competent agent and that alone ground the possibility of autonomy and self determination: the option of saying no to any and all treatment modalities,[26] and of active suicide.[27] Current law thus violates the neonate's status as a person by abridging his autonomy. This cuts against the deontological current of basic legal principles.[28]

It could be argued that the premise of this reasoning is mistaken: the law restrains self-determination where resulting actions would shock the conscience of the community. Laws against obscenity and pornography are examples. 'Autonomy' never implies absolute freedom of choice. The limitations imposed here are therefore consistent with the principle of autonomy, if understood within proper limits.

The objection is wanting. Other limitations are justified[29] by consideration for the rights of others. Rights can be ranked.[30] The right to self-determination with respect to life or death is basic. Interference with it is legitimate only when in conflict with an equally serious right.

---

25. Unless such respect were present, the issue of decision-making itself would never be raised and the whole matter would be disposed of in a routine utilitarian fashion.

26. Unless such options are open, the very confinement of possibilities constitutes a *de facto* constraint on the proxy decision-maker. Any such constraint, however, is a constraint on the freedom of the individual as rested in the proxy. C.F. Lynn and J.F. Childress, "Must Patients Always Be Given Food and Water? ", *Hastings Center Report*, 13:5 (October 1983), 17-21 for a discussion of this and related issues at a general level, especially p. 18 ff.

27. The option of suicide is open to a competent person (see note 10). Making the exercise of that option impossible for the incompetent individual by preventing access, or application of the means thereto, is to constrain choice to only one option: life. That, in turn, is to remove the possibility of choice in any meaningful sense. Therefore, free choice requires the possibility of implementation — which in this case would express itself as agent suicide. Vide Report 20 of the Law Reform Commission, p. 18, for an opposing pragmatically oriented viewpoint.

28. This is one of the more serious flaws in Working Paper 26 of the Law Reform Commission. The mistake focuses in recommendations 3, 10, 18 and 19. The recommendations in effect perpetuate the statutorily sanctioned position of limited autonomy — and thereby limited personhood — for the neonate. See note 23 *infra*.

29. Insofar as they are justified. That, however, is another matter.

30. See Chapter III.

The rights to autonomy and self-determination are hardly outranked by the right not to be subjectively shocked by failure to understand suicide. The comparison therefore fails.

In any case, the objection involves a contradiction. Society allows its competent members to end their existence passively through deliberate inaction, or actively through suicide. The claim of shock and outrage, therefore, cannot be maintained consistently.

Does the fact of the neonate's incompetence make a sufficient ethical difference to allow distinction? We think not because the result would remove the neonate's option to choose not to exercise his right to life. The neonate's right to life would thus become a duty to live.[31] This is precisely what current statutes require. The surrogate's hands are bound with respect to active euthanasia. The right to life of the neonate becomes the duty to live — unless somehow a passive demise can be "appropriately" brought about. This constitutes unjustifiable discrimination, and a contradiction in the law. To be sure, incompetence of the neonate has tremendous significance: "Utter helplessness demands utter protection !"[32] Protection, however, is not the same as perverting right into duty. Protection implies safeguarding rights to the best of our ability. The appropriate course of action is to insure by statute that the proxy administration of the neonate's right to life is carried out as fully, carefully and conscientiously as possible. This requires legislative change.

3. Pragmatic Considerations

The law defines the limits within which an action may or may not be done. Normally, this causes no problem. The congruence between what is legally allowed, ethically correct and practically workable may not always be precise, but the correspondence is sufficiently close to occasion no real difficulty. In the present context, this is not the case. The physician confronted by a radically defective neonate, and faced with the constraints of limited resources, must weigh an ethically acceptable action against the uncertainty of prosecutorial discretion, interpretation of case law, civil suits by parents, interference by welfare authorities, and disciplinary action by his professional association. He is confronted by a series of pragmatic considerations which *prima facie* have little ethical significance, but which he invariably takes into account.

---

31. For the analysis of a specific case, see "In the Matter of Stephen Dawson: Right v. Duty of Health Care," E.-H.W. Kluge, *CMAJ*, 19 (Oct. 18, 1983), especially p. 817.

32. Working Paper 28, pp. 8-9.

Legal threats are the most worrisome. The fact that to date there has been no successful prosecution for failure by a physician to provide the necessaries of life or for promoting neonatal death[33] provides scant comfort to the individual saddled with the burden of decision-making. The letter of the statutory prohibition and the uncertainty of case law hang like the sword of Damocles and interfere with rationality and ethics of the decision process.[34] From a pragmatic standpoint, this is undesirable.

Nor is the reasoning of the Law Reform Commission persuasive on this subject. The Commission claims that the device of prosecutorial discretion and its exercise show "that in the enforcement of the law the justice system is capable of considering the humanitarian and mitigating aspects of the case."[35] That may be true on one level — although it contradicts the criminal law's rejection of motive in contexts such as these.[36] More cogently, discretion can also be construed in another way: as reflecting an awareness by the prosecutorial branch that the law is practically inadequate as it now stands. The Commission's stance equally ignores the pragmatic psychology of decision-making, on which we have just remarked.

Perpetuation of the current state of uncertainty in these quarters is unsettling. As we already documented,[37] it may lead to professional burnout for physicians and nurses. This phenomenon appears to reflect in the exceptionally high turnover in neonatal nursing staff[38] and may well account for the critical shortage of neonatologists.

---

33. The case of Candace Tasczuk in Edmonton may soon constitute an exception. See Chapter I, at p. 36.

34. See Working Paper 28 of the Law Reform Commission of Canada, especially at 26 and 28. The Commission, however, merely states the fact and does not resolve the problem it raises. Furthermore, it will be clear that we cannot subscribe to the Law Reform Commission's opinion (*loc. cit.* at 22) that the ethics of the matter is settled by determining "the degree of social tolerance." That would be true if and only if legal, ethical and social considerations were on the same level. To assume that, however, is to confuse ethics with sociology — an error pointed out by Socrates 2000 years ago. Furthermore, if it were true it would allow the killing of a minority population so long as the practice was socially accepted and sanctioned by law. The assumption speaks for itself.

35. *Ibid.* at 52.

36. Cf. *ibid.* at 25.

37. See Chap. I.

38. *Ibid.*

Few persons engage in professional activities *solely* for personal gratification.[39] Economic necessity constrains individuals to work. This implies adherence to rules, regulations and policies sometimes perceived as archaic and counterproductive. Individuals bear this more or less well so long as the required actions do not threaten their ethical concepts — those concepts that give meaning and direction to life. When that happens, a resulting psychological strain interferes with rational decisional process and personal stability. This imbalance typifies the conflict between legal, practical and ethical motivations in the intensive care nursery. What the professional knows to be ethically correct is legally and therefore practically dangerous; and what be known to be legally and practically correct chafes against his ethical concepts. Our survey suggests that this strain makes burnout a real problem for health care professionals in the intensive care nursery.[40]

But not only the professionals: Parents and other proxy decision-makers are in a similar position. Not, to be sure, with respect to frequency of the situation, but certainly with respect to intensity. They too must attempt a decision under the threat of legal sanction as set forth in statute. The recent B.C. Supreme Court decision in *In Re Stephen Dawson*[41] suggests the judiciary's intention to enforce a strict line, regardless of the catastrophe for parents. In each case, therefore, the conflict between what is ethical and what is legal cannot be dismissed as theoretical. As decision-makers, parents are caught in a real bind.[42]

Even if we ignore these problems, a surfeit of others remain. Hospital administrative structures attempt to operate within the confines of the law. As institutions they cannot routinely formulate policies that are illegal. We know that deliberate death decisions are made within all tertiary care hospitals. Thus, one of two things must occur. Either there is no open analysis of the various criteria and procedures, but decisions are made on an individual and *ad hoc* basis with only a "feel" for what the institution deems right; or there is in-house, informal agreement on such matters which becomes standard practice.

---

39. This is not to say that this is not a partially motivating factor. As to those for whom it is wholly so, the thrust of the ethical difficulties under discussion will be felt less severely because the element of personal necessity is absent.

40. As yet, there is no study of the ethical foundations of burnout.

41. [1983] 3 W.W.R. 613 (B.C.).

42. Currently there is no scientific study on the effect of these constraints on parental decision-making.

In either case pragmatic problems obtain. The first alternative leads to life or death by default.[43] Because no formal parameters have been enunciated, the neonate is treated because it "hadn't been decided not to."[44] Both nature and quality of response under such circumstances will be pragmatically insufficient. In the second scenario there are guidelines, but unique to each centre. Those who work within such units acquire knowledge of them through interaction with their colleagues, on an informal basis. The problem here is failure to profit from inter-institutional fertilization. The perceived necessity of in-house secrecy engenders an isolation which makes consultation across institutional lines difficult. Wide divergence in structures and criteria obtain with no prospect for coherent and harmonious integration.[45]

In the absence of usable guidelines that clearly protect the medical practitioner, a can-do-must-do attitude often prevails.[46] The radically defective neonate may be abused as a result. Medical technology, like medical science, is in the process of rapid expansion. In pioneer hospitals, where newborn intensive care is found, each situation involving a radically defective neonate becomes experimental — an occasion to see how far the limits of medical intervention can be pushed.[47] Qualitative barriers which normally constitute a bar to unmitigated effort are permeable. The practical implications for many neonates is abuse.

Nor is it reasonable to ignore the impact of all this on health care professionals. Legal uncertainty creates an abundance of caution. Professionals tend to go to the limit of what can be done by medical means. The neonate is soon seen as a biological organism, not as a person,[48] to be manipulated in a technically competent fashion so as to achieve maximum results. The neonate becomes "the spina bifida", "the Downs", or "the hydrocephalus" — a depersonalized condition void of rights. He is reduced to the status of a practice object in the eyes of

---

43. Cf. Crane, p. 81 for a similar point.

44. *Loc. cit.*

45. See Chapter I *supra*. See also Crane, *op. cit.*, especially Part II for documentation. See also note 32 *supra*.

46. Cf. Crane, *op. cit.*; and Chap. I, *supra*.

47. Cf. Chapter I, at p. 15. The action amounted to experimentation. For discussion of the latter notion, see D.A. Frenkel, "Human Experimentation: Codes of Ethics," *Legal-Medical Quarterly*, 1:1 (1979), 7-14. On the specific subject of experimentation on children, see Mark S. Frankel, "Social, Legal and Political Responses to Ethical Issues on the Use of Children as Experimental Subjects," *Journal of Social Issues*, 34:2 (1974), at 101-113; and Paul Ramsey, *op. cit.*

48. Cf. Ellis, *op. cit.*

the health care professionals.[49] In the absence of explicit, public and legal guidelines mandating termination, practice may become an end itself. The deleterious effect of this attitude on the morale of non-teaching staff must not be minimized.[50] Pragmatic problems — this time of a staffing nature — will result.

Finally, the problem of resource allocation. The saving and/or sustaining of a radically defective neonate is a resource intensive enterprise with respect to facilities, equipment and personnel. Health care settings in general and hospitals in particular operate within the constraints of a limited budget — limits that are shrinking. Selective allocation of resources is inescapable. In the absence of publicly accessible legal criteria allocation will be *ad hoc*.[51] The statutory restrictions on deliberate death prevent hospital administrations from enunciating as formal policy that which exists in secret. A series of *ad hoc* decisions, each of which may ultimately be illegal, must be scrutinized for underlying rationales, the totality of which must be cobbled together into an informal policy — which may contradict the law. No system of health care administration, whether at the macro- or at the micro-level, can operate efficiently in this setting.

4. The Law Reform Commission Proposal

A solution has been suggested by the Law Reform Commission of Canada in its Working Paper 28. The Commission would decriminalize passive euthanasia for radically defective neonates, but retain in full force the legal ban against active euthanasia.[52] Medical uncertainty in diagnosis and prognosis[53] would therefore present no problem: The possibility of correction would not be ruled out by the act of termi-

---

49. Cf. Crane, *loc. cit.* "In the pediatric nurseries, this was rationalized by saying that if they did not practice on a baby who 'doesn't matter,' they would not know how to use the technique for a normal baby.... . When asked about the influence of professional values upon their decision to treat infants with congenital anomalies, 39 percent of the pediatricians ranked 'Opportunity to learn, practice, or teach new techniques' among the top three out of six items." See also Lynne and Childress, *op. cit.*; Paul Ramsey, *The Patient as Person* (Yale, 1970), p. 128 ff.; Joyce V. Zerwekh, "The Dehydration Question," *Nursing 83* (January 1983), pp. 47-51. But see also Frankel, *op. cit.*

50. See I *supra.* See also Crane, *op. cit.*, p. 79 ff. *et pass.*; and R. and B. Stenson, *The Long Dying of Baby Andrew* (Boston, 1983) for analysis re respirators.

51. See II, *supra.*

52. Working Paper 28, p. 68. This provision is retained in Report 20 of the Commission at p. 31.

53. See 15 *infra.*

nation. Furthermore, the difficulties surrounding non-standard criteria would be avoided by the same criteria for all: palliative treatment only in terminal cases; and in a rather obvious sense the danger of misuse and abuse of treatment modalities would be avoided. Legality would permit public investigation, discussion and analysis — all of which would act as a bar to the idiosyncrasies of individual or local practice. The threat to respect for personal life would not arise because the *raison d'être* of palliative care is the peaceful and dignified demise of the neonate *qua* person. More than this is unnecessary, argues the Commission, because as it says,[54]

> Law exists to meet real needs. The Commission has concluded, inde-
> pendently of all other arguments, that in Canada today, there are
> neither wrongs nor needs sufficiently great to justify overturning a
> well-established tradition based on time-honoured morality.

In short, legalizing active euthanasia is unnecessary.

The Commission's proposals presents difficulties. The facts of the "well-established tradition" which the Commission wishes to legitimate consist in alleviating whatever pain may exist by means of palliative measures and allowing the neonate to die. 'Allowing the neonate to die' translates in practice as death by dehydration and/or starvation.[55] The Commission goes on to justify its position with respect to passive euthanasia as follows:

> [The radically defective neonate] is, at birth, already engaged in the
> process of dying, and medical science is powerless. There is no appro-
> priate treatment, or the treatments which could be applied appear
> to be medically useless. The problem then is identical to that of the
> terminally ill adult. The physician's duty is certainly not to abandon
> the child, any more than he would abandon a dying adult patient,
> but to provide appropriate palliative care and to avoid useless ther-
> apeutic measures.

The views of the Law Reform Commission represent a clearly articulated opposition to the enterprise at hand — at least in its gener-ality — and as such are representative of the type of reasoning legis-lative and professional bodies are wont to employ when considering the topic.[56] For that reason it is important to point out its factual mistakes and to lay bare its logical flaws.

---

54. *Op. cit.*, p. 48.

55. For the use of narcotic analgesics in this context, see *New England Journal of Medicine* (Sept. 15, 1983), p. 614.

56. *Op. cit.*, p. 13.

Let us grant that the law exists to meet real needs. The contention, however, that there is no real need for active euthanasia is mistaken. The mistake is crystallized in the assumption that the radically defective neonate is moribund from the moment of birth, and that the use of "palliative care" does not produce death but merely ensures a qualitatively pleasant demise due to factors other than the withdrawal of the necessaries of life itself. However, as documented by medical researchers,[57] and as the population profile of institutional facilities for congenitally defective individual amply demonstrates, the defect of such a neonate may be so severe that continuation of life would be an assault on the dignity of the person and yet the defect itself may not be inherently fatal.[58] In such a case, there is no possibility of success. Where medical science is powerless, there is no problem. The principle of impossibility applies. One cannot have an obligation to do that which is impossible. Hence no obligation to intervene obtains. Statutory recognition of palliative care only is therefore quite correct. But cases like these do not fall under that rubric. Medical science can save and/ or sustain such a neonate — but only to a life whose quality is abysmal. At this juncture the "time-honoured morality" of the Commission provides no answer because the tradition has never had to face the issue. Here the issue of active euthanasia must be addressed squarely. The Commission fails to do so.

In our previous discussion of the factual parameters of the matter we distinguished four kinds of cases: (1) comatose and vegetative neonates with no reasonable expectation of recovery; (2) neonates with poor quality of life for whom death in all probability is inevitable in the foreseeable future; (3) neonates who will probably not die but whose prognosis is for poor quality of life with no chance for personal development; and (4) neonates whose prognosis as to quality of life is indeterminate if they are kept alive. The Commission does not distinguish between these cases nor does it address the problems posed by them, especially with respect to categories (3) and (4). Yet, these cases have arisen solely out of advances in medical technology. They force us to consider that in particular cases active euthanasia may be preferable to what amounts to torture unto death.

Medical intervention will resolve many indeterminate prognoses into negative ones. In some cases, it will destroy the opportunity for

---

57. Cf. Campbell, *op. cit.*; Duff and Campbell, *op. cit.*; Lorber, *op. cit.*.

58. E.g., severe perinatal trauma, encephalomeningocele, myelomeningocele, etc. See also A.R. Jonsen and M.J. Garland, eds., *Ethics of Intensive Newborn Care* (Berkeley, 1976), for various sorts of cases. See also Keyserlingk, *op. cit.* Chap. III for a general discussion of quality of life — albeit with a different orientation.

passive euthanasia, but fail to produce a life of acceptable quality. Medicine properly intervened when there was hope of success — when the case was indeterminate. The result produced is an unbearable existence. Must medicine become the agent of torture unto death? This constitutes flat contradiction of the ethical foundation on which the decision to intervene is based. Here the same quality of life considerations that mandate passive euthanasia, which the Commission accepts, may entail proxy administration of a person's right to suicide.[59]

Another obvious solution — and one which superficially fits into the Commission's suggestion — is to institute a policy of waiting until conditions arise, like pneumonia or infection, and then restrict treatment to palliation. While this would have the desired effect, it would also abandon the basis on which passive euthanasia is allegedly sanctioned — namely, that the condition itself be fatal — and to use the new and inherently curable condition as a means to effect the desired death. The difference between this and employing medical techniques to bring about death is that the new disease is itself used as a medical tool, and in a deliberate fashion.[60]

All of which brings us to a still more fundamental consideration. The ethical notion which supposedly motivates the decriminalization of passive euthanasia for radically defective neonates is the quality of life criterion. If quality of life dips below a certain minimum, the desire to terminate that life is reasonable. The surrogate may opt for death. In that sense, passive euthanasia is merely passive agent suicide.

The proposed statutory amendment does not focus on quality of life as the enabling condition for passive euthanasia. It concentrates on imminent and inevitable death. By that very token, it does not deal with euthanasia at all: neither active nor passive. The latter deal with the deliberate bringing about of death. The Commission's proposal deals with the nature of prolonged dying: whether it is acceptable to shorten the dying process by palliation or whether all means to prolong life must be employed. At no time has it been legally obligatory to prolong the dying process unreasonably — whether this be the dying process

---

59. The basic assumption here is that to prevent someone from exercising his right unduly is to deprive him of it, and analogously that to allow conditions that prevent that exercise where it is within the power of the second party to remove the impediment is likewise to deprive him of his right. The case of the neonate falls into the latter category. As the person on whom it is incumbent to exercise the neonate's rights, the proxy decision-maker must — if he can — ensure that the latter will not become ineffective because of removable impediments. In these cases, therefore, active euthanasia would simply be agent suicide.

60. See Chap. III, *supra*.

of the neonate or of anyone else.[61] Legalization of passive euthanasia should not ignore the reason for its being proposed in the first instance: the quality of life of the person concerned. Questions of imminent morbidity are beside the point. This means that the enabling condition for application of the statute should be that quality of life has fallen below the level considered acceptable by a reasonable person. The central question from that standpoint is how, most prudently and in the presumptive choices of the neonate under the extant conditions, to bring about an end to unbearable suffering. The distinction between active and passive euthanasia is ethically irrelevant.

The Commission's proposal, and others like it, fail in another respect. Even if imminent death be accepted as the enabling condition for passive euthanasia, there remains the problem of how to determine that condition. Moribundity is not a state that can be absolutely identified independently of all else. Let us recall our discussion about the prognosticative element inherent in any assessment of medical fact. Assessment is a forecast on the basis of an assumption about the action to be taken. A hydrocephalic child usually is deemed moribund unless a shunt is installed; a microcephalic infant with duodenal atresia will die unless the atresia is surgically corrected; and examples could be multiplied. In each instance assessment of imminent morbidity is determined by the amount of intervention and the resources that the practitioner is willing to employ, as well as by the degree of degradation and the quality of life to which the doctor is willing to subject the neonate in his attempt to keep him alive. This last is often the final determinant — which is but to say that whether the neonate is adjudged moribund frequently depends on the evaluative criteria employed in reaching the assessment.

Assessment of the radically defective neonate as unsalvageable and hence moribund is reached by criteria which inherently have little to do with morbidity but have everything to do with whether a given kind of life is deemed worth living. This brings us to the very pragmatic problem of criteria formulation which the rejection of active euthanasia was designed to avoid. From a pragmatic standpoint very little is to be gained by such a move. The ethics has already been made clear.[62]

Finally, there is that most pragmatic of all questions: Will the decriminalization of passive (but not active) euthanasia solve the prob-

---

61. See Working Paper 28 at 65 f. Although the Commission's overall position differs from our own, it appears to agree on this point. It is unclear to us how points (2), (3), (5) and (6) can be reconciled with its overall position on active euthanasia.

62. See Chapter III, *supra*.

lem of resource allocation? Indubitably, it will ameliorate it. The net of passive euthanasia, even when defined in terms of imminent and irremediable death, is sufficiently fine to capture some of the neonates whose attempted life extension would be disproportionately resource intensive. But not all — or even most. Certainly not those who are at the focus of most pragmatically oriented considerations. It is those who despite the low quality of their lives nevertheless can be salvaged and kept alive that constitute the heart of the pragmatic problem. The value of resources committed to their care is out of all proportion to what can be considered reasonable, because it represents resources that must be taken away from other areas of health care. The practical implications of this for the general level of health care are sobering.[63]

All these considerations, whether pragmatically, legally, or ethically oriented, point towards the conclusion for the euthanasia of radically defective neonates, which the Commission dismisses out of hand. It is to consideration of this that we now turn.

---

63. Some indication of an awareness of this is found in Ellis, *op. cit.*, but by and large this aspect has generally been ignored in the present context. Where the parameter has surfaced is in discussion of the nature of death re the question of continuing or discontinuing medical treatment. In this context, however, it is worth keeping in mind that the per diem cost of a radically defective neonate in a hospital or specialized setting is conservatively assumed at $400. If this is multiplied by life expectancy under optimal care conditions, number of individuals affected, the resulting sum staggers budgetary considerations.

III. GENERAL ETHICAL ASPECTS

The primary ethical requisites for an ethically acceptable euthanasia proposal have already been discussed,[64] hence we need merely mention them here. Any such proposal must not be *ad hoc*. It must flow from and be defensible in terms of the same principles that govern ethical behaviour in general. The proposal must be amenable to analysis in terms of proxy administration of an incompetent person's rights in the context of limited resources, competing rights of others, and the expectation of an unacceptable quality of life. The following schematic represents the formal structure of our proposal.

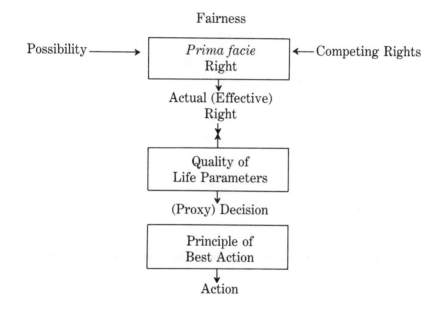

We shall now sketch specific details.

As all other persons, radically defective neonates have the *prima facie* right to health services; in particular, to life saving and/or sustaining treatment. A *prima facie* right is a right considered in isolation. In order to assess its effectiveness in the decisional process, we must consider the context in which it arises. Three parameters are determining: possibility, the competing rights of others, and fairness.

---

64. See Chapter III *supra*.

1. Possibility: Intrinsic and Extrinsic

The principle of impossibility requires the decision-maker to assess whether the neonate's *prima facie* right to life sustaining treatment can be fulfilled. Practically, this entails two considerations; the pragmatic limitations of human actions because of facts of nature, and the particulars of the specific case. These may be called intrinsic and extrinsic possibility respectively.[65]

Intrinsic possibility is well illustrated by the so-called right to health frequently encountered in the literature.[66] To put it bluntly, there is no such right. Health is something which inherently transcends our power to guarantee.[67] Certain biological conditions intrinsic to the individual cannot be overcome, no matter what we do. Genetically determined defects like Tay-Sachs disease and Huntington's chorea fall under this rubric, as do anencephaly and the like. These conditions define the nature of the individual.[68] Their victims cannot be brought to a state of health. The best we can do, even in principle, is to minimize the effects of the condition. That is all.

It follows that the right to health in these circumstances remains *prima facie* only, intrinsically ineffective.

External conditions may also make satisfaction of a right impossible. These conditions may arise from inability on the part of those having the corresponding obligation, or from the circumstances in which the whole situation is embedded. The lack of appropriate expertise, of available resuscitative machinery, incubators, drugs, general facilities and even personnel would be ineffectuating external parameters. Under such conditions, a *prima facie* right to health care remains *prima facie* only, extrinsically ineffective.

2. Ranking of Competing Rights[69]

If a *prima facie* right clears the hurdle of possibility, it must compete with all other rights which also have cleared that hurdle. The task of

---

65. In the logical sense only.

66. Cf. Mark Siegler, "The Physician's Perspective on the Right to Health Care," *Journal of the American Medical Association*, 244:14 (Oct. 3, 1980), 1591-1596; R.M. Veatch, "Just Social Institutions and the Right to Health Care," *Journal of Medicine and Philosophy*, 4:2 (19), 170-173; Gene Outka, "Social Justice and Equal Access to Health Care," *Journal of Religious Ethics*, 2:1 (Spring 1978), 11-32.

67. Cf. Veatch, *op. cit.*, who makes something like this point.

68. E.g., trisomy 13, trisomy 18, anencephaly, etc.

69. What follows must be seen as a propaedeutic to a more completely worked out general ethical structure.

evaluating relative priority arises. Which right takes precedence over which under the circumstances?[70]

Two effectiveness-influencing factors confront the decision-maker. Rights can be ordered on the basis of logic. The right to free speech logically presupposes that the holder be alive. Consequently, if the former right is effective, the latter right exists and is effective. Secondly, certain rights imply actions instrumental to the satisfaction of the right. Under certain circumstances, satisfaction of the right to life is possible only if a certain degree of health care is forthcoming. Under these conditions, the right to life may be said to express itself in the right to health care. Consequently, the right to health care, although itself logically posterior to the right to life, in this instance ranks equally.[71]

Logical relationships as above answer many questions respecting ordering of rights. The real problem concerns conflict between rights of equal rank. Logic provides no solution.

Not all right holders have the same ethical status. Minimally, we can distinguish between competent and incompetent individuals and those who voluntarily remove or subordinate their rights to those of others.[72] Children occupy a special place in the ethical relations that define the social context. Because of their incompetence and greater-than-average need for succor and support, society accords children's rights a preferential status which supervenes competing rights, otherwise of equal rank. Consequently where the right to life (or health care) of a child competes with that of a competent adult, all other things being equal,[73] the former has priority.

We may also distinguish between rights that arise in response to a need and rights that do not. We can then distinguish further situations where the individual is responsible for creating the need, from situations where the need lies beyond his control.[74] Auto-induction of a need, where the individual reasonably could prevent the occurrence,

---

70. We are here assuming exclusivity of satisfaction. If there were no exclusive allocation problem, the question of ranking would have no practical significance.

71. Clearly, more is involved. Completely unrelated, logically independent rights cannot be related in this fashion. However, all rights can be related to the right to life and thus the right to health care. That is all that matters in the present context.

72. Cf. Chapter III *supra*.

73. In other words, the principle of impossibility, etc., not mandating a certain course of action.

74. Or is considered to have no control given the current state of our knowledge and abilities.

lowers a right's priority below competing rights of equal rank which are not auto-induced.

To consider a particular example: Suppose two individuals — a neonate and an adult — suffer from cardio-respiratory conditions that require the use of resuscitative machinery and personnel. Suppose further that the adult's condition results from an imprudence involving smoking, the immoderate use of alcohol, etc., which is preventable. The neonate's condition is not self-induced. Although both persons have the same *prima facie* right, the neonate takes precedence in settings requiring exclusive and discriminatory allocation.[75]

The ranking parameters allow assessment of priority when considering the neonate's medical and paramedical context. This is insufficient. The decision-maker must know how far the priority ranking of others is reduced by these parameters. He also needs to know what to do when, by the criteria just adduced, the ranking of competing *prima facie* rights remains equal.

Everything above provides a decision-schema where individual rights can be evaluated with respect to each other. It is not always possible to engage in one-on-one balancing. In a statistical sense, we know that the rights of *some* individuals will be jeopardized if resources are allocated to make the rights of defective neonates fully effective, because of the effect on the overall resources for health care. The evaluation criteria so far developed are not helpful here. This, however, seems intuitively unacceptable. Is there a way of resolving the problem?

3. Fairness

The answer is yes: in terms of the parameters of fairness. The neonate is not responsible for his health-status, and for that reason his need cannot count against him. However, the cost to satisfy his need can. If the cost oversteps certain limits, his right ceases to be effective.

This solution is *prima facie* reasonable, and meets the misgivings noted above. The difficulty arises with our previous ethical orientation. Are we introducing a calculative utilitarian moment into what had been a qualitative deontological approach? Can we embrace quantitative considerations without contradiction?

---

75. A related question would be, whether the schema thus outlined mandates fetal surgery in preference to adult surgery once fetal development has passed the stage of personhood.

Let us define the problem more precisely. That some rights can be satisfied at lower cost than others of equal rank is not ethically relevant with regard to priorities. To treat matters otherwise would discriminate against the neonate for reasons beyond his control. Nevertheless, no allocation procedure can ignore the impact of the allocation on the rights of others.

When the individuals affected cannot be identified individually, there seems little alternative to considering the rights of the class of individuals we know will be affected. Here the parameters already mentioned come to the fore. Group rights may not be opposed to that of the neonate; nor can the rights of individual members of the group be summed to produce an aggregate to be weighed in the balance.[76] Rights are not additive, nor do they lend themselves to this kind of equation. At the same time, the rights of the group cannot be ignored. That would violate the rights of individual members of the group.

We need to consider the rights of individual members of the group, without falling prey to the temptation of utilitarianism. There is no direct way of doing that. The non-additive, non-calculative nature of rights and obligations excludes direct arithmetic manipulation. We may accomplish this indirectly by considering the rights of individual members of the group as averaged with respect to their health status. The effectiveness of a right is related to the state of affairs that results from its exercise. If that state of affairs can be described as a number, then the effectiveness of the right can also be expressed arithmetically.[77] This allows derivation of a calculative formula for fairness.

That is to say: We are considering the right of access to health care. The state of affairs is the health status of persons. Currently, several evaluative instruments[78] can describe health status. The health status of an individual may be described prior, as well as subsequent, to an allocation of medical resources and these two descriptions may be related as a ratio.[79] A somewhat more complicated procedure, using

76. This is one of the fundamental difficulties besetting the utilitarian approach. It must somehow turn rights into aggregative qualities.

77. It is here assumed that there is a more or less clearly identifiable causal relation between the exercise of the right — in terms of treatment, etc. — and the resulting state of affairs (i.e. health status).

78. The exact choice of which should be adopted will be subject to the same condition of universal applicability as that urged for decision procedures above. As to the complexity of these instruments, modern computerized calculative approaches make evaluation a relatively straightforward matter.

79. The health status before could be represented by $S\frac{B}{P}$, that after as $S\frac{A}{P}$. The relation of $S\frac{B}{P} :: S\frac{A}{P}$ would then be independent of the particular type of instruments used as long as they measured the same factors.

the same instruments but applied to the members of a group, provides numerically expressed health status descriptions which we can average. Once again, we can do this for the group before and after the allocation of resources and represent the result as a ratio.[80] We can then construct a conflict matrix involving the different states of the individual, as opposed to the different average group states. The preferential allocation of resources to the individual over the group is fair if and only if the following conditions are met:

(1) The health status[81] of the individual prior to the allocation of resources is lower than or equal to the average health status of the group prior to the allocation.[82]

(2) The projected[83] average health status of the group after the allocation is not lower than its average health status before.[84]

(3) The projected health status of the individual after the allocation is at least as good as that prior to it.[85]

The principle of justice[86] requires that disparity in health status be equalized.[87] If the health status of a newborn is better than average then, while it would not be unjust to attempt to raise it still further, that attempt must not occur at the expense of the health status of other children. In particular, resources ought not be used that could raise the average neonate's condition to the level of the favoured one. Hence condition (1) above.

The health of a newborn may be average. It would be undesirable to preclude raising the health of the group. This can occur only by raising that of its individual members. This part of (1) allows us to

---

80. I.e., average state of members of the group (calculated by mode, not mean) prior to the action (as opposed to the state projected)

$$\mathop{M}_{S}\,\mathop{B}_{G} :: \mathop{M}_{S}\,\mathop{A}_{G}$$

The reason for using a projected state will be apparent: such a calculation would be useless *ex post facto*.

81. Presumably in such an assessment we would be dealing with a typical health status corrected for momentary variations due to peculiar and non-permanent conditions.

82. I.e., $\mathop{S}_{P}^{B} \leq \mathop{M}_{S}^{B}_{G}$

83. It is here that diagnostic and prognostic competence become crucial. A tutioristic argument might here be raised. For a good example of the latter, albeit in a different context, see D. Walton, *Brain Death*, at 21. For an examination of tutioristic arguments on these points see E.-H.W. Kluge, "Cerebral Death," *Theoretical Medicine*, 5 (1984) 219, 22.

84. $\sim (\mathop{M}_{S}\,\mathop{A}_{G} < \mathop{M}_{S}\,\mathop{B}_{G})$

85. $\mathop{S}_{P}^{A} \geqslant \mathop{S}_{P}^{B}$

86. *Supra*, Chap. III.

87. I.e., the other right-diminishing clauses mentioned above not being operative.

raise the average status of the group by dealing with its members *seriatim*.

The underlying rationale of condition (2) is that rectification of an injustice should not occur by introducing a new injustice, or by unjust means. Therefore, if the lower-than-average health status of a person is considered an injustice, its correction must not perpetuate injustice on others. The individual members of the group are no more responsible for their health status than is the neonate.[88] While the neonate's health should be bettered by the preferential allocation of resources, the limit is reached when the allocation would lower the average health of the group. While preferential allocation is permissible and even mandatory when it keeps within these limits, it becomes unjust when it oversteps them.

Condition (3) reasons that resource allocations which are not expected to maintain even the *status quo* for a damaged newborn must be considered as an attempt to do the impossible. By the Principle of Impossibility, such an allocation can never be an obligation. It may be permissible on a voluntary basis by those whose access to health care resources would be affected, but it will always remain superogatory.[89]

There is also the situation where, although neither retention of nor improvement in the *status quo* is expected, the preferential allocation has the effect of slowing an otherwise rapid deterioration. Is preferential allocation obligatory in such cases? The role of such an allocation is purely palliative. Palliation can be achieved without a loss of rights to others. Ethical principles require a choice of palliative resources which is not detrimental to the health of others.[90]

---

88. A *ceteris paribus* clause again applies.

89. For a discussion of this notion, see Brandt, 1979, pp. 138-148 and 167, etc.

90. We must note an important objection. It is argued that our reasoning is predicated on the false assumption that resource allocation involves disbursement of purely public funds. The reasoning ignores private funding. The availability of private funds changes the situation.

There are several answers to this objection. First, the development of medical technology is not a uniquely medical phenomenon whose results are owned by practitioners of the profession. It is a social phenomenon that draws on the work, resources and even lives of society as a whole over centuries. Private payments to practitioners or institutions on a fee-for-service basis do not defray these costs. Payment to practitioners is for application of the resources; it is not payment to, nor does it oblige society who owns them. Second, there are vast hidden costs in the provision of equipment, buildings, etc. — in short, in the very accessibility of the medical resources. Society defrays them, and individual payment is really no more than a token. Then there is the social cost involved in making trained personnel available in the first instance. Their training, indeed their opportunity to practice, etc., are publicly

It will be apparent that the three conditions outlined are not *ad hoc* — specially tailored to the problem of radically defective neonates. The general schema applies to all allocation problems. This enhances the value of the model since it satisfies the requirement of universality, which is a *sine qua non* of ethical decision-making. The neonatal context is merely a particular application of the general schema. In other words, this approach respects the personhood of all equally while recognizing that the low health status of the radically defective neonate is an ethically relevant feature which requires correction. The point that must be underlined is that here as elsewhere the rectification may not introduce a new imbalance nor may it occur through an injustice.

The question of who constitutes the relevant group, in general as well as in particular applications, is fundamentally important. We have restricted it to children rather than society as a whole. This reflects the thesis that the adult and competent members of society have subordinated their otherwise equal rights to those of the members of society until the latter have attained a state of independence. The only situation in which this does not hold is where any action contradicts the principle of impossibility.

4. Integration

Let us now put all of the above together into a decision-making schema. The process of determining an actual right on the basis of *prima facie* right and its conditioning parameters would look like this:

---

subsidized. Private funding does not reflect this. Finally, health care professions are monopolies. This puts them into a special position. Private funding to defray their cost may well be appropriate, but only so long as it does not interfere with social responsibilities - the responsibilities of fairness to the group — which goes along with the monopoly position.

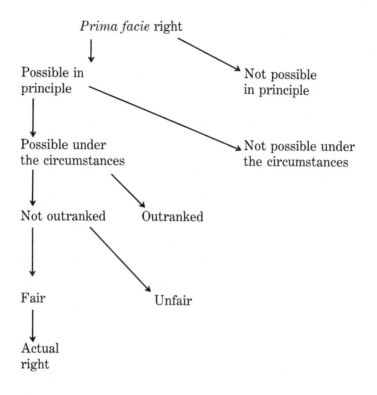

FIGURE 2

The preceding figure does not include the voluntary element, the proxy decision-maker as agent for the neonate. If the neonate's *prima facie* right becomes actual, a question remains whether the proxy decision-maker should insist on those rights. The proxy decision-maker must be as free to reject exercising the right as would be the newborn himself were he competent.

The question that arises at this juncture is what criteria the proxy decision-maker may use to arrive at a decision. Our previous discussion of proxy decision-making here becomes crucial.[93]

Proxy decision-making may be likened to a process of increasing choice limitation as influenced by the constraints we noted in Chapter 3. A graphic representation would look like this:

---

93. Cf. Chapter III *supra*.

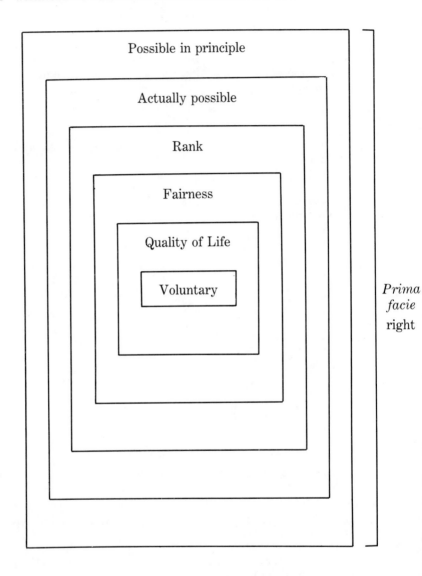

IV. THE ACTION

If the decision favours death, how should that decision be carried out? We have already concluded that active and passive euthanasia stand on the same ethical plane, the choice of one over the other being determined solely by the circumstances. Some conditions which mandate a decision for death are neither painful nor inhumanly undignified. In these cases, all other things being equal,[94] palliation would be entirely appropriate. In others, the individual agonizes or the condition is inhumanly undignified. The proxy ought to have the option of active termination. Our reasoning concluded that it is unethical to foreclose this possibility.[95] A passive stance would not only be logically contradictory; it would commit the injury of continued existence.

1. The Actors

A proxy decision for death is difficult, even when reached in an ethically unimpeachable fashion. The decision that death be actively procured rather than passively allowed to happen is even more difficult. Most difficult of all would be implementing the decision. All participants in the drama of passive euthanasia take solace in the illusion that no one individual can be identified as its agent. Active euthanasia strips the mask from the face of deliberate death. The question of agency moves to the forefront. Who should be the agent to perform the act?

The storm of disclaimers this question produces from professionals and parents alike reflects an important psychological fact. We feel abhorrence when faced with the ethical necessity of active euthanasia. The fear that legalization will start a slippery slide to a horrible social denouement is partly responsible.[96] Yet even when that fear is shown to be groundless, an element of psychological rejection remains.

Our psychological rejection of active euthanasia might be explained by the context in which we are introduced to the notion of active death — murder and execution. This is the only context in which the subject is broached. By the time the acculturation process is complete, it is difficult to approach the topic without the feeling of outrage and revulsion that is appropriate towards such acts in these contexts.[97]

---

94. There being no other overriding duties.

95. See Chapter III *supra*. We are therefore not persuaded by the Law Reform Commission's Report 20, which maintains that active intervention is never acceptable. *Loc. cit.* at p. 18 ff. See also M. Pabst Battin, "The Least Worst Death," *Hastings Center Report*, 13:2 (April 1983), 15. See Ellis, *op. cit.*; Zerwekh, *op. cit.*

96. See Kamisar, *op. cit.*

97. In other words, we are here faced with what in effect is a profoundly effective conditioning process.

That conditioning is distorting. The process of prolonged and agonized dying, of a dehumanized slow slide into death, of a process that is as deliberate on the part of those who are bystanders and more brutal, receives little attention and lacks negative psychological associations. We can speculate over the reasons for this disparity in treatment. Perhaps the frequency of passive euthanasia accounts for our toleration; perhaps the inevitability of death and its accompanying instinctive rejection prompts our refusal to consider the actuality of a passive demise.[98] There may be other factors.[99]

Ethical decision-making must remain uninfluenced by these ethically irrelevant considerations. An ethically responsible participant in the neonatal drama cannot afford the luxury of a psychologically comforting, but ethically reprehensible stance. A society that tortures defective infants to death by starvation and/or dehydration while praising itself on the humanity of its refusal to provide death actively, evidences bizarre contradictions. Those who acquiesce in society's stand on this issue might ask themselves whether the reward of psychological comfort found in conformity to the social norm, and bought at the price of blind conditioning and self-deception, is ultimately worth the price.

With this as a propaedeutic, we return to the question with which we began: Who should be the agent of peaceful, but active and deliberate death?

(a) The Parents

The parents are natural candidates. The considerations that place them first in the order of decision-maker also suggest that they perform the act. They have voluntarily accepted the burden of parenthood. That burden entails the obligations to provide for their child's welfare and to act as his proxy decision-maker. With this burden of care goes the obligation to perform all necessary acts.[100] No one else, the argument concludes, should be saddled with their obligation.

This reasoning is unconvincing. While obligations are implicated in the acceptance of parenthood,[101] this does not mean that all actions

---

98. See Battin, *op. cit.* for some details of the latter.

99. Political and religious considerations come to mind. See Kluge, *The Practice*, Chap. IV. See also Kohl, *Infanticide, passim.*

100. Within limits, of course. We are here exploring one aspect of these limits.

101. We are here assuming voluntary continuation of pregnancy to term under conditions where pregnancy is not itself forced - the usual sort of context. There are exceptions; but it would be a mistake to let the exceptions determine the rule.

that discharge parental obligations must be performed by parents themselves. The parents must decide,[102] but they need not take those actions which they are incapable of performing or which they are not best placed to perform. Parental obligation consists in securing the best qualified, technically competent persons to perform the acts required. Parents do not act as their child's lawyer, nor as his doctor.

Even when parents are health care professionals, the obligation of action does not fall on them, because of the principle of justice. The psychological bond between parent and offspring is usually so strong that to require parental euthanatizing action might do psychological violence. Of course it may not. All depends on the particular case. The parents may see such action for what it is: the ultimate act of respect and kindness. But where this is not the parental attitude, mortal action cannot be required of them. There is only so much that society can expect of its agents. In these cases, and they will be in the majority, the onus of action passes to someone else.

(b) The Nurse

The nurse is appropriately qualified for performing this action. She[103] is responsible for giving medications. She has technical skills.

An argument to the contrary retorts that such an act opposes the ethos of the nursing profession.[104] That ethos — so the argument proceeds — is to promote self-realization for the patient. This is incompatible with the role of death-giver.

A second argument proceeds from the psychological weight of the duty to perform euthanatizing acts. Although nurses are actively and intensely involved in the treatment of radically defective neonates, they have little input into the actual decision process.[105] Consequently, if the burden of carrying out the lethal decision were placed onto her, she would feel forced into a situation where her actions are of ultimate significance but she has no say. Nor would the situation be changed to any appreciable degree were she accorded greater input into the decision process. Formalized health care delivery system entails that there be some persons in position of greater, others in position of lesser authority. In such a system there will always be the danger that those

---

102. See Chapter III *supra*.

103. The use of the female pronoun, here as elsewhere, *mutatis mutandis*, is intended to reflect merely statistical facts.

104. Cf. Storch, *Patients' Rights* (McGraw-Hill-Ryerson, 1982) at 90.

105. See Chapter I *supra*.

who have to perform the delegated tasks will feel cast in the role of someone who has to do "the dirty work" of the decision-maker. In an institutionalized formal health care delivery system the nurse (or her analogue) fulfils the role of the front-line worker and falls into this latter category. The problem would therefore remain. Not all can be decision-makers. The pressures on a front-line worker are tremendous at the best of times; under conditions such as these they would be unbearable.

So the arguments. However, closer consideration shows that they are not unassailable. The argument based on the ethos of the profession is logically unpersuasive. Even if we accept, *arguendo*, the characterization of the profession as correct,[106] the conclusions based on it do not follow. A hopelessly defective biological system may not have functional integrity that could be described as self-realization. Under such circumstances the ethos of the profession would not militate against termination. On the contrary: the argument lies that the ethos would mandate euthanasia because anything else would be to continue that very state of dysfunction which the profession is pledged to fight.

In other words, the refusal to act as death-giver cannot, without more ado, be grounded in the nature of the profession. We can go further: Even in cases where a state of functional integrity could be achieved, the nurse might find it unacceptable to do so. Quality-of-life considerations may well overrule the nurse's professional creed.

The point is perhaps better put in terms familiar from our preceding discussion. The ethics of a profession (as opposed to its ethos) is not something distinct from that which governs conduct generally. Ethical principles are the same for all; the differences reside in the nature of the circumstances in which they manifest themselves. Circumstances may tighten or loosen the obligations that obtain. They do not alter the principles themselves. This means that the rights/obligations that hold for a particular profession cannot stand in conflict with the fundamental ethical principles that govern the behaviour of all. If under certain circumstances it is ethically mandatory that a particular life be ended as quickly and painlessly as possible, and if the principle of best action entails that implementation falls to the nurse, then that act cannot be contrary to the ethics of the profession. To its ethos, yes; but then that has no ethical significance.

The argument based on the nature of the nursing profession therefore collapses; but not the psychological one. This latter is successful

---

106. For a fuller discussion, see E.-H.W. Kluge, "Nursing-Vocation or Profession?", *The Canadian Nurse*, 78:2 (Feb. 1982), 34-36.

because it goes to the heart of the deontological principle that circumscribes social ethics: the principle of autonomy. In the institutional structure where the present problem arises, several professions operate within separate areas of duty and expertise. The nurse's duty entails carrying out decisions made by physicians. Acceptance of a subservient role does not imply voluntary renunciation of ethical autonomy. Every person, the nurse included, retains that right as a condition of personhood. It expresses itself in the right to understand the nature of the action requested as well as in the right to refuse should the act, in her estimation and to the best of her understanding, violate the principles of ethics. Her conscience is here supreme; and forcing her to do the "dirty work" would be a violation of her autonomy. To be sure, there is a risk that she runs when insisting on this option: She may be ethically mistaken. For all that, however, it is her risk to take, and it cannot be removed from her.

At a deeper level, we must remember that the supposed obligation of the nurse is delegated, not original. The basic medical obligation belongs to the physician.[107] Consequently the primary onus of action rests on him. The nurse is employed in these contexts for the sake of pragmatic efficiency and convenience of function.[108] The nurse's request to be excused from performing the lethal act for personal reasons does not amount to a deprivation of rights for the neonate. It means that the obligation of performance reverts to its original base: the physician.

(c) The Physician

But is it really the physician's obligation? We encounter two lines of objection: one based on the social image of the profession, the other on its ethics. The latter argues from tradition: Since time immemorial the code of ethics of the medical profession has expressly forbidden active euthanasia.[109] Consequently, it would be unethical to commit the act.

This reasoning, however, is flawed. What is presented as a code of ethics is not really a code of ethics, but a statement of ethos: a

---

107. *Nota bene*: The medical obligation of service and not, as the Law Reform Commission states, the right/obligation of decision-making, *Op. cit.*, p. 26. See also R.F. Weir, "The Government and Selected Non-treatment of Handicapped Infants," *New England Journal of Medicine*, 309:11 (Sept. 15, 1983), at 663.

108. This is merely a statement about material facts, not ethical desirability. No value judgment is entailed or implied.

109. The C.M.A. *Code of Ethics* (June 1978), "Responsibilities to the Patient" does not explicitly prohibit it but has usually been interpreted in this fashion.

statement of the beliefs and opinions subscribed to by the majority of the profession. While it may have sociological, cultural and even legal significance, it does not guarantee the ethical correctness of its injunctions.

As we previously established, medicine is a monopolistic profession. The monopoly is granted out of consideration for the benefit of society at large. A profession with a monopoly on the administration of medical services must provide those services when there is a legitimate request for them. This holds even when death is an immediate and foreseeable outcome.[110] If the active termination of a particular life is a medical procedure, as it is in the case under discussion, then the monopolistic nature of the profession entails the obligation to perform it. Not, perhaps, on the part of specific physicians, but certainly on the part of the profession as a whole.

The medical profession is in a different position from that of nursing. Ultimate medical responsibility resides in it and its members. The obligation to act medically finds its primary base here. If active euthanasia be required, the responsibility for engaging in it rests on the medical profession which enjoys a monopoly on the neonate's care. Whoever enters the profession voluntarily binds himself to that extent. Merely personal and idiosyncratic reasons lose their force before these considerations. It is inconsistent with the nature of a monopolistic mandate to accept its advantages and then to refuse its duties when they become unpleasant. Only genuine and independent ethical considerations can free individual physicians from such obligation *qua* members of the profession.

We must be careful not to misconstrue the precise line of the medical profession's obligation and the nature of its finality. It is an obligation that rests primarily on the profession as a whole. To be sure, it can be discharged only through the activities of its individual members, and this means that there must be some who will in fact act in the required way. At the same time, however, it does not mean that each and every doctor must so act. Whereas purely personal, non-ethical and idiosyncratic reasons are insufficient to function as an excuse, a refusal on the basis of genuine conscientious objection based on a perception of the ethics of the case is legitimate. In any walk of life,

---

110. In other words, a deontological approach such as ours cannot accept a *post hoc ergo propter hoc* approach. The act itself cannot be defined as unethical because the outcome is unwelcome to those who refuse the right.

conscience is a sufficient reason to refuse a certain activity. The present context is no exception.[111]

But this exception aside: Is the monopolistic nature of the profession really sufficient to ground the physician's obligation to act as death dealer? Even when combined with the assumption that active euthanasia would involve medical tools/techniques in its optimal implementation? Is it not possible to argue that the same service can be supplied with far less serious ramifications by the institution of a professional thanatist: a specialized death-giver? Does not the very nature of the medical profession and its mandate prohibit deliberate and active death-dealing?

We shall address the proposal for a professional thanatist in a moment. As to the nature of the medical profession, the argument equally lies that the nature of the profession embraces active euthanasia within its domain. The charge of the profession is not, the argument would claim, the preservation of life at all costs.[112] Instead, it is to effectuate whatever medical treatment is possible and reasonable under the circumstances. It is to meet the medical needs of members of society insofar as doing so does not violate ethical principles and norms.[113] The actions thus mandated are not invariably curative; not even in intent. Nor are they always in favour of life. They may be merely palliative, as we have seen and as is generally admitted.[114] Medical actions include passive euthanasia. As our previous discussion made clear, passive euthanasia is ethically acceptable, and, in certain cases, obligatory.[115] We argued that when the passive path to death involves an "undue burden" for the suffering individual or otherwise conflicts with the reason for first adopting it, active euthanasia becomes obligatory. If passive euthanasia falls within the domain of medical action, we fail to see why active euthanasia does not as well. The two

---

111. The ethical problem that arises at this juncture — the conflict between what is perceived to be correct and what actually is — is an ancient one which traditionally has been resolved in favour of the primary obligation to follow one's own conscience. At the same time, however, it is recognized that the fact of conviction does not necessarily constitute a complete excuse. The reasonable person standard and the principle of impossibility enter here once again.

112. Cf. Working Paper 28, p. 58 ff.

113. As opposed to medical ethos.

114. Cf. Report 20, L.R.C.C. at 22 ff.

115. Let us emphasize once again that this will be a minority of cases. The smallness of their number does not, however, entail that there is no need for legislation. That need is directly proportional to the need to make sure that the cases are decided in an ethically correct and just fashion.

stand and fall together. Neither the directness of the action nor the speed of its effect constitute ethically relevant differences. If there is ever a medical obligation to "make for a fair and easy passage", then the speed of that passage must be adjusted to the circumstances — and in some cases shortened. Controlling that passage still remains the physician's duty.

The second argument proceeds from the image of the profession. It is claimed that effective medicine requires good will and trust. These qualities would be eroded by an image of the physician as the bringer of death — as "baby killer". Medicine would suffer in consequence.

A certain amount of truth inheres in this reasoning — just as it would in a similar claim raised by any health profession. The elements of trust and goodwill are important to the curative process.[116] Does it follow that the profession's image would suffer if the medical profession assumed responsibility to bring deaths to radically defective neonates? That contention supposes that actively terminating life under the circumstances would be perceived as callous. It is much more reasonable to suppose that if the public were aware that passive euthanasia really means that defective babies die by dehydration, starvation, congestive heart failure, asphyxiation, etc. when "nature is allowed to take its course",[117] the image of the profession would suffer seriously precisely because its members did not actively interfere. Active euthanasia might not be seen as a callous, unfeeling and unspeakable act, but as the kindly intervention of someone who does not falter in his obligation of care.

In short, if any weight attaches to the argument from public image, its conclusion equally cuts the other way. The reason why it currently does not is that the facts of the matter are shrouded in secrecy, opaque to public scrutiny. That situation is changing. In any case, it does not present an ethical barrier to the performance of the act.

(d) The Thanatist

It is tempting to suppose that the problems of a professional nature considered above could be avoided by institutional recognition of a person whose profession is to provide death — the thanatist. Tempting though the suggestion may be, the existence of such a profession would create danger. To see why, we must take a brief excursion into sociology.

---

116. The placebo effect, well know in medical circles, finds its basis here.

117. Cf. Ellis, *op. cit.*; Batin, *op. cit.*

Sociologists are well aware that the existence of an administrative niche for a specialized activity tends to embue it with an aura of legitimacy which allows its practitioners to operate without challenge, independently of the circumstance or occasion. The legal legitimization of a profession gives rise to confusion with the legitimacy of its exercise on a given occasion. Acts of practitioners are presumed legitimate because of the profession's legitimacy. If a profession of thanatists were created, there is danger that questions would not be raised often enough as to the appropriateness of the profession's acts. They would be presumed legitimate.

Furthermore, the profession of thanatist would affect the proxy decisional process by making access to euthanasia too easy. Once the thanatist is a recognized professional, active euthanasia would cease to be an unusual and overwhelmingly weighty decision. Professionalization would give rise to routine. In the absence of professional recognition, the act, though still permissible under the conditions indicated, would remain a more serious, awesome option.

Medicine's traditions and its health-oriented drive operate as pragmatic safeguards against abuse. These work more efficiently than would formal watchdog machinery supervising a new profession. It would be as a mistake to ignore the efficacy of medical tradition as a force that would keep thanatological practice within bounds. Medical traditions would be here appropriate as well as effective. This would be so particularly if the now unjustified concentration of proxy decisional power in the profession were exploded, as we have suggested.[118]

Finally, let us be clear on an important psychological factor. A major reason for the rejection of active euthanasia, both in the public eye as well as from the standpoint of the medical profession, is that the deliberate dealing of death is intimately connected with the image of an executioner. That image would not be shed by isolating the act in a separate profession. It would merely refocus it. What must be seen clearly, through public and medical education, is that the image is artificial and mistaken. Active euthanasia for the radically defective neonate is not an act of execution. It is the compassionate providing of an easy end to an unbearable existence.

---

118. See Chapter III *supra*. For a recent proposal to include the services of an ethicist as part of the decisional process, see *A Proposal for an Ethics Committee,* submitted by the American Academy of Pediatrics in its comments to the Department of Health and Human Services, July 15, 1983, reprinted in *Hastings Center Report,* 13:6 (Dec. 1983) at 6.

2. A Statutory Proposal

It is one thing for the ethics of deliberate neonatal death to be set forth in discussion; another for the conclusions of that discussion to be couched in a form that is implementable in practice. Minimally, there is a bar of legality. The Canadian Criminal Code contains various sections which, if applied, would brand any act of euthanasia, active or passive, as murder.[119] As we have observed, the threat of criminal prosecution prevents many health care professionals and parents from admitting that active and passive euthanasia occur, and restrains informed public discussion of relevant guidelines.[120]

Therein, of course, lies the danger. The physician is not expert in ethics, any more than he is expert in religion. Neither are the parents. By being forced to shroud these decisions in secrecy, physicians and parents must make profoundly ethical decisions without access to ethical consultation, without knowledge of patterns emerging in similar situations, and in an *ad hoc* fashion. The danger of ethical mistake is unreasonably large, and happens too often. The grim drama of lingering neonatal death or of monomaniacal determination to preserve life at all cost occurs every day out of fear of prosecution. There is a sad irony that prosecutions almost invariably fail to materialize because of a prosecutorial discretion that recognizes the ethical validity of deliberate death in the face of an impossible existence.

As we have argued, this situation is unjustifiable. It can be ameliorated by statutory amendment. What follows is a statutory proposal according to the ethical guidelines outlined above.

Section 197 of the Criminal Code is amended by adding immediately after subsection (1) thereof:

S. 197(1.1)
(a) Notwithstanding subsection 1, no one is under a legal duty to provide medical treatment to an infant where the infant displays no reasonable prognosis for cognitive, sapient existence, or no reasonable potential for development to an exist-

---

119. Cf. L.R.C.C., Working Paper 28, p. 8 ff.

120. This is not to say that public discussion and even agreement would settle the ethics of the matter. The consensus approach is no more correct in ethics than it is in sociology, psychology or physics. However, the opportunity for proper analysis would exist and the ethical issues would be clearly identified. Moreover, as was noted above, physicians working in different units would be able to consult and compare notes instead of working in relative isolation. This would undoubtedly be conducive to more trenchant professional discussion, greater awareness and more profound understanding of the issues.

ence of acceptable quality, according to the standards of a person of due discernment.

(b) The prognosis for cognitive, sapient existence and potential for development judgments under paragraph 1.1(a) shall be reviewed as necessary.

(c) The judgments under paragraph 1.1(a) shall be made by the parents or other persons having legal custody of the infant after consultation with the health care professionals directly involved in the case and a third party who is not a health care professional but who has appropriate training in ethics. Where the parents are unable to form judgments under paragraph 1.1(a), upon application, the court shall appoint a guardian for the sole purpose of acting under paragraph 1.1(a).

(d) In all cases that fall under paragraph 1.1(a), upon request by the parents or guardian, the attending physician may employ such measures as he deems, upon due consideration, to be appropriate for terminating the life of the infant as quickly and painlessly as possible.

(e) If the attending physician is unable to act in the manner stated under paragraph 1.1(d) because of conscience or ethical convictions, he shall so advise the parents or guardian and the chief of medical staff immediately. The chief of medical staff shall appoint another physician to act on the case, or assume responsibility for the case himself.

Changes in other sections of the Code will be necessary in order to accommodate these provisions. Sections 205 to 207 and 212 are implicated. These present no further ethical or legal problems, and may be treated as housekeeping matters.

It would be naive to suppose that a statutory proposal like this could be effected easily. The emotional encrustations of the subject are far too great. Still, there is growing recognition, especially from health care professionals, that something like this is necessary. The ethics of the situation demand it. Legislative recognition of passive euthanasia as suggested by the Law Reform Commission[121] does not go far enough; its reasoning is unconvincing, and its ethics are flawed.[122] Prosecutorial discretion, as suggested by the Commission, is an inappropriate mechanism to regulate these serious matters.[123] It is too chancy and erratic to support institutionalization of ethically acceptable active euthanasia.

---

121. *Op. cit.*, at 20.

122. The major one is probably the failure to extend full freedom of choice to the proxy decision-maker.

123. *Op. cit.*, at 20.

We hope that the law, in its statutory expression, will recognize neonates as persons no less than others. If persons have a right to life and not a duty, then *a fortiori* that characterizes the situation of the neonate as well: The neonate's right does not turn into a duty merely because he requires a proxy decision-maker. There is no good reason to deprive the neonate of the possibility of agent suicide — of euthanasia by both active and passive means. This violates the defective newborn's autonomy for no reason other than that he is incapable of acting on his own behalf. We hope Canadian law will recognize that it is unethical to penalize the incompetent newborn for the sole fact of his incompetence.

CHAPTER FIVE

CONTROLLING THE PROCESS

CONTROLLING THE PROCESS

I. INTRODUCTION

What is the best method to regulate medical practice in the intensive care nursery? That is the question we address in this chapter.

Our survey of neonatal medicine, in light of legal and ethical norms, concentrates attention on several discreditable practices common to newborn units. Neonatal units diminish the parents' role in treatment decisions. Experimentation is insufficiently controlled. Consultation among members of the neonatal team is at times inadequate. The use of paramedical data in medical decision making is covert and unscientific, resulting in poor quality data, and insufficient exchange of research about the effectiveness of paramedical facts as a medical indicator. Palliation and starvation are used as slow methods of euthanasia. Few resources of ethical expertise are available to parents in making their momentous decision. Hospitals articulate few or no standards to guide neonatal practice, which in any case is shrouded in secrecy. All of these practices are at best ethically indefensible; in many cases they are open to legal challenge.

On these points neonatal medicine is seriously out of line and requires correction. It is a nice question how best to apply remedial measures and how far to assert continuing legal supervision. The mere enactment of legal prohibitions, as our survey chillingly demonstrates, does not control medical conduct adequately. As we have seen, legal puffery calls forth defiant reactions from organized medicine - "The law be damned".[1] We have seen too that unrefined legal prohibitions can encourage eccentric development of medicine, such as overtreatment of infants who should be allowed to die humanely. Law and medicine chase each other around the mulberry bush, chanting standards unrelated to optimal development of neonatology.

---

1. *Supra*, ch. II, fn. 155b.

Legal regulation of the intensive care nursery ought to incline towards four principal goals: improving neonatal medicine; asserting appropriate societal review and supervision of a self-regulating monopoly; correcting perceived abuses; containing costs. Our survey of neonatal practice implicates all four concerns in any attempt to rethink existing control mechanisms.

Organized medicine has a major stake in insuring that legal regulation of neonatology is sensible and efficient. Unrealistic civil and criminal prescriptions disrupt medicine, producing eccentricities and secrecy. Neonatal decision-making would profit from more specific guidelines on planes where difficult conundrums of law, ethics and medicine intersect. There would be greater possibility for open exchanges between neonatologists themselves. The result would be an improved standard of care for defective newborn children.

Most importantly for a community of honourable and learned professionals who take pride in their traditions and accomplishments, correcting tainted practices will buttress society's confidence that a self-regulating medical profession is able to respond to the perplexing challenges erupting in the intensive care nursery. The privilege of self-regulation rests ultimately on society's confidence that by self-regulation society's interests are best protected, including the interests of its vulnerable newborns.

In Chapter Two we explained how, in theory, civil and criminal liability are relevant to the disquieting practices just reviewed. We might well ask whether, in view of the parents' recourse to civil courts and society's ability by criminal process to compel adherence to its norms, further regulatory machinery is necessary.

To our knowledge civil liability has never been used to control any of the tainted practices we have described as characterizing neonatal medicine. Court actions are unlikely to be so used. The torts system throws the primary onus of action on the parents and requires them alone to bear the staggering costs of a malpractice suit. Our survey demonstrates that parents rarely know that all is not as it should be. Parents are not in a position to question seriously the statement, "We're sorry. Your child just didn't have what it takes to live".[2] They cannot really discover whether their decisional role has been diminished; whether all possible treatment has been provided; whether experimentation occurred; whether appropriate consultation took place according to accepted institutional routines; or whether poor quality

---

2. *Supra*, Ch. I, p. 15.

paramedical data factored into the decisional formula. Even if parents had access to the facts - which they do not - it is unrealistic to expect them to act. They have been numbed by tragedy. Damages recoverable would be insignificant. Costs are prohibitive, and potentially punitive if the suit fails. In truth, civil liability for questionable neonatal practice is more theoretical than real. No serious commentator would suggest reliance on private malpractice suits as a primary regulator of neonatal medicine.[3]

Criminal liability is equally unrealistic. Doctors are not criminals, nor should medicine be regulated by unrestrained application of the draconian criminal sanction. Besides, while prosecution is possible in theory, it virtually never happens in practice. The onus of criminal proof is a formidable obstacle. Doctors are politically powerful; prosecutorial discretion is almost always exercised in their favour. The Crown and courts sympathize with the doctor's difficult position. That is why there are virtually no trials. The few cases which have been reported provoked hostile reaction from legal and medical professions alike.[4] There has never been a conviction.

It is doubtful that these cases increase detection of medical deviance. On the contrary, detection probably becomes more difficult as the medical profession closes ranks out of a sense of self-protection, bolstered by realization of the neonatologist's difficult position and the sense of the harshness of what is done to him (which, after all, is true). Our survey indicates that malpractice and criminal actions produce their own form of medical deviance - overly aggressive treatment, in fear of the law.

Civil and criminal trials are sensational. They weaken the public's confidence in medicine and break down the trust necessary to the doctor-patient relationship. Lawsuits attacking doctors impinge on professional morale. They should be the last resort as a regulatory device,

---

3. The Report of the *Hospital for Sick Children Review Committee* (hereinafter "The Dubin Report") (Toronto: Queens Printer, 1983), p. 70, suggested that hospital liability be intensified to embrace "all physicians practising within the Hospital, be they employees or not". This would reverse the decision of the Ontario Court of Appeal in *Yepremian* v. *Scarborough General Hospital* (1980), 110 D.L.R. (3d) 513. Whatever the merits of this proposal (see J.E. Magnet, *Corporate Negligence as a Basis for Hospital Liability* (1979), 6 C.C.L.T. 121; J.E. Magnet, *Preventing Medical Malpractice in Hospitals: Perspectives from Law and Policy* (1979), 3 Legal-Medical Q. 197), it fails in our opinion to meet the critical questions of the nature and extent of regulation required for the intensive care nursery.

4. Newman, *The Ethical Dilemma* (1983), The Medical J. of Australia 252; *After the Trial at Leicester* (1981), 2 The Lancet 1085.

not the first. For all these reasons, we must look beyond the civil and criminal sanctions to regulate neonatology and to protect defective newborn children.

Apart from civil and criminal liability, three options are available as regulatory mechanisms: external administrative review and enforcement; internal administrative review and enforcement; diffusion of responsibility to ethics committees and prognosis boards.

II. EXTERNAL ADMINISTRATIVE REGULATION

In Canada, there has been little experience with external administrative supervision of neonatal medicine. In theory, Provincial Ministries of Health have widespread powers over hospital administration and treatment. Taking Ontario as a model, the organization and operation of hospitals are subject to plenary ministerial control. The Minister must approve all hospital by-laws; he may require hospitals to enact by-laws.[4a] He may regulate treatment protocols in neonatology directly[4b], by establishing treatment criteria applicable either throughout the Province, to specific hospitals or even to a specific case.

These powers have not been exercised in neonatology to date. The Government has been content to give full sway to self regulation in the difficult dilemmas erupting in the intensive care nursery. The legislation itself premises a self-regulatory structure, including a process whereby treatment criteria may be generated, reviewed and compliance measured in each hospital. The process is three tiered. Department heads have power to advise the Medical Advisory Committee on the quality of medicine in the department and may receive power to make rules respecting treatment.[4c] The Medical Advisory Committee must supervise the practice of medicine in the hospital.[4d] Ultimate responsibility rests with the Hospital Board, through its corporate powers including its corporate and statutory powers to make by-laws, and its duty to enforce statutory and internal rules.[4e]

Nevertheless, there is very little rule-making in neonatal units. While Ministry inaction in neonatology is understandable, and to some extent desirable, failure of hospitals to make internal provision for matters of such critical importance is not. One reason for internal inaction relates to a felt need for secrecy about neonatal practice. What little policy is articulated does not result from systematic research which would insure that the policy embodies the current state of medical knowledge. In fact, this is a problem characteristic of hospital medicine generally: generation of standards is too often an *ad hoc*, unscien-

---

4a. *Public Hospitals Act*, R.S.O. 1980, c. 14, ss. 9, 29. See also discussion in ch. II, note 301 and accompanying text.

4b. *Public Hospitals Act*, R.S.O. 1980, c. 14, ss. 9, 29 (1)(j).

4c. *Public Hospitals Act*, R.S.O. 1980, c. 14, s. 31(1)(2).

4d. *Public Hospitals Act*, R.S.O. 1980, c. 14, s. 32; R.R.O. 1980, Reg. 865, s. 7(6).

4e. R.R.O. 1980, Reg. 865, s.3.

tific process, the chemistry of which is a mystery.[4f] In neonatology certain discreditable practices are too widespread and well known to professionals to be ignored by those responsible to review and supervise the intensive care nursery. Those in positions of responsibility have unjustifiably failed to act.

At Toronto's Hospital for Sick Children, for example, the minutes of the Medical Advisory Committee reveal that the Committee had abdicated its responsibility for supervision to the department heads. The Medical Advisory Committee engaged in "little discussion of clinical care and clinical problems in the hospital. . . the feeling appears to prevail that all clinical matters are the responsibility of the Chiefs of Departments and the assessment of clinical care is entirely the responsibility of the chiefs. . .".[4g] This implies that the Board was inadequately informed about problems in neonatology since it relied principally on advice from the Medical Advisory Committee. At the same time, the department heads were failing to deal with neonatal dilemmas on their own.

The Dubin Committee suggested that "the Medical Advisory Committee should review its terms of reference and its agenda to ensure that it is fulfilling the responsibilities assigned to it by the Board and by the *Public Hospitals Act*."[4h] In our view, the matter cannot be left there. The dramatic deaths at the Hospital for Sick Children concentrate attention to the need for adequate outside input to insure correction of unjustifiable neonatal practices and a more rational development of neonatal medicine. This implies, in our view, gentle exercise of the hitherto dormant ministerial power to stipulate for treatment criteria and protocols in the intensive care nursery.

We suggest that the Ministry require neonatal units to formulate treatment criteria which can withstand scientific and community scrutiny. Initiation of standards should be left as much as possible with hospital organs, as comports with the self-regulatory model. Establishment of a province-wide Standards Review Board would perform the dual role of insuring that standards are set according to which hospitals can meet their obligations to review and supervise neonatal units; and establish a research forum whereby standards generated by different units can be evaluated against each other. The constitution of the Standards Review Board and publicity of its work would provide

---

4f. Weisman *et al.*, *Hospital Decision Making: What is the Nurse's Role?*, The Journal of Nursing Administration, Sept. 1981, p. 31.

4g. *The Dubin Report*, pp. 62, 64.

4h. *Id.*, p. 64.

an effective channel for inputting public conscience into the development of a specialty which profoundly touches public morality. We defer more specific elaboration of this proposal to a later section in this chapter.

Under 1981 amendments to the Ontario *Public Hospitals Act*,[5] the Minister may appoint investigators to report on the quality of care and treatment of patients in a hospital. Upon receipt of an unsatisfactory report the Lieutenant-Governor-in-Council may appoint a hospital supervisor for the purpose of improving the hospital's quality of care. These provisions were used to establish the special Review Committee at the Hospital for Sick Children in Toronto [the "Dubin Committee"]. They are extraordinary provisions, introduced to deal with perception by the public that widespread and uncontrolled criminal acts had resulted in the deaths of thirty-one children under the Hospital's care.

On completion of the Dubin Committee's Report, the Minister of Health forwarded the Committee's recommendations to each hospital with a neonatal unit. The Minister required the hospitals to respond to the committee's criticisms and recommendations. Hospitals were asked to indicate what measures would be taken in response, what recommendations would not be implemented and why. The Ministry has not published a follow-up report to date.

Ontario appointed a second inquiry [the "Grange Commission"] in order to determine the causes behind the deaths at the Hospital for Sick Children. The Commission has held widely publicized hearings on a matter that deeply troubles the public conscience. Its *Report* appears to be inconclusive. The Government of Ontario is now faced with two prickly problems. It must address the highly sensitive question how best to satisfy the public clamor for decisive action against those responsible for perceived wrongdoing. At the same time, Ontario must channel governmental intervention into modalities designed to foster improvements in the hospital's ongoing routines. The Government will have to tread carefully, for if it too intricately involves itself in day-to-day hospital care on an ongoing basis, it may diminish those important benefits flowing from self-regulation by the profession. No external body could ever appreciate as fully as the doctors on the scene the intimate clinical factors which present themselves in every complicated neonatal case. Organization of neonatology, as with other medical disciplines, has been predicated on self-regulation and teamwork by profes-

---

5. S.O. 1981, C. 25, s. 1 enacting ss. 7a and 7b. By Reg. 865 under the *Public Hospitals Act*, R.S.O. 1980, c. 410, s. 61, the Minister of Health receives hospital reports of all neonatal deaths. This appears to be for statistical purposes only.

sionals in the front lines. If the government takes action which effectively replaces self-regulation, it must ensure that it is equal to the critically important regulatory task which the medical profession has so far performed.

Perhaps governments can discharge these functions if this is found necessary to protect the public interest. It is nevertheless worth observing that governmental intervention of this type has never been proven to work. We do know that major disruptions in the machinery of self-regulation can be very expensive, and produce serious negative effects on neonatal, and other fields of medical care, as is occurring through the enforcement by the United States Government of the "Baby Doe Regulations", discussed hereinafter.

The Canadian Council on Hospital Accreditation reserves theoretical power to withdraw a hospital's accreditation if it were to conclude that the hospital's standard of neonatal care was too low. This has never happened, and it would appear an unlikely event. Accreditation teams do survey neonatal units and it would be open to them to make suggestions for improvements in neonatal care in their Report to the hospital. This voluntary process could serve as a useful mechanism to bring to light neonatal deviance hitherto shrouded in darkness. In the normal course of events, the Report would find its way into the hands of the Minister. A combination of embarrassment and the spectre of ministerial review could make this process effective for controlling neonatal deviance, were the C.C.H.A. to examine whether the neonatal ward had seriously attempted to establish a criteria making structure, and to control deviance from accepted criteria.

In the United States external administrative interference is the advancing wave on which the Federal administration is attempting to overrun neonatology with its political judgments and moral positions as to the proper course of treatment. Federal action was prompted by media exploitation of Baby Doe's case. Baby Doe was a Bloomington, Indiana child, who was born April 9, 1982, afflicted with Down's Syndrome and a surgically correctible intestinal blockage. The parents refused treatment; State Courts declined to intervene on the hospital's application for guidance. Baby Doe died six days later.

On President Reagan's instructions, the Secretary of Health and Human Services (HHS) issued a notice to health care providers[6a] stat-

---

6a. 47 Fed. Reg. 26027 dated May 18, 1982, published June 16, 1982. The HHS claims that its general authority to investigate breaches of the *Rehabilitation Act, 1973*, extends to investigation of Baby Doe cases. The so-called "Baby Doe Regulations" do not so much confer additional investigatory powers, but rather place certain

ing that s. 504 of the *Rehabilitation Act, 1973*[6b] prohibited hospitals receiving federal financial assistance from withholding food or medical treatment from handicapped infants. Later, claiming to act under the authority of s. 504, the Secretary issued comprehensive regulations [the "Baby Doe Regulations"] providing for administrative investigations and control over neonatal practice.[7]

The first Baby Doe Regulations required health care providers to post permanently in a conspicuous place in the neonatal ward and visible to parents and hospital visitors, a sign which stated:

"DISCRIMINATORY FAILURE TO FEED AND CARE FOR HANDICAPPED INFANTS IN THIS FACILITY IS PROHIBITED BY FEDERAL LAW".

The sign must further state that any person knowing a handicapped baby was being denied food or medical care should contact HHS. HHS has established a 24-hour hotline for this purpose. Callers are guaranteed anonymity. On receipt of a hotline tip HHS may authorize immediate intervention by an HHS investigatory squad to protect the baby's life and health. Health care providers are required to give 24-hour access to hospital records and facilities. Physicians, families and hospital staff must be available for investigative questioning, even while treatment is in progress.[8]

---

responsibilities on hospitals and state Child Protection authorities, and permit "expedited" action on behalf of the newborn child in cases where discriminatory withholding of treatment is found to have occurred.

6b. 29 U.S.C. para. 794. Section 504 provides: "No otherwise qualified handicapped individual in the United States. . .shall, solely by reason of his handicap, be excluded from the participation in, be denied the benefits of, or be subjected to discrimination under any program or activity receiving Federal financial assistance. . . "

7. 48 Fed. Reg. 9630.

8. The Baby Doe Regulations were challenged by the American Academy of Pediatrics, the National Association of Children's Hospitals and Related Institutions, and The Children's Hospital National Medical Centre. They were struck down in Federal District Court (*American Academy of Pediatrics* v. *Heckler*, 561 F. Supp. 395 (U.S.D.C. 1983)) on the narrow procedural ground that they were promulgated in violation of the *Administrative Procedures Act*, 5 U.S.C. para 551. The thrust of this ruling was sustained in *U.S.* v. *University Hospital*, 729 F. (2d) (U.S.C.A. 2nd Cir. 1984, motion for rehearing denied May 17, 1984) 144 on the broader ground that s. 504 did not invest the Secretary with the regulatory powers claimed.

    Prior to the Court of Appeal decision in *U.S.* v. *University Hospital*, the Secretary issued new regulations to cure the procedural defects: see 45 CFR Part 84, 49 Fed. Reg. 8 (January 12, 1984). However, in light of the broader Court of Appeal ruling, it is apparent that the new regulations are unsupported by sufficient regulatory power. In a third ruling the Federal District Court enjoined HHS from enforcing the new regulations: *American Hospital Association* v. *Heckler*, U.S.D.C. June 11, 1984 (unreported). This decision is on appeal at this writing.

Revisions to the Baby Doe Regulations were published in January, 1984. These include provision for voluntary "Infant Care Review Committees" [ICRC], whose composition includes a practising physician, a representative of a disability organization, a practising nurse, "and other individuals". The ICRC would recommend institutional policy concerning withholding treatment, provide advice in specific cases, and review, on a regular basis, infant medical records where treatment has been withheld. The posting requirements have been changed. The notice now must be visible to professionals, but not to families or visitors. The revised rules require State Child Protection agencies to establish procedures for applying state law to protect children from medical neglect. There are guidelines which soften the impact of HHS investigation squads. HHS will initiate preliminary telephone contact with the hospital, and will involve the institutional ICRC, where there is one in place, before determining the need for on-site investigation. HHS will obtain the assistance of a qualified medical consultant to evaluate medical information.

The fight over the Baby Doe Regulations is only beginning. There will be political battles in Congress and affected institutional governing structures; legal battles in the courts on constitutional and administrative grounds. This makes the final form of the Baby Doe regulatory effort impossible to discern. Nevertheless, the Regulations now on the books provide a pointed example of external administrative intervention in neonatology which has generated wide political support[9], and which, therefore, merits close analysis and evaluation.

The Baby Doe Regulations establish a coercive mechanism whereby the Federal administration, under color of its obligation to enforce the *Rehabilitation Act, 1973*, divests parents of their right and duty to make medical decisions for their children, and erodes the doctors' discretion to assess and treat seriously ill newborns. The Regulations were established to insure that cases such as Baby Doe in Bloomington, Indiana will be treated aggressively, even though parents, doctors,

---

Both Houses of Congress have passed separate bills to supply the regulatory power found wanting under s. 504: H.R. 1904 (1983); S. 1003 (1984). Neither provision is in effect at this writing.

9. HHS received nearly 17,000 comments during the comment period. 97.5 pecent of the comments supported the proposed revised rules, 2.5 percent opposed. It is of interest to note that of 141 pediatricians of newborn care specialists answering, 72 percent opposed the rule, 28 percent were in favour; of 253 physicians other than pediatricians and newborn care specialists, 45 percent opposed, 55 percent favoured; of hospital officials and health related associations, 77 percent opposed and 23 percent supported. All associations representing the handicapped supported; 98 percent of nurses supported; 95 percent of parents supported: 49 Fed. Reg. 8, p. 1623.

hospital and the State courts conclude otherwise. In written comments to HHS, Judge Baker, who presided over the *Baby Doe* case, had this to say:

> "The question in the Infant Doe case was, when parents are confronted with two competent medical opinions, one suggesting that corrective surgery may be appropriate and the other suggesting that corrective surgery and extraordinary measures would only be futile acts, does the law allow the parents to select which medical course to follow? It was the decision of the Indiana Court that the law provided the parents with the responsibility of choosing which medical course to follow *without governmental intervention*" (our emphasis).[10]

The Reagan administration disagrees. In its opinion governmental intervention is appropriate and necessary. Through the instrumentality of HHS, the Reagan adminstration is determined to force compliance with its political and moral views.

HHS's intervention is unparalleled in medical history in the depths to which it carries the intrusion of government into the treatment room. Under the Baby Doe Regulations HHS purports directly to assume ultimate responsibility for treatment decisions. HHS claims authority to say what is medically beneficial treatment and what is not; when treatment is indicated and when it is not. HHS reserves to itself, as an administrative matter, power to investigate alleged violations of its moral judgment as to what treatment is appropriate; and to enforce obedience to its judgment through its power to cut off hospital funding. HHS claims an authority to dictate medical action superior to that of parents, doctors and hospitals, even when these latter are buttressed by approval of the courts.

If such unprecedented intervention were warranted, one would expect HHS to articulate clearly the medical standard it seeks to uphold. HHS's first regulatory effort prohibited denying a handicapped infant "customary medical care". This was rather curious, for as the Federal District Court observed, "even the most cursory investigation by the Secretary [of HHS] would have revealed, *there is no customary standard of care* for the treatment of severely defective infants".[11] The revised Regulation enjoins witholding "medically beneficial treatment". This

---

10. Department of Health and Human Services, Office of the Secretary, *Guidelines and Procedures Relating to Health Care for Handicapped Infants*, Appvd. December 30, 1983; 45 C.F.R. part 84 (hereinafter, *HHS Guidelines*), 49 Fed. Reg. 8 (January 12, 1984), p. 1630.

11. *American Academy of Pediatrics* v. *Heckler*, 561 F. Supp. 395, 400 (U.S. D.C. 1983).

change is designed to blunt the Court's criticism without offering any substantive clarification. HHS's commentary makes clear that the administration has no intent to clarify.[12]

Thus, the new Regulation, like the old "purports to set up an enforcement mechanism without defining the violation, and is virtually without meaning beyond its intrinsic *in terrorem* effect".[13]

The failure to provide articulable standards raises grave questions as to the necessity for governmental interference in the first place. By HHS's own assessment its investigators uncovered only three cases over a decade where treatment was discriminatorily withheld. Even in these cases, further information about available medical procedures led to parents and physicians readily agreeing to treat.[14] One is therefore driven to the conclusion that the draconian regulations have not had the effect their supporters desire. The only problem HHS discovered is a problem related to the adequate diffusion of medical knowledge. One must question seriously whether Baby Doe squads are the appropriate means to upgrade medical education.

The American Medical Association noted[15] that the inevitable result flowing from applying the regulations will be overtreatment and infliction of suffering on many seriously ill newborns. As is evident from our previous chapters, and as HHS itself admits,[16] there are appropriate cases for nontreatment. The difficulty with the Baby Doe Regulations is that medical discretion in identifying these cases is impossibly burdened. Doctors and hospitals, out of fear of HHS harrassment and the descent of Baby Doe squads, "will be required to treat a handicapped infant in all cases".[17] Doctors are virtually forced to tell the parents only those things about their child's condition which will lead them to consent to treatment. This is an unwarranted and unjustifiable violation of the legitimate medical and ethical responsibilities of the

---

12. See especially *HHS Guidelines*, 49 Fed. Reg. 8, pp. 1630, 1632.

13. *American Academy of Pediatrics* v. *Heckler*, 561 F. Supp. 395, 400 (U.S. D.C. 1983).

14. Annas, *Baby Doe Redux: Doctors as Child Abusers* (1983), 13(5) Hastings Center Report 26, 27.

15. *HHS Guidelines*, 49 Fed. Reg. 8, p. 1631.

16. *HHS Guidelines*, 49 Fed. Reg. 8, p. 1653.

17. American Medical Association, Comments to the Proposed Rules in *HHS Guidelines*, 49 Fed. Reg. 8, p. 1631.

doctor.[17a] Fear of the administration ought not to be a primary motivator of medical action.

The Baby Doe Regulations equally interfere with parental discretion to choose the medical course of action they deem appropriate for their child. HHS places the hospital in the unenviable role of policemen by requiring that the hospitals refer to governmental authority all cases where even tenuous arguments could be made that the parents may be inappropriately withholding consent to treatment. HHS requires that "recipient hospitals not fail, on the basis of handicap, to report the *apparently* improper parental decision to the appropriate State authorities. . .so as to trigger the system provided by State law to determine whether the parental decision should be honoured".[18] This

---

17a. In the course of Chapter I, we discussed various practices by neonatal specialists of withholding or manipulating information so that parents would decide to withhold treatment or surgery. However, the HHS's directive applies to a much broader range of cases.

The notice to health care providers of June 18, 1982, 47 Fed. Reg. 26027, contained the following admonition:

> Counselling of parents should not discriminate by encouraging parents to make decisions which, if made by the health care provider, would be discriminatory under section 504.

Arguably, advising the parents of the seriousness of the child's condition and his bleak prognosis could be taken to constitute "counselling" in that such advice would be material in most cases to any decision made by the parents to order that treatment be withheld. Doctors are thus forced to become Polyannas, telling only the bright side, because otherwise the hospital risks being investigated by the HHS. This analysis might strike the reader as exaggerated. However, we refer the reader to note 18, *infra*, where a stikingly similar analysis of discrimination was formulated by counsel for the HHS before the Federal Court of Appeals in *U.S.* v. *University Hospital*.

18. *HHS Guidelines*, 49 Fed. Reg. 8, p. 1631.

The rigour of the HHS's position as to when the hospital is required to intervene and question the parents' decision is demonstrated by its counsel's argument made before the Federal Court of Appeal in *U.S.* v. *University Hospital*, 729 F. (2d.) 144, 149. (U.S.C.A., 1983).

In *University Hospital*, "Baby Jane Doe" was born with multiple defects which included spina bifida, with resultant spasticity of the legs, microcephaly, and hydrocephalus, the latter two combining to produce a high risk of severe mental retardation. The parents refused consent for surgery on the spinal lesions or to implant a shunt to drain the cranial fluid, and elected instead for conservative treatments. Medical evidence revealed that there were risks of severe complications attendant upon surgery, including possible loss of what little muscle control Baby Jane retained to her legs.

In the course of litigation in the New York courts, the Appeals Division of the Supreme Court overturned the trial judge's order appointing a guardian *ad litem* for the child and requiring the hospital to perform surgery. Instead, the Appeals Division held that the parents had chosen reasonably and with concern for the best interests of the child between two reasonable courses of treatment. Therefore, they

means that hospitals will be overly zealous in involving the coercive power of child welfare authorities, for the same reasons they are moved towards over-treatment. Parents suffering under the strain of a difficult emotional trauma will be easily forced to make inappropriate decisions that their child should be treated in accordance with the administration's unarticulated and omnipresent morality.[18a]

Parents have already attested that they find the presence of Baby Doe squads upsetting and humiliating. The squads increase the risk that parents will withdraw the infant from hospital care entirely.[19] HHS offers no reason for taking away the parents' margin of appre-

---

held that there were no grounds for the court to intervene. The Court of Appeals dismissed the appeal from the decision of the Appeals Division.

In the meantime, HHS had received a complaint from an unnamed caller, and referred Baby Jane's case to the New York State Child Protection Service which investigated and decided that there was no cause for state intervention.

Notwithstanding, HHS persevered with the case, and decided to investigate University Hospital for alleged breach of s. 504, arguing that the hospital's failure to refer the parents' refusal to consent to the surgery to the State Child Protection Service constituted discriminatory withholding of treatment. The HHS claimed access to Baby Jane's medical reports, and the hospital refused. The proceedings in Federal Court were launched by HHS to compel University Hospital to divulge the medical reports.

If, even after review of the infant's case by the state courts and child protection agencies, a hospital still can be challenged by HHS for second-hand discriminatory withholding of treatment, then it seems clear that HHS requires hospitals to challenge *every* parental decision to withhold aggressive treatment. Inevitably hospitals are driven to employ coercive measures against the parents to obtain permission for surgery, since even a ruling by the highest court of the state is not enough to satisfy the HHS.

Furthermore, *de facto* coercion of the parents is openly built into the HHS's regulatory scheme. In its notice to health care providers of June 18, 1982, 47 Fed. Reg. 26027, the HHS admonished:

> Health care providers should not aid a decision by the infant's parents or guardian to withhold treatment or nourishment discriminatorily by allowing the infant to remain in the institution.

It seems senselessly cruel - unless the object is coercion - to force parents, traumatized by the birth of a child with severe defects, and agonizing over the terrible decision which they must make for their child, to take the child home to watch it die. Similarly - and this was the case in *New York Hospital* - the HHS would have the hospital deny the child beneficial health care as dictated by a medically reasonable conservative treatment plan, because the HHS insists on aggressive treatment. This must be an intolerable and unjustifiable intrusion into - and obstruction of - the whole medical treatment process.

18a. See especially *supra*, notes 17a, 18 and accompanying text.

19. Incidents of this have already been reported: see *HHS Guidelines*, 49 Fed. Reg. 8, p. 1642; *American Academy of Pediatrics* v. *Heckler*, 561 F. Supp. 395, 400 (U.S. D.C. 1983).

ciation to make the difficult decision in doubtful cases. Moreover the parents' discretion is fully supported by legal and ethical considerations previously explored in Chapters Two and Three.

The descent of Baby Doe squads is highly disruptive to orderly treatment, and normal hospital routines. Doctors and nurses are required to take valuable treatment hours to respond to phone and on-site inquiries from investigators. HHS has received complaints from treatment staff and hospitals that medical records became unavailable during the investigation. In concept, the thrust of the regulations characterizes doctors and nurses as child abusers. This unflattering and unwarranted portrayal infects public confidence in medicine, and makes parents afraid for the safety of their children. It has a serious negative impact on professional morale.

HHS's effort has been a crass political attempt to appease the hard-line opinion in the Right to Life movement. Under pretext of administrative power, HHS has attempted to legislate treatment criteria and the scope of appropriate parental authority - all without articulating its position or goals. It is no secret that little societal consensus exists on these matters. What can flow can ebb. If and when the administration desires to please another group, will it once again don the surgeon's mask? Will it once again establish medical criteria based on some vaguely perceived political advantage? Can we expect the quality of medical care and the integrity of the medical profession to withstand unscathed the onslaught of political tides as the profession honourably attempts to deepen medical discernment, and formulate better medical criteria? It is difficult to perceive how politicization of treatment criteria, through executive instrumentalities, can do other than weaken medicine as a dispassionate purveyor of the healing arts.

III. INTERNAL ADMINISTRATIVE REGULATION

Monitoring of health care quality has preocuppied hospitals and health care professions in the present age of mass institutional medicine. Monitoring efforts originated with attempts to contain costs and to reduce the exposure of health care providers to liability risk. These activities quickly embraced quality control. Quality control programs' are further encouraged by legal recognition of the hospitals' direct responsibility to assure consistently good medical care to the communities they serve. As such, these activities represent a creditable effort to discharge the duty which accompanies the privilege of self-regulation by medicine in the hospital setting.

Quality assurance as a means of monitoring the quality of health care is rapidly becoming a highly technical sub-specialty in the field of hospital administration. It has been responsible for generating a large body of recent specialized literature.[19a] It is not our intention to advocate that specific quality assurance activities be undertaken by all hospitals to monitor neonatal care. Each hospital has its particular problems to address and its own special resources to bring to quality assurance activities.[19b] These will stem from its organizational structures and the skills of its staff. A hospital must tailor its activities accordingly.

There is broad agreement among different organizations and researchers as to the essential components of quality assurance programs. The Canadian Council on Hospital Accreditation identifies five components: problem identification, problem assessment, implementation of measures to reduce or eliminate problems, evaluation, and monitoring of the effectiveness of implemented changes.[19c]

19a. One need only mention some of the learned journals devoted largely or entirely to quality assurance concepts: *Quality Review Bulletin, Health Services Research; Health Care Management Review; Hospital Peer Review; Medical Decision Making.* In addition, the reader will find many articles published in the journals of various medical specialties and of hospital administration. These may be found by consulting volumes of the *Hospital Literature Index* and *Index Medicus* under different subheadings including "Decision Making", "Peer Review" and "Medical Audit".

19b. See, *e.g.*, Marsh, *Quality Assurance and Activities in a Small Community Hospital* (1983), 9(3) Quality Review Bulletin 77.

19c. C.C.H.A., *Standards of Accreditation of Canadian Health Care Facilities* (Jan., 1983), pp. 43-44. See also Joint Commission for Accreditation of Hospitals (U.S.), *Accreditation Manual for Hospitals* (1976), pp. 27-28. For a review of the various theoretical models, see R. Brook, *Quality of Care Assessment: A Comparison of Five Methods of Peer Review* (National Technical Information Service, Springfield, Va., 1973), pp. 1-3.

The diversity of quality assurance activities described in the literature is a tribute to human ingenuity. They attempt to tap the various sources of information available in the hospital: patients' complaints, incident reports, treatment charts, discharge reports, staff interviews, and information observed first hand during routine treatment in the ward. The quality assurance activity itself could be any one of the following: risk management[19d]; medical audit of specific processes[19e]; computer-based monitoring of indices[19f]; professional or peer review[19g]; continuing education, to name only a few.[19h]

In fundamentals, quality assurance activities embody a means for getting at meaningful information from which an assessment can be made of the particular aspects of treatment which are of concern. Therefore, it should not be expected that one technique will be effective in all situations. Those hospitals whose quality assurance programs are reported to be successful conduct a variety of activities at any one time.[19i] The art of quality assurance administration is to be ever alert to signs of weakness in present treatment practice, and then with tact and imagination to select and implement the measurement tool which will gauge the sources and seriousness of that weakness.

Monitoring activities in the form of quality assurance are required by government and institutions. Under Ontario's *Public Hospitals Act* and Regulations hospitals have discretionary power to establish medical audit committees, and must establish tissue committees.[20] The duties

---

19d. See, *e.g.* , Martin, *Hospital Risk Management: A Canadian Perspective* (1981) 2(3) Health Management Forum 23; Jacoby, *Risk Management Rounds: Promoting Quality Care* (1983), 9(3) Quality Review Bulletin 85.

19e. See, *e.g.*, Vanagunas *et al.*, *Principles of Quality Assurance* (Jan., 1981), 7 Quality Review Bulletin 4; Pybus *et al.*, *Clinical Audit of an Intensive Care Unit* (1982), 10(3) Anaesthesia and Intensive Care 233.

19f. See, *e.g.*, Barnett *et al.*, *Quality Assurance through Automated Monitoring and Concurrent Feedback Using a Computer-Based Medical Information System* (1978), 16(11) Medical Care 962; Winegar *et al.*, *A System to Monitor Patient Care in a Perinatal Region* (1983), 145(1) American Journal of Obstetrics and Gynecology 39.

19g. Russo *et al.*, *A Chart Audit Peer Review System in an Ambulatory Service* (1975), 56(2) Pediatrics 246.

19h. For enumerations of quality assurance activities, see Vanagunas *et al.*, *Principles of Quality Assurance* (Jan, 1981), 7 Quality Review Bulletin 4; C.C.H.A.; *Standards for Accreditation of Canadian Health Care Facilities* (Jan. 1983), pp. 44-45; Mason and Paige, *Perceived Usefulness of Quality Assurance Activities* (1983), 9(1) Quality Review Bulletin 20, 21-22.

19i. See, *e.g.*, Rosenberg, *A Self-Policing Program That Works*, Medical Economics, April 4, 1983, p. 215.

20. R.R.O. 1980, Reg. 865, s. 7(1)(e)(v).

and powers of these committees are established by hospital by-law. Ideally their mandate is wide, allowing the committees to operate an ongoing monitoring process, and also to pinpoint specific problems, or problem areas, and investigate accordingly. The Canadian Council on Hospital Accreditation has emphasized the importance of the quality assurance process in its *Standards for Accreditation.*[21] Most investigators studying the quality assurance process have discovered widespread acceptance by doctors of the necessity for a quality assurance effort.[22]

The research into quality assurance is divided as to its effectiveness. To date, it appears that quality assurance programs do not substantially curtail costs or reduce inefficient utilization.[24] Some programs actually increase costs by imposing requirements for unnecessary or redundant protocols. To the extent that quality assurance routines require doctors to focus on prepackaged, possibly outdated or irrelevant treatment steps, they may affect medical treatment negatively.[25] Scarce treatment time is occupied with irrelevant detail; the doctor's treatment imagination may become cluttered with bureaucratic preoccupations.[25a]

---

21. C.C.H.A., *Standards for Accreditation of Canadian Health Care Facilities* (Jan. 1983), p. 46. Although approved January, 1983, the new standards did not come into effect until January, 1984. Therefore, we are not yet in a position to assess the effect they will have in spurring hospitals toward more effective quality assurance activities.

22. Anderson and Shields, *Quality Measurement and Control in Physician Decision Making: State of the Art* (1982), 17 Health Services Research 125; Winegar *et al.*, *A system to monitor patient care in a perinatal region* (1983), 145(1) American Journal of Obstetrics and Gynecology 39.

24. Brook, *et al.*, *Use, Costs, and Quality of Medical Services: Impact of the New Mexico Peer Review System* (1978), 89 Annals of Internal Medicine 256; Anderson and Shields, *Quality Measurement and Control in Physician Decision Making: State of the Art* (1982), 17 Health Services Research 125, 137.

25. See Anderson and Shields, *Quality Measurement and Control in Physician Decision Making: State of the Art* (1982), 17 Health Services Research 125, 128-29, 138.

   See also Eddy, *Clinical Policies and the Quality of Clinical Practice* (1982), 307(6) New England Journal of Medicine 343, 346, where this problem in quality assurance is tied in with the problem of setting clinical policies in the following way: "The common assumption is that the existing policies are correct and that the task of quality control is to identify and investigate cases that deviate too much from the average. These methods do not reevaluate [sic] the policies themselves; they evaluate only whether current policies are followed. This tends to lock existing policies in place; it may threaten anyone who applies a different policy, even though the new one may be correct; it misses an opportunity to improve the policies themselves[.]"

25a. See Mason and Paige, *Perceived Usefulness of Quality Assurance Activities* (1983), 9(1) Quality Review Bulletin 20, 22, who after surveying the psychiatric service

Some fundamental shortcomings of quality assurance programs would appear to be structural. The medical profession inadequately understands the relationship between medical interventions and desired clinical outcomes.[26] It is widely suspected that many procedures have no clinical value. The net result is that quality assurance programs may monitor adherence to specific procedures when those procedures might be useless.

The failings of quality assurance techniques appear to be the same as those characteristic of any new science. The mass bureaucratic structure which increasingly characterizes modern medicine demands effective monitoring processes. Even those commentators who concentrate on deficiencies of quality assurance do so in order to advocate research capable of refining the technique, not to discredit the concept. In the meantime, they suggest that quality assurance programs should focus on specific, validated clinical procedures.[26a] With time, quality assurance should assist medicine in validating or rejecting many procedures hitherto supported merely by received, but unscientific wisdom.

Notwithstanding these shortcomings, the research literature suggests that quality assurance techniques have some positive impact on the quality of medical care.[27] Furthermore, the literature has been particularly useful in concentrating attention on the necessity to involve those affected by quality assurance programs in all components of the system. This involvement is emphasized to such an extent that 'Peer Review' - the term of art for involvement of doctors - is central to most quality assurance activities. It has become clear that treatment protocols cannot be imposed effectively upon medical practitioners, if large numbers of practitioners are not persuaded of their validity.[29] In order

---

of a hospital found that the paperwork required by quality assurance activities was perceived as a cause of declining staff morale and of staff burnout, and as "affect[ing] patient care adversely by emphasizing quantity rather than quality and by decreasing the time available for teaching and research."

26. Uberla, *Methodological Limitations in the Analysis of Medical Activities* (1980), 19(1) Methods of Information in Medicine 7.

26a. Anderson and Shields, *Quality Measurements and Control in Physician Decision Making: State of the Art* (1982), 17(2) Health Services Research 125; R. Brook, *Quality of Care Assessment: A Comparison of Five Methods of Peer Review* (National Technical Information Service, Springfield, Va., 1973).

27. Anderson and Shields, *Quality Measurement and Control in Physician Decision Making: State of the Art, supra,* note 26a, at 149; Brook *et al., Use, Costs and Quality of Medical Services: Impact of the New Mexico Peer Review System* (1978), 89 Annals of Internal Medicine 256.

29. Rosen and Feigen, *Quality Assurance and Data Feedback* (1983), 8(1) Health Care Management Review 67, 68-69.

to compel compliance, widespread punishment would be required. Experience teaches that this is ineffective and demoralizing in the hospital setting. Imposition of treatment protocols without medicine's acceptance is one of the principal failings of the Reagan administration's approach to neonatal care in its Baby Doe regulatory effort.

Quality assurance techniques are workable only to the extent that standards are tolerable to the doctors such that over the course of time the standards are internalized as norms. Once internalization occurs, deviation becomes less frequent and thereby is more readily detected. On the other hand, if doctors do not accept the standards, they are unwilling to monitor deviance. It is therefore critical that doctors be energetic and willing participants in problem identification. To this end, doctors must perceive as problems those practices quality assurance programs seek to inhibit. If doctors fail to accept that there is a problem, quality assurance programs will be ineffective as a control device.

We began this chapter by refocusing attention on several discreditable practices common to newborn units. We reach an impasse upon the realization that many doctors do not perceive these practices as discreditable. Many neonatologists strenuously defend them - but at the same time refuse to articulate and publicize their practices as official policy. Without acceptance by a substantial number of doctors that these practices call for change, it is difficult to see how quality assurance techniques can be useful as a control device in the intensive care nursery.

The way out of this dead end would appear to be establishment of a process which requires that criteria for neonatal care be clearly articulated, especially in the contentious areas of parental consent, experimentation, interdisciplinary consultation, use of paramedical data, palliation and recourse to ethical expertise. As we stipulated earlier, criteria should be established by a three tiered process: proposed rules emanating from the neonatal unit; review by the Medical Advisory Committee, review by a provincial Standards Review Board.

A schematic of the proposal follows.

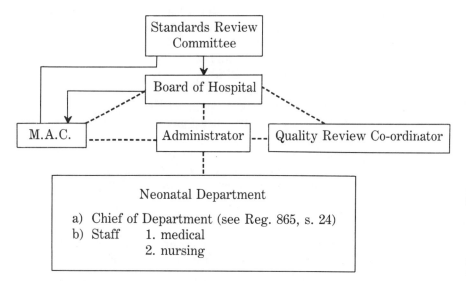

We would emphasize the following points.
1. Criteria proposals would ordinarily originate from the Neonatal Department, either from the Chief of Neonatology, the treating staff, or the nursing staff.
2. The Chief of Neonatology would receive the proposal. He would appoint a committee of staff, with a nursing component, charged to study the feasibility of the proposal, *to review current medical literature*, and to compile a report, including a recommendation.
3. The proposal would be subject to vote by departmental doctors and nurses.
4. The department would be required to prepare a statement of dissenting reasons when a proposal receives less than 2/3rds approval, and would be required to attach a statement of dissenting reasons in all cases where dissenters desire to express their views. After departmental approval, the proposed criteria would be sent to the Medical Advisory Committee for ratification.
5. The Medical Advisory Committee would have initiating power to recommend to the neonatal department that criteria be developed as to a given subject or concern. If the department refused to comply, it would be required to give reasons. Upon a refusal, the Medical Advisory Committee would notify the Standards Review Board and the Hospital Board of the recommendation and refusal.
6. The Medical Advisory Committee would submit a copy of the criteria approved, as well as its own recommendations, to the provincial *Standards Review Board*.

7. The composition of the Standards Review Board would be:
   a. Neonatal specialists working within the province's hospitals;
   b. Representative of the provincial College of Pediatrics;
   c. Professor of Neonatal medicine;
   d. Professor of Medical Law;
   e. Professor of Medical Ethics;
   f. Professor of Nursing;
   g. Representative of the Ministry of Health;
   h. Representative of the general public appointed by the Minister of Health.
8. The Committee would have power to review the appropriateness of all criteria submitted. It would have initiating power to request that hospitals rewrite criteria, or to invite criteria development on a particular subject or concern.

The authority for setting the criteria, therefore, rests in three places: The Department, the Medical Advisory Committee, the Standards Review Board.

There are several lines of reporting and consultation. The Administrator must receive a report of all proposals from the Department and from the Medical Advisory Committee. This reflects the reality of his responsibility for enforcing the *Public Hospitals Act* and Regulations, and the By-Laws of the Hospital. We have added a Quality Review Co-ordinator to the structure. He would be an employee of the Ministry of Health, independent from the hospital. His responsibility would be to co-ordinate the quality assurance process in the hospital, and as such would work closely with the Administrator. All proposals submitted by the Department or originating from the Medical Advisory Committee would be submitted to the Co-ordinator. He would be without formal power to reject or recommend, but would have informal authority to discuss his concerns with the Medical Advisory Committee or the Department. The Co-ordinator would also report to the Hospital Board, who are ultimately responsible under the *Act* for the quality of health care in the hospital. The Board of the Hospital would receive reports through the Medical Advisory Committee, the Administrator, and the Co-ordinator in the regular way.

These procedures for criteria development insure that standards governing contentious practices in neonatal care will be publicly articulated and defended. They insure, too, that doctors will be the primary actors in the criteria generation process. In requiring doctors to go through this exercise, we express our belief that by so doing doctors will come to perceive the merit in what others have been saying: that on important points where law, medicine and ethics intersect, neonatal practice requires change.

We have suggested a program to detect and evaluate deficiencies in neonatal care, a process to articulate treatment criteria, and follow-up techniques to monitor and evaluate the degree of compliance by doctors and the extent to which patient care is improved. May we be satisfied that medical practice will change in response to problem identification, criteria setting and compliance monitoring?

The question might appear to jar common sense. Is it not self-evident that once a problem is identified and doctors made aware of it, they will immediately mend their ways, especially where the accepted practice is set out before them? Would not peer pressure have this effect?

Our survey leaves room for doubt. In Chapter One we considered the case of a neurosurgeon who failed routinely to consult his colleagues,[29a] even though it was widely known neonatology was premised on inter-specialty consultation. Peer pressure did not change the surgeon's ways. Nor did the departmental chief or the hospital administration force him into line. This situation persisted despite the annoyance and anger of the Chief of Neonatology.

The case is not unique. The research literature outlines numerous cases where monitoring programs uncover an aspect of medical activity - for example, charting behaviour - where the medical staff is not performing according to desired standards. Even after ongoing peer review and data feedback, and *even given a general perception by the staff that the monitoring program was useful to improve charting behaviour*, the follow-up reports found no substantial objective improvement in charting practices.[29b]

If monitoring processes cannot by themselves insure improved compliance with professional standards, even in cases where staff accepts the result, it is hard to see how monitoring processes can be expected to control behaviour effectively in cases where the delinquent doctor does not embrace the standards, as in the case of "loner" specialists.

The apparent lack of will to enforce standards in neonatology is alarming. On the one hand, the literature reports vigorous action by

---

29a. Ch. I, at p. 20.

29b. Greene *et al.*, *Effect of Resident Peer Review on Charting Behavior* (1981), 68(6) Pediatrics 840.

hospitals in all departments to insure compliance with standards through processes of peer pressure, education, and, where necessary, direct discipline.[29c] On the other hand, the Dubin Committee[29d] discovered a complete failure to enforce standards in neonatology, and a general reluctance to rein in staff.

Therefore, short of some increased effort in the way of enforcement, the best that can be hoped for is that over the long term the educative process involved in criteria setting and quality review will gradually diminish the abuses we have identified. In our view, the interests of society and protection of the newborn demand more. A meaningful process of enforcement ought to be implemented now.

We do not advocate draconian intervention. Internal disciplinary processes appear to be best, and least disrupting of self-regulation.[29e]

The Medical Advisory Committee is responsible to recommend to the Hospital Board whether a particular doctor should be granted privileges to practise in the hospital, or whether the doctor's privileges should be renewed, restricted, or cancelled.[29f] The Chief of Neonatology, as head of the department, can be given more precise authority and responsibility to supervise the practice of neonatal care, and to insure that rules of the department are observed.[29g] In theory, once appropriate criteria are set according to the process earlier described, the Chief of Neonatology should discipline staff for breaches of rules and criteria. When the time comes to renew the doctor's privileges, the Medical Advisory Committee ought to consider whether the doctor's record of non-compliance with departmental rules and criteria renders him inappropriate to be privileged to act in the neonatal ward. As a last resort, privileges could be restricted or cancelled.

How can we insure that the processes of discipline and privilege review are performed in a meaningful way? We suggest that an important step would be to render the mandate for the process more explicit. Hospital by-laws should require that the Medical Advisory Committee and the Chief of Neonatology give close consideration to a doctor's record of non-compliance with departmental rules and criteria when considering applications for additional or continuing privileges. To this

---

29c. Rosenberg, *A Self-Policing Program that Works*, Medical Economics, April 4, 1983, p. 215.

29d. *The Dubin Report*, pp. 61-64, 68-70.

29e. See text, *supra* at note 4d.

29f. R.R.O. 1980, Reg. 865, s. 7(6)(5).

29g. *Public Hospitals Act.*, R.S.O. 1980, c. 14, s. 31(1)(2).

end, section 7 of the Regulations under the *Public Hospitals Act*,[29h] which sets out the mandatory contents of hospital by-laws, could be amended to stipulate for this change.

As part of his duties set out in the by-laws the Chief of Neonatology should be required to discuss with offending staff members any breach of criteria or departmental rules. A written notation of all such discussions should be made. Further disciplinary action or intervention in specific cases would be according to the processes already called for by legislation, the medical profession's own processes, and internal hospital regulations.

While this might appear unduly severe to some, we believe the criticism to be unwarranted. Doctors cannot expect to violate rules and criteria with impunity, especially when the medical profession itself articulates the rules. Of course, there are breaches, and then there are breaches. Some endanger the welfare of the patient, for which the guilty doctor should be strictly reined in. Others are much less consequential and call only for a gentle reminder. We believe that we have respected this reality, by leaving to the senior medical authorities in the hospital the Chief of Neonatology and the Medical Advisory Committee - to assess the gravity of the breach, and to determine what action is appropriate.

We insist only that they give this matter due consideration. To that end, the process for internal rule and criteria enforcement must in itself be subject to review by the quality assurance process. As earlier outlined, each hospital should have a Quality Assurance Co-ordinator on staff. He should be the employee and appointee of the Ministry of Health, because in that way his independence is enhanced, along with his ability to probe meaningfully the shortfalls in the hospital's health care delivery. The Co-ordinator should develop specific investigatory processes to detect efforts to circumvent or ignore the enforcement processes outlined above.

To examine the role of the Co-ordinator, imagine the following scenario. A pediatric neurosurgeon repeatedly refuses to involve his colleagues in meaningful consultation. He does not want or need the advice of other specialists. He is one of the city's foremost pediatric surgeons, and has been on staff for ten years. The Chief of Neonatology is aware of the surgeon's idiosyncratic behavior. He has received several complaints from the medical and nursing staff, as has the Medical Advisory Committee. The Chief never raises the matter with the neuro-

---

29h. R.R.O. 1980, Reg. 865, s. 7.

surgeon, who is feared for being temperamental and unreceptive of criticism. The Medical Advisory Committee duly renews his privileges each year: he is difficult to replace.

Because of the reluctance of hospital authorities to act, the Quality Assurance Co-ordinator assumes a key role. His mandate would require that he insure that the Chief addresses incidents of nonconsultation, and that both the Chief and the Medical Advisory Committee give serious consideration as to whether there was a *medical justification* behind the neurosurgeon's actions. The Co-ordinator would not assess the medical justification. However, where neither the Chief nor the Medical Advisory Committee address the issue on its medical merits, the Co-ordinator would report the case to the Hospital Board. In a very serious case, he might feel compelled to refer the surgeon's case to the Complaints Committee of the Provincial College of Physicians and Surgeons.

It is believed that such an enforcement and review process is in line with our stated concerns of leaving with neonatal practitioners the principal function of judging what action is necessary and commensurate with the medical realities of the neonatal ward and each clinical case. At the same time, our suggested system would assure society, by a system of independent quality assurance monitoring, that the doctors are performing this function: that in exchange for the privilege of self-regulation, they are discharging their responsibility for self-discipline and enforcement.

If physician acceptance of the need for change can be secured through a process for criteria generation, quality assurance techniques become an appropriate means to implement and monitor compliance to or deviations from the articulated standard. If doctors cannot be persuaded of the need for changes in neonatal practice, it is likely that neonatal issues will become increasingly charged politically, as American pediatricians now living under the "Baby Doe Regulations" learned to their chagrin. The longer term impact of the inquiries into the deaths at Toronto's Hospital for Sick Children will likely be significant public clamor for action. Responsible internal action in neonatal units now, which generates defensible criteria and monitors their implementation through serious quality assurance efforts, will go a long way towards forestalling precipitous, dramatic action by governments, spurred on by the popular American "Baby Doe" example.

We cannot overemphasize the necessity for those in governments and hospital administrations to involve doctors significantly in the process of criteria generation and quality assurance. It would be unrealistic

to expect criteria imposed from Ministry or Hospital governing structures to be effectively implemented. In order for our proposal to succeed,
doctors themselves must be the primary problem-identifiers, solution
proposers, monitors and enforcers. The reason is that hospitals are not
organizations like the traditional model. In the industrial firm, roles
are sharply differentiated: administration, sales, production and
research. Different people are assigned to different roles. In hospitals,
roles are blurred: patient care, research, teaching and administration,
with one person straddling all roles. In industrial firms, administrators
are on top, capable of charting direction and giving orders. In hospitals,
administrators are on the bottom, incapable of giving orders to medical
staff in clinical matters. This idiosyncrasy of hospital organization
necessitates that doctors accept the legitimacy of hospital efforts in
matters of a clinical nature. If the doctors' acceptance is not forthcoming, the plain reality is that the best laid plans of hospital administrators and legislators will rarely have any significant impact on clinical
practice.[30]

---

30. Weisbord, *Why Organization Development Hasn't Worked (So Far) In Medical
Centers* (1976), 1(2) Health Care Management Review 17.

IV. PROGNOSIS BOARDS AND ETHICS COMMITTEES

A final control device is the establishment of variously constituted ethics committes which may or must be consulted to provide advice on the correct course of action. Approximately 70 such committees (1% of acute care hospitals) now operate in the United States, with a smaller number established in Canada.[31]

There is energetic debate about the role such committees ought to play. An ethics committee composed of physicians, social workers, lawyers and clergy was first called for by the *Quinlan* Court to confirm or reject decisions to withdraw treatment from the terminally ill.[31a] Application of the concept to the neonatal ward produced change in the committees' composition to include members with neonatal expertise, ethicists, nurses, representatives of disability organizations and developmental disability experts.[31b]

Committees so composed have been sharply criticized by certain commentators. The committees, it is said, are too amorphous, use nonmedical personnel to reach essentially medical decisions, and bureaucratize death.[32] In consequence, certain commentators and courts would move away from the diversely composed ethics committee concept. They would retain the idea of an institutional committee, but restrict its function to medical review, and eliminate all but doctors from its composition.

This latter committee has been termed the 'prognosis board'. As envisaged by the Courts, prognosis boards are composed of a small number of doctors, including at times the attending physician. The committee's function is to confirm or reject the attending doctor's diagnosis that no reasonable probability exists for reversing the patient's path toward imminent death.[33] As so envisaged, the concept is only an elaboration of the idea that a second medical opinion should be obtained in difficult cases. In that form, the concept has been endorsed

---

31. Randal, *Are Ethics Committees Alive and Well?* (Dec., 1980), 13(6) The Hastings Center Report 10.

31a. *Matter of Quinlan*, 70 N.J. 10, 355 A. (2d) 647, 671-72 (1976).

31b. Fleischman and Murray, *Ethics Committees for Infants Doe?* (Dec., 1983), 13(6) The Hastings Center Report 5, 6-7.

32. Annas, *Reconciling Quinlan and Saikewicz: Decision Making for the Terminally Ill Incompetent* (1979), 4 Am. J.L. and Med. 367, 379; Cantor, *Quinlan, Privacy and the Handling of Incompetent Dying Patients* (1977), 30 Rutgers L. Rev. 243, 255. The criticism has found judicial support: *Matter of Colyer.* 660 P. (2d) 738, 749 (Wash. 1983); *Eichner* v. *Dillon*, 426 N.Y.S. (2d) 517, 549-50 (App. Div. 1980).

33. *Matter of Colyer, supra,* note 32 at 749; *Eichner* v. *Dillon, supra,* note 32 at 550.

by the Canadian Medical Association, Canadian Nurses Association and Canadian Hospital Association, in a 'Joint Statement on Terminal Illness'.[34]

The difficulty with the Prognosis Board concept is that it presumes that decisions to discontinue treatment are based principally on medical factors, the function of the prognosis board being to confirm the medical probabilities.[35] Prognosis committees, therefore, reinforce the doctor's role in decision making. Doctors appear to be on strong ground when insisting that the decision making prerogative is theirs, because a committee of their peers stands behind them to confirm the basis on which the doctor's decision is reached.

It is also significant that cases where prognosis committees were relied on as central to the decision making process are cases where the patient is adult and in an irreversible coma. The central question addressed in these cases is the correctness of the doctor's prognosis that no reasonable possibility exists for the patient to return to a cognitive sapient state.

These special factors reduce the utility of the 'prognosis board' concept in cases of radically defective newborns. Numerous paramedical factors are relevant to assess neonatal cases. The key questions are often developmental potential and quality of life, not reversibility of coma and inevitability of death. Neonatal cases raise searching questions that transcend the expertise offered by a committee of doctors. As our survey has shown, the doctor's role in deciding the appropriate action for cases of radically defective newborns needs to be trimmed, not enlarged. For these reasons, we would reject application of the prognosis board concept in the intensive care nursery.

It has been suggested that committees with multi-disciplinary composition ["ethics committees"] may usefully serve at least five different functions. First, they may provide ethical expertise, helping decision makers to identify ethical principles, competing and conflicting values and interests, and point them towards possible reconciliations. They thus facilitate ethical analysis of the important non-medical issues presented by serious pediatric cases. Secondly, the committees may play an educative role, informing hospital personnel of legal and moral norms relevant to recurring ethical dilemmas in the hospital. They could serve as an important catalyst for the making of hospital policy.

---

34. 130 Canadian Medical Association Journal 1357 (May 15, 1984).

35. *Matter of Colyer*, 660 P. (2d) 738, 749 (Wash. 1983): "The prognosis determination is a medical one."

Thirdly, the committees may play a supportive role for parents, doctors and nurses forced to grapple with traumatic ethical dilemmas. Fourthly, the committees may provide a forum for venting of disagreements which experience teaches arise between various actors in the intensive care nursery. The opportunity before the committee to give explanations, provide information and receive the committee's further input can lead to resolution of disputes which might otherwise continue to cause tension or lead to court action. Finally, the committees may reduce the hospital's exposure to liability risk, functioning as an early warning system for ethical problems that might involve the hospital in avoidable litigation.[36]

The public response to committees of this type has been favourable, where the committee is limited to an advisory role. A survey conducted at one large urban hospital indicated that most patients viewed the committee positively as a facilitator of the decisional process, on the condition that ultimate decisional responsibility is left with the patient.[37] It is hardly surprising that the response should be favourable considering the alternatives: direct action by the government through coercive machinery like HHS; slow, expensive, adversarial litigation; or no help at all. By contrast, the ethics committee will be speedy, close to the treatment situation, informal, private, non-coercive and advisory, able to reconvene easily and, at the very least, "provide an opportunity for discussion in an open reasonable atmosphere,"[38] where different disciplines can lend their various perspectives to resolving a difficult dilemma.

The ethics committee concept certainly has potential to remedy the deficient practices in neonatology disclosed by our survey. In our view, ethics committees are properly invested with an advisory function. Ethics committees should not be given decisional power, as this would amount to another institutional mechanism for divesting the ethical and legal authority of parents to make decisions on behalf of

---

36. Robertson, *Ethics Committees in Hospitals: Alternative Structures and Responsibilities* (Jan., 1984), 10(1) Quality Review Bulletin 6, 7-8, identified these five functions, which we have adopted.

37. Youngner, *et al.*, *Patients' Attitudes Toward Hospital Ethics Committees* (1984), 12 Law, Medicine and Health Care 21, 23.

38. Cohen, *Interdisciplinary Consultation on the Care of the Critically Ill and Dying: The Role of One Hospital Ethics Committee* (1982), 10 Critical Care Medicine 776, 784. See also President's Commission for the Study of Problems in Medicine and Biomedical and Behavioral Research, *Deciding to Forego Life Sustaining Treatment: A Report on the Ethical, Medical and Legal Issues in Treatment Decisions* (1983), pp. 168-69.

their children. Use of the committee's processes should be at the option of parents. There is little point in imposing on parents an advisory mechanism, the opinion of which they are not obligated to follow and which they feel they may not need. The hospital still has recourse to the Child Welfare authorities should it feel that the parents' decision is unjustified.

While the process is optional for parents, it would be useful to require doctors to alert the committee in cases where withholding treatment is considered a serious medical option. The committee would then contact the parents independently, explain the committee's function and offer its services.

Utilization of the committee will reduce the risk that doctors will not provide parents with adequate information, or usurp the parents' decisional role. The quality assurance process should detect those cases where the doctor unjustifiably fails to notify the committee. It appears unlikely that the attending doctor would present selective, biased information before the committee. The committee will normally contain his most prestigious peers, and other persons well able to recognize inadequate presentation of the case. Unjustifiable experimentation would likely be inhibited by awareness that the case might come before the committee at some point. The ethics committee could be called on by the Quality Assurance Co-ordinator to review ethical factors arising in cases appropriate for withholding treatment.

The committee would be able to encourage the consultation process by its ability to call for further medical information from the various pediatric specialties. An awareness that the committee routinely requires interdisciplinary presentation of the case might well dissuade recalcitrant doctors from their 'loner syndrome'.

The committee could serve a particularly useful function in developing policies for use of paramedical facts in neonatal decision making. It could lift the shroud of secrecy from the use of paramedical data, by requiring neonatal staff and parents to articulate those paramedical facts thought relevant. A consistent requirement for articulation of paramedical factors would assist the hospital to formulate and refine policy and standards in this area. The committee would have special expertise with respect to paramedical data through the contributions made by its sitting ethicists and developmental experts. In the same way, the committee would be able to help the hospital wrestle with the difficult questions of palliation and starvation.

The ethics committee is not the perfect vehicle for resolving all dilemmas in the intensive care nursery. It is not available at two o'clock in the morning when many emergency life and death decisions must be made. There is no assurance that its opinions will be consistent, or that its treatment of ethical dilemmas will be defensible in terms of consistency.[39] The committee may be impractical or expensive for smaller hospitals, although in many cases this could be overcome by pooling of resources on a regional basis.

Despite obvious shortcomings, ethics committees would appear able to provide an important safety valve for pressures building in neonatology. They may head off the advent of more direct, distasteful and politicized governmental intervention. We advocate that hospitals scrutinize their utility carefully.

---

39. A study of institutional review boards established to approve research proposals found widespread inconsistency in their decisions. The study concluded that I.R.B.'s "approve inappropriate investigations and inhibit appropriate investigations. . . only the most glaring problems are identified": Goldman and Katz, *Inconsistency and Institutional Review Boards* (1982), 248(2) Journal of the American Medical Association 197, 202; see also Veatch, *Problems with Institutional Review Board Inconsistency* (1982), 248(2) Journal of the American Medical Association 179.

BIBLIOGRAPHY

Books

Annas, George, J. *The Rights of Hospital Patients*. New York: Avon Books. (1975).

Bacon, Francis. *Advancement of Learning*.

Baxter, Ian F.G. and Eberts, Mary A. (Eds.). *The Child and the Courts*. Toronto: The Carswell Company Limited. (1978).

Beauchamp, Tom L. and Perlin (eds.). *Ethical Issues in Death and Dying*. Prentice Hall. (1978).

Beauchamp, Tom L. and Walters, LeRoy. *Contemporary Issues in Bioethics*. Belmont: Wadsworth Publishing Company, Inc. (1978).

Beauchamp, Tom L. and Childress, James F. *Principles of Biomedical Ethics*. Oxford. (1979).

Bell. *The Court of Wards and Liveries*. (1953).

Bartin, David (ed.). *Dying and Death*. Baltimore: The Williams & Wilkins Company. (1977).

Bentham, Jeremy. *The Principles of Morals and Legislation*. (1789).

Bergsma, Daniel. *Ethical, Social and Legal Dimensions of Screening for Human Genetic Disease*. New York: Stratton Intercontinental Medical Book Corporation. (1974).

Blackstone's Commentaries (1st U.S. ed.).

Bodenheimer, Edgar. *Jurisprudence: The Philosophy and the Method of the Law*. Cambridge. (1967).

Bok, Sissela. *Lying: Moral Choices in Public and Private Life*. New York. (1978).

Bracton, *Rerum Britannicarum Medi Aevi Scriptores* (Rolls Series), p. 459, Kraus Reprint Ltd. (1964).

Brandt, R.B. *Ethical Theory: The Problems of Normative and Critical Ethics*. Prentice-Hall, Inc., Englewood Cliffs. (1959).

Brandt, R.B. *A Theory of the Good and the Right*. Oxford. (1979).

Broad, C.D. *Five Types of Ethical Theory*. Harcourt, Brace & Co., N.Y. (1934).

Brody, Howard. *Ethical Decisions in Medicine*. Boston: Little, Brown and Company. (1976).

Brook, R. *Quality of Care Assessment: A Comparison of Five Methods of Peer Review*. National Technical Information Service: Springfield, Va. (1973).

Cahn, Edmond. *The Moral Decision: Right and Wrong in the Light of American Law.* Bloomington: Indiana University Press. (1955).

Campbell, Alastair V. *Moral Dilemmas in Medicine,* London: Churchill Livingstone. (1975).

Chitty on Medical Jurisprudence.

Cohen, Bernice H., Lilienfeld, Abraham M. and Huang, P.C. (eds.) *Genetic Issues in Public Health and Medicine.* Springfield: Charles C. Thomas. (1978).

Cohen, S.F., *Ethical Systems and Legal Ideals.* Westport, Conn.: Greenwood. (1976).

Coke on Littleton.

Corovitz et al. (ed.) *Moral Problems in Medicine.* Englewood Cliffs: Prentice Hall Inc. (1976).

Costa, Joseph J. and Nelson, Gordon K. *Child Abuse and Neglect: Legislation, Reporting and Prevention.* Lexington Books. (1978).

Cox, Archibald. *The Role of the Supreme Court in American Governments.* New York: Oxford University Press. (1976).

Crane, Diana. *The Sanctity of Social Life: Physicians' Treatment of Critically Ill Patients.* New York: Russell Sage Foundation. (1975).

Cross and Jones. *Introduction to Criminal Law.* (R. Card, ed., 9th ed. 1980).

da Costa, M. (ed.). 2 *Studies in Canadian Family Law.* (1972).

D'Arcy, Eric. *Human Acts.* London: Oxford University Press. (1963).

Devine, Philip E. *The Ethics of Homicide.* London: Cornell University Press Ltd. (1978).

Dorlands Illustrated Medical Dictionary (25th ed.).

Driedger, E. *The Construction of Statutes* (2nd ed. 1983)

Dworkin, Ronald. *Taking Rights Seriously.* Harvard University Press. (1977).

Englehardt, H. Tristan and Callahan, Daniel (eds.). *Morals Science and Sociality.* New York: The Hastings Centre. (1978).

Englehardt, H.T., Jr. and Daniel Callahan (ed.). *Science, Ethics and Medicine.* Hastings Centre. (1976).

Everleigh on Domestic Relations (6th ed., 1951).

Farndale, W.A.J. *Law on Hospital Consent Forms.* Beckenham Press. (1979).

Feifel, Herman, Susan Hanson, Robert Jones, Lauri Edwards. *Physicians Consider Death,* Reprinted from the proceedings, 75th Annual Convention, American Psychological Association. (1967).

Feinberg, J. *Doing and Deserving: Essays in the Theory of Responsibility.* Princeton. (1970).

Feinberg, Joel (ed.). *The Problem of Abortion.* Belmont, Calif. (1973).

Frankena, W.K. *Ethics.* Prentice-Hall, Englewood Cliffs. (1963).

Freidman, Paul R. *Legal Rights of Mentally Disturbed Persons.* New York: Practising Law Institute. (1979).

Halsbury's Law of England (4th).

Hamilton, William P. and Lavin, Mary Ann. *Decision Making in the Coronary Care Unit.* Saint Louis: The C.V. Mosby Company. (1976).

Hare, Richard M. *The Abnormal Child — Moral Dilemmas of Doctors and Parents, Moral Problems Concerning Life and Death.*

Hart, H.L.A. *The Concept of Law.* Oxford. (1961).

Harris, John. *Violence and Responsibility.* London: Routledge & Kegan Paul Ltd. (1980).

Holder, *Legal Issues in Pediatrics and Adolescent Management.* Toronto: John Wiley & Sons. (1977).

Holdsworth, *A History of English Law.*

Humber, James M. and Almeder, Robert E. *Biomedical Ethics and the Law.* New York: Plenum Press. (1977).

Hunt, Robert and Arras, John (eds.). *Ethical Issues in Modern Medicine.* Palo Alto: Mayfield Publishing Company. (1977).

Illich, Ivan. *Limits to Medicine.* (1976).

Jarcho, Saul and Brown, Gene (eds.). *Medicine and Health Care.* New York: The New York Times Arno Press. (1977).

Jonsen, A.R. and Garland, M.J. *Ethics of Newborn Intensive Care.* University of California, Health Policy Program and Institute of Governmental Studies, Berkeley. (1976).

Katz, Jay and Capron, Alexander Morgan. *Catastrophic Diseases: Who Decides What?* New York: Russell Sage Foundation. (1975).

Kenny's Outlines of Criminal Law. (J.W. Cecil Turner, ed., 19th ed. 1966).

Kluge, E.-H.W. *The Ethics of Deliberate Death.* Kennikat. (1981).

Kluge, E.-H.W. *The Practice of Death.* Yale University Press. (1975).

Kohl, Marvin (ed.). *Beneficent Euthanasia.* Buffalo: Prometheus Books. (1975).

Kohl, Marvin. *Infanticide and the Value of Life.* Buffalo: Prometheus Books. (1978).

Kohl, Marvin. *The Morality of Killing.* London: Peter Owen Limited. (1974).

Leichter, Howard M. *A Comparative Approach to Policy Analysis.* Cambridge: Cambridge University Press. (1979).

Linden, A. *Canadian Tort Law.* (1977).

Lowe and White. *Wards of Court.* London: Butterworth. (1979).

Ludlam, James E. *Informed Consent.* Chicago: American Hospital Association. (1978).

Maguire, Daniel C. *Death by Choice.* Garden City: Doubleday & Company, Inc. (1974).

Magnet, J.E. *Constitutional Law of Canada* (2nd ed.). Toronto: Carswell. (1985).

Mannes, Marya. *Last Rights.* New York. (1974).

Mappes, Thomas A. and Jane S. Zembaty. *Biomedical Ethics.* New York: McGraw-Hill Book Company. (1981).

Maundeville, Sir John. *The Voiage and traivaile of Sir John Maundeville.* (1400, repr. 1839), V. 47.

Mayrand, A. *L'inviolabilité de la personne humaine.* (1975).

Melden, A.I. (ed.). *Essays in Moral Philosophy.* Univ. of Washington Press. (1958).

Michalos, Alex C. *Foundations of Decision-Making.* Canadian Library of Philosophy, Ottawa. (1978).

Mill, J.S. *Utilitarianism.* (1863).

Ostheimer, Nancy C. and Ostheimer, John M. *Life or Death — Who Controls?* New York: Springer Publishing Company. (1976).

Pacela, Allan F. and Sloan, Anne B. *The Guide to Biomedical Standards.* Brea: The Quest Publishing Company. (1980).

Parizeau, Alice. *Protection de l'enfant: échec?* Montréal: Les Presses de L'Université de Montréal. (1979).

Picard, E. *Legal Liability of Doctors and Hospitals in Canada.*

Pollock on Torts (14th ed.).

Ramsey, Paul. *Ethics at the Edges of Life.* London: Yale University Press. (1979).

Ramsey, Paul. *The Patient as Person.* New Haven: Yale University Press. (1979).

Rawls, John. *A Theory of Justice.* Harvard University Press. (1971).

Roy, D. (ed.). *Medical Wisdom and Ethics in the Treatment of Severely Defective Newborn and Young Children.* Montreal: Eden Press. (1978).

Russell, O. Ruth. *Freedom to Die.* New York: Human Sciences Press. (1977).

Schiff, S. *Evidence in the Litigation Process* (2nd ed., 1983).

Shapiro, Martin. *Getting Doctored.* Kitchener. (1978).

Sharpe, David J., Salvatore F. Fiscina, and Murdock Head. *Law and Medicine: Cases and Materials.* St. Paul: West Publishing Company. (1978).

Sharpe, Steven Blair. *Informed Consent.* Toronto: Butterworths. (1979).

Sieverts, Steven. *Health Planning Issues and Public Law.* Chicago: American Hospital Association. (1977).

Smith, Roger. *Children and the Courts.* London: Sweet and Maxwell. (1979).

Smith, Selwyn M. *The Battered Child Syndrome.* London: Butterworths. (1975).

Smith's *Blood Diseases of Infancy and Childhood.* Miller, D.R. and Pearson, H.A. (eds.). Saint Louis: C.V. Mosby Company. (1978).

Sobel, Lester A. (ed.). *Medical Science and the Law: The Life and Death Controversy.* New York: Checkmark Books. (1977).

Stenson, B. *The Long Dying of Baby Andrew.* Boston. (1983).

Stephen. *Digest*, Article 311.

Toulmin, Stephen. *An Examination of the Place of Reason in Ethics.* Cambridge. (1950).

Storch. *Patient's Rights* McGraw-Hill Ryerson. (1982).

Swinyard, Chester A. *Decision Making and the Defective Newborn.* Springfield: Charles C. Thomas. (1978).

Swyer, P. *The Intensive Care of the Newly Born.* New York. (1975).

Tapell, Edward. *The History of Fourefooted Beasts.* (1607).

Trubo, Richard. *An Act of Mercy: Euthanasia Today.* Nash. (1973).

van den Berg, Jan Hendrik. *Medical Power and Medical Ethics.* New York: W.W. Norton & Company, Inc. (1978).

Veatch, Robert M. and Branson, Roy. *Ethics and Health Policy.* Cambridge: Ballinger Publishing Company. (1976).

Wadlington, Walter, Waltz, Jon R. and Dworkin, Roger B. *Cases and Materials on Law and Medicine.* Mineola: The Foundation Press, Inc. (1980).

Walton, D.N. *Brain Death.* Purdue Research Foundation. (1980).

Walton, D.N. *On Defining Death*. McGill-Queens. (1979).

Weber, Leonard J. *Who Shall Live ? The Dilemma of Severely Handicapped Children and its Meaning for Other Moral Questions*. Paulist Press.

Wecht (ed.). *Legal Medicine Annual*. (1977).

Weir, R. *Ethical Issues in Death and Dying*. Columbia University Press. (1977).

Williams, G. *Criminal Law : The General Part*, (2d ed. 1961).

Williams, G. *The Sanctity of Life and the Criminal Law*. New York : Alfred A. Knopf. (1970).

Wilson, Jerry B. *Death by Decision*. Philadelphia : Westminster Press. (1976).

Wojick, Jan. *Muted Consent*. West Lafayette : Purdue Research Foundation. (1978).

Articles

Natalie Abrams, *Defective Newborns : A Framework for a Case Analysis*, (1983) 2 The Westminster Institute Review.

After the Trial at Leicester (1981), 2 The Lancet 1085.

Anderson and Shields, *Quality Measurement and Control in Physician Decision Making : State of the Art* (1982), 17 Health Services Research 125.

Leslie G. Andrews, *Spina Bifida Cystica : A Follow-up Survey* (1967), 97 C.M.A.J. 280.

Annas, *Baby Doe Redux : Doctors as Child Abusers* (1983), 13(5) Hastings Center Report 26.

Annas, *Denying the Rights of the Retarded : The Phillip Becker Case* (1979), 9 Hastings Center Report 18.

Annas, *Reconciling Quinlan and Saikewicz : Decision Making for the Terminally Ill Incompetent* (1979), 4 Am. J.L. and Med. 367.

Lennart Aquist, *Modal Logic with Subjunctive Conditionals and Dispositional Predicates* (1973), 2 Journal of Symbolic Logic 1.

James A. Baker, *Court Ordered Non-Emergency Medical Care for Infants* (1969), 18 Cleveland Marshall L. Rev. 296.

Barrett *et al.*, *Quality Assurance through Automated Monitoring and Concurrent Feedback Using a Computer-Based Medical Information System* (1978), 16(11) Medical Care 962.

Charles Baron, *Assuring Detached but Passionate Investigation and Decision : The Role of Guardians Ad Litem in Saikewicz-type Cases* (1978), 4 Am. Journal Law and Med. 111.

Charles H. Baron, Margot Botsford and Garrick F. Cole, *Live Organ and Tissue Transplants from Minor Donors in Massachusetts* (1975), 55 Boston Univ. L. Rev. 159.

M. Pabst Battin, *The Least Worst Death* (1983), 13 Hastings Center Report 15.

W.H. Baughman, J.C. Bruha and F.J. Gould, *Euthanasia : Criminal, Tort, Constitutional and Legislative Considerations* (1973), 48 Notre Dame Lawyer 1203.

H. Baunenann, *Life Devoid of Value ?* (1976), 115 C.M.A.J. 1086.

D.F. Beauchamp, *Public Health and Social Justice* (1976), 13 Inquiry 3.

Henry K. Beecher, M.D., *Ethical Problems Created by the Hopelessly Unconscious Patient* (1968), 278 The New England Journal of Medicine 1425.

David A. Birnbaum, M.D., *The Iatrogenesis of Damaged Mothers and Newborns*, Medical Trial Technique Quarterly 177.

John D. Bonnet, M.D., *Bill of Rights of the Dying Patient* (1975), 27 Baylor L. Rev. 27.

Brook *et al.*, *Use, Costs, and Quality of Medical Services: Impact of the New Mexico Peer Review System* (1978), 89 Annals of Internal Medicine 256.

Judge Howard G. Brown, *Opinions of Trial Judges: In re Henry Green* (1966), 12 Crime & Delinquency 377.

R.H. Brown and R.B. Truitt, *The Right of Minors to Medical Treatment* 28 De Paul Law Rev. 289.

Bryn, *Compulsory Lifesaving Treatment for the Competent Adult*, 44 Fordham L. Rev. 1.

Allen Buchanan, *Medical Paternalism or Legal Imperialism: Not the Only Alternatives for Handling Saikewicz-type Cases* 5 American Journal of Law and Medicine 97.

A.G.M. Campbell, *Which Infants Should not Receive Interim Care?* (1982), 57 Archives of Disease of Childhood 569.

Norman L. Cantor, *Quinlan, Privacy and the Handling of Incompetent Dying Patients* (1977), 30 Rutgers L. Rev. 243.

A.M. Capran, *A Functional Approach to Informed Consent* (1974), 123 University of Pennsylvania Law Review 364.

Rosemary Carter, *Justifying Paternalism* (1977), 7 Canadian Journal of Philosophy 133.

J.-G. Castel, *Nature and Effects of Consent with Respect to the Right to Life and the Right to Physical and Mental Integrity in the Medical Field: Criminal and Private Law Aspects* (1978), 16 Alberta L. Rev. 293.

Robert S. Chabon, *You May Face a Nightmare in the Newborn Nursery* (June 1979), Legal Aspects of Medical Practice 43.

G.W. Chance, *The Severely Handicapped Newborn: A Physician's Perspective* (1980), 1 Health Law in Canada 34.

John R. Claypool, *The Family Deals with Death* (1975), 27 Baylor L. Rev. 34.

Cohen, *Interdisciplinary Consultation on the Care of the Critically Ill and Dying: The Role of the Hospital Ethics Committee* (1982), 10 Critical Care Medicine 776.

Donald G. Collester, Jr., *Death, Dying and the Law: A Prosecutorial View of the Quinlan Case* (1977), 30 Rutgers L. Rev. 304.

Vincent J. Collins, M.D., *Limits of Medical Responsibility in Prolonging Life* (1968), 206 J.A.M.A. 389.

Comment, *North Carolina's Natural Death Act: Confronting Death With Dignity*, 14 Wake Forest L. Rev. 771.

R.E. Cooke, M.D., *Whose Suffering?* (1972), 80 J. Pediatrics 906.

E.M. Cooperman, *Meningomyelocele: To Treat or Not to Treat* (1977), 116 Can. Med. Assn. J. 1338.

Diana Crane, *Physician's Attitudes Toward the Treatment of Critically Ill Patients* (1973), 23 Bio Science 471.

Paul-A. Crépeau, *Le consentement du mineur en matière de soins et traite-ments médicaux ou chirurgicaux selon le droit civil canadien* (1974), LII La Revue du Barreau Canadien 247.

Cross, *Wards of Court* (1967), 83 L.Q.R. 200.

Barbara J. Culliton, *The Haemmerli Affair: Is Passive Euthanasia Murder?* (1975), 190 Science 1271.

William J. Curran, *The Saikewicz Decision* (1978), 298 The New England Journal of Medicine 499.

Rosalyn Benjamin Darling, *Parents, Physicians, and Spina Bifida,* (1977) Hastings Center Report 10.

Deborah DuBois Davis, *Addressing the Consent Issues Involved in the Sterili-zation of Mentally Incompetent Females* (1979), 43 Albany L. Rev. 322.

J.A.P. Davis, *Defective Children — Who Should Decide?* Family Law, p. 203.

J. De Mol, *Troubles psychiques au cours d'hydrocéphalie normotensive* (1978), 78 Acta neurol. beig. 321.

L.L. De Veber, M.D., *On Withholding Treatment* (1974), 111 C.M.A.J 1183.

Dickens, *The Use of Children in Medical Experimentation* (1975), 43 Medico-Legal Journal 166.

Raymond S. Duff, M.D. and A.G.M. Campbell, *Moral and Ethical Dilemmas in the Special-Care Nursery* (1973), 289 The New England Journal of Me-dicine 890.

Lee J. Dunn, Jr., *Who "Pulls the Plug": The Practical Effect of the Saikewicz Decision,* (1978) Medicolegal News 6.

Gerald Dworkin, *Paternalism,* 56 no. 1 The Monist.

Eddy, *Clinical Policies and the Quality of Clinical Practice* (1982), 307(6) New England Journal of Medicine 343.

John Elliott, *Controversy in Medicine: Access to Employee Health Records,* 241 J.A.M.A. 777.

T.S. Ellis, *Letting Defective Babies Die: Who Decides?* (1982), 7 American Journal of Law and Medicine 393.

H.T. Engelhardt, *Euthanasia and Children: The Injury of Continued Existen-ce* (1973), 83 Journal of Pediatrics 170.

Euthanasia, 1,700 Doctors Speak out (1974), 29 Modern Medicine in Canada 657.

Horatio Fabrega, "Concepts of Disease: Logical Features and Social Implica-tions" (1972), 15 *Perspectives in Biology and Medicine* 583.

J. Fischhoff, M.D. and N. O'Brien, *After the Child Dies* (1976), 88 The Journal of Pediatrics 140.

George P. Fietcher, *Legal Aspects of the Decision Not to Prolong Life* (1968), 203 J.A.M.A. 119.

George P. Fietcher, *Prolonging Life* (1967), 42 Washington L. Rev. 999.

Fleischman and Murray, *Ethics Committees for Infants Doe?* (1983), 13(6) The Hastings Center Report 5.

John Fletcher, *Abortion, Euthanasia, and Care of Defective Newborns* (1975), 292 The New England Journal of Medicine 75.

Joseph Fletcher, *Ethical Aspects of Genetic Controls* (1971), 285 The New England Journal of Medicine.

Percy Foreman, *The Physician's Criminal Liability for the Practice of Euthanasia* (1975), 27 Baylor L. Rev. 54.

Percy Foreman, *Indicators of Humanhood: A Tentative Profile of Man* (1972), 2 Hastings Center Report 1.

R.M. Forrester, *Ethical and Social Aspects of Treatment of Spina Bifida*, (1968) The Lancet 1033.

Mark S. Frankel, *Social, Legal and Political Responses to Ethical Issues on the Use of Children as Experimental Subjects* (1974), 34 Journal of Social Issues 101.

J.M. Freeman, *Is there a Right to Die Quickly?* (1972), 80 J. Pediatrics 904.

J.M. Freeman, M.D., *The Shortsighted Treatment of Myelomeningocele: A Long-Term Case Report* (1974), 53 Pediatrics 311.

J.M. Freeman, *To Treat or Not to Treat: Ethical Dilemmas of Treating the Infant with a Myelomeningocele*, 20 Clinical Neurosurgery 134.

B.M. Freeston, *An Enquiry Into the Effect of a Spina Bifida Child Upon Family Life* (1971), 13 Dev. Med. Child Neurol. 456.

D.A. Frenkel, *Human Experimentation: Codes of Ethics* (1979), 1 Legal-Medical Quarterly 7.

Charles Fried, *Terminating Life Support: Out of the Closet!* (1976), 295 The New England Journal of Medicine 390.

C. Anthony Friloux, Jr., *Death, When Does It Occur?* (1975), 27 Baylor L. Rev. 10.

Susan K. Gauvey, Susan B. Leviton, Nancy B. Shuger, and Judith K. Sykes, *Statute Informed and Substitute Consent to Health Care Procedures: A Proposal for State Legislation* (1978), 15 Harvard Journal on Legislation 431.

Beverly A. Gazza, *Compulsory Medical Treatment and Constitutional Guarantees: A Conflict?* (1972), 33 Univ. of Pittsburg L. Rev. 628.

D.A. Geekie, *Report of the Seventy Second Meeting of the Alberta Medical Association* (1977), C.M.A.J. 922.

Bernard Gert and G.M. Calver, *Paternalistic Behaviour* (1976), 6 Philosophy and Public Affairs. 1.

D.P. Girvan and C.A. Stephens, *Congenital Intrinsic Duodenal Obstruction* (1974), 9 J. Pediatric Surgery 883.

Leonard H. Glantz, *Post-Saikewicz Judicial Actions Clarify the Rights of Patients and Families*, (1978) Medicolegal News 9.

P.R. Glazebrook, *Criminal Omissions: The Duty Requirement in Offences against the Person* (1960), 76 The Law Quarterly Rev. 386.

Goldman and Katz, *Inconsistency and Institutional Review Boards* (1982), 248(2) Journal of the American Medical Association 197.

Goodman, *Continuing Treatment of Parents with Congenitally Defective Infants* (1964), 9(1) Social Work 92.

Christina M. Gow, and J. Ivan Williams, *Nurses' Attitudes Toward Death and Dying: A Causal Interpretation* (1977), 11 Social Science and Medicine 191.

Guides to the Judge in Medical Orders Affecting Children (1568), 14(2) Crime and Delinquency 109.

Gurney, *Is There a Right to Die ? — A Study of the Law of Euthanasia* (1972), 3 Cumberland-Sanford L. Rev. 235.

J.M. Gustafson, *Mongolism, Parental Desires and the Right to Life* (1973), Persp. Biol. Med. (summer) 529.

Lawrence B. Guthrie, *Brain Death and Criminal Liability*, Criminal Law Bulletin.

F.M. Gutman, *On Withholding Treatment* (1974), 111 Can. Med. Assn. J. 520.

Bruno Haid, *The Prolongation of Life* (1957), 4 The Pope Speaks 393.

Michael J. Hardman, and Clifford J. Drew, *Life Management Practices with the Profoundly Retarded: Issue of Euthanasia and Withholding Treatment,* (1978) Mental Retardation 390.

E.H. Hare, K.M. Laurence, H. Payne, and K. Rawnsley, *Spina Bifida Cystica and Family Stress* (1966), 2 Brit. Med. J. 757.

Harold L. Hirsch and Richard E. Donovan, *The Right to Die: Medico-Legal Implications of in Re Quinlan* (1977), 30 Rutgers L. Rev. 267.

Philip B. Heymann and Sara Holtz, *The Severely Defective Newborn: The Dilemma and the Decision Process* (1975), 23 Public Policy 381.

Dennis J. Horan, *Euthanasia, Medical Treatment and the Mongoloid Child: Death as a Treatment of Choice ?* (1975), 27 Baylor L. Rev. 76.

W. Glen How, *Religion, Medicine and the Law* (1960), 3 Can. Bar. J. 365.

W. Glen How, *What Should Be Done for Patients Who do not Want Blood Transfusions ?* 2nd National Conference on Health and the Law, Ottawa, May 2-4, 1979.

Douglas Husak, *Paternalism and Autonomy* (1980-81), 10 Philosophy and Public Affairs 27.

D.W. Hyde, H. Williams, H.L. Ellis, *The Outlook for a Child with a Myelomeningocele for Whom Early Surgery was Considered Inadvisable* (1972) 14 Dev. Med. Child Neuro. 304.

F.J. Ingelfinger, *Bedside Ethics for the Hopeless Case* (1973), 289 N. Eng. J. Med. 914.

F.S. Ingelfinger, *Informed (But Uneducated) Consent* (1972), New England Journal of Medicine 287.

Jacoby, *Risk Management Rounds: Promoting Quality Care* (1983), 9(3) Quality Review Bulletin 85.

Patrick Jamieson, *Modern Biomedical Questions Challenge Christians,* Catholic Hospital 4.

A.R. Jonsen and M.J. Garland, *Critical Issues in Newborn Intensive Care: A Conference Report and Policy Proposal* (1975), 55 Pediatrics 756.

A.R. Jonsen, R.H. Phibbs, W.W. Tooley, M.J. Garlan, *Critical Issues in Newborn Intensive Care: A Conference Report and Policy Proposal,* (1975), 55(6) Pediatrics 756.

Journal of Medicine and Philosophy: (1978) 1:3, Concepts of Health and Disease; (1980) 5:2, Social and Cultural Perspectives in Disease.

Y. Kamisar, *Some Non-Religious Views Against Proposed "Mercy-Killing" Legislation* (1958), 42 Minn. L. Rev. 969.

Ronald P. Kaplan, *Euthanasia Legislation: A Survey and A Model Act* (1976-77), 2 American Journal of Law and Medicine 41.

Miriam Kass and Margery W. Shaw, M.D., *The Risk of Birth Defects: Jacobs v. Theimer and Parents' Right to Know* (1967-77), 2 Am. Journal Law and Med. 213.

M. Katyen, *The Decision to Treat Myelomeningocele on the First Day of Life* (1971), S. Afr. Med. J. 345.

Beverly Kelsey, *Which Infants Should Live? Who Should Decide?*, (1975) Hastings Center Report 5.

Ian Kennedy, *The Legal Effect of Requests by the Terminally Ill and Aged not to Receive Further Treatment from Doctors*, (1976) Crim. L. Rev. 217.

Kerengi and Chitkara, *Selective Birth in Twin Pregnancy with Discordancy for Down's Syndrome* (1981) 304 New England Journal of Medicine 1525.

E.W. Keyserlingk, *Sanctity of Life or Quality of Life*. Ottawa: Law Reform Commission of Canada, 1979, p. 132.

E.-H.W. Kluge, *The Calculus of Discrimination: Discriminatory Resource Allocation for an Aging Population*, Proceedings of the Conference on Ethics and Aging, U.B.C., 1984.

E.-H.W. Kluge, *Cerebral Death* (1984), 5 Theoretical Medicine 209.

E.-H.W. Kluge, *The Euthanasia of Radically Defective Neonates: Some Statutory Considerations* (1980), 6 Dalhousie Law Journal 238.

E.-H.W. Kluge, *Human and Persons: Normative Concepts in Contemporary Biomedical Decision-Making*, invited paper for the *Symposium on Human and Person*, Law Reform Commission of Canada and the Centre for Bioethics, Montreal, (May 10-11, 1979).

E.-H.W. Kluge, *In the Matter of Stephen Dawson: Right v. Duty of Health Care* (1983), 19 C.M.A.J. 817.

E.-H.W. Kluge, *Nursing — Vocation or Profession?* (1982), 78 The Canadian Nurse 34.

E.-H.W. Kluge, *The Profession of Nursing and the Right to Strike* (1982) 2 *The Westminster Review* 161.

Bartha M. Knoppers, *Les notions d'autorisation et de consentement dans le contrat médical* (1978), 19 C. de D. 893.

G.E. Knox, *Spina Bifida in Birmingham* (1967), 13 Dev. Med. Child Neuro. 14.

John Kohring, *Seeking a Judicial Determination that Treatment May be Withheld from a Seriously Ill Newborn* (1979), 7 Medicolegal News 10.

Luis Kutner, *The Living Will — Coping with the Historical Event of Death* (1975), 27 Baylor L. Rev. 39.

Kenneth Kysnis and Gailynn M. Williamson, *Nontreatment Decisions for Severely Compromised Newborns* (1984), 95 Ethics 90.

John Lachs, *Humane Treatment and the Treatment of Humans* (1976), 294 The New England Journal of Medicine 838.

Ron Lapin, M.D., *Major Surgery in Jehovah's Witnesses* (1980), 2(9) Contemporary Orthopaedics 647.

K. Laurence, *The Survival of Untreated Spina Bifida Cystica* (1966), 11 Dev. Med. Child Neuro. Supp. 10.

A. Linden, *The Negligent Doctor* (1973), 11 Osg. Hall L.J. 31.

A. Linden, *Custom in Negligence Law* (1968), 11 Can. Bar J. 151.

Arthur A. Levisohn, *Voluntary Mercy Deaths, Socio-Legal Aspects of Euthanasia* (1961), 8 Journal of Forensic Medicine 57.

J. Lorber, *Ethical Problems in the Management of Myelomeningocele and Hydrocephalus* (1975), 10 J. Roy. Coll. Phys. 47.

J. Lorber, *Results of the Treatment of Myelomeningocele* (1971), 13 Dev. Med. Child Neuro. 279.

C.F. Lynn and J.F. Childress, *Must Patients Always Be Given Food and Water?* (1983), 13 Hastings Centre Report 17.

Elizabeth S. MacMillan, *Birth-Defective Infants: A Standard for Nontreatment Decisions* (1978), 30 Stanford L. Rev. 599.

Reverend Everett MacNeil, *Cessation of Treatment — Euthanasia — Suicide of Patients*, Catholic Hospital 12.

McCartney, *The Development of the Doctrine of Ordinary and Extraordinary Means of Preserving Life in Catholic Moral Theology Before the Karen Quinlan Case* (1980), 47 Linocre Q. 215.

Richard A. McCormick, *To Save or Let Die, The Dilemma of Modern Medicine* (1974), 229 J.A.M.A. 172.

J.E. Magnet, *Corporate Negligence as a Basis for Hospital Liability* (1979), 6 C.C.L.T. 121.

J.E. Magnet, *Preventing Medical Malpractice in Hospitals: Perspectives from Law and Policy* (1979), 3 Legal-Medical Q. 197.

J.E. Magnet, *Liability of a Hospital for the Negligent Acts of Professionals* (1978), 3 C.C.L.T. 135.

S.R. Magnet, *The Right to Emergency Assistance in the Province of Quebec* (1980), 40 R. du B. 373.

Mandelbaum and Wheeler, *The Meaning of a Defective Child to Parents*, (1960) Social Casework 360.

Marsh, *Quality Assurance and Activities in a Small Community Hospital* (1983), 9 Quality Review Bulletin 77.

Martin, *Hospital Risk Management: A Canadian Perspective* (1981), 2(3) Health Care Management Forum 23.

Mason and Paige, *Perceived Usefulness of Quality Assurance Activities* (1983), 9(1) Quality Review Bulletin 20.

Neil H. Mickenberg, *The Silent Clients: Legal and Ethical Considerations in Representing Severely and Profoundly Retarded Individuals* (1979), 31 Stanford L. Rev.

Bruce Miller and Howard Brody, *Contracting the Principles of Medical Ethics: A Critique of Veatche's, A Theory of Medical Ethics* (1983), 2 Westminster Institute Review II.

Charles H. Montange, *Informed Consent and the Dying Patient* (1974), 83 Yale Law Journal 1632.

Daniel Mark Mueller, *Involuntary Passive Euthanasia of Brainstem-Damaged Patients: The Need for Legislation — An Analysis and a Proposal* (1977), 14 San Diego L. Rev. 1277.

Richard A. Mueller and G. Keith Phoenix, *A Dilemma for the Legal and Medical Professions Euthanasia and the Defective Newborn* (1978), 22 Saint Louis Univ. L. Journal 501.

Newman, *The Ethical Dilemma* (1983), The Medical J. of Australia 252.

Nielsen, *A Longitudinal Study of Psychological Aspects of Myelomeningocele* (1980), 21 Scandinavian Journal of Psychology 45.

Note, "Last Rights: Hawaii's Law on the Rights to Choice of Therapy for Dying Patients", 1 Hawaii L. Rev. 144.

Note, "The Tragic Choice: Termination of Care for Patients in a Permanent Vegetative State" (1977), 51 N.Y.U.L. Rev. 285.

Russell Noyes, Jr. and Terry A. Travis, *The Care of Terminally Ill Patients* (1973), 132 Arch. Intern. Med. 607.

Sheff D. Olinger, M.D., *Medical Death* (1975), 27 Baylor L. Rev. 22.

Optimum Care for Hopelessly Ill Patients, A Report of the Clinical Care Committee of the Massachusetts General Hospital (1976), 295 The New England Journal of Medicine 362.

David A. Ott, M.D., and Denton A. Cooley, M.D., *Cardiovascular Surgery in Jehovah's Witnesses* (1977), 238 (12) J.A.M.A. 278.

Gene Outka, *Social Justice and Equal Access to Health Care* (1978) 2 Journal of Religious Ethics II.

Position Paper on Withholding Treatment (1979), 24 Can. J. Psychiatry 75.

Pybus *et al.*, *Clinical Audit of an Intensive Care Unit* (1982), 10(3) Anaesthesia and Intensive Care 233.

Mitchell T. Rabkin, M.D., Gerald Gillerman and Nancy R. Rice, *Orders Not to Resuscitate* (1976), 295 New England Journal of Medicine 364.

James Rachels, *Active and Passive Euthanasia* (1975), 292 The New England Journal of Medicine 78.

Jane A. Raible, *The Right to Refuse Treatment and Natural Death Legislation* 5 Medicolegal News 6.

Randal, *Are Ethics Committees Alive and Well?* (1980), 13(6) The Hastings Center Report 10.

Diane Redleaf et al., *The California Natural Death Act: An Empirical Study of Physician's Practice* (1979), 31 Stanford Law Review 913.

Hilda Regier, *Judge Rules...:* (1975), 3 Journal of Legal Medicine 10.

Robert Reid, *Spina Bifida: The Fate of the Untreated*, (1977) Hastings Center Report 16.

Religion, Medicine and the Law (1960), 3 Can. Bar J. 365, 409.

Arnold S. Relman, M.D., *Viewpoint — Saikewicz Decision* (1978), 4 Am. Journal Law and Med. 233.

Return Adolph! All is Forgiven, (1976) C.A.M.R. 30.

Robertson, *Ethics Committees in Hospitals: Alternative Structures and Responsibilities* (1984), 10(1) Quality Review Bulletin 6.

J.A. Robertson, *Involuntary Euthanasia of Defective Newborns: A Legal Analysis* (1975), 27 Stan. L. Rev. 215.

John A. Robertson and Norman Fost, M.D., *Passive Euthanasia of Defective Newborn Infants: Legal Considerations* (1976), 88 The Journal of Pediatrics 883.

Rosen and Feigen, *Quality Assurance and Data Feedback* (1983), 8(1) Health Care Management Review 67.

Rosenberg, *A Self-Policing Program That Works* (April 4, 1983), Medical Economics 215.

Reverend David Roy, *The Severely Defective Newborn*, (1979) Health and Christian Life 16.

Russo *et al.*, *A Chart Audit Peer Review System in an Ambulatory Service* (1975), 56(2) Pediatrics 246.

Thomas St. Martin, *Euthanasia: The Three-in-one Issue* (1975), 27 Baylor L. Rev. 62.

St. Thomas, *Abortion and Euthanasia* (1981), Philosophy Research Archives.

Walter Sackett, Jr., *Euthanasia: Why No Legislation?* (1975), 27 Baylor L. Rev. 3.

R. Sade, *Medical Care as a Right, A Refutation* (1971), 285 New England Journal of Medicine 1288.

K.J.P. Sargeant, *Withholding Treatment from Defective Newborns: Substituted Judgment, Informed Consent and the Quinlan Decision* (1978), 13 Gonzaga Law Rev. 781.

Savage, *As a Family Practitioner Must You Consult With Other Specialists?* (1979), 7 Legal Aspects of Medical Practice 35.

R. Savatier, *Impérialisme médical sur le terrain du droit, le permis d'opérer et les pratiques américaines* (1952), XXXII Recueil Dalloz 32.

C.G. Schoenfeld, *Mercy Killing and the Law — a Psychoanalytically Oriented Analysis* (1978), 6 J. of Psychiatry and Law 215.

Ronald B. Schram, John C. Kane and Daniel T. Roble, *"No Code" Orders: Clarification in the Aftermath of Saikewicz* (1978), 299 Medical Intelligence 875.

K. Scott and M. Goddard, *Assessment of the Role of Antenatal Referral in Reduction of Neonatal Deaths* (1978), 11 Ann. Roy. Coll. Phys. Surg. Can. 79.

H. Scott, *Outcome of Very Severe Birth Asphyxia* (1976), 51 Arch. Dis. Child. 712.

K. Scott and M. Goddard, *Assessment of the Role of Antenatal Referral in Reductions of Neonatal Deaths* (1978), 11 Ann. Roy. Coll. Phys. Surg. Can. 79.

Searle, *Life with Spina Bifida* (1977), 24 Brit. Med. J. 1670.

Barry B. Shapiro, *Legal Aspects of Unauthorized But Necessary Emergency Treatment* (1963), Law Society of Upper Canada Special Lectures 255.

Thomas H. Sharp, Jr. and Thomas H. Crofts, Jr., *Death with Dignity — The Physician's Civil Liability* (1975), 27 Baylor L. Rev. 86.

Anthony Shaw, M.D., *Dilemmas of "Informed Consent" in Children* (1973), 289 The New England Journal of Medicine 885.

Sherman, *The Standard of Care in Malpractice Cases* (1966), 4 Osg. Hall L.J. 222.

D.B. Shurtleff, P.W. Hayden, J.D. Loeser, and R.A. Kronmal, *Myelodysplasia: Decision for Death or Disability* (1974), 219 N. Eng. J. Med. 1005.

Helen Silving, *Euthanasia: A Study in Comparative Criminal Law* (1954), 103 Univ. of Pennsylvania L. Rev. 350.

Mark Siegler, *The Physician's Perspective on the Right to Health Care* (1980), 244 Journal of the American Medical Association 1591.

P.D.G. Skegg, *Consent to Medical Procedures on Minors* (1973), 36 Mod. L. Rev. 370.

P.D.G. Skegg, *A Justification for Medical Procedures Performed Without Consent* (1974), 90 The Law Quarterly Review 512.

P.D.G. Skegg, *Medical Procedures and the Crime of Battery,* (1974) Crim. Law Rev. 693.

P.D.G. Skegg, *The Termination of Life-Support Measures and the Law of Murder* (1978), 41 The Modern L. Rev. 423.

Eliot Slater, *Health Service or Sickness Service* (1971), 4 British Medical Journal.

G. Keys Smith and E. Durham Smith, *Selection for Treatment in Spina Bifida Cystica,* (1973) British Medical Journal 189.

M. Somerville, *Medical Interventions and the Criminal Law: Lawful or Excusable Wounding?* (1980), 26 McGill L.J. 82.

Steven S. Spender, *"Code" or "No Code": A Nonlegal Opinion* (1979), 300 The New England Journal of Medicine 138.

W.B. Stason, *Foundations of Cost-Effectiveness Analysis for Health and Medical Practice* (1972), New England Journal of Medicine 716.

Steel, *The Right to Die: New Options in California* (1976), 93 Christian Century.

H. Steiner and G. Nelligan, *Perinatal Cardiac Arrest: Quality of Survivors* (1975), 40 Arch. Dis. Childh. 696.

Stephen M. Stewart, *The Problem of Prolonged Death: Who Should Decide?* (1975), 27 Baylor L. Rev. 169.

Stone, *Jurisdiction over Guardianship and Custody of Children in Canada and in England* (1979), 17 Alta. L. Rev. 532.

C. Strong, *The Neonatologist's Duty to Patient and Parent,* 14 Hastings Center Report 13.

Hon. Michael T. Sullivan, *The Dying Person — His Plight and His Right* (1973), 8 New England L. Rev. 197.

Swardon and Himel, *Legal Opinion on Position Paper: Withholding Treatment* (1979), 24 Can. J. Psychiatry 81.

Switching Off Life Support Machines: The Legal Implications, (1977) The Criminal L. Rev. 443.

The Technical Criteria Fallacy, (1977) Hastings Center Report 15.

Karen Teel, *The Physician's Dilemma, A Doctor's View: What The Law Should Be* (1975), 27 Baylor L. Rev. 6.

Elizabeth Telfer, *Justice, Welfare, and Health Care* (1976), 2 Journal of Medical Ethics 107.

Thayer, *Public Wrong and Private Action* (1914), 27 Harv. L. Rev. 317.

David Todres et al., *Pediatrician's Attitudes Affecting Decision-Making in Defective Newborns* (1977), 60(2) Pediatrics 197.

Michael Tooley, *Abortion and Infanticide* (1973), 2 A Philosophy & Public Affairs Reader 52.

The Tragic Choice: Termination of Care for Patients in a Permanent Vegetative State, 51 N.Y.U.L. Rev. 285.

Uberla, *Methodological Limitations in the Analysis of Medical Activities* (1980), 19(1) Methods of Information in Medicine 7.

Vanagunas *et al.*, *Principles of Quality Assurance* (1981), 7 Quality Review Bulletin 4.

Donald VanDeveer, *The Contractual Argument for Withholding Medical Information* (1978-80) 9 Philosophy and Public Affairs 198.

R.M. Veatch, *Just Social Institutions and the Right to Health Care*, 4 Journal of Medicine and Philosophy 170.

Robert M. Veatch, *Models for Ethical Medicine in a Revolutionary Age* (1972), 2 Hastings Center Report 2.

Veatch, *Problems with Institutional Review Board Inconsistency* (1982), 248(2) Journal of the American Medical Association 179.

Waitzkin and Stoeckle, *The Communication of Information About Illness* (1972), 8 Advanced Psychosomatic Medicine 180.

D.N. Walton, *Modal Logic and Agency* (1975), 69 Logique et Analyse 103.

Josef Warkany, *Terathanasia* (1978), 17 Teratology 197.

R.F. Weir, *The Government and Selected Non-treatment of Handicapped Infants* (1983), 309 New England Journal of Medicine 663.

Allan J. Weisbord, *On the Bioethics of Jewish Law : The Case of Karen Quinlan* (1979), 14 Is. L.R. 337.

Weisbord, *Why Organization Development Hasn't Worked (So Far) In Medical Centers* (1976), 1(2) Health Care Management Review 17.

Glanville Williams, *Euthanasia* (1973), 41 Medico Legal Journal 14.

William P. Williamson, M.D., *Life or Death — Whose Decision ?* (1966) 197 J.A.M.A. 793.

Winegar *et al.*, *A System to Monitor Patient Care in a Perinatal Region* (1983), 145(1) American Journal of Obstetrics and Gynecology 39.

William J. Winslade, *Thoughts on Technology and Death: An Appraisal of California's Natural Death* (1977), 26 D Paul L. Rev. 717.

James Woodward, *Paternalism and Justification* (1982), 8 Canadian Journal of Philosophy 67.

E.W.D. Young, *Caring For Disabled Infants* (1983), 13 Hastings Center Report 15.

Robert Young, *Autonomy and Paternalism* (1982), 8 Canadian Journal of Philosophy 47.

Stephen Grant Young, *Parent and Child — Compulsory Medical Care Over Objections of Parents* (1963), 65 West Virginia L. Rev. 184.

Younger *et al.*, *Patient's Attitudes Toward Hospital Ethic Committees* (1984), 12 Law, Medicine and Health Care 21.

R.B. Zachary, *Ethical and Social Aspects of Treatment of Spina Bifida*, (1968) The Lancet 274.

Joyce V. Zerwekh, *The Dehydration Question* (1983), Nursing 8347.

Reports ; Statements

Ad Hoc Committee of the Harvard Medical School to Examine the Definition of Brain Death, *A Definition of Irreversible Coma* (1968), 205 J.A.M.A. 337.

Ad Hoc Committee of the Harvard Medical School to Examine the Definition of Brain Death, *Report* (1968), 205 J.A.M.A. 85.

Alberta, Institute of Law Research and Reform, *Report of the Institute of Law Research and Reform on the Consent of Minors to Health Care*, Dec. 1975.

American Academy of Pediatrics, *A Proposal for an Ethics Committee* rep. (1983), 13 Hastings Center Report 6.

American Hospital Association. *Hospital Statistics*. Chicago: American Hospital Association (1976).

American Medical Association, Comments to the Proposed Rules in *HHS Guidelines*, 49 Fed. Reg. 8, p. 1631.

Anglican Church of Canada, Whytehead, L. et al., *Considerations Concerning the Transit from Life to Death*. Report of the Task Force on Human Life (1972).

British Columbia, Royal Commission on Family and Children's Law, 12th Report, *The Medical Consent of Minors*, Aug. 1975.

Bureau of Surveillance Services, Surveillance System of Congenital Anomalies, Surveillance Period: 1 Jan. 1975 — 31 Dec. 1975.

Canada, Law Reform Commission, Report No. 15, *Criteria for the Determination of Death* (1981).

Canada, Law Reform Commission, Report 20, *Euthanasia, Aiding Suicide, and Cessation of Treatment* (1983).

Canada, Law Reform Commission, Working Paper, 28, *Euthanasia, Aiding Suicide, and Cessation of Treatment* (1983).

Canada, Law Reform Commission, *Protection of Life Project* — Excerpt from the "7th Annual Report".

Canada, Law Reform Commission, Queen's University at Kingston, Department of Community Health and Epidemiology, *Survey of Health Care Professionals Concerning their Experience with, and Opinions Regarding, Adult Patients who Want to Die*. Professor A.S. Kraus to Justice Antonio Lamer.

Canada, Law Reform Commission, Report — Canadian Doctor's Special Study re: Medical/Legal Issues (February, 1980).

Canada, Law Reform Commission, Working Paper 26, *Medical Treatment and Criminal Law* (1980).

Canada, Statistics Canada, Causes of Death — Provinces by Sex and Canada by Sex and Age, 1977.

Canada, Statistics Canada, Vital Statistics — Volume I, Births, 1975 and 1976.

Canada, Statistics Canada, Vital Statistics — Volume III, Deaths, 1976.

Canada, Statistics Canada, *Vital Statistics*, Vol. III, Mortality.

Canadian Council on Hospital Accreditation, *Standards of Accreditation of Canadian Health Care Facilities* (Jan. 1983).

Canadian Medical Assn. (1968), 99 Can. Med. Assn. J. 1266.

Canadian Medical Association, Canadian Nurses Association and Canadian Hospital Association, *Joint Statement on Terminal Illness* (1984), 13 Canadian Medical Association Journal 1357.

Canadian Medical Association, Council on Community Health, General Council, 1974.

Canadian Medical Protective Association, *Annual Report* (1976).

Declaration of Tokyo, The Canadian Medical Association Statement, *Guidelines for Medical Doctors Concerning Torture in Relation to Detention and Imprisonment.*

Draft Declaration of Tokyo, *Guidelines for Medical Doctors Concerning Torture and other Cruel, Inhuman or Degrading Treatment or Punishment in Relation to Detention and Imprisonment,* September, 1975.

Dubin Report (see: Ontario, *Report of the Hospital for Sick Children Review Committee*).

Grange Commission Report (see: Ontario, *Report of the Royal Commission of Inquiry into Certain Deaths at the Hospital for Sick Children and Related Matters*).

Joint Commission for Accreditation of Hospitals (U.S.) *Accreditation Manual for Hospitals* (1976).

Joint Committee of Society of Obstetricians and Gynaecologists of Canada and the Canadian Pediatric Society on the Regionalization of Reproductive Care in Canada, *Regional Services in Reproductive Medicine,* P.R. Swyer and J.W. Goodwin (eds.), Toronto. (1973).

Manitoba, Task Force on Human Life, *"Dying", Considerations Concerning Passage from Life to Death,* An Interim Report. Winnipeg, Manitoba. June, 1977.

Ontario, Department of Health, Ontario Council of Health, *Perinatal Problems,* Toronto (1971).

Ontario, Department of Health, *Second Report of Perinatal Mortality Study in Ten University Teaching Hospitals in Ontario.* Toronto. (1967).

Ontario Ministry of the Attorney General, *Reports of Family Law,* Second Report of the Attorney General's Committee on the Representation of Children. (September 1978).

Ontario, Ministry of Health, *A Regionalized System for Reproductive Medical Care in Ontario,* Report of the Advisory Committee on Reproductive Medical Care to the Ministry of Health for Ontario, September, 1979.

Ontario, Ministry of Health, Interministerial Committee on Medical Consent, *Health Services Consent Act, s. 13,* Dec. 1979 (draft).

Ontario, Ministry of Health, Interministerial Committee on Medical Consent, *Options on Medical Consent,* Sept. 1979.

Ontario, *Report of the Hospital for Sick Children Review Committee* (The Dubin Report) Toronto: Queen's Printer (1983).

Ontario, *Report of the Royal Commission of Inquiry into Certain Deaths at the Hospital for Sick Children and Related Matters* (The Grange Commission), Toronto: Queen's Printer (1984).

President's Commission for the Study of Ethical Problems of Medicine and Biomedical and Behavioural Research, *Deciding to Forego Life Sustaininl Treatments: A Report on the Ethical, Medical and Legal Issues in Treatment Decisions* (1983).

Quebec: Ministry of Social Services, *Perinatal Intensive Care after Integration of Obstetrical Services in Quebec: A Policy Statement of the Quebec Perinatal Committee* (1973).

Report of the HCMT-UTHA Joint Committee on High Risk Pregnancy — Phase II, October, 1979.

W.W. Sackett, M.D., Member of the House of Representatives of the State of Florida, Statement, *Death With Dignity*, Part 1 — Washington D.C., August 7, 1972.

Saskatchewan, Law Reform Commission, *Tentative Proposals for a Consent of Minors to Health Care Act*, Nov. 1978.

Saskatchewan Medical Association, Position Paper on the Report of the Committee on Rights in Relation to Health Care.

The World Medical Association, Inc., *Declaration of Helsinki*, Recommendations guiding medical doctors in biomedical research involving human subjects, October, 1975.

Newspaper and Periodical Articles

Acquittal of Paediatrician Charged after Death of Infant with Down's Syndrome (1981), 2 The Lancet 1101.

Allegedly left to die, Siamese twins saved, Globe and Mail (Toronto), May 18, 1981, p. 12.

Babies with defects allowed to die — M.D., The Ottawa Citizen, January 22, 1977.

Baby deaths, handicaps could be cut, (a hospital study conducted jointly by the Hospital Council of Metropolitan Toronto and University of Teaching Hospitals Association), The Globe and Mail, December 4th, 1979.

Brain-damaged baby denied operation that may have averted starvation, The Globe and Mail, October 8, 1974.

Can cut life support, New York Court rules, The Globe and Mail, December 7, 1979.

The Citizen (Ottawa), Nov. 18, 1981.

Court Saves Mongoloid Baby, The Toronto Star, Jan. 21, 1977, p. 1.

Euthanasia "happening everywhere" doctor says, Toronto Star, June 6, 1983.

Euthanasia raised as motive for baby deaths at hospital, The Globe and Mail (Toronto) Aug. 26, 1983, p. 1.

Girl needed blood, Witness trial is told, The Globe and Mail (Toronto), June 12, 1981, p. 13.

Judge Acquits Jehovah's Witnesses, but warns others against negligence, The Whig-Standard, September 12, 1981, p. 3.

Judge Demands How Apologize, The Chronicle Journal, Wednesday, June 24, 1981, p. 23.

Sidney Katz, *Life and death ethics*, Maclean's, March 17, 1980.

Let hopeless cases starve to death : M.D., Toronto Star, June 2, 1983.

MDs abort two of woman's quads, The Globe and Mail (Toronto), Thursday, September 24, 1981, p. T9.

Most low weight preemies grow normally, study finds, The Globe and Mail (Toronto), 6/1/82, p. 15.

The Ottawa Citizen, Jan. 23, 1977, p. 90 (decision of Judge Morris Genest of Family Division of the Ontario Provincial Court, Middlesex Co.).

Parents Bar Surgery and Lose Son's Custody, The New York Times, August 9, 1981.

Parents of Siamese twins charged, The Globe and Mail (Toronto), June 13, 1981, p. 13.

Patients do have rights, Ottawa Journal, February, 2, 1978.

Psychiatrists condemn practice of letting retarded babies die, The Globe and Mail, February 17, 1979.

A. Shaw, *Doctor, Do We Have a Choice?* The New York Times Magazine, Jan. 30, 1972, p. 54.

Siamese Twins' Parents Accused of Attempted Murder, New York Times, June 12, 1981, p. A12.

Robert and Peggy Stinson, *On the Death of a Baby,* The Atlantic, July, 1979.

"Useless" baby allowed to die, The Gazette, October 5, 1974.

Values reflected in baby's death, B.C. Doctor says, The Globe and Mail (Toronto) August 16, 1978, p. 11.

Windsor girl is disconnected from respirator, The Globe and Mail, November 17, 1979.

TABLE OF CASES

TABLE OF STATUTES

INDEX

.